YOUNG NELSONS

Boy Sailors during the Napoleonic Wars 1793–1815

Foreword by
ALEXANDER KENT

D.A.B. RONALD

In Memory of Colonel David Bruce Ronald CBE

First published in Great Britain in 2009 by Osprey Publishing, Midland House,
West Way, Botley, Oxford OX2 0PH, United Kingdom.
443 Park Avenue South, New York, NY 10016, USA.
Email: info@ospreypublishing.com

Every attempt has been made by the Publishers to secure the appropriate permissions for materials
reproduced in this book. If there has been any oversight we will be happy to rectify the situation and
a written submission should be made to the Publishers.

A CIP catalogue record for this book is available from the British Library.

D.A.B. Ronald has asserted his right under the Copyright, Designs and Patents Act, 1988, to be
identified as the author of this book.

ISBN: 978 1 84603 360 5

Page layout by Myriam Bell Design, France
Index by Fineline Editorial Services
Typeset in Minion Pro
Originated by PDQ Media, Bungay, UK
Printed in China through Worldprint Ltd

09 10 11 12 13   10 9 8 7 6 5 4 3 2 1

Front cover: National Maritime Museum

For a catalogue of all books published by Osprey please contact:

NORTH AMERICA
Osprey Direct, c/o Random House Distribution Center
400 Hahn Road, Westminster, MD 21157, USA
E-mail: uscustomerservice@ospreypublishing.com

ALL OTHER REGIONS
Osprey Direct, The Book Service Ltd., Distribution Centre, Colchester Road, Frating Green,
Colchester, Essex, CO7 7DW
E-mail: customerservice@ospreypublishing.com

Osprey Publishing is supporting the Woodland Trust, the UK's leading woodland
conservation charity, by funding the dedication of trees.

www.ospreypublishing.com

CONTENTS

FOREWORD

by Alexander Kent

Having shadowed the footsteps of my fictional hero, Richard Bolitho, from midshipman to admiral, I found *Young Nelsons* vivid, lively and approachable. Meticulously researched, it illuminates aspects of Nelson's navy and times hitherto unrecorded: the lives and careers of those taking the first tentative steps up the uncertain ladder from 'young gentlemen' – midshipmen – and those boys, less fortunate or less privileged, whose experience was a harder beginning on the lower-deck.

Some were very young indeed. It is sobering to recall that when 'Bounty Bligh', as he was known to the end of his tempestuous life, was first packed off to sea in a disciplined ship-of-the-line, the *Monmouth*, he was seven years and nine months old. The rigours of life at sea from this tender age can without doubt have ensured that Bligh, who was by no means the tyrant of legend, had absolutely no sense of humour, which I believe contributed in no small measure to the unfortunate events for which he will forever be blamed.

I think it is worth noting, too, that when Bligh was a captain in command of his own two-decker, the *Glatton*, at Copenhagen in 1801, he was summoned aboard the flagship after the battle and commended for his performance and support. The admiral was none other than Horatio Nelson, who, incidentally, had joined his first ship aged 12 in 1771, under the auspices of his maternal uncle, Captain Maurice Suckling.

The author of *Young Nelsons* also examines the flood of contemporary literature, particularly the work of Marryat, who wrote from a lifetime's experience at sea, and whose novels undoubtedly gave rise to modern naval fiction. Lovers of that very popular genre are already prepared for descriptions of being aloft, reefing and furling sails, or sponging out a gun in the aftermath of close action, when we read eyewitness accounts from those who were actually there.

That these voices from the past can speak to us with such clarity and immediacy can have its disadvantages, of course, requiring accuracy and experience from the novelist. My hero Richard Bolitho has a bad head for heights. I blame that on my own service at the naval training establishment HMS *Ganges*, which was dominated by a towering mast from the original vessel of that name, the last sailing line-of-battleship to serve in the Royal Navy. You were expected to climb up and over the mast, no matter what. I can still feel it!

Of all those termed 'Young Nelsons', I still consider William Hoste the best candidate for the title. He first went to sea at the age of 12 and served as an eager midshipman aboard the third-rate *Agamemnon* under the command of Captain Horatio Nelson. In his letters home, Hoste often described the encouragement and paternal interest Nelson regularly offered his midshipmen, qualities which Hoste would soon recognize as the essence of leadership by example. Hoste was always a favourite of Nelson's, described by him as 'brave, bright, and enterprising'. Praise indeed from one already regarded as one of England's heroes.

Although Nelson did not live to see it, Hoste would repay that faith in him, in 1811 at the battle of Lissa, fought in the disputed waters of the Adriatic. Captain Hoste, in command of the frigate *Amphion*, with three other similar ships, *Cerebus*, *Active*, and *Volage*, was confronted by a French-Venetian force of twice their strength, under the flag of Commodore Bernard Dubordieu. Lissa was to prove one of the last major battles fought under sail. Hoste had been well trained, and bore in mind Nelson's edict: *the best form of defence is attack*. But before he opened fire against such daunting odds, he made one more signal: *Remember Nelson*.

It was enough. For his men, and those who followed.

Many years later a memorial was erected on Lissa, renamed Vis, at the Old Naval Cemetery, as a fitting tribute to all British sailors and soldiers who perished in the Mediterranean theatre of war. The last lines on it read:

> Life to be sure is nothing much to lose,
> But young men think it is, and we were young.

Our Nel would have approved.

A.K.

PREFACE AND ACKNOWLEDGEMENTS

T he idea for *Young Nelsons* has been percolating for some while. As a parent, I have been fascinated trying to understand how differently children see the adult world around them. Nothing could be more 'grown-up' than nations, races and religions at war with each other, yet all too often children find themselves, for better or worse, thrust into the thick of the resulting maelstrom. As far as I am able to deduce from the archives, an ancestor of mine entered the British Navy aged ten in the early 1800s. His trail has gone cold. Fortunately this is not so for many other 'young Nelsons'.

The Revolutionary and Napoleonic Wars, spanning the period 1793 to 1815, were, by some measures, the first 'world' wars and truly modern ones. Young boys and, indeed, girls found their voices and began articulating what they thought of the adult world around them gone mad. The story of these Wars has been told from many angles, through many lenses, but never before by the 'young gentlemen' of the quarterdeck and the 'boys' of the lower-decks. Who were these 'young gentlemen'? Who were these 'boys'? What did life at sea in a man-of-war hold for them? *Young Nelsons* is their stories, their 'Wars'.

At the same time as working on *Young Nelsons*, I have been undertaking a research thesis at the University of Exeter, a major centre of excellence for the study of maritime history. My research aims to carry on where *Young Nelsons* must leave off.

PREFACE AND ACKNOWLEDGEMENTS

As with all works of non-fiction, I have been dependent on the expertise and generosity of many individuals and institutions. I would like to thank the extremely helpful and knowledgeable staff at the Royal Archives, who, by permission of Her Majesty Queen Elizabeth II, gave me invaluable access and guidance for my 'Royal Sailor' chapter. The archives at the London Marine Society, the Caird Library at the National Maritime Museum, the Royal Naval Museum, Portsmouth, the Royal Marines Museum, Southsea, the British Library, London, the Bodleian Library at the University of Oxford, and the library at the University of Exeter were stalwarts of my research, and I am very grateful to all of the staff at these institutions for their assistance.

From my bibliography it will be evident that I have relied on a wide range of learned works by historians and biographers. I thank them all, especially Tom Pocock, sadly recently deceased. In order to find and hold on to the original voices of the young Nelsons, I have drawn on many memoirs and collections of letters, some edited by later historians. The Navy Records Society has been especially diligent in this regard and is thanked and congratulated for its tireless efforts as a vital source of reference for me and future historians. Two reference sources stand out and deserve my special thanks: the 2003 thesis by Roland Pietsch on the early days of the London Marine Society, and the collection of Nelson letters compiled by, among others, George Naish. I am particularly grateful to my supervisors at the University of Exeter: Professor Jeremy Black, Professor Nicholas Rodger and Professor Gerald MacLean for their support and guidance throughout on my thesis. Last, but certainly not least, my thanks go to my commissioning editors, Ruth Sheppard and Jaqueline Mitchell and their colleagues at Osprey Publishing for working with me on this project.

On a personal note, my heartfelt thanks and love go to my wife, Susan, who has inspired and helped nurture this endeavour, listening with me each day for the patter of tiny feet echoing along the decks of Britain's 'wooden walls' from two centuries ago and waiting with bated breath as one young Nelson after another has struggled to find his voice.

My one regret is that my father, Colonel David Bruce Ronald CBE, and my mother, Elizabeth, did not live to see *Young Nelsons* in its final form. *Young Nelsons* is dedicated to my father's memory thanking him for who he was. I already have a second project in progress and the resulting book will be dedicated to my dear mother.

PROLOGUE

They 'behaved like young Nelsons',[1] Thomas Dalrymple, a schoolmaster, had noted, writing from aboard the *Mars* after the Battle of Trafalgar. His words bore witness to the skill and valour of his classroom charges in the heat of battle, and, by likening them to the nation's greatest naval hero, Dalrymple was paying them the highest compliment imaginable.

Yet there was one of Dalrymple's young pupils, 13-year-old Norwich Duff, who stood out for his bravery long after the cannons had fallen silent that day. Following the 'Great Battle' at Trafalgar, young Norwich had the painful duty of writing to his mother waiting back home in Edinburgh for news that all was well. He was safe and sound but, sadly, he must report the death of the captain of the *Mars* – his father, her husband. Struggling for words, Norwich described to 'my dear Mamma' how 'dear papa … died like a hero having gallantly led his Ship into Action'.[2]

Surprisingly to us today, Norwich was one among hundreds of 'young Nelsons' in the fleet of 27 British warships forming in line to confront the combined fleet of France and Spain on 21 October 1805. 'Tomorrow, I will do that which will give you young gentlemen something to talk and think about for the rest of your lives',[3] Nelson had told a group of midshipmen with him aboard HMS *Victory* ahead of the Great Battle. Indeed, across the horizon wherever Britain's navy was on patrol around the globe, there were yet more young Nelsons, some no more than ten years old, who had joined the British Navy in the years leading up to and following the declaration of war by France in February 1793. To be in on the Great Battle, whenever and wherever it happened, was what these youngsters had been striving for all those years, and to have missed out was too cruel. Writing home soon after hearing news of the victory, William Hoste, who had first gone to sea in 1793 aged 12, and whose ship, the *Amphion*, had been ordered away from the fleet by Nelson only days before the Great Battle, would ruefully remark: 'Not to have been in it is enough to make one mad.'[4]

Who were these youngsters and why were they so 'mad' for battle? To answer those and other questions about a whole generation of Britain's youth, we must begin their story long before the Battle of Trafalgar, before even the start of the Wars.

For one young gentleman, as his friend Bat James recalled, the story started as he lay fast asleep one cold winter's morning as 1767 turned into 1768:

> Never shall I forget, O my friend and old messmate, Richard Marsinghall, thy good old mother's joy at communicating the news of her success to thee, nor can I help smiling at the flattering picture she drew of thy situation when she awoke thee on that day before thy usual hour.
>
> 'Richard,' said she, 'my dear son Richard, get up, thou art made for ever.'
>
> 'What am I made, Mother?' replied my friend Marsinghall, in the utmost surprise and astonishment.
>
> 'Oh,' said she, 'Richard, my tender life, thou art made a midshipman…'[5]

If Richard's mother were to be believed, all he had to do was haul himself up, slip into one of 'the most fashionable midshipmen's uniforms'[6] that she had had made up specially, have himself royally conveyed by carriage down to the harbour at nearby Torbay, strut on board some mighty ship-of-the-line waiting to do his bidding and, in the twinkling of his mother's eye, he was 'made for ever'. Nothing could be simpler to the boy's mind. No matter that the Marsinghalls were not a naval family, nor that Richard was just one of a 'great many youngsters who had never before been to sea.'[7] Mother Marsinghall had said he was 'made for ever', and mothers were there to be trusted.

What blind faith. Would that Mother Marsinghall had read about young Tom Bowling, in Tobias Smollett's immensely popular *Adventures of Roderick Random*, venturing on the high seas back in the 1740s, or seen a production of Shakespeare's *Henry IV Part 2* portraying ship-boys at sea from an even earlier time:

Wilt thou upon the high and giddy mast
Seal up the ship-boy's eyes and rock his brains
In cradle of the rude imperious surge,
And in the visitation of the winds,
Who take the ruffian billows by the top,
Curling their monstrous heads and hanging them
With deaf'ning clamour in the slippery clouds,
That, with the hurly, death itself awakes?[8]

Surely, reading these, Mother Marsinghall would have thought twice and even if, unbelieving of novelists and playwrights and preferring facts to fiction, she could have imbibed the true histories of all those 'younkers' described in Hakluyt's 1600 *Principall Navigations, Voiages and Discoveries of the English Nation* ranging across the globe in Sir Francis Drake's shadow. If she were minded to, she could even have tracked back into ships' records in the 1300s, where as many as one in eight of a ship's complement might be boys.[9] With the legacy of Britain's great naval tradition to draw on, it was inconceivable that Mother Marsinghall had no 'apprehension of the dangers that attend the profession'[10] of a mariner. So why did she, like so many mothers before and after her, risk her son at sea? Again, the answer to this starts long before the Wars, all the way back to the reign of Queen Elizabeth I, when Britain began its first tentative steps in search of empire and boys began to reach out from the pages of history.

'YOUNKERS IN THE TOP CONTINUALLY'

Hakluyt compiled his great work of English naval history over many years, finally completing it in 1600. Drawing on many sources, including eyewitness accounts, he recorded the great 'voiages' of the period, including one that, by 26 November 1578, had brought its explorers to the shores of the Island of Mocha deep in the South Pacific. There, a drama unfolded:

> The general himself was shot in the face, under his right eye, and close by his nose, the arrow piercing a marvellous way under the *basis cerebri,* with no small danger of his life; besides that he was grievously wounded in the head. The rest, being nine persons in the boat, were deadly wounded in divers parts of their bodies, if God almost miraculously had not given cure to the same. For our chief surgeon being dead, and the other absent by the loss of our vice-admiral, and having none left us but a boy, whose good will was more than any skill he had, we were little better than altogether destitute of such cunnings and helps, as so grievous a state of so many wounded bodies did require.[1]

A tale of bows and arrows. A far-off island few have heard of. A general dangerously wounded; nine others injured, at death's door; the surgeon dead. Their fate in the hands of 'a boy'. Surely no 'Great Battle' this. True, but, given that the 'general' who came within a whisker of death was Francis Drake, it was nevertheless a seminal moment. By the time of his encounter with the tribe of Araucanians on Mocha Island, Drake had safely navigated through the treacherous waters of Magellan's Strait and, blown off course, discovered the southernmost point of the Americas by accident. No mean feats, but mere trifles compared to what lay ahead for him and his crew, among them 'younkers', as boys serving on ships were often called in those days. Drake had not yet decided that the only route home lay westwards out across the vast Pacific, leading him, perforce, to circumnavigate the globe. He would achieve this momentous task over the next two years, arriving home in September 1580. Nor had he led the English Navy to its ultimate trial of strength with the mighty Spanish empire. This would happen in the coming years, culminating in the defeat of the Spanish Armada in 1588. This victory would establish England as a maritime power to be reckoned with in the race to carve up the known world: an ever-present threat to the established empires of newly united Spain and Portugal, and fast rival to the other upstart empire-builders, Holland and France.

The foundations for England's so-called 'wooden walls', laid down earlier by Henry VIII and nurtured by his daughter Elizabeth I, would creak at times during the coming centuries, but in 1588 a line had been drawn in the sand by a fleet of 54 English sails ranged along the English Channel. So far, no further, the cry rang out. And for every Englishman, the hero was Drake, scourge of the Spanish Main, greatest mariner of his time and heroic embodiment of the English Crown's swashbuckling ambitions. From behind this line in the sand, England would increasingly project its imperial destiny, culminating with seeming inevitability in the Battle of Trafalgar 217 years on, after which date Britain really could claim to 'rule the waves'.

Yet in 1578, on the shores of the Island of Mocha, for one brief moment Drake's destiny was in the hands of a mere youngster, 'a boy, whose good will was more than any skill he had'. Hardly what Drake needed at this critical moment. No young hero this boy. No fight, no skill; just bags of goodwill. Fortunately for Drake, or so Hakluyt's eyewitness reassured his readers, there were other, more powerful, more reliable forces at work and 'God by the good advice of our general, and the diligent putting to of every man's help, did give such speedy and wonderful cure, that we all had great comfort thereby, and yielded God the glory thereof'.[2]

When, by contrast, Thomas Dalrymple reported all those years later on the exploits of his pupils at the Battle of Trafalgar, there was no mention of divine intervention. Why should he? All around him, for months on end, Thomas had witnessed the discipline, training and expert seamanship that was Britain's now well-honed naval fighting machine. Add a healthy dose of bravery and valour on the day of battle, and victory was the only possible outcome. They 'behaved like young Nelsons'. These were no empty words, soothing balm to ease the suffering of a grieving widow. Thomas meant them, as only survivors of a titanic life and death struggle could mean them. And, more telling, his words embraced not only Mrs Duff's son, Norwich, but all the young gentlemen aboard the *Mars* that day. No cowards here; one and all were cut from the same cloth.

And they had names. Not so the boy on Mocha Island, nor the other two boys listed among the '164 able and sufficient men'[3] on the five ships that started out on this expedition in 1577. Their anonymity is no surprise, but at least these three made it into the official records. There would almost certainly have been more boys on the five-ship expedition. A ship's complement in the time of Henry VIII allowed for between one and five boys per vessel depending on the rate (size) of the ship. 'Boys' had been an official naval crew classification on Crown vessels since the 1200s, when Exchequer Pipe Rolls gave standard rates of pay for various grades of sailors as 6d per day for masters and constables, 3d per day for sailors and 1½d for 'boys'. However, come the 1582 Scale of Sea Pay and Complements, 'boys' had already disappeared as a separate classification and may have been subsumed into other titles such as 'Yeoman's Mate', 'Steward's Mate', 'Carpenter's Mate' or 'Swabber'. Additionally, boys often came on board ship as apprentices to learn a specific trade. The fact that they were at sea rather than on land was incidental. 'Boys' only reappeared in the 1626 Scale of Pay and Complements, by which time they were earning 7s 6d for a 28-day month.[4]

Whatever the exact number of boys on the Famous Voyage of Circumnavigation, they were starting out young, just as Drake had done. By the age of eight Drake was already afloat, albeit living in a hulk moored in the River Medway. By the age of ten, if not earlier, he was at sea proper, his father having placed him 'with a neighbouring pilot, who, by daily exercise, exercised him to the sailor's labour with a little bark, wherewith he sailed up and down the coast, guided ships in and out of harbours, and sometimes transported merchandise into France and Zeeland.'[5] Still only in his teens, Drake became proud owner of the bark, having fallen heir to it on the master's death. By age 20 he was voyaging to the Guinea coast, having teamed up with the other great mariner of the age, his distant cousin John Hawkyns, working the slave routes.

Records from an unlikely source, the Spanish Inquisition, show that younkers also took other roles on board ship. In one account sent back to Madrid by the Portuguese pilot Nuno da Silva, one of the prisoners captured by the English during Drake's Famous Voyage, we hear how 'Francis Drake kept a book in which he entered his navigation and in which he delineated birds, trees and sealions. He is adept in painting and has with him a boy ... who is a great painter.'[6] Another account by Don Francisco De Zarate, a Spanish aristocrat who joined Drake and his crew on the *Golden Hind* in prayers, mealtimes and evenings of entertainment, reveals how the evening ended with a pageboy entertaining the ship's company by dancing 'in the English fashion'.[7] However, Zarate soon moves on to the more sinister purpose of his account: 'He also carries with him painters [mapmakers] who paint for him pictures of the coast in its exact colours. This I was most grieved to see, for each thing is so naturally depicted that no one who guides him according to these paintings can possibly go astray.'[8]

By noting every headland, every bay, every shoreline along these distant coasts, these 'painters', so detested by the Spaniards, were recording a maritime world known until then only to the Spanish and, maybe, the Portuguese. And it was another cousin of Francis Drake, John Drake, who filled this position on the Famous Voyage. Aged 15 at the time of the Voyage, John had already been at sea with his cousin for at least two years. The records of an expedition to Ireland in 1575 financed by Walter Devereux, Earl of Essex, list John in the crew of his cousin's ship, the frigate *Falcon*. This expedition was no gentle cruise easing young John into the ways of life at sea. The orders from Essex were to destroy the Scottish galleys marauding in the waters between Scotland and the north Irish coast. Exceeding these orders, the expedition landed on the Scottish stronghold of Rathlin Island, off County Antrim, rounded up hundreds of Scots who had surrendered in the besieged castle or were in hiding around the island and systematically slaughtered every man, woman and child. What, if anything, John witnessed of these atrocities has been left unrecorded.

After his exploits on the Famous Voyage, advancement came quickly for John, as cousin of the greatest mariner of his time. In 1581 Sir Francis Drake was organizing an expedition to the East Indies via the Cape of Good Hope and appointed John, still only 20, captain of the 40-ton *Bark Francis*, one of the fleet ships. Obliged by domestic politics to remain in England, Sir Francis made Edward Fenton, a soldier of fortune with no maritime expertise, Admiral of the Fleet. At sea, tensions soon erupted between the 'mariners', with John as their ringleader, and the 'soldiers' in the expedition. The mariners wanted to go in search of Spaniards and plunder, but Fenton's instructions from the Muscovy Company, chief backers of the expedition, were to eschew any confrontations. Reaching the coast of South America and remembering how easy and rich the pickings had been playing at 15-year-old pirate alongside his older cousin on the Famous Voyage, John deserted, taking the *Bark Francis* south towards Cape Horn in search of his precious plunder.

Heaping incompetence on indiscipline, if not mutiny, John would soon learn the harsh lesson of the sea: there were no short-cuts for a master mariner. As ship's mapmaker on the *Golden Hind*, he may have digested the theory of navigation, but had he mastered the practical skills of ship-handling? With one eye, maybe, on the lessons to be learnt from the mixed fortunes of England's mariners in the reign of Elizabeth I, Captain John Foxe, writing two generations later, would deride what he called 'Mathematicall sea-men'[9] instead praising the 'painefull Seaman ... who must be taught to practice by long and industrious use'[10] and was not 'a good Sea-man that hath not undergone the most Offices about a Ship, and that hath not in his youth bin both taught and inured to all labours'.[11] John was now to realize his shortcomings as a 'good Sea-man' for, en route to Cape Horn, the *Bark Francis* was shipwrecked off the River Plate. Struggling ashore, many of the crew were promptly killed by the local Indians. John should have died then. Instead, the Spaniards captured him. Once they discovered his name, his fate was sealed.

Despite Sir Francis Drake's abhorrence of his cousin's 'mutiny', John was family, and Drake made strenuous efforts over the coming years to find his whereabouts. Prisoner exchanges and ransoms were not uncommon even between sworn enemies such as England and Spain. However his efforts proved fruitless, as the Spaniards were not letting on where they held John. In this most personal battle of wills between Sir Francis and Philip II, King of Spain, a prisoner with the name 'Drake' was special. The Spaniards may not have been able to capture the hated El Draco [*sic*] – 'The Dragon' – bane of their existence. Still, having at their mercy his namesake, a cousin to boot, was some small revenge. And with those state secrets locked up in John's head, there was never any chance the Spaniards would set him free. Persuaded by the Inquisition to repent his Lutheranism, John was glimpsed briefly in a procession for the auto-da-fé of 1589 wearing the red cross of those who had rediscovered the 'true faith'. He then disappears from view, except that a 'John Drake' does, tantalizingly, show up in the records of the Spanish Inquisition in 1650, when John would have been 88 and Sir Francis was long dead.

Another younker to suffer at the hands of the Inquisition was Miles Philips, just 14 when one of those put ashore in 1568 by Hawkyns whose ship became overcrowded with survivers from an attack against the English fleet at San Juan de Ulla in Mexico. More than a hundred mariners, men and boys, were left stranded on the American shoreline in the Gulf of Mexico, somewhere between modern-day Galveston and New Orleans. Along with Miles Philips was Hawkyns' nephew, Paul Horsewell, aged ten. Hawkyns vowed to return with ships and provisions to carry the men and boys home to England, but he broke his promise. Abandoned to their fate, Miles and Paul survived an attack by natives from the Chichemici tribe, who killed others of their companions but, dying of thirst and starvation, they finally surrendered to the Spanish in a nearby town. Miles described how he and his fellow captives 'remained prisoners in the said house [of the Viceroy] for the space of four moneths after their coming thither at the end whereof the fleete being readie to depart from St John de Ullua to goe to Spaine, the said Gentlemen were sent away into Spaine with the fleete where as I have heard it credibly reported, many of them died with the cruell handling of the Spaniards in the Inquisition house.'[12]

Miles was lucky. For five years, being deemed too young, he was spared the harshest punishments, instead being put to work as a servant 'to serve sundry gentlemen'. Then the Inquisition arrived in Mexico, and all those captives not already sent to Spain were rounded up and interrogated. Some were given '200 stripes on horsebacke, and some 100, and condemned for slaves to the gallies, some for 6 yeeres, some for 8 and some for 10'.[13] Others were burnt at the stake. Only the youngest, Miles included, were spared the worst punishments, the Inquisition judging them free of Lutheran heresies, since they'd left England before they were old enough to receive religious instruction:

> And then was I Miles Philips called, and was adjudged to serve in a monasterie for
> five yeeres, without any stripes, and to wear a fooles coat, or S. Benito during all that

time. Then were called, John Storie, Richard Williams, David Alexander, Robert Cooke, Paul Horsewell and Thomas Hull: the sixe were condemned to serve in monasteries without stripes some for three yeeres and some for foure and to weare the S. Benito during all the said time.[14]

Only in 1582 'after 17 yeeres absence, having sustained many and sundry great troubles and miseries'[15] did he return home to England.

What motivated these younkers to venture their lives in unknown lands and uncharted waters, where vengeful enemies and hidden dangers lurked everywhere? For some, the warm embrace of the Press Gang left them no choice. Young Richard Temple claimed that 'he being in the said port of Plymouth the said general John Hawkyns under commission he held from the Queen of England ordered him to go on board the flagship'.[16] William Cornelius, who had been at sea since he was 12, described how 'one day as he was going along the street unsuspectingly they fell upon him suddenly and hurried him on board as they were short of people owing to the fact that they were going to Guinea which had the reputation of being an unhealthy country where they would die from fever'.[17] As for John Drake and the boy with no name on Mocha Island, it was all about 'gold come as plentiful as this wood unto the ships',[18] or so Sir Francis Drake told them when, faced with mutiny in his fleet, he issued a rallying call to those aboard the *Elizabeth* just weeks before they ventured into the treacherous Magellan's Strait on the Famous Voyage. Addressing himself to the youngest boys among those assembled, 'he declared what wealth the worst boy in the fleet should get by this voyage, and how the worst boy should never need to go to sea again, but should be able to live in England with [like] a right good gentleman'.[19]

For Sir Francis Drake, 'worst boy' was, doubtless, a mere figure of speech, and if there was a worst boy back then he remained hidden from view. Not so some two centuries on when the Industrial Revolution spawned an avalanche of candidates for the title of 'worst boy', many of whom, seemingly, were to be dumped on Britain's navy. What is more, with so many candidates to choose from, Britain's cast-offs could no longer remain invisible, anonymous. They must have a name, height, colour of hair, everything that was necessary to distinguish them from other cast-offs. Like it or not, it would be possible for Britain to begin identifying its 'worst boy'.

SCAPE GALLOWSES

'A sprightly boy, his character doubtful, read midling.'[1] Short, sharp and to the point. No call for heavy-duty psychological profiling. The captain, seeing this entry in a column marked 'Character' and taking on this boy in September 1786, knew pretty much what to expect. Add to this the information logged in the other columns of a ledger book entitled *Register of Boys Received – Discharged*, and the picture was complete:

Date when received: Sept 13 1786

Number: 1

Name: Ja's Sidaway

Age: 13

Stature: 4ft 8inches

Description: Brown hair with two scars in his head

When discharged: Sept 29 1786

To whom discharged: Gunner on the *Pearl*, Deptford

In what capacity to serve: Servant

No. of days victualled: 17.[2]

Here is none of the anonymity of Drake's 'worst boy', nor the facelessness of John Drake aboard the *Golden Hind*. This boy from 1786 had as good as a passport: name, age, height, even some distinguishing features. And he had done enough in 17 days to warrant his own sharply etched personality, all this despite being only

13 years old. Once out at sea, Sidaway might well have receded into anonymity, and his destiny be no different to that of the younkers of 200 years before but, whatever that fate – living to a ripe old age, or being invalided out, shipwrecked, killed in action, or carried away by one of the many diseases that afflicted sailors – for a brief time in his life young Sidaway hit an official register.

To what body of late Georgian officialdom did Sidaway owe this, by the standards of the times, meticulous record? The organization in question is The Marine Society, founded in 1756, and the largest and most successful of a number of ventures launched about this time, including the Foundling Hospital, Christ's Hospital School and the Royal Hospital School, whose boys were to have a 'Destination to Navigation'. The first meeting of the Society was held in the King's Arms Tavern, Cornhill on 25 June of that year to approve 'A Plan of the Society for contributing towards a supply of Two or Three thousand Mariners for the navy'.[3]

The first batch of 41 boys was inscribed in the *Entry Book for Boys* (an early version of the *Register of Boys Received – Discharged*) on 5 August 1756. The very first boy entered was Anthony J. Philips. Unsurprisingly for a new organization, record-keeping was rudimentary and, in contrast to the relative wealth of detail given to Sidaway 30 years later, the entry for Philips has the bare minimum of information. Apart from his date of entry, his age, 15, and his place of abode, Bloomsbury, the only other detail given is in a column headed 'Parents or Fatherless', where Philips is listed as 'friendless' – meaning he was worse off than an orphan, having no relative to claim responsibility for him. Nor do we know where Philips began his seagoing career. To all intents and purposes, he vanished. The only clue to his whereabouts comes in the minutes of the Society's next meeting on 12 August:

> John Fielding having procured 24 boys for the sea service, they were all clothed by the Society... Order'd that 10 of the said boys be sent to Admiral Broderick and 14 to Capt. Barber of the *Princess Royal* at the Nore and that each Boy shall have a Testament, Common Prayer Book, Clasp Knife and a printed list of their Cloths.[4]

Philips was not the only boy passing through the Society in 1756 to have no official past and no future. Of the first 100 boys registered in the *Entry Book*, 29 were recorded as 'friendless' and another 21 as 'fatherless' or 'mother only'. Seventeen came from outside London, from as far afield as Somerset (Wm. Stacey, aged 14, friendless), Shropshire, Newcastle, Lancashire and Dublin (Patrick Furtel, aged 14, father 'Worsted Weaver'). Only occasionally are personal details given, as with six of the boys who had links to the sea, among them Gamaliel Shannon, aged 14, described as 'Father dead, was Lieut of a Man of War'.[5]

The perfunctoriness of these early entries relative to 30 years on could be a measure of an organization still in its birth-pangs. More likely, it is a reflection of the different pressures on the Society. In 1786 Britain was at peace, and there was time for the Society to be methodical in its bookkeeping. As a result, all 25 boys in the 'class' of 13 Sept 1786 enrolling with Sidaway had the same level of detail. There was Daniel Cameron, aged 15, height 4ft 6in., whose 'Description' was marked down as 'light brown hair, fair complexion, troubled with Trotts', and 'Character' as 'a wicked boy, reads well'.[6] Also, because it was peacetime, Daniel Cameron's 'No. of days victualled' at the Society was a leisurely 43 days, after which he was discharged as a 'servant' to 'Carpenter Merritt' on board the 'Canada, Portsmouth'.

John Drangsill, another boy from that year's intake, spent an even more leisurely 153 days at the Society. No reason is discernible from the records why he spent so long there. Maybe without the pressure of war and captains baying at the Society's heels for 'volunteers', there was time to ensure that boys recovered from their ailments. Additionally, with Drangsill's 'Character' being 'a very good boy reads well', there is a possibility that his potential had been spotted and he was being groomed for a career in the merchant service, hence why he was discharged as an 'apprentice', not 'servant' to 'James Mather, Owner of the Ship Nancy'.[7]

Back in 1756, however, Britain was on edge, about to embark on another in the interminable string of deadly conflicts with France – this one the Seven Years' War – which bedevilled this period of the two nations' histories. Within weeks of its formation, the Society came under pressure from the 'Right Hon'ble the Lords of the Admiralty' to deliver on the 'Plan…towards a supply of Two or Three Thousand Mariners',[8] which it had submitted following its 1 July meeting. The minutes of the Society's 29 July meeting hinted at the urgency: 'A letter was read from John Fielding Dated 26 July Instant, signifying that the Commander of His Majesty's Ship the St George had applied for Thirty Boys'.[9] Not yet in a position to supply boys by its own efforts, the Society resolved instead to 'send Mr Fielding sixty pounds for the Clothing, Bedding and convoying to Portsmouth 30 boys on board His Majesty's ships'.[10]

The growing feverishness of the war effort is palpable in the *Entry Book*, whose entries become ever more perfunctory. All we know of Boy 152 from the *Entry Book* is his name, Thomas White, and his date of enrolment, 30 September. White could have appeared from, and vanished back into, thin air for all the world knew; hardly a reassuring fact, especially given the speed at which these boys passed through the Society's doors before being whisked off to their port of embarkation – one week. This frenzy is further evidenced in the growing intensity of the Society's recruitment campaign. With the navy's manpower requirement rising from 10,000 to 80,000 during the Seven Years' War (1756–1763), Fielding's '24 boys for the sea service'[11] were a drop in the ocean. From 1700, navy regulations allowed an admiral of the fleet 50 servants, an admiral 30 servants, a vice-admiral 20 servants, and a rear admiral 15 servants.[12] A captain was allowed four servants for every 100 crew, which, on a first-rate 100-gun ship-of-the-line with a crew of 800, equated to 32 captains' servants. These 'servants' were the future officers of the navy. Drawn from the ranks of 'young gentlemen', they were quite definitely not candidates for recruitment by the Society. Other officers and warrant officers were also allowed a quota of servants and it was these more lowly servants and cabin boys that the Society needed to find for the navy. Overall, this meant that between five and ten per cent of a ship's complement would typically have been 'servants' – be they 'young gentlemen' or 'boys'.

By the Society's calculations, some 4,500 servants alone were required at the outbreak of the Seven Years' War, and yet there were only 1,000 sons of gentlemen and 'reputable persons' considered available to fill this requirement. The Society launched a massive recruitment drive, with 2,000 advertisements placed in 'all the Daily Papers for One Week' and 'pasted up in the streets'[13] across the capital. There was no patriotic call to arms, instead a matter-of-fact statement of conditions of employment:

All stout Lads and Boys who incline to go on board His Majesty's Ships, as servants, with a view to learn the duty of a seaman, and are, upon examination, approved by The Marine Society, shall be handsomely clothed and provided with bedding, and their charges borne down to the ports where His Majesty's Ships lye, with all proper encouragement.[14]

Thus were spelt out the key ingredients in the three-way compact between the boy, the Society and the navy. The boys had to be 'stout', meaning able-bodied, which was in turn defined by the Society as no younger than 14 and no shorter than 4ft 3in. Practical considerations overriding all others, there was a job waiting for boys at sea, and there was no point sending weaklings to His Majesty's Ships: captains would only complain or reject them. Nevertheless, the Society's records are full of underage, undersized boys, such as Richard East, 3ft 11in. tall, aged ten. The Society's flouting of its own rules is best explained in light of the age limit set by the navy, which was 13, or 11 in the case of sons of naval officers, such as Richard Philip, aged 12 and 4ft 1in. tall, whose father was on board the ship he was being sent to.

'Upon examination' in the advertisement referred to the medical checks undertaken to identify 'the various Distempers which are the Constant Consequences of Poverty and Nastyness'[15] namely the 'trotts' and scurvy, both treatable. The 'pox' (smallpox), was an endemic condition and, again, no obstacle to entry. The 'itch' not a problem if the cause was the curable scabies, but a barrier to entry if it was symptomatic of the dreaded lice-borne disease known as ship fever (typhus), which could sweep away a whole ship's complement should just one new recruit come aboard infected with it. The Society retained on its staff a surgeon, John James, who checked for and treated the minor, curable skin afflictions and had its own lodgings in Grub Street, where the latest intake were sent to be scrubbed, disinfected and treated.

The word 'incline' in the advertisement points to boys being invited to join as 'volunteers'. Better a willing than an unwilling recruit was the reasoning, and a young one to boot. Although the Society would expand its role over the years to handle recruitment of landsmen, in the words of Jonas Hanway, driving force behind the foundation of the Society: 'It is beyond contradiction that those bred to the sea from the earliest part of life, generally become the ablest mariners ... being inured to hardship they are not only rendered the more active and intrepid, but they can bear long voyages, winter cruizes and change of climate.'[16] He had evidently read all about Foxe's 'painefull Seaman'.

In return for agreeing to become 'servants', the boys would be clothed and given bedding, both not inexpensive items. According to the Society's own calculations, these costs were as follows:

1756/7:   £3,739 for 2,046 boys [= £1.83 per boy or c. £58.56 today]

1758:   £1,770 for 930 boys [= £1.90 per boy or c. £60.80 today]

1759:   £1,282 for 710 boys [= £1.81 per boy or c. £57.92 today]

A boy's kitbag typically included a felt hat, two worsted caps, a kersey pea jacket, waistcoat, shirts, up to three pairs of drawers, trousers and a couple of pairs of shoes. Bedding comprised a mattress, pillow and blanket. Kitting out the boys was the most important contribution the Society made, not only in financial terms but also in enabling the boys to feel at one with seaboard life. More significantly, a set of new clothes and bedding 'detached' the recruit from his disease-carrying lice.

The reference to 'proper encouragement' in the advertisement meant a wage of 40 shillings a year (c. £60 today), a considerable improvement on what a boy would receive for a land-based apprenticeship. With all these blandishments, what more could a boy want, especially if he were 'friendless' and, in Hanway's words, one of the 'distressed orphans, who wander about like forsaken dogs'?[17] Much more, in Hanway's opinion, for he saw his brainchild as having a higher purpose than that of mere recruitment agency. In tune with the enlightened philanthropy that swept Georgian Britain in the middle of the 18th century, Hanway and the other worthy founders of the Society cloaked their new venture in a thick veil of good intentions. Hanway loftily described his vision:

> You ask me if I am a philanthropist; well, yes Sir, I am… I am flattered you perceive in
> me more than the street urchins to whom I am known as a curiosity … they know that
> I can fit them for the sea… Without parents who should patronise them but persons
> like myself? Witness the wretched condition of the Climbing Boys [chimney sweeps]…
> The excuse is the urchin must have employment, or starve. What nonsense; there is
> employment enough at sea… In this wise we may save the climbing boys and prepare
> others for service with the fleet that being the chief purpose of The Marine Society.[18]

To reinforce the broad charitable roots of the Society, the early advertisements issued a general offer of assistance to the needy, whether suitable for the navy or not: 'If, in the meanwhile, any are in distress for want of the necessaries of life the same shall be provided for them, in the most satisfactory manner at the Society's house, under the care of Mr Fluyd, in Grub-street.'[19] Further emphasizing the evangelical message of noble intentions, the Society's committee resolved that it would be Society policy to 'take care of their souls as well as their bodies'.[20] Prior to being frogmarched by a 'conductor' to the coast – a journey, to Portsmouth, which took four days – the boys received religious instruction from a dominie, and the Society for the Propagation of Christian Knowledge provided a Testament and Common Prayer Book. In addition, the Society gave each boy a copy of Archbishop Synge's *Essay towards making the Knowledge of Religion Easy to the Meanest Capacity*, whose title spoke volumes for what earnest messages awaited those who could read its contents. The boys may be forgiven for thinking that their other standard-issue bedtime reading, the *Seaman's Monitor*, offered lighter fare. Not a chance. Written by Reverend Woodward, it had precious little to do with practical seamanship and everything to do with strictures on sailors' indiscipline, godlessness and inveterate blaspheming. Emphasizing that there was no escape for the wicked, the message in the 1772 *Regulations of the Marine Society* was that 'religion makes the steadiest warriors'.[21]

With such a morally weighty reading list awaiting these boys on board ship, it is no wonder that the column marked 'Character' in the *Register of Boys* had, by the time Sidaway was passing through the Society's doors in 1786, an obligatory reference to literacy, be it 'very good boy, reads well', or 'an idle bad boy, very dull in learning, cannot read' or, somewhat ambivalently, 'a smart willing boy, can't read'.[22]

However philanthropic the intentions of the Society's founders, there is no disguising the more sinister means it used to fulfil its aims. Writing in 1758, Hanway set out how the Society was 'a means to render our highways and our streets more secure; and by a gentle or compulsive means remove the wretched crouds who disturb the peace of civil society'.[23] Compulsion was a direct contradiction of the Society's 1757 advertisements claiming that it was 'resolved not to infringe on the Liberty of the Subject'.[24] The resolutions of the Society's meetings show how it wrestled with this contradiction in practice. An overseer, called a 'providetor', responsible for housing the boys during their sojourn at the Society was expected to forewarn captains about the conduct of certain boys, but only by way of 'Private Intimations'. Especially wayward boys were shipped straight to a tender on the Thames where they were close confined, prior to joining their designated ship.

The *Entry Book* left open whether some boys arrived at the Society's doors, if not under compulsion, certainly on the horns of Hobson's choice, as in the case of John Britchard (Entry 86), whose record does not indicate any crime but who still came by order of the Lord Mayor. As for Sam Hardman, aged ten, the only 'crime' he committed was one of association: his father was recorded in the *Entry Book* as a smuggler. Still, Hardman may have been placed with the Society with the consent of his father. As for the numerous orphans arriving from around the country, it is inconceivable that they did so under their own steam or with the consent of a parent. Rather, they arrived as a result of the Society's early recruitment drive with local magistrates, parish officers, aldermen, beadles and bishops. So successful was this campaign that the Society had to issue an advertisement telling local officials not to send further boys without prior agreement. If these boys' only 'crimes' were that they were 'friendless', 'distressed orphans, who wander about like forsaken dogs', it is difficult to square the Society's philanthropic aspirations with its means of compulsion, which were tantamount to the Press Gang, the only difference being that boys were too weak to resist its embrace.

However, in the case of the Higgins brothers (Entries 803, 804 and 805), registered as 'Three Thieves', there was no need for the Society to wrestle with any contradictions. These were out-and-out criminals, and it is implausible that they arrived at the Society of their own free will and made such an unabashed admission. More likely, they were accompanied, compelled by a court official who made the declaration on their behalf.

Going by the *Entry Book* alone, the Higgins brothers were the exception, in which case the Society's 'Doorkeeper' registering them on arrival could doubtless lay claim to having found Britain's worst boys. For Hanway, however, the Higgins brothers were just three among a cast of hundreds, if not thousands, of Britain's worst boys. By the *Regulations of the Marine Society* in 1772, he had Society boys classified according to whether they were good, or not so good and with 'little or no guard against temptation', or were so 'abominably corrupted [by the] most wicked company, in the most wicked parts of these kingdoms' that they were 'hardened in iniquity'.[25] Hanway concluded that the majority fell into the last category.

The magistrate John Fielding echoed Hanway's cynicism, describing 'numberless miserable, deserted, ragged, and iniquitous pilfering Boys that at this Time shamefully infested the Streets of London'.[26] He also knew where to lay blame, referring to 'Shoals of Shop-Lifters, Pilferers, and Pick-pockets who, being deserted Children of Porters, Chairmen and low Mechanics, were obliged to steal for their Subsistence'.[27] And Fielding should know, because, as a senior magistrate for the Covent Garden district, he witnessed the human detritus of social dislocation passing daily through his courts. Henry Fielding, John's half-brother and himself a Justice of the Peace, dramatized the plight of these illegitimate offspring in *Tom Jones*, published in 1749, when he had Mrs Deborah say of the foundling Tom that 'it is, perhaps, better for such creatures to die in a state of innocence than to grow up and imitate their mothers, for nothing better can be expected of them'.[28]

Queen Anne's Act of 1703, allowing for vagabonds as young as ten to be sent to sea as maritime apprentices, was meant to have removed these unfortunate children from Britain's streets, so it was not as if the problems identified by the Fieldings, or indeed the proposed cure, were new; only more acute, more widespread, more intractable. Hanway and the Fieldings were seeing the Industrial Revolution begin to cast its shadow over the nation's towns and cities, fracturing traditional family and social structures and leaving in its wake thousands of cast-offs to fend for themselves. With the Poor Laws and Apprentice Laws militating against a wrongdoer whatever his age, and an offender's capacity to distinguish good from evil, often the only measure applied when deciding on the level of punishment, boys as young as 14 could be deemed fit for the gallows. By 1775 Hanway was noting that the majority of criminals being hanged were aged 16 to 21.

Faced with this crisis where 'for want of a seasonable relief, carts full of these unhappy wretches have ended their days in the vigour of their youth, at the dreadful tree',[29] it is no wonder Hanway would accept the necessity of compulsion, 'for by thus checking them in the very dawning of their iniquity, Tyburn might be left a desert'.[30] The Society offered Britain's street urchins a choice: the gallows or the sea, hence the nickname given to Society boys by their fellow mariners: 'Scape Gallowses'. Choose the sea, however, and they might find themselves side by side with the most unlikely of naval companions, one who, to read King George III's letters from just a few years on, had his own claim to be Britain's 'worst boy'.

A ROYAL SAILOR

I n October 1781, Yorktown surrendered to rebel forces under the command
of General George Washington, ending British resistance in Virginia. Surely
this was the beginning of the end for the British in the American colonies?
Yet, six months on, the British were still doggedly holding out in New York. The
city might be their last stronghold in the American colonies. Notwithstanding,
it was defended by a formidable force of thirty thousand Redcoats. To give
the British further solace, tensions were evident between the republicans of the
American cause and their haughty royalist French allies, Canada remained
stubbornly loyal to the British Crown, and Britain's unrivalled navy controlled
the strategically vital sea routes along the eastern seaboard.

So the game wasn't up yet, which presented General Washington with a
political problem. The war had already lasted five years. Washington firmly
believed that final victory was in sight, but not all his fellow Americans saw it that
way. Voices, wearying of the seemingly endless war, were raised in Congress and
among the people. There was talk of compromise, truces, a peace treaty, anything
rather than the prospect of an attritional fight to the last man standing. Fearful that
total victory would be snatched from under his nose, not by the enemy but rather
through lack of fortitude among his own, Washington desperately began casting
around for a single tactical masterstroke that would shock the British, rock them
to the core, shorten the war and mercifully end the bloody misery.

In March 1782, Washington's prayers seemed to be answered. Encamped in
Morristown, New Jersey, news reached him via his all-seeing spy network that no

less a personage than Prince William Henry, third son of King George III, had arrived in New York. What was this mere stripling of a boy doing 3,000 miles from the British court? Nothing, it seemed, apart from manifesting what one genteel New Yorker euphemistically referred to as 'a decided fondness for manly pastimes'[1] and ice-larking around on 'a small freshwater lake in the vicinity of the city, which presented a frozen sheet of many acres: and was thronged by the younger part of the population for the amusement of skating'.[2]

According to local reports, 'as the Prince was unskilled in that exercise, he would sit in a chair fixed on runners, a crowd of officers environed on him, and the youthful multitude made the air ring with their shouts for Prince William Henry'.[3] So the prince was having a high old time. No surprise, given his age, but what madness could have possessed the king to let his 16-year-old son come all this way to frolic and gambol within sniper's range of the rebel enemy? Certainly not the porphyria that incapacitated Britain's king in later years; the disease had not yet taken hold. So what, if anything, was the king's ploy?

The answer to this question begins four years earlier, in 1778, when Prince William's parents started agonizing over a fitting education for the third in line to the throne. Their eldest son, George, was already manifesting wild tendencies to debauchery, but, as heir to the throne, he must be kept close to court so as to best prepare him for kingship. Frederick, their second son, was destined for the army, the latest in a long line of soldier princes. As for William, he was already proving troublesome and must be kept gainfully employed, or he'd make mischief with his elder brothers.

A solution came staring the king and queen in the face during a visit they made to Portsmouth in the spring of 1778 for a long-overdue review of the navy. Britain had been at loggerheads with the renegade American colonies for the past two years, and the king saw the rebellion increasingly as a personal challenge to his royal power. However, away from court, opinion was divided about the justness of the rebel cause. The war was unpopular in the country, and the Whigs in Parliament were outspokenly sympathetic to the rebels. There were even captains in the navy refusing to serve on the American station.

Nevertheless, France's recent entry into the war on the side of the Americans should change all that. France was the old enemy. No loyal Englishman could possibly doubt any longer the justness of this war. Still, if the king were to trump the Whig waverers, the circumstances called for a masterstroke of statesmanship. He would show the nation that his royal family, the House of Hanover, was prepared to lead from the front, take the fight to the enemy. And what better way than to enrol his own 12-year-old son, William, in the navy? The Crown and the navy, the two supreme guardians of the national interest, would thus become one in the eyes of the people.

Affairs of state might dictate this tactical manoeuvre, but the king and queen were nothing if not caring parents, and there was no question of their third son being offered up as a sacrificial lamb. Therefore, before deciding on this novel form of royal education, they must see for themselves the life that a boy sailor could expect to lead. Arriving in Portsmouth and boarding the 90-gun flagship, *Prince George*, the king 'visited the three Decks to see the Men exercise as in Action…then saw the whole economy of the Ship'.[4] However, as with all official inspections, there was the inevitable *trompe l'œil*: the sailors kitted out in their best uniforms, the ship all spick and span, any evidence of the harsh reality that was a sailor's lot hidden from view. Hosts and guests alike colluded in the charade that official protocol dictated. Next came a 'surprise' inspection of the Portsmouth Naval Academy, one of the earliest institutions to provide shore-based training for future generations of naval officers. The king and queen were not impressed. No matter; the composite impression of discipline, natural order and camaraderie that they had witnessed first hand among the sailors and officers on board the *Prince George* fully convinced them that the navy was, coinciding fortuitously with the exigencies of statecraft, the ideal environment in which to complete the education of their handful of a third son. Prince William Henry had an alarming tendency to temper tantrums, a fact the king only alluded to some years later: 'William has ever been violent when controuled [*sic*]. I had hoped that by this time He would have been conscious of his own levity and that in his Station his conduct must be more studied than in that of Persons who from the privacy of their birth cannot be held out as examples for others to look up to…'[5]

The navy would soon sort that out – and more besides. The prince might even make a career of it in the navy. The decision taken, the king threw himself with gusto into preparations for his son's new life, even down to the smallest detail of attire, as the Governor of the Naval Academy, Sir Samuel Hood, soon discovered when the king wrote to him shortly after returning to London to ask 'what cloaths, necessaries and books he ought to take. This will enable me to be ready when called upon by the Captain for this Young One; he has begun Geometry and I shall have an attention to forward him in whatever you hint of as proper to be done before he enters into that glorious Profession.'[6]

Sir Samuel duly responded, providing a clothes and sundries list that included:

2 uniforms,

a short blue coat of the jacket make, with uniform buttons and waistcoat & breeches the same.

3 dozen of shirts & stocks – part of the latter black ones.

3 dozen pairs of stockings some silk, some cotton or thread & some worsted

Six pairs of shoes & a pair of boots

2 Hatts & 2 round ones / Hatts are liable to be lost overboard!

Mattrass, bolster & Pillows 3 blankets & a Quilt

Six pair of sheets & Pillow Cases

2 Dozen of Hand Towels

Pocket handkerchiefs, night caps or netts.

Basons, washballs, brushes, combs etc[7]

A royal prince must look and live the part, even at sea. Next came a long list of textbooks, including the following weighty tomes:

'…Robertson's Elements of Navigation…'

'Patoun's Navigation…'

Mariner's New Calendar,

'Nautical Almanac…'

Sherwin's Mathematical Tables.

The prince's heart must have sunk when he saw this list, and sunk further at the sight of the remaining items on the list: 'Pens, ink powder & paper – Mem'd Books, Log Books & Journal Books – Slate & Pencil.'[8]

The prince was being left in no doubt that he would be expected to study and keep a daily log. The logbooks, which the prince filled in assiduously, at least in his early years at sea, highlight the exceptional problems for the 'Young Sailor' of adjustment to his new life. Knowing that his every move was watched, his every word scrutinized, these logs were written with an audience in mind. As a result, there is a discernible tension between William the boy, the prince and the sailor.

Generally, the logbooks strictly confine themselves, as was naval convention, to the daily routine of shipboard life. Occasionally, however, the boy in him – especially when he had been naughty – burst out, as on 23 June 1779, a week after going to sea, when he wrote: 'Nota Bene at half past 5 o'clock I was not awaked by a gun.'[9] Here is the merest hint that the prince had overslept his watch and was using his logbook to explain away the transgression. The 13 July entry 'I went on shore to Farmer Lilington where I drank some milk'[10] begs the question: was the little cherub drinking cow's milk or, in the naval slang of the time, quaffing 'milk-water', a vicious alcoholic distillation of milk and herbs officially described as 'an intoxicating drink resembling egg-nog'?[11]

It is difficult at times to discern whose actions the prince is describing. This was another of his ploys. With an entry 'caught a bonetta'[12] recorded for 4pm on 16 June, it is a safe assumption that the prince was the hero of that hour. However, other entries, such as 'washed between decks with vinigar'[13] on 13 July, were, it seems, left deliberately ambiguous. As this is one of the few references to this chore, here may have been a reluctant admission that he had committed some misdemeanour and this was his punishment.

Two months into his time at sea, the prince employed the same ambiguity to cover his tracks, but, as all parents know, children can only lie for so long, and this time he gave himself away. Two entries, one on 5 August, 'served beer',[14] followed by another on 19 August, 'lost in sounding a Deep Sea lead and line',[15] seem at first sight unconnected. Check the handwriting in the logbook and a different story emerges: it progressively deteriorates during August to the point where it is virtually illegible, only to improve dramatically the day after *he* lost the 'Deep Sea lead and line'.

'Cloaths, necessaries and books' taken care of between the king and Sir Samuel Hood, there remained the thorny question of the young sailor's prospective accommodation on board ship: 'I trust you will, whenever my intentions become publickly known, throw out to your friend the propriety of his allowing a small place to be made with light sufficient for William's following his studies as I should rather wish this appear'd politeness of the Captain than an application.'[16]

The king was attempting to balance his 'whole plan' as a stern father bent on ensuring that his son would 'be treated with civility but no marks of respect'[17] with the pragmatic awareness that, as son of the monarch, Prince William Henry must inevitably be set apart, not only from the seamen, but also from the young gentlemen who would, at least nominally, be his peers. There would be other small but significant ways in which William would be marked apart from the day he came aboard. Although initially set to fulfil the official duties of 'captain's servant', the lowest of the low for aspiring officer material, he would nevertheless carry the more exalted title of 'Midshipman' from day one, thus taking him effortlessly one rung up the steep ladder of a ship's officer hierarchy. Furthermore, he was to have his own tutor, Reverend Majendie, who would also, somewhat incongruously, carry the rank of 'Midshipman'. Majendie would teach his young charge Christian religion, and Latin and English composition.

History was also on the curriculum, but the king insisted in his instructions to Majendie that history meant 'That the Study of the English History will be a pleasant as well as useful occupation, Mr Majendie should in the first course merely teach him the Facts and omit much Political Reasoning that will take more effect when his mind is more enlightened'.[18] His son might be a political pawn in the king's game of chess with his subjects, but there was no point prematurely muddling the head of one so young with the arcane subtleties of statecraft.

For Majendie, this new calling would be a mixed blessing. It was one thing to be the prince's tutor but quite another to act as watchdog, charged round the clock with keeping the boy out of trouble. A difficult enough task on land, it would be a well-nigh impossible one at sea, given that Majendie had rarely before set foot outside the cloisters of Cambridge, had never left terra firma and was wholly unfamiliar with the ins and outs of a ship and all the attendant temptations. Prince William, once he learnt the ropes, would run rings round his tutor.

Before wishing his son 'God Speed', the king wrote him a long, plaintive epistle, the first of many over the years to come, exhorting his young sailor to the highest pinnacles of exemplary behaviour, beginning portentously with, 'You are now launching into a Scene of Life, where you may either prove an Honour, or a Disgrace, to your Family' and culminating in mounting crescendo with:

Though when at home a Prince, on board the *Prince George* You are only a Boy learning the Naval Profession: but the Prince so far accompanies You that what other Boys might do, You must not. It must never be out of Your thoughts that more Obedience is necessary from You to Your Superiours in the Navy, more Politeness to Your Equals and more good nature to Your Inferiours, than from those who have not been told that these are essential for a Gentleman.[19]

On 15 June 1779, aged 13, His Royal Highness Prince William Henry boarded the *Prince George*. Marking the start of a career at sea spanning 11 years, the prince made a first entry in his 'Logg Book' (a misspelling he did not repeat): 'I went away to every part of the ship, where I was received with universal joy,'[20] Presumably advised that a logbook was no place for displays of egocentric emotions, he quickly reverted to the matter-of-fact of sea life, concluding this first entry with a befitting economy of words: 'Moored at Spithead. Variable winds. Light airs and fair.'[21]

Bed for the young sailor that first night at sea was in a canvas cot slung from a beam, located, of course, in his own quarters. However, except for this privilege and dinner most evenings at the admiral's table, William's life at sea revolved around the after-cockpit, the dank, dark nether region at the end of the lower gun deck and below the waterline, where the normal run of midshipmen and captain's servants relaxed, ate, slept, brawled ... and played, which for William, who especially liked his theatricals, meant stage-managing an impromptu canvas theatre on the orlop deck, or burlesquing his favourite role of Prince Hal in *Henry IV*.

From eyewitness accounts of those early days on board the *Prince George*, it is clear that William was keen to integrate with his peers. How a prince was addressed could be a barrier, which William overcame by announcing to his fellow midshipmen: 'My father's name is Guelph and you are welcome to call me William Guelph.'[22] An early entry in his log – 'I went on deck and saw the anchor catted and fished',[23] – shows a ready ear for mess-room slang and an intuitive understanding that language was the surest passport to being accepted. That and a willingness to pull no punches. A taunt that 'the son of a whore is as good a fellow as the son of a king'[24] rolled off the young royal's back, but future challengers received no such clemency. Lieutenant George Moodie of the then much reviled Marines goaded the prince one time with: 'If it was not for your coat, I would give you a basting', to which the prince replied, 'My coat shall not stain my honour'[25] and, discarding his coat, prepared for fisticuffs. They did not come to blows, but a later confrontation with fellow midshipman, Mr Sturt, did.

Nor was the prince averse to rolling up his sleeves in other ways. As the two newcomers on board ship, William and Majendie were expected to take turns cooking for the midshipmen's mess. They did so without demur, but took advantage of the chore to help themselves to more than their fair share of flour rations, not because their bellies were any more deserving, but rather so as to powder their hair ahead of dinner at the admiral's table.

As to the prince's duties on board ship, without pretending to comprehend the specifics of a midshipman's routine at sea, the king had written to Admiral Digby, spelling out in general terms what he expected, namely that the 'Young Sailor' should be 'obliged to perform most rigidly every duty of the Station in which he is placed... [and] That a proper Lieut. be always on the Watch when it is his T[urn] of Duty who must report very exactly how he has behaved...'[26]

To what extent the navy respected the wishes of the king in practice can be seen in the list of rules Admiral Digby later claimed he applied during the three years he supervised the prince at sea:

> ...never to dine or lay out of the ship without his Royal Highness – and ... that his Royal Highness should not go out of the ship without me, that he should receive no visits and never be sent for but to the Commander-in-Chief, nor dine with anybody but the officers of the Fleet and Commissioned officers on shore, that when any officer his Royal Highness had not seen was in the Fleet, I always invited him to dinner and introduced him before we sat down. It was a rule that he employ his morning in studying mathematics till noon when his Royal Highness with all the young people in the ship went to their exercise. That he should every day write his logbook, that he should wear the same dress as the midshipmen and that he should not on any account go off deck in his watch and should not frequent the wardroom.[27]

The prince's logbooks give a better insight into his ordinary and extraordinary duties. The frequent references to soundings as on 1 June 1779, 'sounded in 67 fathoms. Fine brown sand and shells',[28] suggests that this was one of the prince's daily duties, as was signal activity: 'The Adml. made the Sig'l to Rendez-Vous off the Lizard.'[29] On occasional Sundays, because of his royal status, the prince led the crew and 'performed divine service'.[30] On 2 December, six months into his time at sea, William referred for the first time to specific duties allocated to him: 'Variously empl'd: at 10am struck the L.G. Masts. Sent the Pinnace after the Long Boat which went adrift. Empl'd in stowage the Hold and refilling the rigging.'[31] The captain-to-be was starting to give, as well as take, orders.

The prince's early experiences at sea were a curious juxtaposition of raw reality and puerile pursuits. The log entry 'punished Jn. Wright with 12 lashes for being absent without leave'[32] on his second day at sea, was followed soon after by a letter home telling his parents how 'I have been three times on shore with Admiral Digby. He has allowed me to begin to swim & I have been twice in the water with which I am very much delighted.'[33] A few months later the prince went pheasant-shooting and, again, it is the voice of a child seeking sympathy who describes how 'We had to deal with brambles & thorns & at last got into a swamp. When we returned on board the cutter, we had a fire lighted & I pulled off my shoes and stockings to dry. As I was sitting by the fire side, a cinder fell out & burnt my foot. This has turned into a sore, which is troublesome & makes me limp a little.'[34]

After two months at sea, his logbook recorded the dreaded 'cleared for action' for the first time, and his next letter immediately struck a different tone:

> ...we received information from the Southampton of the French & Spanish fleets being in the Channel. We were, as Your Majesty may suppose, very much surprised & allarmed [sic] being apprehensive of their invading England... In the evening of the 30th, we saw some cutters making signals, as was supposed, to the combined fleets. Next morning we saw from the masthead upwards of sixty sail. We were in a very disagreeable situation all day... I wish that the Queen's health may not have been impaired by the anxiety of the mind occasioned by the sudden news of the combined fleets appearing in the Channel.[35]

Words such as 'apprehensive' and 'disagreeable', doubtless chosen by his tutor, enabled William to strike the correct pose of an official dispatch to his sovereign, the king, reporting news vital to the nation's defence. Still unable to contain his enthusiasm, he briefly reverted to the role of son writing to father, when 'we saw from the masthead' placed him with a group of fellow midshipmen high up in the crow's nest, eyes fixed on the horizon, each of them eager to be first to spot and relay to the quarterdeck news of enemy sail on the horizon.

It was a false alarm. The fleets shadowed each other, but each for their own reasons avoided giving battle. William was disappointed, but he would not have long to wait. On 8 January 1780 more enemy sail were sighted. Decks were cleared, furniture stowed and strapped down, gun ports opened. William took his place on the quarterdeck next to Admiral Digby and waited. This time the British would not hold back. William's log described the unfolding battle: 'Saw a strange fleet to w'ward: after which the whole fleet chaced [*sic*] by signal. At 8 tack'd after the strangers, who had tack'd before. At 10, the *Edgar* and *Dublin* brought to several of the chace. Rep'd the signal for the convoy to make sail and for the ships astern to board the Prizes.'[36]

Writing home, William repeated news of the battle, then again struck his official pose:

> I am very happy to congratulate Your Majesty upon the success of the fleet under Sr George Rodney & give you an account of what I myself saw.
>
> Yesterday morning we fell in with a fleet, which proved to be a Spanish fleet of Merchantmen bound from St Sebastian to Cadiz under the Convoy of a 64-gun ship, 4 Frigates and 2 Sloops, laden with corn & naval stores… I have been present at the taking of the first line of battle ship this war.[37]

Caught up in the euphoria of the moment, William could not, however, resist finishing off his account with the jingoistic flourish: '& hope to see such a number of them taken before the end of it as that our enemies, who have undertaken the war upon such unfair grounds, may suffer for their temerity.'[38]

Such intemperate opinions were considered unworthy of a royal prince for whom restrained diplomacy must rule his every utterance, and Admiral Hood had this in mind when, in response to some ill-judged remarks by the prince on the wisdom of the Peace of Versailles a few years later, he 'most strongly recommended to Him that whatever His thoughts are to keep them to himself except in our private conversations.'[39]

William could be forgiven his youthful exuberance this time. He had good, personal reason to celebrate. He had 'rec'd from Cpt MacBride the Colours and Pendant of the Spanish 64-gun ship named the *Prince William Henry*'.[40] His first enemy encounter, a ringside view of the whole engagement and a captured ship-of-the-line named after him to boot. His cup runneth over. So what that MacBride's gesture was doubtless made with one eye to his own promotion prospects. Yet for William there was still no cut and thrust; no blood and guts. No matter; he wouldn't have long to wait. A few days later, another enemy fleet sighted, another action, but this time no tame surrender by the enemy. His 16 January log entry recorded that 'the *Bedford* made the signal for a fleet to the s'ward. At 1, re'd the signal for a line of Battle abreast and at 2 to prepare for action. Made all clear. At 6 or 7 minutes past 2, re'd the signal for a general chace and made sail. At 12 minutes past 2 re'd the signal to engage to Leeward. Made the chace to be a Spanish Fleet of the Line.'[41]

At last William had his opportunity to witness at close quarters a no-holds-barred sea battle, starting with the merciless bombardment and total disintegration of a once-mighty ship-of-the-line. At first William wasn't sure whether the stricken ship was British or Spanish: 'a most shocking & dreadful sight. Being not certain whether it was an enemy or a friend, I felt a horror all over me,'[42] he later wrote to his father. Happily, it turned out to be Spanish. Meantime, the battle was reaching its climax and William was in the thick of the action:

> At 10 mins past 4 came up with a Spanish ship without top mast, who had been engaged by the *Invincible* and was making off. We fired 4 broadsides. At 10 mins before 6, she struck and proved to be a Spanish line of battle ship of 70 guns named *St Julian*. Sent Mr Williams, an offr of Marines, 2 Petty Offrs and 30 men on board her and took possession of her. Took out of her the 2 Captains (the 1st being wounded) 4 Lieuts and 14 men. It blew too hard to ship any more. The Adl. and some of ships in sight. Had 4 men wounded and one mortally. During the action (the first I was ever in) I was quartered near Adl. Digby and the Captain to receive their orders. 4 shot went through our main and maintop sails. Another wounded our F mast. Fresh gales and very hard squalls.[43]

The battle over and his thirst for action finally assuaged, the prince's log entry the next day was altogether more muted, and with good reason. 'Ditto weather…

Departed this life Jn. Smily Seaman wounded in action.'[44] A lower-deck man, in death a comrade-in-arms, had fallen in battle.

Victory was near total. Seven Spanish ships had surrendered, others had sunk or blown up, and Don Juan de Langara, the Spanish admiral, had been captured. Obeying the courtly niceties that applied to such occasions, Don Juan visited Admiral Digby on board the *Prince George*, by then riding at anchor in Gibraltar harbour. When Don Juan was ready to depart 'his Royal Highness appeared in the character of a midshipman and respectfully informed the admiral that the barge was ready'.[45] So much appears to be fact. According to an English historian of the time, the Spanish admiral is then purported to have exclaimed: 'Well, does Great Britain merit the empire of the sea, when the humblest stations in her navy are filled by princes of the blood!'[46] Given the questionable source of this report, there must be some doubt whether Don Juan uttered these words, but to judge by the cannon fire raining down simultaneously on the British fleet from nearby Spanish shore batteries, it is safe to say that, if Don Juan did say these words, he was surely alone among Spaniards prepared that day to contemplate such flattering sentiments about Britain.

Prince William's reputation inflated by such stories, he was accorded a hero's welcome on his return to England two months later. As a tangible symbol of royal commitment to the national cause, he had fulfilled all his sovereign could have wished for. 'I am sincerely happy that Your conduct has been such as to deserve the Approbation of Your Admiral,'[47] the king wrote. Recording the official victory ceremony, William described in his logbook how he 'had the happiness of presenting to the King the Colours taken from the *Prince William*, *St Julian*, and *Prothee*, the first Spanish and French ships of the line taken this war of which I was a Spectator'.[48]

On the streets of London, the public cast him as the single-handed victor of this Battle of Cape St Vincent. Poems lauding the victory alluded to the youthfulness of this, the country's new hero. One entitled 'The Royal Sailor' soared to unimaginable heights of praise:

> When Neptune arose from his wat'ry throne
> In a coral-red suit he most beautifully shone
> He called for his Tritons and bade them repair

> To the Court of Great George, for young William was there
> He's Royal, he's Noble, he's chosen by me
> This Isle to protect and reign Prince of the Sea
> O'erjoy'd at the message, the youth rear'd his head
> 'I'll fight like a Prince', were the words that he said...[49]

Another verse celebration by Henry Pye, the Poet Laureate, referred to 'the young eagle' and 'the intrepid boy'.[50]

Forgotten in all the euphoria, at least temporarily, by the king and queen, were the mounting signs of their son's wayward behaviour, including reports filtering back of his brawling on the streets of Gibraltar, arrest by a military patrol and night spent in the town jail. For the moment the royal couple could bask in the glow of Admiral Digby's fawning report that the prince would make 'a very great sea officer' and that 'the moment he [the prince] saw that they were preparing for action his spirits rose to that degree that he was almost in a state of insanity ... the moment the fleets were separated, his spirits sank very low'.[51]

Alas, the euphoria would not last for long. Wherever the king came by his information, it is clear that parental disillusionment soon set in. The queen may have burst into tears on receiving an earlier letter from William nonchalantly reminding her that 'I may be killed',[52] and the king may have bought into William's early self-portrait of a cherub at sea bathed in innocence:

I hope Sir, that by my conduct it will appear that I have learnt nothing bad; I should be sorry to show any bad example to my Brothers, & particularly to my Sisters. I hope on the contrary by the accounts Your Majesty will receive from the Ad[l] [Admiral] it may be known that I am in the way of proving an honour to my country & a comfort to my parents; that my moral conduct is not infected by the great deal of vice I have seen; nor my manners more impolite by the roughness peculiar to most Seamen... I have translated French, Latin, & English in all which I hope I am improved. The Drawing has not gone on quite so well. I am sensible I have been negligent about it, it is at present more attended to.

By this method of living I have learnt many things in common life I never knew before; amongst others keeping accounts. I have seen the manners practised in the world, & things begin to appear to me in a very different light from what I had seen before. I have seen martial discipline kept up, & the severity arising from it executed: the manner Courts Martial are held: the justice, that is done in a free country.[53]

However, the king was not be fooled for long. Long before Prince William's heroics in battle, letters from the king were peppered with complaints about his son's 'love of improper company' and how his 'manners are still compared to the frequenters of the forecastle'[54]. In one particularly blunt letter, the king accused his son of 'persisting in doing what you knew would displease me then thinking to get off like a child by saying you will not do the like again'.[55]

Now back home in England and on shore leave, opportunities for mischief were boundless. Entanglements of the heart and Prince William Henry's propensity to fall under the spell of his dissolute eldest brother were his undoing and brought about the first of his many banishments from England. Deciding where to pack their 'worst boy' off to was easy. If the latest reports from across the Atlantic were anything to go by, the American colonies were the place for the prince. There he would get action aplenty locking horns with the renegades. And, with one eye on the demands of statecraft, the dispatch of a royal – forget that he was only 15 – to the American colonies could be just what the colonials needed to abandon their rebellious ways and return to the royal fold.

So it was that on 21 July 1781 Prince William recorded in his logbook: 'Rec'd on board 18 boxes of money, made the signal for weighing [anchor]'.[56] The *Prince George*, with William on board, set sail for America. Two months later, at 8pm on 24 September, the prince saw 'Extremes of land from W.S.W. to N.W. 5 leagues'.[57] At midnight 'the Neversunk', a strip of land along the coast, came into view. At 4am the *Prince George* 'made the signal to anchor'. The British fleet had arrived at Sandy Hook, the entrance to the great harbour of New York, headquarters of British administration in the American colonies. Two days later 'the Admiral and myself … anchored at a little distance from the City at 5pm' and 'at our landing we were received on the Beach by Sir Henry Clinton, Commander-in-Chief'.[58]

Prince William, the first member of the British royal family to visit North America, came ashore to a rapturous welcome. The king had anticipated the mood correctly. In this loyalist stronghold eager for a royal banner to rally to, the prince became the focal point of new hope. Patriotic ballads were composed in his honour, time and again emphasizing his 'Royal Youth' come 'to share our dangers and soothe our pains'.[59]

According to Prince William Henry's record of his 'Occurrences on shore',[60] elevated to the status of King's Representative he 'went to the Parade [and] to dinner to the Governor's to meet the Council'.[61] However, the prince's functions were to be more than ceremonial. Trusting his son more than his political or military advisers, the king had given Majendie orders that William be schooled in the art of intelligence-gathering. History was no longer to be 'the Facts and omit much Political Reasoning'. The prince may have only been 16 when he arrived in New York but, with the American colonies slipping away, the king needed reliable, on-the-spot intelligence, hard facts, and the more the better. As a royal prince, William was to be trusted. Here was an opportunity to get back into his father's good books, and Prince William Henry duly obliged.

Soon after arriving in New York he advised his father that 'With Mr Majendie I am writing an extract, that he has collected from different people, relative to the present state of affairs in this continent.'[62] Some of this information would come from a Council of War he attended between Admiral Digby, Admiral Hood, recently arrived from the West Indies, and Captain Russell of the Hussars, where strategic decisions on how to quell the revolt were taken. The prince's log recorded this meeting. Entitled 'Intelligence collected on our Arrival off Sandy Hook, Wednesday September 24 1781',[63] he recorded how 'they had intelligence that Mon. de Graves' fleet from the West Indies were anchored in order to assist and cooperate with the Rebel Army against Earl Cornwallis [and] would soon reduce Lord Cornwallis to the utmost distress if he were not soon relieved.'[64]

Finally, on 28 September, he dispatched the long-awaited report to his father, commenting firstly on the stronghold of New York: 'There is but one Church, all the others being converted either into magazines or Barracks ...[and]... there is great scarcity of lower masts in short of all stores here,'[65] and then on the state of the navy on the American station – 'in a most wretched condition'[66]. Lastly came a report on the limited troop numbers at the king's disposal: 'The inhabitants of the town are in number 25,000. They have 3,000 Militia, besides which there are about 1000 men raised at their own expense.'[67]

However not all was doom and gloom, and in his next report the prince offered a glimmer of hope, suggesting that 'There is a very great disunion between the

French & American[s]… The French treat the Americans with a great deal of hauteur…'[68] To reinforce the point that this weakness could be exploited, William referred to an incident where an American had mistakenly ignored a French sentry's challenge and been lashed to a gun and given 24 strokes with a sabre.

Such rays of hope were few and far between, and uplifting though the presence of a royal might be to New Yorkers, more was needed if the American colonies were to be saved. By now, might and right were firmly on the side of the rebel cause. The time had come for action. And so it was that two weeks after landing in New York William was back on board the *Prince George* in the fleet sent to relieve Yorktown. The fleet arrived off Yorktown on 29 October and the prince's log for that day recorded the dramatic news: 'Rec'd from N.Y. certain information that Lord Cornwallis surrendered on the 19th after having had two of his redouts taken by storm.'[69] Closing this chapter of the war, William wrote three days later: 'Bore away with the whole Fleet for New York, where we arrived on Nov 1.'[70]

Despite the news of this crushing defeat, the loyalists still refused to yield New York. And so it was, five months later in March 1782, that General Washington began casting around for some masterly ruse that would hasten the demise of British rule in the American colonies. With these thoughts in mind, he eagerly seized on a daring plan conceived by Colonel Ogden, commander of the 1st Jersey regiment camped across the Hudson river opposite New York. The plan would climax as follows:

> The order of debarkation to agree with the mode of attack as follows:
>
> First – Two men with a guide, seconded by two others, for the purpose of seizing the sentinels, these men to be armed with naked bayonets and dressed in sailors' habits: they are not to wait for anything but immediately execute their orders.
>
> Second – Eight men, including guides, with myself, preceded by two men with each a crow-bar, and two with each an axe – these for the purpose of forcing the doors, should they be fast – and followed by four men entering the house and seizing the young Prince, the Admiral…[71]

Immediately alive to the possibilities, Washington gave Ogden the go-ahead. Kidnap the third in line to throne and ransom him, not for money, but for liberty … the liberty of the American colonies: a brilliant plan. There was only one problem: through their own spy network, the British got word of the plot and doubled the guards protecting Prince William. Reluctantly, Washington abandoned the plan. The opportunity for a masterstroke, to strike at the heart of the royal family, had been lost. The war rumbled on for another nine months and only with the signing of the Peace of Versailles in January 1783 were the American colonies finally free.

With the end of the American Revolution (sometimes called the American War of Independence), Prince William Henry's fighting career was over. Leaving the Americas, there was however one crumb of comfort that the prince could draw from his time on the American station: in his four years at sea, he had met and dined with many a captain, admiral, governor and general. As a royal prince, nobody was supposed to excite awe in him. And yet, one did:

> …the merest boy of a captain I ever beheld … and his dress was worthy of attention … his lank unpowdered hair was tied in a stiff Hessian tail of an extraordinary length; the old-fashioned flaps of his waistcoat added to the general appearance of quaintness of his figure… I had never seen anything like it before, nor could imagine who he was, or what he came about. My doubts were however removed when Lord Hood introduced me to him. There was something irresistibly pleasing in his address and conversation; and an enthusiasm when speaking on professional subjects that showed he was no common being.[72]

Thus began a lifelong friendship that only ended when Horatio Nelson fell at Trafalgar.

For the king, Prince William Henry returning to England in 1783 had little to show from four years in the navy. As an instrument of royal statecraft, the prince had failed his king: the American colonies were lost for ever. As for it being a novel experiment in royal education, the prince's naval career had also left a lot to be desired. Mindful of his son's 'two uncles the Dukes of Gloucester and Cumberland, who at this alarming moment are', as the Prince's brother remarked, 'at home unemployed because it is impossible to give them any commands as they are so totally ignorant of the Professions into which they have entered',[73] the king had insisted from the outset on a professional naval education for the prince. Yet, seemingly at every turn, William's behaviour was cause for rebuke.

Nevertheless, for all that the father was disappointed in his son, there might still be a bonus, albeit unintended: the king's choice of a naval career for a royal prince might make the navy fashionable for the swelling ranks of younger sons of the aristocracy who had previously shunned a career at sea, but were desperately needed as, with each passing year, the list of Britain's enemies mounted remorselessly.

A SINK OF VICE AND
ABOMINATION

At one end of Britain's social ladder Prince William, budding young sailor, arrived at Portsmouth harbour on 15 June 1779 in a royal carriage attended by his personal tutor, Reverend Majendie, the two all set to climb aboard the *Prince George,* their individual cabins awaiting them. At the other end of that same ladder, stuck on the bottom rung, clinging on for dear life, the latest batch of Scape Gallowses waited their turn to scramble aboard. They, however, were destined not for their own cabins but, with any luck, for the gun room where, for a few days, they might be shielded from the stark realities of lower-deck life by the maternal ministrations of the gunner's wife. Each knew their station in life and at sea.

What, meanwhile, of all those social climbers, neither royal princes nor strangers to beds, caught halfway up or down the ladder, for whom the navy, with all its glittering promises of adventure, a dashing career and limitless prize money, might be a hoped-for lifeline to higher standing and financial advancement? If they had patronage, their progress through the service would be smooth, but for 'want of interest to secure situations that could lead to promotion'[1] their best chance of advancement was with a good naval education. What were their options? Not for James Grant and Mr Sturt, Prince William's fellow midshipmen, the close coaching of a private tutor nor, mercifully, the philanthropic entreaties of the *Seaman's Monitor.* Instead it was either a classroom at sea, sharing, if they were lucky, one of the few schoolmasters spread thinly round His Majesty's ships, or a shore-based naval school, the most famous – or rather infamous – of which was the Portsmouth Naval Academy, the institution visited, but rejected, by King George III in 1778 when deciding on a naval career for Prince William.

Founded by the Admiralty in 1729, the Academy's official mission statement was for 'laying aside the Establishments in force relating to Volunteers at Sea, and for establishing in lieu thereof an academy at Portsmouth for the better education of forty young gentlemen to be trained up for your majesty's said service at sea.'[2] In terms of naval policy, its purpose was being made abundantly clear: to break the long-standing stranglehold individual naval captains and the Crown exercised over the recruitment of the naval officer corps. Until then, families looking to put a son to sea had first to secure the patronage of either a serving captain, whose personal prerogative it was to choose which boys to appoint as a captain's servant – the so-called 'Volunteer-at-Sea'– to his ship, or the Crown, who could issue a King's Letter (hence a 'King's Letter boy') – commanding a captain to take a boy on board. With increasing pressure on the navy to modernize in order to meet new challenges to Britain's 'wooden walls', the Admiralty wished to lay the foundations for a professional cadre of naval officers, appointed and nurtured by it rather than at the whim of personal or royal patronage.

The Academy's founding *Articles and Orders* further confirmed the Admiralty's plan to break with the past. Article 1 stated that 'None shall be admitted into the Academy but the Sons of Noblemen or Gentlemen, who shall not be under thirteen years of age nor above sixteen at the time of their admission.'[3] In a period when it seemed there was no door that was not open to 'sons of Noblemen or Gentlemen', such a statement of positive discrimination in their favour appears redundant, except that this new policy flew in the face of long-standing practices whereby captains drew their volunteers-at-sea from a tightly knit circle of naval and merchant service families. By discriminating in favour of 'Sons of Noblemen or Gentlemen' for entry to the Academy, the Admiralty was intending to kill two birds with one stone: break the captains' stranglehold over naval preferment and widen the net of recruitment at a time when the national interest required a larger navy.

To ram the point home, the Admiralty even ordered ships' captains to accept these 'Sons of Noblemen and Gentlemen' on board their ships after they had graduated from the Academy, by issuing a standard certificate to each graduate which read:

'Whereas Mr.—— has been educated at the Royal Academy at Portsmouth and is well qualified to serve His Majesty at sea, you are hereby required and directed to receive him on board H.M. —— under your command and enter his name as one of her complement.'[4]

The Admiralty may have been looking to favour these 'Sons of Noblemen and Gentlemen' on entry and exit from the Academy, and thenceforth on board ship, but there was an additional problem lamented by, among others, Barnaby Slush in his *Navy Royal* pamphlet published in 1709. Slush observed that these sons of noble birth faced the daunting prospect on board ship of being herded 'at nights among a gang of sorry scabs, the very outcasts of a parish' and expected to 'swing most vilely in some louzy berth surrounded with the noise and stink of rotte-ye-dogs and blackguard boys.'[5] Maybe no bad thing, but hardly conducive to attracting the crème de la crème of Britain's noble crop. Accordingly, during their time at the Academy these sons of noblemen were to be subjected to a regime of deliberately egalitarian utopia. That way, when their time came to 'swing most vilely in some louzy berth' on board ship, the shock would be less. Article 9 stated that '...the Master is to treat all the Scholars with equal care and attention ... there being no preference or distinction to be suffered among the Scholars, either in Boarding, Lodging, Schooling or otherwise', and Article 10 that 'No Scholar shall be allowed to keep a Servant.'[6]

Article 13 spelt out a broad 'plan' of education for the boys' two, maximum three, years of study: 'It being intended that the Master of the Academy shall instruct the Scholars in writing, arithmetic, drawing, Navigation, Gunnery, Fortification and other noteful parts of the Mathematics, and also in the French Language, Dancing, Fencing and the exercise of the Firelock.'[7] This remained substantially the basis of the Academy's curriculum throughout its existence. In a letter dated 10 March 1773, James Trevenen, an 'Academite' from 1772 to 1775, reported to his 'Honoured Father': 'Though I do not like to praise myself I may safely say I have won the affections of my masters, particularly of Mr Jeffrey's, the drawing and arithmetic master in whose hands I now am. Spencer the Irishman, when I first began my plan was above fifty before me and now is not upwards of thirty seven.'[8]

Each boy had a Plan – a coursebook – into which they transcribed the daily exercise-work they performed. Francis Austen, brother of Jane Austen, enrolled at the Academy in 1786 and the 500 pages of *A Plan of Mathematical Learning Taught in the Royal Academy Portsmouth performed by Francis Austen. A student there 1788* [9] set out, in neat, legible handwriting, the work done by him during the two years from 1786, when he enrolled at the age of 11, through to 1788, when he graduated. Francis' Plan provides an intimate insight into not only the training regime of the Academy, but also the rhythm of the scholars' lives during their time there.

On page one Francis faithfully transcribed his tutor's first dictum: 'Arithmetic is a science which teacheth the properties of Numbers and how to compute and estimate the value of things.'[10] By page three he had moved on to a series of tests and it is clear his teacher wanted his pupil thinking himself into the swing of life on board ship. Francis' skill in 'Liquid Measures' was tested with water, wine, ale and, finally, beer.

Example 6 combined subtraction and history in a suitably patriotic note:

How many years since the Spanish Invasion, it being in the year 1588 and the present being 1786?[11]

Example 7 offered a colourfully day-to-day exercise to work out:

A miser has 3 bags of Money containing in all £2984.6.0 of which the first contains £324.10.0 and the second £913.0.6. What doth the 3rd contain?[12]

By Example 8, Francis was being thrust into the raw language of commerce:

A Merchant had 5 Debtors. A B C D E together owe him £1115.6. Now together B C D E owe him £737. What is A's Debt?[13]

One might assume that the world of 'Debt' and 'Debtors' was beyond the comprehension of a 12-year-old boy. Surely this was no subliminal lesson in the vagaries of personal finances. Quite the contrary. Money and so-called 'economy' were part of the harsh realities of life for sailors, whether from the lower or upper decks. Long voyages, interminable delays between being paid, the temptations of distant ports: all these meant that money worries were ever-pressing. After Francis finished at the Academy, and before he set sail for the Far East, his father wrote to him with guidance on 'economy': 'Keep an exact account of all money you receive or spend, lend none but where you are sure of an early repayment, and on no account be persuaded to risk it by gaming.'[14] This and other homilies in the same letter were important lessons for the 14-year-old Francis starting out in life, and the letter was found, dog-eared and well worn, among his personal papers on his death 77 years later.

Contrary to the inference in its full title, the Academy's Plan went further than the study of mathematics and embraced the whole gamut of technical training for a budding naval officer. There were sections on 'The Description and Use of the Terrestrial Globe', 'Geography', 'Chronology', 'Navigation', 'Spherics', 'Astronomy', 'Latitude', 'Longitude', 'Day's Work' and 'Marine Surveying'. Interestingly, whereas 'Arithmetic' and 'Geometry' were described as a 'science', 'Geography', 'Chronology' and 'Navigation' were referred to as an 'art'.

Bearing in mind that Britain had been at war with one or more of its enemies off and on for the past 30 years, the final three sections of the Plan, 'Fortifications', 'Gunnery' and 'Mechanics' should have left Francis in no doubt he was being

Sketch by Thomas Carter in his Plan of Mathematical Learning *while a scholar at the Portsmouth Naval Academy from 1796–1800. (Royal Naval Museum, Portsmouth)*

prepared for a life of war and danger. Whether the point struck home is difficult to tell, but, if the well-crafted drawings or watercolours that headed each section of his Plan are anything to go by, Francis still imagined himself sallying forth into a world of peace and tranquillity. The images depicted in his Plan are not unlike those of other Academites that have survived. Each betrays the individual vision of its author: the imaginings of the youngster about the world outside waiting for him. Their composition is worthy, in imagery if not in skill, of a Poussin or Lorrain. Indeed, many Academites and young gentlemen learning these drawing skills went on to become accomplished artists in their own right and, in the case of J. Theophilus Lee, who was born in 1787 and went to sea in 1795 aged seven, regularly contributed to the *Naval Chronicle*.

Typically, a lake or bay was the centrepiece of Francis' compositions. He would pick out a small sailing ship or rowing boat crossing the water, with, on the shoreline, a bucolic cottage or imposing house complete with classical pediment. High up on the hill overlooking the waters, a castle-ruin evoked a gothic novel. Not a man-of-war in sight; not a soldier or a sailor to be seen. Whereas Francis' vision of the outside world was uniformly idyllic, other Academites such as Francis Phipps, who entered in 1774, and Thomas Carter, who entered in 1796, did at least occasionally draw in a fortified castle or man-of-war.

Given his idealized vision of the outside world, it is no surprise that Francis excited misgivings in his father about his son's choice of career. James Trevenen, an earlier Academite, had no such illusions when he wrote to his brother on 5 September 1775, still three months shy of his graduation. Belying his tender years, James made clear that he fully understood, indeed embraced, the risks in his chosen career: 'There are two ships now here fitting out to go round the world and to carry Omiah the Tahitean back to his native country. Now if Mama and Papa please I should like to go out in one of them... In their last voyage they lost but four men. It will be a most excellent breaking in for me. I shall experience all climates, hot and cold to an extremity, and consequently shall always be prepared for any other station whatever. Charlton, another Academite, intends to go.'[15]

For all that these exercises in drawing served to excite the imagination, in James' case they also had a practical purpose, which was redolent of John Drake aboard the *Golden Hind* over 200 years earlier. At the same time as James was going through the Academy, Admiral Digby may have been able to report dismissively that Prince William 'wants application… His Log should never be omitted above one day and if it could be made an entertainment by inserting little drawings of the land, tho' by another hand, it would be worth any trouble.'[16] However, Prince William was a royal and allowances could be made. For Francis Austen and, more especially, James Trevenen, learning how 'to draw the appearance of head lands, Coasts, Bays, Sands, Rocks and such like'[17] was still a vital skill they would need at sea. Times and knowledge may have moved on since Sir Francis Drake ranged across the globe, but there were immense areas of the world still uncharted, as James discovered on his first ship after leaving the Academy. Appointed to the *Resolution*, he accompanied Captain Cook on his famous voyage to open up and map the South Seas, and just how much Britain's mariners still needed to learn about the outer reaches of the known world can be deduced from the 'Geography' section in Francis' Plan:

> There are generally reckoned four continents: Europe, Asia, Africa, America. The Northern and Southern Continents not being sufficiently known to Geographers, all that need be said of them is that Terra Artica is too cold for the residence of mankind and that part which is known of Terra Antartica appears to be very barren and the natives very little superior to Brutes.[18]

It was all very fine the Academites imbibing wholesome doses of bookish knowledge about 'Brutes' but the products of the Academy would open themselves up to ridicule if they were not armed with practical skills. Leaving nothing to chance, therefore, after year one the Academites were expected to do time in the rigging house in the nearby docks and learn 'the manner of preparing and fitting the rigging of ships.'[19] Additionally, the master attendant was 'likewise to take them afloat, when any works are doing that are fit for their knowledge, and even to employ them in such works as are proper for them.'[20] From the Academy's inception, the emphasis on practical training was carried down to the minutest detail, as evidenced by an order issued by the Admiralty in 1735: 'having represented that the rigging and Gear of His Majesty's Ship … is too large and ponderous to be handled or managed by the Scholars in the said Academy with any dexterity and proposing to have a block of about 5 or 6 feet long cut into the form of a Ship with Mast's rigging etc made of suitable dimensions in order of their being taught the method of rigging and unrigging a Ship.'[21]

In Francis' case, it is possible to pinpoint from his Plan the moment when his sea training begins: page 381, the 'Day's Work'[22] section. On 16 June 1788 he began *A Journal of a Voyage from England towards Madeira*, in which he noted, much as Prince William had done in his 'Logg Book', the time, speed, course, and winds. From the 'Remarks' column it is possible to plot Francis' precise location:

> At 5 saw the Needles bearing NNW 7 miles (16 June)
>
> At 1/4 past 2 saw the cape Finisterre bearing SW – W Distant 7 Leagues (21 June)[23]

By 23 June Francis was back in Portsmouth, and in December he graduated. Recalling this moment in his *Memoir* many years later, Francis wrote with limited self-deprecation how:

> …although rather small of stature, of a vigorous constitution and possessing great activity of body, [he] was not long in acquiring a competent knowledge of the practical parts of seamanship to which he was urged by the natural energies of his mind and a general thirst for knowledge.[24]

Like James Trevenen, Francis was a model student as were the six boys who wrote to the Admiralty in 1742 complaining that 'The model of the *Victory* is so small, her rigging so slight that we cannot learn anything from it, neither do we know anything of rigging or the stowage of anchors or cable, we are quite ignorant of anything that belongeth to sails.'[25] The six scholars who put their name to this letter also petitioned for an old yacht to be made available to the Academy to enable them to improve their technical skills. The petition was granted.

The question is whether James and Francis were the exception or the rule: on that might hang the success of this whole experiment in shore-based education. Judging by the flurries of correspondence between the Commissioner of the Dockyard and the Admiralty, the impression emerges of a *Marie Celeste* adrift in a sea of iniquity and debauchery, and it is easy to conclude that its inmates were 'wasters' with more money than sense; rakes bound for the Hellfire Club. Surely then, from behind the walls of this Academy would finally appear the candidate for Britain's 'worst boy'.

In January 1734, for instance, the Lords of the Admiralty wrote in high dudgeon to the Commissioner instructing him to look into 'the indecent and insolent behaviour of the young gentlemen who have been admitted to the Academy'.[26] On closer examination, however, it turns out that the incident that provoked the Admiralty's outrage was little more prankish than a midnight raid on the Academy's kitchen stores, admittedly with sword in hand, occasioned, no doubt, by hunger and cold as it was January, and by dissatisfaction over another, presumably abysmal, school dinner. Indeed, the Commissioner's report to the Admiralty comes as somewhat of an anticlimax, with the then headmaster, Mr Hasleden, being ordered 'not to suffer them to go into the kitchen for the future, nor any of them to be permitted to wear a sword, but at such time as they shall actually be at their exercise; as also to consider what sort of meat may be proper, and he can conveniently allow them each day in the week, and what he proposes to supply them with, for breakfasts and supper'.[27]

In a second incident a few weeks later, a nocturnal pub crawl to the out-of-bounds Sun Tavern in town ended up with seven boys – the full complement of the Academy at that time – spending 'for wine and brandy, etc no less than one pound and two shillings' and returning 'very drunk, and Mr Dashwood (I presume not being used to drink much strong liquor at one time) had like to have been destroyed. He was almost dead drunk, and so very bad that Mr Hasleden was obliged to call on the surgeon of the yard for assistance and relief'.[28] The ringleaders, Peregrine Baber and Francis Colepeper, who at 16 were the oldest scholars then at the Academy, were expelled, being judged to have 'seduced the others.'[29]

Yet again, on closer examination, these latest high jinks, far from representing a worrying pattern of behaviour, turned out to be an attempt to institute an initiation ceremony, each new arrival being expected to 'make a treat'[30] for the other scholars. So it is no surprise to find, a year on, the Admiralty regretting its earlier heavy-handedness and authorizing the Commissioner to welcome Messrs Baber and Colepeper back to the Academy, albeit so long as they made 'promises of amendment'.[31]

From these incidents and the Admiralty's overreaction each time, it seems that its earnest desire to make a success of the Academy clouded its judgement.

So if the official accounts give a misleading impression of the Academy, what did the inmates have to say for themselves? Few letters have survived. One, dated 15 November 1774, would seem, however, to justify the Admiralty's worst fears. Writing to his 'Honoured Mother', James Trevenen recounted yet another expulsion, this time of William Delater 'for eloping and for decoying Henry Wray and for having a bad character'.[32] Studiously, James did not linger on the events leading up to the expulsion, doubtless a signal that he did not want to hold the Academy to blame and thereby risk his parents removing him. Instead he waxed lyrical on the salacious events after the expulsion, thereby cloaking his story in the moral tones of Hogarth's *Rake's Progress*:

> I believe I told you that Delater ran away from hence and was afterwards expelled, but I will now tell you of something worse. He lately wrote a letter to Charlton… He says that when he arrived in London he was almost dead, for having disobliged all his friends (who now refuse to have anything to say to him) and that later having spent all the money he had, in gambling and brothels, he pined away for about a month with hardly anything to support him, lying all night in the streets…[33]

At least, James could report a happy ending of sorts:

> one day walking in the Strand after having eaten nothing for two days and nights he met an acquaintance who gave him two or three shillings, treated him to dinner and hired a lodging for him … his landlord soon began to dun him for money and threaten him; that one day walking out he happened to see a bill for enlisting soldiers and that he went and listed himself as a common soldier in the 70th Regiment of foot.[34]

For James, it was no surprise that Delater had come to no good. Describing to his father, in his very first letter home, what he made of the 16 other scholars in the class of '72, James had marked Delater down as one of 'two ill natured fellows'.[35] Barely 12, James could already give a to-the-point, thumbnail sketch of his contemporaries, pigeon-holing them as good or bad, swearers or non-swearers:

> A few days after I arrived here there came another from London, so I have got a junior already. His [James Ward's] warrant and mine came down together, but as I had been

here the longest I am the senior. He is a good natured young gentleman and always keeps his word, but swears greatly... Next a *macaroni*, viz Abbott is taller than Mackie, a great swearer and a great drunkard – what a waster! Stays out whole nights drinking at bawdy houses, together with Phipps, who is just the same character ... spends all the money he gets as soon as he has it, does not swear, is idle and throws away his time. Gwatkin is coming fast in wickedness, very fast. Spencer and Delater come next, are two ill natured fellows, and are at Coventry, id est, none of the young gentlemen speak to them. I am next and then Ward.[36]

Many of James' characters are easily recognizable. As for Abbott being dubbed a 'macaroni', James' father would have instantly recognized the allusion, a macaroni being 'a member of a class of travelled young Englishmen of the late 18th and early 19th centuries that affected foreign ways'.[37]

Unlike with Prince William Henry, James' letters seem to have exited the Academy uncensored as is clear when, describing the antics of Abbott and Phipps, he told his father how: 'they conceal from Mr Witchell [the headmaster] I can't tell how. I beg you not speak about it.'[38]

Francis Austen, James Trevenen, the model scholars; Baber, Colepeper, Delater, the wasters. Surely no worse, no better than any other academic institution. So why, 60 years after the Academy's founding did Sir Henry Martin, Commissioner of the Academy in 1788, still feel the need to take advantage of Francis Austen's stellar performance at the Academy to lobby the Admiralty as if fighting for the Academy's very existence:

Herewith I enclose a Letter from the Headmaster of the Academy signifying that Mr Francis William Austen has finished his Plan of Mathematical Learning and in consequence thereof is judged qualified to serve in His Majesty's Navy which you will please to communicate to their Lordships for their information and further directions. I beg leave to observe to their Lordships that this Young Gentleman has completed his Plan of Mathematical Learning in a considerably shorter time than usual, his acidity [*sic*] has been uncommon and his conduct during the whole time he has been at the Academy has been in all respects so perfectly correct that I have never had a complaint or unfavourable report of him from any master or usher, altho' he has a lively and active disposition. From these circumstances, I am induced to hope their Lordships will not think it improper in me to recommend him to their particular favour, and to request that he may be discharged into His Majesty's Ship *Perseverance* as Captain Smith will be glad to receive him, and if their Lordships should be pleased to recommend him to Commodore Cornwallis for promotion when he shall have served his time, I think it might tend to induce other young people educated at the Academy to exert themselves in the hope their Lordships upon such very favourable reports, may be induced to shew them some marks of their approbation.[39]

This was more than a plea on behalf of one exemplary Academite. Sir Henry's message was political: 60 years after its foundation and, despite major reforms in 1773 that had opened 15 of the 40 places to sons of naval officers on a free scholarship, reduced the entrance age to 11 and improved the school fare by requiring it to keep a decent and proper table, the Academy was still failing. In Sir Henry's opinion, the Admiralty was to blame for not providing the continuing patronage so necessary if Academites were to progress on board ship. Without this incentive, why would parents choosing a naval career for their sons abandon the time-honoured practice of sending them directly to sea under the patronage of an influential captain?

Important though patronage was, this was not the issue. In spite of, or maybe because of, the Admiralty's high ambitions, the Academy had consistently failed to live up to official expectations. From the outset, scholar numbers had consistently fallen well short of capacity. Nor was the problem the quality of intake. Rather it was the poor calibre of student, a few notable exceptions such as Francis Austen apart, graduating after three years at the Academy. The end product served to confirm the naval hierarchy – at least the part of it that was at sea – in its prejudice that shore-based training was no substitute for sending young gentlemen straight to sea. The problem came down to the specific institution: the Academy was the author of its own mediocrity. There were many other better naval schools, as the *Naval Chronicle* pointed out when it wrote that 'the subject of our memoir [William King, born 1776] being designed for a sea-life, was sent, in the spring of the year 1788 to the Naval Academy at Chelsea, supposed at that period, to have been one of the best institutions for a maritime education.'[40]

Writing some years later, Thomas Byam Martin, son of Sir Henry and himself a Portsmouth Academite in 1785, couldn't put his finger on it exactly and instead concluded with a dismissive flourish that 'there was a screw loose somewhere, and the machinery did not work well'.[41]

It took Charles Penrose, a contemporary of James Trevenen, to hit the nail on the head when, again writing some years later, he identified the fault line:

> Although at this period, the masters were gentlemen of extensive knowledge in the several branches they superintended ... yet the unfortunate declension of discipline had rendered it too much the pupil's option whether he would or would not pay attention to his studies. Consequently this noble institution had lost great part of its intended value. For from its excellent regulations and fortunate position it certainly is, in preference, to any other place, calculated to form officers for the British Navy.[42]

'Declension of discipline' had been the problem right from the start, but among the staff not the scholars. Back in 1735, according to a deposition before Portsmouth justices, John Ham, the second mathematics master 'did then and there ... threaten to murder the French Dog [John Bellonet, the French master]...'[43] With Ham for an example, how could the boys be expected to knuckle down? As for 'the disputes which have arisen between the masters and the scholars'[44] in 1766 that led to the expulsion of the Academite Charles Cuthbert for 'ill behaviour', the headmaster and mathematical usher were also dismissed.

Add to this the comment by James Anthony Gardner, a scholar briefly at the Academy in 1780, that 'the Master of this school was Orchard, a very good man he was; but who taught him navigation is more than I can say'[45] and it is no wonder that the Academy had a 'screw loose', that Sir Henry felt the need to fight for the Academy's very survival, but that Lord St Vincent, with all the weight his words as First Lord of the Admiralty carried, declared in February 1801 that 'The Royal Academy at Portsmouth, which is a sink of vice and abomination, should be abolished and a naval military school established upon the footing of that at Marlowe *caeteris paribus*.'[46] When Lord Barham added his weight in 1805 in a letter to William Pitt referring to the Academy as 'a nursery of vice and immorality'[47] its days were numbered.

The Academy duly closed in 1806. However that was not the end of the story. The institution may have failed, but not the principle of shore-based training.

Sketch of a man of war by Thomas Carter in his Plan of Mathematical Learning *while a scholar at the Portsmouth Naval Academy. (Royal Naval Museum, Portsmouth)*

In 1808 the Academy was replaced by the Royal Naval College, also at Portsmouth, thereby ensuring that shore-based training became a permanent feature of the education for naval cadets.

However, that is to run ahead. With all these youngsters – the street urchins, the occasional royal and now the young gentlemen – all lined up more or less willingly to go to sea, they, along with the rest of Britain, were about to face their greatest challenge. The decisions they made and the spirit they displayed from behind Britain's 'wooden walls' would determine the nation's destiny for the foreseeable future. The Wars were about to begin.

YOUNG SQUEAKER

Anyone glancing down the order of business for the House of Commons on 12 February 1793 could at first be forgiven for thinking this day would be like any other: the committee meeting to discuss the Land Tax Bill; the Malt Bill debate; and, the penultimate item on the day's agenda, the Pawnbrokers' Petition. Nothing could be more routine. Yet few Members attending that packed session were concentrating on the doubtless legitimate complaints of the pawnbrokers. Ringing in their ears was the message delivered to the House by King George III the previous day:

> His Majesty thinks proper to acquaint the House of Commons that the Assembly now exercising the powers of government in France have, without previous notice, directed acts of hostility against the persons and property of His Majesty's subjects … and have since, on the most groundless pretensions, actually declared war against his Majesty…[1]

Britain and France were about to confront each other again. The War of the Austrian Succession, the Seven Years' War and the American Revolution were just three conflicts involving France in the past 50 years. This time, however, was different, and the Members sensed it. Britain had been catching whiffs of the fatal brew intoxicating France since 1789, but news reaching London that Louis XVI of France had been guillotined on 21 January 1793 had shaken everyone to the core, once again raising the spectre of Charles I shivering outside Banqueting House 140 years earlier. Even 14-year-old Betsy Wynne, travelling on the Continent with her parents at the time uttered the *cri de coeur*, 'what a terrible century this is'[2] in her diary, when she heard the news.

Yet abhorrent as was the king's execution, far more sinister was the French Convention decree of 15 December 1792, in which France had 'avowed the most insatiable ambition, and greatest contempt for the law of nations'.[3] No longer satisfied with the trifles of plunder and territory, France wanted total war according to Britain's Prime Minister, William Pitt, and its instrument would be a revolutionary cocktail of *liberté, égalité et fraternité* designed to challenge not merely the old dynastic order, but also the very existence of other countries. With heavy irony, Pitt laid bare the sword of Damocles suspended over Europe: 'They have explained what that liberty is which they wish to give to every nation; and if they will not accept of it voluntarily, they compel them.'[4]

So it was that on 12 February, the routine business of the day completed, the House of Commons declared, as the last item on the order of business, that 'Your Majesty may rely on the firm and effectual support of the representatives of a brave and loyal people in the prosecution of a just and necessary war...'[5] Still, there were democratic conventions to be honoured. France had declared war on Britain on 1 February. This required a formal response; there must be a vote. Accordingly, on 18 February, 'a motion was made and the question being proposed, it is not for the honour or interest of Great Britain to make war upon France. The House divided.'[6] The result of the vote was:

'Tellers for the Yeas: 44.

Tellers for the Noes: 270.'[7]

Britain was officially at war. Meantime, towns and cities all across the country had already begun their preparations. Anticipating the French declaration of war by two days, Portsmouth and Portsea were first to mobilize on 30 January, their local committee proposing and passing unanimously a motion 'to raise a fund for the purpose of granting a bounty to a certain number of able and ordinary seamen, who may voluntarily enter into His Majesty's Navy at that port, after a declaration of war.'[8] Recruitment notices were posted in other towns calling for volunteers and offering, in the case of Flintshire with its County Bounties for Seamen: 'Two Guineas a-piece (not Eight or Four as the Public have been misinformed) to the first Twenty Able Seamen ... and One Guinea a-piece to the first twenty ordinary seamen or Landmen [those from an agricultural background].'[9]

Those who would fight this war on its front line – the captains – had moved even more quickly. For them, the moment Louis XVI was guillotined, war was inevitable. There was no time to waste: the quicker a ship was crewed up, the quicker the captain got to sea and stole the best station. Captains placed advertisements in their chosen localities and bombarded the Marine Society, requesting between 10 and 20 boys depending on the size of ship. This was the moment for the Society to come into its own. In the first week following the guillotining of the French king, 96 boys were 'requested'. This compared to 66 boys requested in the previous week. By the second week, requests rose to 112 boys and by the week of 14 February the figure had shot up to 220, peaking at 385 in the week of 30 May, thereafter tailing off as ships set sail.

Responding to this barrage, the Society launched a recruitment drive but, despite the pressure of war, unlike in 1756 there would be no cutting corners in the records. The details of each boy were faithfully entered into the *Register of Boys sent as Servants to Officers in the Royal Navy, 1793, Lady Quarter,*[10] including how they came to the Society: whether they were volunteers, albeit at their parents' behest, in which case they had S for 'Sober Parents', F for 'Father attended' or M for 'Mother attended' annotated beside their name, or had suffered some form of compulsion, in which case the annotation varied depending on their circumstances: with O for 'Orphan', D for 'Destitute', V for 'Vagabond', M for 'From Magistrates', D.P. for 'Discharged Apprentices' and P for 'Parish Boy'. Whether any boys were volunteers in their own right is unclear. Few of these or any other boys going into the lower-decks would ever have found their voice during the long Wars ahead. One who volunteered in 1805 aged 17 and did find his voice, albeit only in 1836, was William Robinson, whose 'father was an honest tradesman, but in humble circumstances, as a shoemaker'.[11] He claimed he was speaking on behalf of all lower-deck boys when he asserted that 'to the youth possessing anything of a roving disposition, it is attractive, nay, it is seductive'.[12]

Whatever the levels of coercion, the Society was never able to match the requests suddenly flooding in from captains. The number of boys 'clothed' by the Society increased from 49 in the week preceding the guillotining of the French king to a peak of 99 by 3 March, then tailed off to 34 in the week of 30 May. In all, 764 boys were sent to His Majesty's ships by the Society in the three months to 22 April 1793. Measure this against Britain's fleet totalling 276 ships-of-the-line and cruisers at the outbreak of war, each of which required as many as 20 boys, and it is clear that street urchins would not be the bountiful source of recruits that Hanway had anticipated back in 1756. Indeed, taken in the context of the total numbers mobilized by Britain in the first two years of the Wars, they were a drop in the ocean. Navy strength rose from 16,000 men to 86,000 during that period, yet there were only 2,343 'Boys Clothed' and sent 'as servants on board the King's Ships' by the Society in the same period.

Aware it was failing to meet the navy's demands, the Society stopped sending boys to merchant ships. Between 1786 and 1793, 620 boys had been sent as apprentices to merchant ships. However John Hatton, discharged as an apprentice to the *Grant Conway* on 16 February, and Geo Cheverill, discharged as an apprentice to the *Boyd* on 23 February 1793, were the last of these pre-war commitments to the merchant service. Thereafter, the Society threw its full weight behind the war effort, and in the next four years only nine boys were sent to the merchant service.

The Society also stepped up its recruitment drive for landmen, with regular dispatches to ships of 80 to 90 a week. However, captains preferred boys to landmen. Boys were more pliable, quick learners and didn't grumble. Sir Gilbert Blane, physician to the fleet, writing in 1780 went to the heart of the matter: 'The formation of a seaman depends upon a long habit and a practical education from an early age of life.'[13] Hence the very precise request made by one captain who was more than usually impatient to be on his way in 1793. Addressing his letter of 6 February that year to 'The Governors of the Marine Society',[14] he wrote:

> Gentlemen
>
> I have to request that you will have the goodness to furnish me with Twenty Lads from your Society and the greatest care shall be taken of them on board the *Agamemnon* under my command at Chatham.[15]

The letter was signed Captain Nelson. What a relief it must have been for him to be writing this letter. The friendship he had formed with Prince William in the Americas in the early 1780s had subsequently come back to bite him on the tail. Out of favour with the Admiralty and the court, for, wrongly so Nelson claimed, 'taking part of the Kings Son'[16] against the king, and told by Lord Hood that 'the King was impressed with an unfavourable opinion'[17] of him, Nelson had fretted away the past five years, 'cultivating his garden' at the family home in Norfolk, reduced to writing letters reporting that 'the sheep etc have been until Wednesday last kept in the Marshes [and] Mrs Nelson thanks you for the offer of the pigs'.[18]

Nelson's war started in December 1792 when he received a letter from the Secretary to the Admiralty saying: 'Sir, I have received your letter of 5th instant, expressing your readiness to serve, and I have read the same to my Lords Commissioners of the Admiralty.'[19]

Reading between the lines, this could only be a precursor to active service. By 7 January, Nelson knew he would have a ship and by the time the news of Louis XVI's death came through from Paris, he had been told it would be the 64-gun *Agamemnon*. His news buzzed round the family, Nelson's father describing in his letter of 4 February to Nelson's sister, Catherine Matcham, the immediate fever of activity:

> My Dear: Your Good Brother having received from the Admiralty notice that the Agamemnon is in readiness to be commissioned for Him: this morning left Thorpe in Health and Great Spirits. He will be Commissioned on Wednesday and means, God willing, to get to Chatham on Thursday and enter into the busy Scene of getting all things in proper Order. If you can send Him any good Sailors they will be acceptable. Severall [*sic*] men in and around the Burnhams are Entered for him. Indeed his Character commands respect and Esteem wherever it is known.[20]

There was no time to waste if he was to bag the plum station, which, for him, had to be the Mediterranean, a point he made in a letter of 15 March to his wife telling her that 'we go down the River tomorrow, and are ordered to proceed to Spithead with all possible dispatch as we are wanted. Lord Hood writes me word for immediate service, and hints we are to go a cruise and then to join his fleet at Gibraltar: therefore I am anxious to get to Spithead.'[21]

'Any good sailors' was top of the agenda. Before Nelson could sail, he needed a full complement, which, for the *Agamemnon*, meant a crew of 500, hence why, after setting his family on the hunt round Norfolk, his next port of call was the Marine Society. Nevertheless, desperate though he was to crew up the ship, he knew he must limit the number of boys. Too much on board ship was man's work, which explains his request for only 'Twenty Lads'. By promising 'the greatest care', he might hopefully ensure himself the cream of the crop. Tangible evidence of the 'greatest care', which would have played so well with the Marine Society, was in the letter Nelson sent to Dr Gaskin of the Society for Promoting Christian Knowledge on 4 March in which he asked 'for a donation of Bibles and Prayer Books for the use of the Ship's Crew under my command consisting of 500 men'.[22]

Within two weeks of his letter to the Marine Society, it was supplying a first batch of boys to the *Agamemnon*. A column in the Society's *Register* summed up each boy's physical and mental state and had at its heading the following annotations: 'Reads: r, Writes: w, S.pox: p'.[23]

The entry for the first boy drafted onto the *Agamemnon* read as follows:

Number: 7910

Name: Jeremy Newton

Age: 19

Stature (F.I.): 5.3

Reads: r, Writes: w, S.pox: p

Parish connections and where living: Destitute

How he was employed: Drew beer

When sent to sea: Feb.y 19

Officer to whom sent: Captn. Nelson

To what ship: *Agamemnon*

What port: Chatham.[24]

A further seven boys were sent to the *Agamemnon* on 19 February including John Green, recorded as aged 14, height 4ft 2in., who had been 'Apprentice to Mr Banks, Taylor. No 36 Holywell Lane',[25] and Tho Amery, the youngest, aged 13, height 4ft 5in., who was 'p.r.w.'[26] and had been an 'Errand Boy'[27] working at Wide Gate Alley and whose mother was a servant living at 27 Barbican. Another batch of 12 boys was dispatched to the *Agamemnon* on 21 February. The vast majority of boys passing through the Society had the marks of smallpox and those joining the *Agamemnon* were no exception: all save one of the 20 Society boys sent to the *Agamemnon* were afflicted. However, seven could read and write, and a further two could read but not write.

Importantly, none of the 20 was classified as 'V' for 'Vagabond' or 'M' for 'From Magistrates',[28] and only three were listed as 'Destitute'.[29] Eight had previous 'Sea' employment, 13 were aged 15 and under, and all 20 were from London and had been trained in 'knotting yarns'[30] as well as 'exercising guns'.[31] All told, not a bad bunch. Nelson may not as yet have established himself as the nation's talismanic captain, but the quality of these 20 boys and the speed of their dispatch suggests he was already held in high regard at least in naval circles.

By contrast, Captain George Duff, father of then one-year-old Norwich, drew the short straw as he began crewing up the *Nemesis* in Portsmouth: he received just seven boys from the Society, three only of whom could read and write. Worse still, six of the seven were 'destitute', aged 16 and over, and variously from distant Yorkshire, Lancashire or Ireland. Parishes around the British Isles were evidently using the war as an opportunity to offload their dregs on to the Society, which, given the exigencies of war, did not protest, instead palming them off on to an unsuspecting junior captain who could hardly protest if he wanted to be on his way quickly.

As with Nelson, most captains' requests at this time came in for 20 or so boys. Any more and the balance of the crew would be compromised. Captain Collins, who, like Nelson, had got in ahead of the pack, took 21 for the *Berwick* between 2 and 11 February. The Hon G. K. Elphinstone, who was slower off the mark, took from 22 February until 15 March to fill his requirement for 19 boys for the *Robuste* at Chatham. Captain Pasley, who was evidently less well regarded, commissioned his ship, the *Bellerophon*, on 16 March, but come May was still sending out Press Gangs in search of crew and eventually took 24 Society boys – 23 under his own name between 6 and 7 May and a further boy via his chaplain, Freselicque, on 10 May. So whereas Nelson was already at sea by mid-April and bound for the Mediterranean, Pasley had to wait until mid-June before he was fully crewed up. As a result, he ended up joining the Channel Fleet for the tedious task of blockade duty.

The 20 Society boys set to join the *Agamemnon* were more or less 'volunteers', and, arriving at the Society, they were quickly vetted, clothed and discharged. Other boys arriving at the Society could not be fast-tracked whatever the exigencies of war: they were either in poor health or, with a record of ill-discipline or criminality, were non-volunteers. They had to spend more time under the care and supervision of the Society. Among these was William Whitaker, aged 15, whose discharge record read, 'Run from ship and took his clothing'.[32] His 'No. of days victualled'[33] was only 11, but still long enough for the Society to sum up his 'Character' as: 'A thief, reads well'.[34] By contrast, it took 101 'days victualled'[35] to come to much the same conclusion about Thomas Brown, aged 13, whose discharge record read, 'Sent to prison'[36] and 'Character' was described as 'A thief. Reads a little'.[37]

These special cases were the ones lodged 'at the Society's house, under the care of Mr Fluyd, in Grub-street'[38] in its early years. By 1793, however, the Society had its own ship, the *Marine Society*, originally a merchantman acquired in 1786, which served as a training/schooling vessel for these special cases. Nevertheless, despite having a ship in which to confine or minister to them, supervision of the Society's special cases would appear to have progressed little since the early days. Of the first five special cases registered following France's declaration of war in 1793, one boy ran and three others were promptly discharged home, including 14-year-old Luke McCarthy, who arrived on 2 February and was discharged on 14 February for 'Having fitts'.[39] The *Register* summed up the fate of the fifth boy, Thos March (No: 1945), who arrived on 1 February:

Age: 15

Stature: 4ft 6in.

Description: Sandy brown hair, grey eyes, pale complexion. Left sop washed.

  Go with fitts.

When discharged: Apr 6

To whom discharged: Died in consumption

In what capacity to serve: -

No. of days victualled: -

Character: A good disposition. Very grateful for favorites.[40]

Some of these boys did eventually make it on to a ship in service despite a prolonged period of convalescence or probation on board the Society's ship. On occasions they were held back for no more nefarious reason than that the Society was waiting for the ship making the request to be ready for service. This happened with 19 boys sent to the *Duke of Clarence* on 3 August 1793, some of whom had been on the Society's ship for 53 days and others for as long as 85 days. However, many of the boys held on the Society's ship were troublesome, or, as non-volunteers, were likely to be a burden to any captain receiving them. Accordingly they were sent singly, as with the first boy to be discharged from the *Marine Society* following the declaration of war by France. His entry in the *Register* highlights the problem:

Date when received: 1793, Mar 7

Number: 1950

Name: John Stokes

Age: 14

Stature: 4ft 7in.

Description: Brown hair, very dark amber eyes, very much pitt smallpox

When discharged: Mar 26

To whom discharged: Admiral Gill of *St George*

In what capacity to serve: Servant

No. of days victualled:

Character: A very good boy but unformed.[41]

Fortunately for all concerned, the number of these special cases was not significant: 38 in the first year of the Wars, all bar one of whom were 16 and under. Of these, 26 went to king's ships, including 19 to the *St George*, and six ran away. Three, however, were discharged home, one 'not liking the sea'[42] and two 'as apprentice tailors'.[43] Of the remaining three, one died while in the Society's care, and two were 'discharged having Fitts'.[44]

These figures echo the perennial problem the Society had reconciling its volunteer charter with the realities that required some degree of coercion if street urchins were to be kept out of mischief. Of the 1,618 boys who passed through the Society's ship between 1786 and the outbreak of war, 208 had run away.

No such mishaps for Nelson with his merry band of 20 fast-track 'volunteers'. No fits; no runs; no deaths. All arrived safely on board but, taking no chances, being as the *Agamemnon* was laid up in Chatham, very likely one of Nelson's own officers would have come to the Society's offices on Bishopsgate in person on 19 and 21 February and accompanied the boys to the tender, the *Sandwich*, moored on the Thames, from where they would have been transferred downriver. Nelson described the likely arrangements in his letter of 26 January to

Commodore Locker: 'Lord Hood tells me I am now fixed for the *Agamemnon* at Chatham and that whatever men are raised for her, will be taken care of on board the *Sandwich*.'[45]

In typically polemical style, William Robinson described in *Jack Nastyface. Memoirs of an English Seaman* his own experience being 'taken care of' in the meat-grinders that were, firstly, the receiving ships:

> Whatever may be said about this boasted land of liberty, whenever a youth resorts to receiving ship for shelter and hospitality, he, from that moment, must take leave of the liberty to speak or to act. On being sent on board the receiving ship, it was for the first time I began to repent of the rash step I had taken, but it was of no avail… After having been examined by the doctor, and reported *seaworthy*, I was ordered down to the hold, where I remained all night (9th May 1805) with my companions in wretchedness, and the rats running over us in numbers.[46]

The next meat-grinder for 'Jack' was the 'Admiral's tender [where] we spent the day and the following night huddled together for there was not room to sit or stand separate: indeed, we were in a pitiable plight, for numbers of them were sea-sick, some retching, others were smoking, whilst many were so overcome by the stench, that they fainted for want of air.'[47] As if that was not bad enough, it was on from there to another receiving ship, this one down on the Nore where the fleet was moored. Here he was: 'supplied with slops, the price of which is stopt from our pay by the purser, and in due time we were transferred and distributed among the different ships, where we awaited an order for a supply of men and boys, to complete each ship's complement. From this ship I was drafted on board a line of battle ship.'[48]

In the case of the *Agamemnon*, it had been laid up for ten years and it was all hands to the deck provisioning and making it seaworthy. Since his appointment, Nelson had been abuzz with activity, recruiting here there and everywhere, especially in his most favoured spot, East Anglia, where 'I have sent out a Lieutenant and four Midshipmen to get men at every Sea-port in Norfolk, and to forward them to Lynn and Yarmouth; my friends in Yorkshire and the North tell me they will send what men they can lay hands on to the Regulating Captains at Whitby and Newcastle.'[49]

So strong was his preference for Norfolk stock that he had even asked the Admiralty to delay posting bills for the *Agamemnon* in London until he could appear in Norfolk in person and have his own bills posted locally. He enlisted Commodore Locker for these tactics: 'The name of the ship was fixed for the avowed purpose of my raising men for her, therefore I hope if any men from London are inclined to enter for her, you will not turn your back on them, as although my bills are dispersed over this County etc. I have desired that no bills may be stuck up in London, till my Commission is signed.'[50]

With help from his friends, he set about filling the important posts of surgeon, surgeon's mate, master, purser and lieutenants. Prince William – now the Duke of Clarence – arranged for Joseph King, a boatswain who had earlier served under the prince, to be drafted to the *Agamemnon*. However, crewing up from a standing start to a full complement of 500 was always going to be challenging and, if Nelson was to get to sea quickly, he would, like all captains, have to consider the Press. In a letter to his brother dated 10 February, he alludes to the problem: 'I have only a few men, and very hard indeed they are to be got, and without a press I have no idea our Fleet can be manned.'[51] According to the logbook of the *Agamemnon*'s lieutenant, the recruitment work began bearing fruit on 18 February, when he 'received on board 20 men'.[52] On 19 February, it was 'rec'd 20 men from the *Sandwich*',[53] doubtless including the eight boys sent that day from the Marine Society.

Nelson used the Press, but to what extent is not clear. One of his Pressed men was John Wilkinson, who, writing in 1840, described how 'on the breaking out of the French Revolutionary War in February 1793, Wilkinson was serving in a transport out of which he was taken when lying in long reach in the Thames, and sent on board the guardship at the Nore, from whence he was drafted into the *Agamemnon*, Captain Nelson, almost as soon as that ship was commissioned.'[54]

Much has been written about the adult Press during these Wars but little is known about the use of the Press for boys. The Impress Service, introduced in 1788 to regularize this iniquitous but necessary system of enforced recruitment, limited impressment to able-bodied seamen or watermen between the ages of 18 and 55, which meant that boys were exempted. However, what boy walking the streets of Portsmouth or Chatham had a birth certificate, let alone one about

The Press Gang in action. The Impress Service received £1 for every person entered into the navy. Etching by Barlow and Collings, 1790. (National Maritime Museum, Greenwich, London)

his person, to prove that he was 17 or younger? Abuses were common and of long-standing. Writing in 1710 in a tract called *Fighting Sailor turn'd Peaceable Christian*, Thomas Lurting described his own experiences at sea, including how he had been impressed at the age of 14. Apprentices were also exempted by law but were especially easy pickings for the Press Gangs. If a master wanted to be shot of a recalcitrant apprentice, he had a choice: offload him on the Marine Society – hence the annotation 'D.P.' in the Society *Register* meaning 'Discharged Apprentice'; or tip off a local Press Gang. A ballad from late in the 1700s entitled *The Lighterman's Prentice Prest and Sent to Sea* describes the process:

> A prentice I was at Wapping-new-stairs,
> And a smart young lad was I;
> But that old blackguard old W——d,

He inform'd, and had forty shillings for me,
It was on the last day of February,
In the year of forty-five:
He had me taken out of bed;
When my parents heard it, lord! How they cry'd.
My mother and my cousin both
They on board of the tender came with speed,
And thro' the grates to them I talk'd,
It was enough to make any heart bleed
And, now, my lads, we're come to an harbour
We can go to rest with great content.
So all young men that row in the lighters,
Keep yourselves free from a press-gang.
And whenever you come athwart old W____d
For my sake give him a hearty damn.[55]

For Nelson, there were no such problems. The Marine Society had given him the 'Twenty Lads' he needed for below decks and they were all from London, which would help them bind together once at sea. As for the dozen or so young gentlemen he needed as captain's servants to walk the quarterdeck, he had his pick of the local talent in Norfolk and as many as possible of them would come from there. That way, they would be fellow brothers-in-arms during the tough, dangerous days, months and years away at sea, their careers closely woven in with that of their 'sea-daddy', Nelson, until premature death or rapid promotion would pull them asunder.

The moment Nelson returned to Norfolk in early February following his appointment to the *Agamemnon*, the family home in the village of Burnham Thorpe became the mecca for any young gentleman within a radius of 30 miles aspiring to a career in the navy. Trying to identify the archetypal young gentleman joining the navy is almost impossible. Some, like Prince William, were second or third sons, if not in royal, then certainly in noble line. Many, like Francis Austen, were younger sons of clergymen or from naval families, with interest and little money. If there was a common denominator among them, it was the perception that the navy could be a route to fortune. As for the young gentlemen beating a path to Nelson's door, if 'giving up their whole care to profit themselves and not the King's service'[56] was what drove them, they had better tread carefully. They were about to run up against a man for whom 'True honour, I hope, predominates in my mind far above riches'.[57]

From the sitting room at Parsonage House Nelson held court, his father, the Reverend Edmund Nelson, doubtless in attendance to add an atmosphere of pastoral caring to the proceedings. Influence, patronage, interest, all currencies totally alien to Nelson's 20 Marine Society 'Lads', were the levers exercised on behalf of the young gentlemen presenting themselves one after the other for an interview with Captain Nelson.

Some choices were easy. Family came first, which meant William Bolton, Nelson's nephew from the nearby village of Hollesby, was quickly accepted. More difficult must have been the decision to take his own 12-year-old stepson, Josiah Nisbet. The acute problems between Nelson and his wife Fanny were still in the future and would await the advent of the beguiling and colourful Emma Hamilton some years on before bursting into public view. Nevertheless, Nelson had already realized during his enforced garden-leave in Norfolk that marriage to Fanny was not all it was cut out to be, especially given her constant illusions of ill-health. 'Poor Mrs Nelson has, indeed, a severe Tryall,'[58] Nelson's father commented in a 4 February letter. About to escape to sea, Nelson fired off some pointed remarks, first reminding her, in a letter of 15 March, 'that a handsome fortune for Josiah depends on your surviving Mrs Hamilton [another, not *the* Lady Hamilton]',[59] then chiding her with the words: 'I hope you intend a new lease of your life.'[60]

In this fraught emotional environment, honouring his obligation to favour Josiah risked only exacerbating the tensions of the union. Josiah was not – at least not yet – the problem. It was the mother. Fanny was ever overweaning when it came to Josiah and this could make for complications in the orderly running of a ship-of-the-line. For all his misgivings, determined on being the dutiful husband Nelson set out the choices starkly, but left the final decision about Josiah's future to Fanny: 'Mr Suckling thinks it would take our whole income to keep him [Josiah] at the Temple, and I suppose we must think of some other walk of life for him. My objection to the navy now he will be certain of a small fortune is in some measure done away. You must think of this. Would you like to bring him up with you? For if he is to go, he must go with me.' Betraying to what extent the subject preyed on his mind, Nelson reverted to it later in the letter which closed with the words 'Think about Josiah'.[61]

Nelson waited while mother and son agonized, impatiently sending a chaser in the letter of 15 March telling Fanny: 'Have not heard from Josiah which I am sorry for. Tell him to write to me and inclose it to my brother.'[62] Finally they made up their minds, and by the time of his next letter, dated 5 April, Nelson could report from Portsmouth that 'Josiah and myself came down very comfortably yesterday morning and he seems quite settled, we slept on board last night...'[63] One more young gentleman was on his way. Time would tell how well stepson and stepfather would rub along and whether war would bring them together or tear them apart.

However fraught the decision to take Josiah, only a little less troubling was the request made on behalf of another young gentleman, 12-year-old William Hoste, who, in company with his father, came knocking at the front door of Parsonage House. In echoes of James Trevenen's ambitions 'to go round the world',[64] for William too 'it was first intended that he should begin a naval career in a vessel about to make a voyage around the world',[65] but the advent of war had changed all that.

Unlike Josiah's situation, the problem was neither William nor his parents. The Reverend Dixon Hoste was, after all, rector of the neighbouring parishes of Godwick and Tittleshall and, with his own father a parson, Nelson had no objections to extending his favour to embrace other sons of the clergy as he had just done for Thomas Weatherhead, whose brother was already in the navy and whose father was rector in the neighbouring parish of Sedgeford. What caused Nelson to arch his eyebrows was who had effected William's introduction: Lord Coke, local Member of Parliament and a leading light in Whig circles. The navy was, supposedly, blind to politics but old allegiances ran deep. Nelson was Tory through and through, and frowned on all Whigs: they had treacherously supported – at least with lip service – the rebels during the American Revolution and more recently flirted dangerously with the revolutionary fervour wafting across the Channel. Burnham Thorpe was not two miles from Holkham Hall, seat of the Coke family, yet Lord Coke and Nelson had met just once in the past five years. William's father must be very important indeed for Lord Coke to favour the humble Captain Nelson with this sudden lavish attention, but, for all that, Nelson would have looked askance at the origins of this patronage.

What convinced Nelson to take William Hoste is anyone's guess: pragmatism in the face of a common enemy, political expediency, a rapport with the boy's likeable father, or a keen eye for the boy's officer potential? In any event, remembering the treachery of the Whig sailors during the American Revolution his first advice to William was 'you must always implicitly obey orders, without attempting to form any opinion of your own respecting their propriety'.[66]

Nelson was never short of homilies, as evidenced in a letter he wrote some years later to another young gentleman about to set out on a naval career:

Dear Charles:

As Captain Hillyer has been so good as to say he would rate you MID, I sincerely hope that your conduct will ever deserve his kind notice and protection, by a strict and very active attention to your duty… As you from this day start in the world as a man, I trust that your future conduct in life will prove you both an officer and a gentleman: recollect, that you must be a seaman to be an officer; and also, that you cannot be a good officer without being a gentleman.[67]

As for William, lecture over, political honour satisfied, the decision to take him was made without further ado. Conscious, however, of William's extreme youth and aware that, like all the young gentlemen set to join the *Agamemnon*, they would be vulnerable on board if the ship's officer hierarchy were not fully constituted to ensure rigid discipline, Nelson advised William's father that he would call for the boy only once the *Agamemnon* was ready to sail. Remembering his own lamb-to-the-slaughter arrival as a 12-year-old on board the *Raisonnable* back in 1771, Nelson had promised himself that the captain's servants in his care would not suffer the same anguish. This was a subject dear to his heart, one which Nelson came back to when he asked Midshipman George Parsons, whom he had invited to dine with him on the *Foudroyant* in 1799, 'You entered the service at a very early age, to have been in action off St Vincent?'[68] When George replied, 'Eleven years, my lord',[69] Nelson muttered, 'Much too young.'[70]

Nelson formally entered William on the *Agamemnon*'s books as of 15 April and wrote to Dixon Hoste notifying him to have his son ready to join the ship by the end of the month. Accordingly, 'at the beginning of April 1793, William (accompanied by his father with his elder and beloved brother) left Godwick Hall, the scene of his childhood, and proceeded to London. From thence, in the course of a few weeks, he went to Portsmouth where he was placed under the care of Nelson himself, then just arrived at Spithead.'[71]

William arrived in Portsmouth ahead of the *Agamemnon*, which was still undergoing sea trials and did not come into port until 28 April. William's letters are silent on what he did while waiting to go aboard, although a later letter referred to a 'Mr Noble who showed us round the fleet when we were at Portsmouth'.[72] Each young gentleman would have had his own unique experience of waiting to go on board ship. For 11-year-old George Parsons, arriving unaccompanied:

On my alighting from the heavy coach, early in the year 1795, at the India Arms, Gosport, the first person who noticed me was this eccentric [the oldest] midshipman [in His Majesty's service]; he was seated on a low settle by the large kitchen fire of that respectable house, with an outsized rummer of darkish liquor.

'What cheer, young squeaker? And what ship are you bound for?

'The *Barfleur*, sir.'

'Do you like grog?'

'I don't know, sir; for I never tasted it.'

'Here, then,' said he, kindly getting off the settle, and putting it to my lips; 'take a swig, and let me know if it is stiff enough. Old Mother does not make good nor'-westers this month, the last score not being paid up.'

All this was lost on my comprehension, and the only thing I understood was, that I must give an opinion on its merits, and accordingly swallowed some with great difficulty, for to me it was nauseous.

Billy contemplated my wry faces and aversion with astonishment and indignation. 'You must alter very materially to make a sailor, young squeaker.'[73]

In his brief time at Portsmouth, William may have rubbed shoulders with scholars from the Academy. If so, he would have discovered that, unlike the Marine Society, the Academy had higher priorities than the war effort. Jealously endeavouring to foster its reputation, the Academy resisted the general call to arms and only released Academites to ships once it was satisfied they had completed their Plan.

This can have done the Academy few favours. One of the scholars held back during this period was Charles Austen, youngest brother of Jane Austen. He had followed his elder brother, Francis, into the Academy in 1791 but was obliged to serve out his full time of schooling, only being discharged 18 months into the war on 14 September 1794 'to go to sea in the *Daedelus* [*sic*]'[74] aged 15.

To judge by his school reports, Charles was not the stellar student that Francis had been. Year by year there was a steady decline in Charles' performance. His headmaster's reports read: 1791: 'Has a very good Capacity, is very attentive to his studies and of a good disposition.'[75] 1792: 'Is of a good disposition and capacity; diligent and makes good progress.'[76] 1793: 'Has a pretty good Capacity and is very attentive to his studies.'[77] Very good had progressively become pretty good. The Governor's Report repeated the trend, only the adjectives were different: 1791: 'Good capacity & behaviour with very considerable industry.'[78] 1792: 'Of good capacity, well disposed and industrious.'[79] 1793: 'Of a tolerable Capacity & very attentive and well behaved.'[80] Including his teachers' reports, 1793 had three 'pretty' adjectives scattered around. In addition to the headmaster's report, his French was 'pretty diligent'[81] and he 'writes and draws pretty well'.[82] This decline is no surprise: Charles was a restless youngster, itching to be off to sea where the action was. Holding him back was a mistake for him and the navy.

Reading those reports, Reverend Austen would doubtless have composed much the same – only more chastening – letter to Charles as he had done to Francis some five years before. 'The little world of which you are going to become an Inhabitant',[83] imagined by their father, would still 'consist of three Orders of Men – All of whom will occasionally have it in their power to contribute no little share to your pleasure or pain…'[84] It would remain to be seen how Charles Austen and all the other young Nelsons-to-be, descending on ports around England over the coming years, would come to terms with the 'little world' that they were about to inhabit and handle 'the three Orders of Men' they would encounter there.

RITES OF PASSAGE

A s young gentlemen and boys converged, more or less willingly, on ports around the British Isles in 1793, absent from the navy at sea would be any royal blood. Prince William Henry may have been received with 'universal joy' when first going to sea 14 years before, but, returning from North America in 1783, he quickly fell out of favour. Promoted too rapidly, then deliberately marooned ashore after the *Andromeda*, the ship he captained, was paid off in 1789, he entered Parliament and, as the duke of Clarence, set about becoming, at least in the eyes of King George III, the bad – if not the worst – boy of Britain. 'Politics, that bane and curse of military men'[1] did for the naval career of the duke who had 'the superlative culpable folly to make himself conspicuous in his hostility to the war measures of the minister … [and] to make a speech in the House of Lords condemnatory of the minister's proceedings. Mr Pitt … went forthwith to the King to tell his Majesty that a political admiral, and one who thought the war objectionable, was not a proper person to be placed as a flag-officer in the grand fleet.'[2]

There could no longer be any doubt: the experiment in royal education had failed. Nevertheless, the king had unwittingly done right by the navy. Its choice as a career for a prince of the realm made the navy fashionable for many younger sons of the great houses, such that one frigate was:

so crowded with bantlings of the aristocracy that one of the lieutenants of the ship, a rough hand, but with some humour, had been reading the King's Speech to Parliament, and presently after, being officer of the watch, he was desired to 'wear the ship' [to cause a ship to go about, so that the vessel's stern is presented to the wind], and in doing so he called out to the young noblemen and honourables stationed at the different ropes: 'My Lords and gentlemen, shiver the mizen [the mast aft of the main mast] topsail.' This parliamentary language on the quarter-deck became quite the joke in the squadron.'[3]

By the time the Wars broke out in 1793, there were 'Honourables' to be found everywhere: among the captains requesting boys from the Marine Society and in daily reports of ships leaving and entering Plymouth and Portsmouth. Against the backdrop of Britain's rarefied social hierarchy and surrounded at sea by so many Honourables, one youngster who had claim to the lofty but somewhat obscure title of 'Baronet of the Holy Roman Empire' could have been expected to style himself as such on entering the navy. However William Dillon did not, for the simple reason that there were doubts about his legitimacy. The exact date of William's birth remains a mystery, but he was about ten when he went to sea in 1790. His *Narrative of My Professional Adventures* provides an intriguing insight into the sinister pitfalls for a youngster first going to sea. William starts off his memoirs wide-eyed in wonderment: 'During my stay on board the *Royal William*, how shall I describe the scenes that presented themselves to my view? I was completely lost in contemplating the immense size of the ship, the busy motions of the seamen, the noise of Boatswain's Mates piping, the officers giving orders: in short, the whole machine was beyond my comprehension.'[4]

When the time came for his father to leave the ship, the tug of homesickness was made more acute because the sea was not the youngster's choice. William's preference was for the army, having 'already formed a taste for a military life',[5] but his father had decided: 'You are too young for the army. The navy is an honourable profession, the favourite one of this country. What should we do without the wooden walls of Old England?'[6] With stiff-upper-lip understatement, William merely hints at the dim distant pangs: 'The moment was now rapidly approaching when I was to take leave of my Father. The new career I was about to enter occupied all my thoughts, starting alone, without any friend to advise me. My Father noticing my pensive mood, cheered me with soothing expressions, and alluded to the brilliant prospects before me… My Father then, taking an affectionate leave of me, quitted the ship.'[7]

His father gone, William was left to fend for himself. Initially, this posed no problem as he:

> ...was shown down to the Cockpit. My entrance into this place I shall never forget – total darkness: under water. I was introduced into the starboard Midshipmen's berth, and presented to some very fine young men, all of whom appeared to be above the age of twenty ... occupied with books, by candle light... I went out into the open space of the Cockpit, where my attention was attracted towards two young gentlemen hard at work pipe claying [cleaning with pipe-clay] their smalls by the light of a small tallow candle. So soon as they understood that I had joined the ship, they both shook me by the hand, with merry laughing countenances. They told me of their being anxious to make themselves smart, as one of them was to dine with the Captain, the other with the officers in the Ward Room.[8]

Dining at the captain's table was a special privilege accorded only to the most illustrious of young gentlemen arriving on board ship for the first time. Even William Parker, a captain's servant aged 11 going aboard the *Orion* of 74 guns in February 1793, had to wait three months until 'Yesterday, my Capt. invited me to dine with him where I met four or five other Capt. I was dressed in uniform and I assure you we had a very nice dinner at the Top, very nice salt fish at the bottom, a leg of fresh mutton in the middle very excellent pea soup on one side Potatoes and on other side stued cabbage and very nice boiled Rice. After that Cranberry and Apple Tart and Plumb pudding. Some redishes and other little necessarys.'[9]

No such luck for Jeffrey Raigersfeld. Son of the Austrian Chargé d'Affaires, he could reasonably expect an invitation to the captain's table aboard the *Mediator* when he first went to sea aged 12. Yet his memoirs, *The Life of a Sea Officer*, are silent, instead describing the plain fare he could look forward to on his first voyage, bound for the West Indies shortly before the beginning of the Wars: 'As the ship was soon to sail, the sea stock for mess was laid in; it consisted of a few pounds of tea and brown sugar, a couple of sacks of potatoes, and about sixty pounds of beef taken up from the purser, which was salted down and put into a small cask for to serve as fresh provisions during the voyage ... some celery seeds and onions to make pea soup savoury, was all the stock midshipmen at that time thought of taking to sea.'[10]

No more invitations to the captain's table for William Dillon either, once his father had left. Prioirity for William was to come to terms with his new surroundings, which were increasingly bewildering: 'I went on the Lower Deck to look about. There was a strong breeze, the ship inclined over to the left, the ports were all open, the guns out, and the sea, to me, appeared to be entering. I was alarmed thinking the ship must fall over and sink. My fears were noticed by some of the marines, whose quarters I had got into...'[11] Reassured by them, William boasts that 'I very soon became used to the ship, and was much noticed by my messmates. I was extremely anxious to keep watch. My proposal was not approved of. Everyone said I was too young; the fatigue would be too much for me.'[12]

However he was about to get a rude awakening to the realities of life on board ship. All seemed fine at first:

> One evening a very fine young man, Mason by name, who seemed desirous of making himself agreeable, offered to take charge of me during the first watch – that is from eight o'clock to midnight. I was punctual and a few minutes after eight I attended on the Quarter Deck. My friend met me, and replied to all my questions with extreme kindness. The first thing that drew my attention was what they call the setting of the watch, at nine o'clock at that time of the year. The Admiral's ship fires an evening gun; the others fire muskets. By that is meant that the lights are put out, and the crews, excepting those who have the look-out, go to bed: or as the sailors say 'turn in to their hammocks'.[13]

Suddenly, matters took a sinister turn: 'My friend held me by the hand nearly the whole watch. I kept walking by his side, at its termination receiving the compliments of the elderly Mids, and went to my hammock shortly after 12 o'clock.'[14] Acute anxiety creeps into young William's narrative as he struggles with the painful and embarrassing memory of all the attention that he is receiving from older men in the crew: 'When I joined the ship, I had been led to believe that she should soon sail for Torbay. But delays constantly occurred, which weighed upon my anxious mind. I felt I was not in my right position, although several of the midshipmen, particularly my messmates, were all cordiality – and, what was still more strange, one or two of the seamen devoted themselves to me, and would often carry me in their arms to explain several parts of the ship in answer to my inquiries. I did not feel comfortable. I wrote to my Father as often as I thought it necessary.'[15]

His father should have taken action, but did nothing. William was on his own. His solution was to pick a fight, but not with his unwanted 'friend' Mason, instead with the resident bully, 18-year-old Sanders, who: 'messed in the opposite berth. He watched his opportunities to vex and torment me… When I thought myself rid of him, I made my way quietly to the Gun Room, where I generally retired that I might read my letters by daylight. However, whilst I was in the act of perusing it, the letter was suddenly snatched out of my hands to my great surprise by Sanders…'[16] One thing led to another, ending with a sword-fight: 'Closing then upon Sanders, I drew my sword and attacked him. I soon perceived that he did not know how to defend himself, and made him feel the point of my steel against his ribs.'[17] Sanders fled but soon after:

> …all the Mids were hastened on deck, where I was ordered before Mr Shields [the Lieutenant]. To him I stated all that had happened from first to last: in short that Mr Sanders had been the plague of my life, and that I was determined to convince him I would no longer submit to the continual annoyance he had inflicted on me. When the Lieutenant heard all I had to say (which could not be contradicted by Sanders), he censured him in such terms of severity that he was humbled beyond description, and was ordered not appear on the Quarter Deck for some time. Then Mr Shields … shook me by the hand, expressing his approval at my knowing how to take my own part… In consequence … Sanders was turned out his berth by his messmates, and sent to Coventry, as it is called, by all the Mids in the ship, whilst on my side, I was noticed by the Ward Room officers, and called 'the manly boy'.[18]

William had made his point. Staking out territory was the obligatory rite of passage for youngsters going on board ship, the usual resolution being fisticuffs as in the case of Prince William, or the sword in William Dillon's case. However William's story was not just one of the young 'bucks of the navy'[19] boasting about his early exploits. William had an ulterior motive but, with Victorian prudishness, did not want to spell it out in so many words. Instead, the sword-fight enabled him to declare euphemistically that 'This affair made an impression very much in my favour on board the *Saturn*, and stuck to my name very many years. No one after this ever attempted to take liberties with me.'[20]

William Dillon waited until he had the benefit of maturity before recalling his first impressions but, in the process, his account lost some of its immediacy. William Hoste, finally aboard the *Agamemnon*, was too impatient to wait. He was living the moment and wanted his family back home to know then and there what his 'little world' was really like. And so the letters flooded home, bursting with immediate news. On 4 May 1793, a few days after joining the *Agamemnon*, William wrote to his father, brimming with excitement:

> We did not sail from Spithead till 1st of May; the wind not proving fair enough. We had a very pleasant cruise, but it would have been more so if we had taken two Dutch frigates and two men-of-war brigs, which we found riding at Cape la Hogue. In all probability we should have captured them if we could have got a pilot to take us in. They ran their ships amongst some rocks. Night coming on, we left them; no doubt rejoicing in their narrow escape. From thence we proceeded to Cherbourg; we went so near it that we could perceive with glasses, the people walking on the shore. It is remarkably well fortified; the officers on board all considered it to be one of the strongest places they ever saw. The country around it looked in very high cultivation. All attempts at getting anything here being fruitless, we sailed along the coast till we came to the island of Alderney, where we made a signal for a pilot. A boat accordingly came off with two, but both being ignorant of the pilotage of the aforesaid cape, we were obliged to desist from any further attack upon those dastardly Frenchmen among the rocks. Our time being fixed for returning this morning, we were obliged to steer for Old England without a prize, and are at this moment entering Spithead. So much for our cruise. Now for a little about myself. I like my situation very much. Captain Nelson treats me as he said he would; and as a proof, I have lived with him ever since I have been on board.[21]

This is William's first letter home. On the surface, he gives the illusion of a world untouched by the realities of war, as he describes his living 'situation' in glowing terms. However, by taking his parents to the front line, he unwittingly puts on display some, if not all, of the key dynamics of the maritime Wars of the next 22 years: the enemy immediately on the defensive; the British Navy at once eager for the fight; its crews better trained and better led. In 1793 Nelson may have been little known outside naval circles, just one of many captains who had served honourably at sea in previous conflicts. Similarly, the sentiments prompting William's letter may have been hero-worship. After all, what youngster wouldn't idolize the swashbuckling captain who had plucked him from the dull, drear backwaters of Norfolk? Nevertheless, in this small story William captures the genius-to-be, Nelson at his simple best: at once strategically inspired and tactically sound. It is this perfect cocktail that would make Nelson the quintessence of all that would be 'great' about Britain's fighting spirit at sea during the Wars.

Setting out on the cruise, Nelson's orders were simple: the *Agamemnon* was to undergo sea trials. However, sighting 'two Dutch frigates and two men-of-war brigs', he could not pass up the opportunity to have a go at the enemy. Nevertheless, there was nothing foolhardy about his actions, and the moment the enemy took refuge in unfamiliar rocky shoals, and a local pilot could not be found, Nelson abandoned the chase. After five years 'cultivating his garden' and newly in command of a motley crew of old hands and raw recruits drafted to a ship that had been laid up in ordinary for ten years, Nelson was testing his own mettle, the sea-worthiness of the *Agamemnon* and the fighting qualities of his officers and men. What better way than a dry run at the enemy?

As for the young gentlemen standing beside him on the quarterdeck, they may have been mere spectators in this little skirmish, but Nelson was giving them an early masterclass in what it took to be a good officer. Their job was to watch, listen and learn. William certainly did, hence his comments about 'the pilot' and the officers on board 'who all considered it to be one of the strongest places they ever saw'. He was doubtless regurgitating what he had heard officers debating on the quarterdeck or in the wardroom. He may even have been quoting his hero directly, since Nelson made a similar comment in a later letter to Fanny: 'We fell in with two French frigates, and two armed vessels who got into La Hogue harbour where we could not follow for want of a pilot.'[22] This was on-the-job training par excellence that no number of years at the Portsmouth Naval Academy could mimic. No wonder that one Academite could 'think a well-regulated man-of-war, and a really good schoolmaster, and where the captain really takes an interest about his boys, is a preferable course of education.'[23]

Still, the dry run was not just about training. Nelson understood that first impressions counted for much. Instil in these young gentlemen the thrill of the chase, offer them the promise of riches, and they would go to the ends of the earth for their captain and their country. Honour may have been more important to Nelson than prizes, or at least so he said, but he knew that for many families of young gentlemen joining the navy, if not the youngsters themselves, prizes and profit must count somewhat. And he was right. For William, returning 'without a prize' would, he knew, disappoint his father.

Josiah Nisbet had no such complex thoughts. As he made clear in a two-line postscript added to an early letter Nelson sent Fanny, his Wars were meant to be all about prizes: 'We have taken nothing at present nor are likely to take any thing. I am very well at present and hope you are the same.'[24] Such meagre fare would be typical of the boy's letters throughout the Wars: long silences punctuated by the occasional cryptic missive. Instead, Fanny would have to rely on Nelson for news on how Josiah was adjusting to life at sea. Well enough, according to the early letters: on 5 April, 'he seems quite settled, we slept on board last night and are now at home… Josiah seems to like his situation very much'[25] and on 11 May, 'Josiah is in high spirits.'[26] Like William's parents, Fanny could rest easy for the moment.

Still, there were other ordeals for the youngsters to endure in those early days, one of them being the dreaded *mal de mer*. Typically, Josiah was silent on the subject, so it took a letter from Nelson on 18 April for the truth to filter back that 'Josiah is with me: yesterday, it blowing a smart gale, he was a little sea-sick.'[27] William Hoste, in his letter home of 19 May, let slip his fears of much worse to come. By then the *Agamemnon* was on its way to the Mediterranean and William had fallen prey to the scaremongering of old hands: 'Hitherto, we have had fine weather and pleasant sailing, though scarcely wind enough to give a sickening motion to our vessel. I have not been sick since our last cruise but expect to have a touch of it as we are rolling through the Bay of Biscay.'[28]

William never got round to telling his parents how bad seasickness was Biscay-style. However, Jeffrey Raigersfeld, crossing the Bay, did not hold back. He revelled in the gruesome details, recounting how 'no sooner were we out of sight of land, than I became so very sea sick as to be unable to assist myself in the least; indeed when crossing the Bay of Biscay, the waves ran so high, and the water out of the soundings caused so bad a smell on board, from the rolling of the ship as it washed from side to side in the between decks, that had any one thrown me overboard as I lay helpless upon the gangway I certainly should not have made the smallest resistance.'[29]

Jeffrey seems to have endured more than his fair share of rites of passage. In addition to *mal de mer*, he was victim of another plague visited on newcomers to a ship. Jeffrey's tale of woe started off innocently enough as he described being 'taken on board his Majesty's ship *Mediator*, of 44 guns on two decks, lying at Spithead, in the Commissioner's barge, with my large chest of clothes, which including ten pounds that was in it, in halfpence and silver, cost my parents one hundred pounds, besides bed and blankets that were bought for me before I left the Commissioner's.'[30]

The trouble began once on board the *Mediator*:

> I had not been long on board before I perceived that my large chest began to attract the notice of those about me whenever I went to unlock it, indeed, although it had been so well packed that when I wanted anything out of it, assistance was necessary to close the lid down before it could be locked up, it was not long before I could do this myself, for I began to lose my clothes, and noone knew anything about them; a leather cap, which I usually wore in the morning when I wanted to put it on; at last it struck me, that the blackguard boy of the mess seemed very quick at finding it when I offered sixpence to the finder; he then instantly went into the pump well, and in a little brought it up, sometimes wet, at other dry... As to the mess things that I brought on board in my chest, such as tea, sugar etc, they had been consumed long before for the public good, and my pewter wash-hand basin, the only visible remains of all my more than ample fitting out, was only mine when others were not using it.[31]

No point complaining; he got short shrift: 'In this way I was often gulled; at last, however, I complained of the boy to the mate of the berth, who took no notice of it, which soon convinced me that complaining would do me no good; therefore after a good crying when I was alone, I became more heedful of those around me.'[32] But just when he needed to be most vigilant, he was struck down by seasickness, and afterwards:

> Upon this partial recovery, I went to visit my chest, but found it nearly emptied of all superfluities, and excepting three or four shirts and a scanty portion of other necessaries, little remaining of all the abundant stock my parents had so carefully put together for a three years' stations. What could I do? The key of the chest was in my possession, and it was locked when I went to it, so my loss was deemed fancy by

those around me, and I was only laughed at, but given to understand that unless I could prove my loss, my complaint would do me harm than good, and I wisely followed this advice which certainly afterwards contributed to my not being made the general fag.[33]

Jeffrey's experience of a 'little world' beyond the law could simply be put down to one barrel of rotten apples. After all, theft was considered a serious crime and punishable by flogging. Furthermore, Jeffrey's captain, Cuthbert Collingwood, was known to be most caring and solicitous especially towards youngsters on his ship. There is no reason to doubt Jeffrey's account: he retold the saga of his 'chest of clothes' without rancour, portraying the whole experience as a badge of honour. Yet there was not one word in any of the letters from Josiah Nisbet and William Hoste about petty larceny and other such shenanigans. Could it be they were honouring a code of silence, which Jeffrey only dared break years later from the safety of his armchair? Maybe, or it could be that, as with William Parker, they found a way round the problem.

Like William Hoste and Josiah Nisbet, William Parker was in his element and had only good to say about his early days at sea, writing in his second letter home on 24 February 1793 that: 'I am very happy and as comfortable as if I was at home, and like it of all things.'[34] William Parker also had many fine things that he had brought on board. In a letter to his brother before sailing, he wrote that: 'I have been very busy laying up (what we call) a sea store such as Gingerbreads...'[35] Again, in his second letter to his mother, he described how: 'I bought with my Aunt's present the 4 volumes of Ye Arabian Knights ... you cannot think what nice presents my Brothers made me. They brought me Music etc and a large jar of honey. It will be a nice thing to eat with Biscuits out at sea when our salt butter is out. I am completely rigged out with Fiddle Strings, Drawings and Eatables.'[36]

Yet there is not a word about any of his possessions going missing. The solution for William was, as he explained in his letter of 24 February, that Mr Nevill, a junior officer on the *Orion*, 'tells me also to lay anything, if it would be more convenient to me, in his cabin.'[37] By stowing his prized possessions in the quarters of Mr Nevill, a junior officer, William was keeping them out of harm's way. No 'blackguard boy of the mess' would dare enter the quarters of an officer and steal his effects.

William Parker, Jeffrey Raigersfeld and other young gentlemen had plenty of fine 'superfluities' that could attract covetous eyes. Not so Jeremy Newton making the journey partway on foot, partway by boat down the Thames from the Marine Society's offices on Bishopsgate to join the *Agamemnon* at Chatham. Jeremy also had possessions – but only the 'necessaries' provided by the Society and certainly no 'superfluities'. Meagre though they were, these 'necessaries' would, nevertheless, have attracted their fair share of sticky fingers. Unsurprisingly, Jeremy left no letters recording his first impressions. Despite being able to read and write, he was 'destitute', which meant he had no one to write home to. Nor did he write his memoirs later.

However another lower-deck boy did. In *The Autobiography of Pel Verjuice*, Charles Pemberton described his first impressions going on board a man-of-war, albeit a few years on in the Wars: 'How invitingly beautiful I thought her then,'[38] was followed in the next sentence by 'Reader, she was a hell afloat.'[39] With clunking irony, Charles was setting out his polemical stall. Notwithstanding, his description of those first hours 'coming on board His Majesty's Frigate' in 1806 were refreshingly matter-of-fact: 'Registered on her chronicles by name Peregrine Verjuice, aged 17 years, by trade a quill driver, by birth a Welshman: then I was tucked under a sort of gallows to ascertain my height: 5 feet 5 inches; white, soapy complexion, bleached oakum hair, high cheek bones, and deep ditches beneath them; eyes indigo, or pepper and salt. Just as the sun or light chose they should be; a nose nothing particular, only it seemed to belong to me: no brands, marks, or scars. All these particulars were duly noted.'[40] A very straightforward account until the explanation why all these details were being recorded: 'in order that if I deserted the "Hue and Cry" might have a description of me.'[41] Just as the Marine Society recorded every boy passing through its doors, so to the navy needed a detailed description of each 'volunteer'. Both might need to track down deserters.

In the sorry saga of lower-deck boys going to sea, 'Jack Nastyface' picks up the story where Charles Pemberton left off. After being processed through the various meat-grinders and finally reaching his 'line of battle ship … we were now fast getting our ship ready for sea, and in a few days sailed past the Downs to Portsmouth, and joined the Channel Fleet. Here we began to feel discipline with all its horrors.'[42] With remorseless inevitability, Jack describes how there was 'a regular system of

plunder observed on board of those ships, on the *birds of passage*, as we were called…
Some lost their shoes in the open day, while others had their blankets taken from
them as they lay on the deck at night; they would disappear instantaneously, as if by
magic. The mode resorted to, I learned, was by using fish-hooks and a line, which
were contrived so dexterously, that, aided by its being dark between decks, it was
almost impossible to detect them.'[43] Jack's experience was no surprise given that his
companions were: 'a number of the Lord Mayor's Men, a term given to those who
enter to relieve themselves from public disgrace, and who are sent on board by any
of the city magistrates, for a frolic or a night charge.'[44]

For all the wide social gulf between Jack Nastyface and Jeffrey Raigersfeld, they
had one thing in common when they came on board. They were alone, which
made them easy prey for onboard thieves. As a runaway apprentice, Jack did not
benefit even from the modicum of camaraderie that might have come from being
one of the 'Scape Gallowses' arriving from the Marine Society. Jeffrey Raigersfeld
had started off his education at a girls' school on Paddington Green before being
sent to a school in Whitehaven, Cumberland, prior to joining the *Mediator*.
Therefore he enjoyed neither the mutual support Charles Penrose and James
Trevenen could give each other as fellow Academites from the Portsmouth Naval
Academy on their first sea voyage exploring the South Seas together, nor the
camaraderie of being Norfolk lads all from neighbouring villages, as was the case
for William Hoste, William Bolton and the Weatherhead brothers. Jeffrey, for all
his connections at court and 'having a letter of introduction to the Hon Rowland
Burton'[45] whom he stayed with on shore when he arrived in Antigua, had no young
gentlemen he could claim as friends when he arrived on the *Mediator*; instead:
'My messmates consisted of one mate, four grown-up midshipmen, a younker,
who had been at sea, myself, and a blackguard boy, that served the mess as cook
and all else besides.'[46]

Left to his own devices like William Dillon, Jeffrey decided 'after a good
crying when he was alone'[47] that the solution to survival in his lonely little world,
full of rules but devoid of laws, was to make himself useful by 'betaking myself
again to climbing the rigging, attending in the round tops, and observing the
different shifting and trimming of the sails … indeed the officers appeared much
pleased at my quickness, and I very soon became a favourite, not only with them,
but with the common sailors likewise.'[48]

William Parker had no such problems as he stepped on board the *Orion*. For starters, he was messed in with a group of young gentlemen as well connected as himself, including, 'Mr Baker/Son of Mr Baker Member of Parliament for Hartfordshire',[49] and Mr Lane, son of a 'Captain of the navy' [who] says he knows our family'.[50] Furthermore, he had a bevy of mentors lining up to protect him, guide him, minister to his every needs. It was a given for young gentlemen that their captain would be their sea-daddy, acting in *loco parentis*. Hence, William Hoste could gush about how 'Captain Nelson is uncommon kind to me'[51] and 'Captain Nelson treats me as he said he would; and as proof, I have lived with him ever since I have been on board',[52] and William Parker could muse how 'I think I have every prospect of doing well, particularly under the care of so good a gentleman as Captain Duckworth, who is like a father to us all',[53] and that 'Captain Duckworth is so good as to send for some plums, and other good things, for Messrs Lane, Baker and me'.[54]

However, as Jeffrey Raigersfeld had found 'on my arrival on board',[55] once 'the Captain sent for the mate of the berth he intended me to mess in and I found myself consigned to the main hatchway berth',[56] nefarious forces were free to operate unseen in the nether regions of a ship, and no captain could hope to protect a young gentleman from these day in, day out. The forces ranged from the Jeffrey's 'blackguard boy of the mess' to William Dillon's 'friend'. Young gentlemen going to sea needed other allies, closer to hand than the captain. The older of the two Weatherhead boys was nominated by William Hoste's parents as his protector and, acknowledging the importance of this role, William made frequent references to Weatherhead in letters home. On 5 August 1793, 'Mr Weatherhead is made Mate. I like him very much',[57] and in May 1794 William repeated his praise, noting that 'To Weatherhead, I am greatly indebted for every friendly office; I assure you, he has never forgot the charge he took of me upon your leaving us.'[58]

However, having Weatherhead as guardian angel was nothing to compare with the resources William Parker could mobilize. His uncle by marriage and cousin by blood was Admiral Sir John Jervis, who 'has told Mr Nevill (who he knows very well) to take care of me, and I assure you does, and is by far the best friend I have on board (Captain Duckworth excepting); tells me to ask him anything I want, and often asks me questions in those rules of navigation I have gone through.'[59] William's letter of February 24 1793 shows patronage at work: not just in the important moments of a young gentleman's naval career – entering the navy, transferring ships or gaining promotion – but day to day at sea, especially as the youngster was finding his sea legs. With Mr Nevill, a junior officer, at his beck and call, little could go wrong. In addition to Mr Nevill, others on board the *Orion*, with one eye on their own promotion prospects, queued up to offer themselves up as his mentor, including Mr Gray who 'is so good as to say he will take me to watch with him in a year'[60] and, as if that were not enough, William had a schoolmaster who seemed more than usually attentive to his needs: 'I like our schoolmaster very much, and he brings me on amazingly, and explains everything very plainly to me. I have begun navigation. He tells me if I ever feel the least sick to tell him; in short he tells me to acquaint him with whatever I want, and he is one of my best friends.'[61]

For William Dillon, the enduring memory of spending that first night on board ship was the noise and the smells: 'I did not enjoy much sleep that night in the cable tier where I was slung up. The effluvia from the cables was not very agreeable. But, knowing that there was no bettering my position, I calmly resigned myself to my fate. The noise of the chain pumps in the morning was a regular nuisance…'[62] William Parker, on the other hand, had very snug sleeping arrangements his first night on the *Orion* and, knowing this would interest his sister especially, wrote to his parents to 'pray tell Patty that I do not sleep in a hammock, but a cot, which is a much more comfortable thing, and that is not swung yet, so I manage very well.'[63] By April, he wrote with an update. 'My Cot – tell Patty – is serving and I get in very well but I believe we are all to have Hammocks since in time of Action they may not make splinters.'[64]

Any moment soon would come the 'time of Action', but not just yet.

THE LITTLE WORLD

The novelty, the excitement, the bewilderment and, in some cases, the horrors of those first few days on board ship over, next came the grinding adjustment these young gentlemen and boys must make to life day in, day out in the 'little world' they had entered.

Back in the 1770s, King George III had conceived the notion of a 'whole plan' to govern Prince William's early career at sea. The prince wilfully circumvented the plan, but when he in turn became captain of the *Pegasus*, instituted his own regime for youngsters, whereby, as one of them later commented admiringly, 'from nine in the morning until noon we were engaged with the schoolmaster and never left unoccupied during the rest of the day.'[1]

Also, when setting up the Portsmouth Naval Academy, the Admiralty tried extending its remit into King's ships by stipulating a set of rules to regulate how Academites should be received once they left the Academy and went on board ship. Order 31 of its *Articles and Orders* stated that: 'The Scholars in His Majesty's Ships shall be kept to the duty of Seaman, but have the privilege of walking the Quarterdeck, and shall be allotted a proper place to be in, without setting up any Cabbins for them, and they shall be rated on the Ship's Books with the title of Volunteers per order and receive Able Seaman's pay.'[2]

As for Scape Gallowses, they would be on their own, at the mercy of the boatswain, and his rules were simple: they were 'to come at a whistle and run at a blow.'[3]

Whatever the background of these young gentlemen and boys, however, once on board ship, their prospects were best off with 'a well-regulated man-of-war, and a really good schoolmaster and where the captain really takes an interest about his boys'.[4] Nelson was typical of the 'parental commander'[5] who took 'an interest about his boys',[6] but he also led by example. Lady Hughes, briefly a passenger on board the *Boreas* commanded by Nelson before the Wars, commented on:

> …his attention to the young gentlemen who had the happiness of being on his quarter-deck. It may reasonably be supposed, that among the number of thirty, there must have been some timid spirits, as well as bold; the timid he never rebuked; but always wished to shew them, he desired nothing that he would not instantly do himself: And I have known him say – Well Sir, I am going a race to the mast head, and beg I may meet you there. No denial could be given to such a request, and the poor fellow instantly began to climb the shrouds. Captain Nelson never took the least notice in what manner it was done; but, when they met in the top, spoke in the most cheerful terms to the midshipman, and observed – How much any person was to be pitied, who could fancy there was any danger, or even any thing disagreeable, in the attempt.[7]

With Nelson as their captain it is no wonder then that, six months after putting to sea, William Hoste could write in a letter dated 5 August 1793 how 'I like the sea very much…'[8] and that Josiah Nisbet could, by his standards, wax lyrical in a letter of 12 October 1793 that 'I have been very well since I wrote you last… I still like being at sea and think I always shall.'[9]

As for William Dillon, after the near disaster of his first three months at sea aboard the benighted *Saturn*, he was moved to the *Alcide*, whose captain 'Sir Andrew [Douglas] was a strict officer and had a good judgment',[10] ran a 'well-regulated man-of-war', and 'sent for me into his cabin, accompanied by the Schoolmaster [Mr Humphreys]. After being with him a full quarter of an hour, he explained to me that I was to consider myself entirely under the control of Mr Humphreys',[11] who, to ram home the point, later that same day, 'placed himself at the head of the table, laying down the law as he thought proper',[12] which meant everything from William's schooling to his duties and leisure time. Where he ate, drank and slept was the first priority and Humphreys arranged that the first lieutenant, Mr Dalby, 'conducted me below to the Gun Room where our mess was established. I made the twelfth in number, and the youngest in age, of the party. My reception on board was truly gratifying. I very soon experienced the difference between the two ships.'[13]

William was harking back to his experience on first going to sea: the *Alcide* was a well-regulated ship; the benighted *Saturn* was not at all so. The captain of the *Saturn* should never have put ten-year-old William in the cockpit with the midshipmen, some of whom might be 40 years old, and even the youngest of whom would, in normal circumstances, have been two years older than William. It was just such lax crew-management that could lead to a serious breakdown of discipline; hence the strictest of Admiralty regulations when it came to 'unnatural acts'. William's place was in the gun room with the other volunteers and captain's servants just going to sea, 'as fine a set of youths as I had ever met in my school days… Most of these young gentlemen were highly connected – the names of some of them will satisfy you.'[14] At least, William was finally among peers of his own age.

On the Alcide Captain Douglas ran a tight ship and had Humphreys on hand to oversee the young gentlemen and their well-being. Humphreys was well 'aware of the good opinion Sir Andrew had of him, acted as he thought proper'[15] and, relishing his authority, was: 'very fond of keeping up a certain discipline among us. He had provided himself with a light yellow cane, studded with black circular spots, on which account we called it the Zebra. This was hung up in his cabin, and when he intended to chastise any delinquent, he would in the first instance order the youth to bring him the Zebra. Some would not obey his order, being perfectly aware of his object in sending for it.'[16] Under this iron regime, Humphreys imposed a routine covering every aspect of these young gentlemen's lives.

William was one of the majority of boys whose naval training and education began at sea:

> … school hours were from 9 o'clock in the morning till 12: in the afternoon from 2 till 4…
> I had now in my career two separate duties to learn – Seamanship and Navigation. The
> nautical terms alone were nearly a language of itself: such (in the former) as bowlings,
> braces, backstays, bobstays, shrouds, buntlines, clewlines, tack, sheets, earrings, reef
> tackle, luff tackles, brails, and many other names too numerous to mention; then again
> (in the latter) logarithms, sines, tangents, cosines, secants, cosecants, horizontal parallax,

semidiameter, meridian altitude. Next came all the heavenly bodies, the planets, the details of which you are not desirous of my communicating.[17]

Captain Douglas considered education a priority. As a result William 'had nothing to do with keeping watch, but my whole time was taken up with my studies'.[18]

Humphreys may have been a disciplinarian, but William was lucky with him as his schoolmaster, as was William Hoste with his schoolmaster, writing in August 1793 that 'we have a schoolmaster on board, who is very clever'.[19] Other young gentlemen were not so lucky. All too often ships did not even have a schoolmaster, the chaplain occasionally doubling up in the function, albeit reluctantly by all accounts.

The title of 'schoolmaster' was first introduced to naval regulations in 1731, and his duties were to instruct volunteers 'in the study of navigation and in whatsoever may contribute to render them artists in that science'.[20] In a first nod towards the concept of free education, he was 'likewise to teach the other youths of the ship, according to such orders as he shall receive from the Captain, and with regard to their capacities, whether in reading, writing, or otherwise'.[21] Further regulations in 1806 would extend the duties of schoolmaster to include 'to attend to their [the Young Gentlemen's] morals and to report 'any disposition to immorality or debauchery, or any conduct unbecoming an officer and a gentleman'.[22] For all this progress, however, the reality was that there were only 500 schoolmasters estimated to have been employed at sea in the whole period from 1712 to 1824.

An additional problem was the quality of schoolmasters. Many had gone to sea to escape complications on shore and were not suited to the life. Mr Mears, the schoolmaster brought on board the *Pegasus* by its captain, Prince William, in the late 1780s, was one such maverick. The first indication that Mears was a problem came, as Prince William recounted, when 'I was asleep on the sofa in the after-cabin dreaming that Mears was going to kill me, when suddenly I awoke and found he had hold of my wrist with one hand, and a penknife in the other. I started up and said "Good God! Mears, what are you about?" He replied, "I was merely going to tell your Royal Highness that you would be likely to lose your life by sleeping here with the windows open."'[23]

Rear Admiral Sir Horatio Nelson on board the Vanguard *after the Battle of the Nile receiving a French officer's sword from a midshipman. Painting by Guy Head. (National Portrait Gallery)*

The Naval Academy established in His Majesty's dockyard, Portsmouth, from a design by John Theophilus Lee who was a pupil at the academy in the years 1800, 1801 and 1802. (Royal Navy Museum, Portsmouth)

His Royal Highness Prince William Henry on board the Prince George *(National Maritime Museum, Greenwich, London)*

Midshipman James Ward, c.1759–1806 after attending the Naval Academy at Portsmouth, 1772–1775. Ward went as a midshipman on Captain Cook's third voyage and was present in a boat offshore when Captain Cook was killed. (National Maritime Museum, Greenwich, London)

Johnny Newcome leaving home: 'The coach stopp'd at the garden gate, and first the father took his seat.' (The Adventures of Johnny Newcome in the Navy)

Johnny Newcome: The Captain's table: 'The dinner over and table cleared, the bottles and desert appeared.' (The Adventures of Johnny Newcome in the Navy)

Cabin Boy: The first in a series of images of sailors designed by Thomas Rowlandson, published in 1799. (National Maritime Museum, Greenwich, London)

Mary Anne Talbot, otherwise known as John Taylor, Foot Drummer and Soldier. 1778–1808. (National Maritime Museum, Greenwich, London)

King Henry V dressed as a naval captain for Jane Austen's History of England *(1791). (© British Library Board. All rights reserved, 014604)*

Emma Hart, later Lady Emma Hamilton. One of a number of portraits by George Romney of Emma Hamilton, this one painted in 1785–6 showing her as Ariadne. (National Maritime Museum, Greenwich, London)

Master Blockhead finding things not exactly what he expected. (National Maritime Museum, Greenwich, London)

Master Blockhead on the middle watch: 'Cold blows the wind and rains coming on.' (National Maritime Museum, Greenwich, London)

The Brunswick *and* Le Vengeur du Peuple *at the height of the Battle of Glorious First of June, 1794. (National Maritime Museum, Greenwich, London)*

Lord Howe on the deck of the Queen Charlotte, *1 June 1794. (National Maritime Museum, Greenwich, London)*

Rear-Admiral Nelson wounded at the landing at Santa Cruz, 24 July 1797, here being supported by his stepson, Josiah Nisbet. (National Maritime Museum, Greenwich, London)

The recapture of
Hermione, the
frigate whose crew
mutinied and took
the ship into La
Guira, in Spanish
Puerto Rico, 1797.
(National Maritime
Museum,
Greenwich, London)

The explanation was accepted, as 'the fact of Mears being in the cabin at such an hour in the evening (probably about six o'clock) … was by no means unusual. He had always free access to the foremost cabin in the morning to schoolmaster the youngsters; and at all other times to write the Prince's log … to trace the ship's course on the chart, and to go on with a series of drawings he always had in hand for the captain.'[24] So Mr Mears was not confined. It was only when a second incident occurred that it became 'evident that Mears intended to murder the Prince'. This second time, 'Mears stole up to the half-deck, and into the cabin of the captain's servants, a place merely shut off by a canvas screen; there he armed himself with a large carving knife'[25] and went on a rampage. Mears ended up confined in 'the hospital at Antigua'.[26]

Mad and murderous Mears was an extreme case. However, in general, the standard of onboard teaching was so uneven that the good reputation of an individual schoolmaster could often be the very reason for parents choosing to send their son to a particular ship. This happened in William Parker's case. When a career in the navy was first mooted for him in 1792, his uncle objected, writing to William's father that:

> …with respect to educating one of your sons for the navy, I cannot possibly recommend it, on the score of expense, which daily experience convinces me will be too heavy for you. The allowance stipulated for by captains when they receive a recommendation, being double to what it was ten years ago – £50 per annum (exclusive of clothes on the outfit) and no pay coming in for the first two years and when you consider that I am approaching three score, and the small probability, from the aspect of foreign affairs, of any warfare happening in my time, I think you will be of the opinion with me that a worse profession cannot be chosen.[27]

Yet nine months later in a letter dated 22 February 1793, with Britain already on a war footing, these objections evaporated and instead Sir John was writing to Mrs Parker that: 'In my judgment William is placed with the very best man in the navy for training youth, and there being a very scientific schoolmaster in the *Orion*, the strong objections I had to his going to sea, before he had been taught navigation, are in a great degree removed.'[28]

The three Williams – Parker, Hoste and Dillon – were lucky to have captains who set store by a good schoolmaster, but theory was only the start. Captains' servants were supposedly not meant to carry out seamen's duties. However there were exceptions, as when an emergency arose in the Channel while the *Alcide* was laid up in Portsmouth for repairs. With some of the crew taken off to fill other ships' complements:

> …our remaining people, a few marines, boys etc., had extra work in attending to the ship's duty. However, it was a case of necessity, and we made the best of it. The marines rowed our boats: The Mids remaining exerted themselves to perfection, more especially when crossing the top gallant yards. I made one of eleven that hoisted a cask of water out of the main hold. Sir Andrew, ever thoughtful of some useful improvements for our advantage, had selected from among the crew a clever rigger. This seaman taught us to knot and splice: we learned how to use the marling spike, serving mallet etc. Very few captains would have taken so much interest in behalf of youngsters.[29]

Nevertheless, there were other skills – the ones that would make officers of these young gentlemen – that needed to be tested in practice. William Dillon's opportunity came a year into his time at sea when in August 1791 he was temporarily transferred from the *Alcide* to the *Hebe*, a 40-gun frigate patrolling the coast of Ireland on anti-smuggling duties. William recounted how 'we had no schoolmaster to control us, but had to keep watch, go aloft and attend to the reefing of the topsails etc.'[30] and when stood down, still 'the youngsters were not allowed to be idle. We had plenty of exercise at reefing, learning how to use the single stick and also the musket drill.'[31]

Midshipmen were often called on to command small-boat operations against enemy positions on shore or in raiding parties against other ships. William was not as yet rated a midshipman and, even if he were, was still too young to participate in these operations. With one eye to the future, he was keen to learn how to shoot as soon as he could, but 'the Captain, watching us one afternoon while we were under the tuition of the Sergeant of Marines at the latter training, and noticing the slightness of my person, asked me if I did not feel the ship's musket too heavy. I replied that I was trying to make the best of it. "I think it is too heavy for you," he remarked: then, sending for his servant, ordered him to bring up his fowling piece. When the servant had delivered it over to his master, he instantly handed the same to me, saying "Make use of that gun as long as you remain on board."[32]

Back on the *Alcide* and laid up briefly in Portsmouth, William had the opportunity to perfect a skill all aspiring officers were expected to have and, in a rare moment when Britain was not at war with the French, did so 'under the denomination of a French fencing master. Those who had taken lessons from him reported favourably of him. Sir Andrew, hearing this, immediately thought his presence to our advantage. He sent to enquire whether any of us would like to learn the use of the small sword.'[33]

The cost of these lessons raised the thorny issue of William's allowance. Sir John Jervis had broached the question in connection with his nephew, William Parker. Now it was the Dillons' turn. Each family had to confront the problem of money: until new regulations came into force in 1794, a captain's servant received no pay. Only when made up to a midshipman would these young gentlemen receive pay, but the earliest they could expect promotion was after having served on board for two years. Until that time, as the captain had explained the day William Dillon came aboard the *Alcide*, 'my Father would be called upon for an allowance of £50 per annum to keep up my respectability... He [the captain] enquired what cash I had brought with me. Thinking it not sufficient, having to contribute £5 5 0 entrance to my mess, he directed Humphreys to make out a draft upon my Father for £10, which he would endorse, stating that he would write to him and explain what was required, as well as other particulars relating to me. There was also a pecuniary consideration to be made annually to the Schoolmaster.'[34]

By these calculations, the allowance was enough for William's routine lifestyle, but did not stretch to exceptional expenditures such as fencing lessons. William decided to check with his father before engaging in the expense. He was wise. The arrangements made for him when he first arrived on the *Alcide* show that captains were used to advancing money to young gentlemen on their ship. However, this could pose difficulties if the parents did not then honour their responsibilities. Nelson had particular problems, and his letters to Fanny were increasingly peppered with references to arrears due on at least two of the Norfolk lads, William Bolton and William Hoste. The latter's father, Dixon Hoste, was especially troublesome, and by April 1796 Nelson's frustration got the better of him and he wrote to Fanny to say that it was 'extraordinary, I have not had a line from Mr [Dixon] Hoste since I drew the last bill, although it must be known I advanced the money every day for 14 months before I asked for it, and another is rising very fast. I am very angry.'[35] With Nelson busy fighting the Wars, Fanny was deputized to ring the arrears out of poor William Hoste's father.

There were no such problems for William Dillon, or at least none that he recounted, and 'having obtained my Father's sanction, I joined several others of my messmates who had also received authority from their parents. We repaired to the Frenchman's apartments and made our terms with him. Three days in a week he was to teach us. There were six of us, and it was settled that he should occasionally come off to the ship, the Captain having placed his Fore Cabin at our disposal for that purpose.'[36]

Reading William Dillon's account of these fencing lessons, it is difficult to judge whether they were considered sport or officer training. For all that it was imperative that 'the youngsters were not allowed to be idle', they still had plenty of leisure time. In William's case, this meant that 'in the midst of our studies we were occasionally allowed the use of one of the ship's boats, in which we went to visit the Isle of Wight, and take a stroll in Carisbrook Castle.'[37] Swimming was another pastime. Sailors were superstitious about swimming, yet many young gentlemen made a point of learning. Jeffrey Raigersfeld, on the West Indian station, recounted that:

> my great delight was to play about in the water, and the patroon of the boat, who was a black man, very soon taught me to swim and dive as well as play off many pranks while swimming. The launch carried eight butts of water, which generally required an hour to fill, for the water was led through a canvass hose from the beach to the boat, and during that time I had quite practice enough in swimming before she returned on board, where we generally arrived with water in good time for the pipe to breakfast.[38]

Among other leisure-time pursuits, music was the backbone of entertainment on board ship, and while in port, as William Dillon recounted, 'Sir Andrew, desirous of making the *Alcide* cut a conspicuous appearance in the Fleet, established a band of musicians on board. The 4th Lieutenant, Mr Rogers, undertook the collection of men for that purpose, and in the course of a few weeks the *Alcide*'s band was all the vogue.'[39] The gifts bought for William Parker by his elder brother George anticipated the importance of music for young gentlemen: 'I have bought the Fiddle things and 2 modern songs which you ordered for William – The songs are my presents and called "Tom Hatchaway" and "When fair Susan". They are quite new and the favourites of the day.'[40] As for William Dillon whiling away his long watches, 'my messmate Ribouleau never failed during our watch at night in fine weather to entertain us with a song – "the Shipwreck". Generally speaking, too, Saturday night was never passed without the favourite song of "Sweethearts and Wives"...'[41] Music was especially important on the lower-decks, and many of the boys arriving from the Marine Society were taught to be fifers so that they would immediately be useful on board ship as 'at one bell the fifer is called to "Nancy Dawson" or some other lively tune, a well-known signal that the grog is ready to be served out.'[42]

Theatricals were another regular form of onboard entertainment, as Prince William had shown, but each ship had its own idiosyncratic pastimes, some more or less official. In William Dillon's case, on board the *Alcide*, 'on Saturday night the Captain generally entertained most of his officers in his cabin. We had on board a ventriloquist, one of the Carpenter's crew, who, with a monkey that he had tutored, amused us amazingly, and always attended upon our chief on those occasions.'[43]

Below decks, the men occasionally resorted to blood sports for their entertainment, one particularly gruesome variation on the theme being described by Jeffrey Raigersfeld from his time in the tropics:

> The scorpion often afforded entertainment to the men, for being easily provoked, it was soon made to vent its rage upon itself to its own destruction, in the following manner: – When one of these were seen, a small piece of wood was held right over its body, it instantly erected its tail, by which the venom is communicated, and on making of hitting it, it darted its tail with such violence at the bit of wood that it struck itself, and in the course of a couple of minutes its own venom would render it giddy, it would then go round and round in a small circle, decreasing its circumference, and in a few seconds cease to exist.[44]

When young gentlemen weren't studying or relaxing, and occasionally performing ship duty, they were eating. The mess was the focal point of a sailor's early years at sea. In William Dillon's case, on the *Alcide* 'our mess was established between two of the lower-deck guns, 32-pounders. A canvas screen fitted to the beams was triced up and let down, as deemed convenient...'[45]

William perfunctorily describes his meals: 'We breakfasted at eight o'clock, at sea on burgoo, in harbour on tea.'[46] Burgoo is defined in the Marine Dictionary of 1815 as 'a sea-faring dish, made by adding two quarts of water to one of oatmeal, so that the whole may mix smoothly; then boiling it for a quarter of an hour, stirring it constantly: after which a little salt, butter and sugar is generally added.'[47]

His other meals of the day are described with equal economy: 'One o'clock was the dinner hour: fresh meat in harbour with vegetables, and salt at sea accompanied with potatoes and such, puddings, pea soup etc: generally some refreshment in the evening, but that was very precarious. Or we might have a slice of cheese and biscuit previous to turning in.'[48] Simple fare, but a cut above what awaited William Parker once the *Orion* reached the West Indies, if Jeffrey Raigersfeld's earlier experiences were anything to go by.

As with William Dillon, 'pea soup savoury' was the staple in Jeffrey's diet during his voyage to the West Indies. Once there, he survived on ship's biscuit which, when 'served to the ship's company, was so light, that when you tapped it upon the table, it fell almost into dust, and thereout numerous insects, called weevils, crawled; they were bitter to the taste, and a sure indication that the biscuit had lost its nutricious particles: if, instead of these weevils, large white maggots with black heads made their appearance, then the biscuit was considered to be only in its first state of decay; these maggots were fat and cold to the taste, but not bitter.'[49]

If he were lucky, he came by the occasional delicacy, for instance: 'by foraging locally, one day when climbing a tree, I observed large funguses, and I was agreeably surprised to find under them large clusters of oyster, with very fine shells, about the size of a crown piece, bedded together; they had a most excellent flavour.'[50] Saturdays were 'fresh beef days'.[51] However, such delicacies were the exception and 'so seldom was it that fresh provisions could be had at this time in the West Indies, that the captain of the hold used to catch rats (of which there was an abundance in the ship) in the night, and by eight in the morning, generally four or five rats were readily cleaned and spread out as butchers dress sheep for the inspection of the amateurs; and those who purchased the rats for a relish, had only to pepper and salt them well, broil them in the galley, and they were found nice and delicate eating.'[52] To make the prospect of broiled rat palatable to his readers, Jeffrey further explained what sumptuous diet the rats had been fed on: 'the best of the ship's provisions, such as biscuit, flour, peas and they were full as good as rabbits, although not so large.'[53]

In view of Jeffrey's unsavoury experiences, it is difficult to feel sympathy for William Hoste's complaint, when, after two years on the Mediterranean station he wrote home that 'Two or three brace of Partridges would be very acceptable down in the Cockpit instead of salt beef and pea soup,'[54] or with William Dillon when, removing to the *Niger* on the eve of war, he commented that 'our table was amply supplied, so that I felt as comfortable as the situation of a Middy would allow'.[55] William Dillon was lucky to be in the Channel Fleet: food was not a problem even for those ships at sea for long periods on blockade duty along the coast of France. Conscious that sailors as well as soldiers fought best with a full belly, the Admiralty's 'Victualling Office' began arranging regular shipments of fresh produce to the Fleet, as when 'This day sixty fine bullocks were embarked on board the ship going to join the Channel Fleet.'[56]

William Dillon may have been satisfied with the food on board ship; not so the drink. On the *Alcide* 'we did not trouble ourselves much about grog, as small beer was our principal beverage.'[57] However, it was not what he had to drink that he was complaining about. It was others' drinking. From the lofty heights of retirement but, doubtless, self-conscious that his *Narrative* was written specifically for his children and grandchildren, his writing often strikes a superior moral tone, never more so than on the subject of drink. Drunkenness was the arch-enemy of a well-regulated ship, but with grog – rum in diluted, measured daily doses – being one of the few pleasures allowed to seamen, captains sometimes tolerated wild binges, only to order the requisite dose of plus or minus 100 lashes the next day. Recording his first impressions going aboard the benighted *Saturn*, William was unable to resist self-righteously recounting that 'what shocked my young mind the most was the scenes of licentiousness, drunkenness, swearing and immorality to which I could not help being a witness. I avoided them as much as possible.'[58] According to Jack Nastyface, among these would have been lower-deck boys, 'as every man and boy is allowed a pint, that is one gill of rum and three of water, to which is added lemon acid, sweetened with sugar.'[59]

William's disapprobation of the men was, if not a literary, certainly a moral convention. However, he did not stop there. He also criticized Humphreys, recounting how 'the Schoolmaster had a cabin between the next two guns to our mess in which he used to entertain one or two of the elderly Mids with a glass of grog. On these occasions he did not spare his allowance.'[60] Next came the turn of the 'elderly Midshipmen [who] established a club in the Cockpit, to be held every Saturday night. On those occasions they sent invitations to their acquaintances of the other ships... They met at 8 o'clock to the number of near one hundred convivial souls.'[61] Still not satisfied, William finally lashed out at 'the Ward Room officers of our ship [who] would sometimes join in these festivities, which on some occasions ended in noise and confusion. There were some very fine voices, but I cannot say much for the decency of the songs. The entertainment generally terminated about 11 o'clock. We of the Gun Room were not admitted to these scenes. I did not regret the omission, as I had not the slightest taste for drinking bouts.'[62]

Frowning on these 'festivities' from the safe sanctuary of the gun room was easy. However in 1792, when he had been at sea the best part of two years, if his career was to follow the normal path laid down by the Admiralty in its *Articles and Orders*, then 'after two years at sea, the captain of the ship shall rate them Midshipman Ordinary, and oblige them to do the duty of Midshipman';[63] in which case he would be leaving the gun room and going into the cockpit, assuming, of course, that he had caught the eye of the captain. According to his *Narrative*, he undoubtedly had – as had William Parker who was made up to midshipman, apparently without his knowledge, after only one year, one month, one week and six days at sea. William Parker's eagerness for promotion is palpable, never more so than when he wrote to his brother, George: 'I am not rated midshipman yet, for Mr Neville told Captain Duckworth that my aunt Jervis was very anxious to know whether I was or not; and he said that I was not, but that I was only captain's servant. I think I shall soon be rated, as I believe one of the midshipmen will leave the ship.[64]

It seems William Dillon had to wait longer for advancement. Recording his move to the *Niger* in October 1792, William's promotion appears to have come through when he wrote that 'I shall not readily forget my first introduction to the Starboard Midshipmen's berth.'[65] However, the same mistake had been made as on the benighted *Saturn* two years earlier. This time the error was quickly corrected and 'the next day my quarters were shifted to the other side, where there was a Schoolmaster, with several youngsters under his care'.[66]

So what was so aberrant to a 12-year-old about the cockpit and the midshipmen who berthed there? George Parsons gives some inkling in his *Nelsonian Reminiscences*, first published in 1843, recalling his time as a midshipman in the Wars. It was 1799, George was aboard the *Foudroyant* in the Mediterranean and Lady Emma Hamilton, a passenger aboard, being 'pronounced ill … stillness was observed in all parts of this Noah's ark, save and except the infernal regions, where the jolly reefers held their carouse, and played all manner of boyish pranks with impunity. I can aver that there is more happiness to be found in these dip-lighted abodes than in the splendid cabin or wardroom. Divested of all responsibility, the midshipman enjoys the present day without a thought of the morrow'.[67] It is small wonder then that the captain of the *Niger* wanted young William Dillon kept as far away from the Mids and the cockpit as possible.

The 'infernal regions' were no place for a youngster at the best of times, but certainly not during battle, when, as George explained, the cockpit doubled up as surgeon's operating theatre, and on being sent below to ascertain 'the number of wounded from the surgeon …[he] entered the cockpit and … after stumbling against some of the wounded … approached the medical tribe who, with shirt-sleeves tucked up to the shoulders, their hands and arms bathed in blood, were busily employed…'[68]

Relief for the midshipman whose lot it was to inhabit the 'dip-lighted' world of the cockpit came in the form of the occasional invitation to dine at the captain's table, whereupon vanity instantly transformed the 'jolly reefer' into 'Cockpit Beau'.[69] George, when ordered by 'Lord Nelson's favourite servant … [to] dine with his lordship today', pleaded that 'I have no clean shirt, and my messmates are in the same plight [and] the admiral … good-naturedly said I might dine in any shirt, but must celebrate … at his table at three o'clock. This was the first time I dined with the heroic Nelson'.[70]

Dinner over, it was back down to the cockpit there to await 'yonder voice the MID to DUTY calls!'[71] The duties of a midshipman were more demanding than those of a captain's servant. As a petty officer he was senior to, for instance, the boatswain's mate, but junior to the boatswain, gunner or carpenter. There was little euphoria in William Dillon's tone when recalling how on 5 January 1793, aged 13, he was finally made up to a midshipman with his entry on the books of the *Thetis*, a frigate of 38 guns: 'This rating having been obtained, I considered it my first step in the navy.'[72] He was remembering exactly what awaited him all those years ago, unlike Mother Marsinghall, who, sending 'poor Richard' to the navy in blissful ignorance, 'little knew what a sea of trouble thy son had to go through; little didst thou conjecture what innumerable difficulties he was about to encounter, and "the snubs that patient mids from their superiors take", or thou wouldst not have supposed by his being a midshipman he was made for ever.'[73]

When still a captain's servant, William Dillon had already performed some of the duties of midshipman, including acting as 'one of the midshipmen of the watch to visit the lower part of the ship every half hour to see that there is no unauthorised light burning, and that all is quiet; he reports all well or otherwise, to the officer of the watch.'[74] Other responsibilities meant mustering the seamen at divisions and supervising their deck duties. This gave a midshipman direct responsibility over the men and exposed 'the Danger of giving too much power into the hands of young officers'.[75]

Jack Nastyface remembered 'a mid-shipman on board our ship of a wickedly mischievous disposition, whose sole delight was to insult the feelings of the seamen, and furnish pretexts to get them punished. He was a youth not more than twelve or thirteen years of age; but I have often seen him get on the carriage of a gun, call a man to him, and kick him about the thighs and body, and with his fist would beat him about the head; and these, although prime seamen, at the same time dared not murmur.'[76] Retaliating against an officer, even a petty officer, was punishable by death, as one sailor discovered when sentenced to be hanged 'for striking a midshipman in the execution of his duty and for other mutinous conduct'.[77] So the men had to wait until, as Jack explained, it 'was ordained by Providence that his reign of terror and severity should not last; for during the engagement, he was killed on the quarter-deck by a grape-shot, his body greatly mutilated, his entrails being driven and scattered against the larboard side; nor were there any lamentations for his fate! – No! for when it was known that he was killed, the general exclamation was: "Thank God, we are rid of the young tyrant." His death was hailed as the triumph over an enemy.'[78]

Other less controversial but still demanding duties for a midshipman included acting as signal-officer or as aide-de-camp to the captain on the quarterdeck, in which instance he was charged with carrying messages round the ship and also between ships. This could bring a midshipman his first command, albeit only of the cutter or jolly-boat used to convey him round the fleet. William Dillon described such duties with pride as in January 1793 when 'during our stay at the Nore, I was sent one day with a message to Captain Riou, then commanding the *Rose*'[79] and later, on convoy duty, 'it became necessary to issue instructions and signals to all the valuable ships of the convoy. I was selected for this duty. Therefore I went in succession from one ship to another, delivering to each the official documents by which their future proceedings were to be regulated.'[80]

And when he wasn't up to his boyish pranks, eating at the captain's table or carrying out – reluctantly or otherwise – his routine daily duties, how did the Mid fill up his days? According to William Falconer's poem 'The Orlop', published in the 1799 edition of the *Naval Chronicle*, which would have done the rounds of wardrooms and gun rooms during the Wars:

> In canvass'd birth, profoundly deep in thought,
> His busy mind with sines and tangents, fraught,
> A MID reclines – in calculation lost!...
> And now to make a pudding he pretends.'[81]

The midshipman studies and lazes about, but also 'pretends' to cook, his pretensions to cookery most likely only brought on because the 'blackguardly, rascally son of a sea-cook' was the bane of the midshipmen's mess, his poor cooking the constant butt of insults, as in the post-war novel *The Naval Surgeon*, which has a midshipman berating his boy, 'do you call this soup, or the water you washed the dishes in last night, warmed up again?'[82] Often a Scape Gallows, the luckless boy serving in the midshipmen's mess was typically 'a dirty-looking lad, without shoes or stockings, dressed in a loose pair of inexpressibles, fitting tight round the hips, a checked shirt, with the sleeves turned up to the elbows – his face as black as a sweep's, and his hands as dirty as a coalheaver's who was leaning against the locker, and acted in the dignified capacity of midshipmen's boy.'[83]

If caught thieving, he was punished, subject only to the summary justice of the midshipman's court. George Parsons recalled how 'our black servant (a prince by his own account), acting in the capacity of steward, cook and butler, was brought up before a self-constituted court, and charged with stealing from divers midshipmen (his then masters) their pots of pomatum… The case was proved to an amazing extent… Punishment followed closely on the sentence, which was fifty strokes with the sheath of a sword on the shin bones, the most susceptible part about a black…'[84]

As to other duties of cabin boys, the likes of Pel Verjuice and Jack Nastyface aside, lower-deck boys are mute once more. Occasionally, however, their duties appear in contemporary accounts, as when the *Naval Chronicle* reported in April 1803 that 'the *Royal Sovereign*, Captain Curry: and the *Britannia*, Captain Kittoe, of 100 guns each, have, by the exertions of about forty Marine Society boys, and the convicts belonging to the Captivity hulk, been got in a state to proceed to Spithead.'[85] In literature during and after the Wars, the plight of the cabin boy reached near-epic proportions as his youth was subsumed into the heroic lifecycle of Jack Tar. A poem called 'The Tar', circulating in the navy during the Wars, was subtitled 'A Parody of Shakespeare's Seven Ages' and starts Jack Tar off as 'the cabin boy, cleaning guns, and clearing out the decks'[86] until in the 'last scene that ends this advent'rous history, is Greenwich pension: mess, tobacco, grog.'[87]

Of course, the midshipman's life at sea was not just about the 'saucepan and the book'[88] and taking his 'blackguardly boy' to task. In the 15 months after war was declared in February 1793 there were numerous small skirmishes, and Britain captured, then lost, the strategic Mediterranean port of Toulon, defended by, among others, a very young Napoleon. William Hoste and the other Norfolk lads aboard *Agamemnon* may have glimpsed their first action off Toulon, albeit from afar, and Jeffrey Raigersfeld may have acted as aide to Captain Elphinstone, briefly appointed governor of Toulon during its short occupation. However, for William Dillon, William Parker and the young gentlemen and boys on the 'wooden walls' cruising up and down the English Channel in defence of the homeland, day after day was all too often a journal of empty horizons. Not for long. The time was past for playing the 'sage, the hero, the cook'.[89] It was late May 1794 and any day soon, a mighty enemy fleet would appear on the horizon: youngsters in the Channel Fleet would finally be facing their baptism of fire.

INTO THE GLORIOUS FRAY

I n the January 1799 launch edition of the *Naval Chronicle*, the Reverend James
Clarke, whose brainchild it was, chose as the first anecdote, for what would
become a regular 'Naval Anecdotes, Commercial Hints, Recollections Etc.'
section, the following story:

> Lord Howe, on the first of June, observing a little boy standing in a dangerous position,
> and feeling for his tender years, yet unaccustomed to endure the shock of such
> contention as was about to take place, said to him, 'You had better go below, you are
> too young to be of service here.' – 'My Lord,' replied the blushing boy, 'what would my
> father say, if I was not to remain upon deck during action?'[1]

Billed as 'containing a General and Biographical History of The Royal Navy of the
United Kingdom,'[2] the *Naval Chronicle* was to be published throughout the
remaining years of the Wars, ceasing publication only in 1818. It would become
the *vade mecum* of all things maritime, read by sailors, by their families and by
the general public.

The choice of this vignette, true or apocryphal, with which to launch the
magazine was surely no accident. What many had thought would be a short war
when it started in 1793 was, by 1799, shaping up to be a conflict like no other Europe
had experienced. With ideology and revolution as France's main weapons of choice,
this was war on a world scale, total warfare, a fight to the death. Propaganda and
the battle for heart and mind would be important weapons in Britain's arsenal

of counter-attack. The *Naval Chronicle* would be at the forefront of this war of persuasion, and Clarke, who had himself been a chaplain at sea and been recently appointed personal chaplain to the Prince of Wales, was under no illusions as to what was at stake.

The anecdote was emblematic, and the characters Clarke chose talismanic, of what Britain needed to win. First and foremost, there was the man of the hour: Lord Howe, the 68-year-old admiral of the fleet, hero of previous wars against France, nicknamed 'Black Dick', brought out of retirement in Britain's moment of direst need, but in this anecdote cast *in loco parentis*. Then there was the 'blushing boy' standing in Black Dick's fearsome shadow: another boy with no name, one of the so-called 'young gentlemen' privileged to walk the quarterdeck of a mighty ship-of-the-line and invited to voice the virtues Britain most needed to survive: attention to duty, a keen sense of family honour, and, above all, the intrepidness that would inspire the hundreds of youngsters serving in Lord Howe's fleet that day. Finally there was 'the father': absent from the scene, anonymous also, maybe far away at home waiting anxiously for news of his dear son, but just as likely to be one of the many in the Grand Fleet that day whose 'wives ... were on board some of the English ships [and] fought with the most determined valour, at the guns; encouraging and assisting their husbands.'[3] Here was Britain's secret weapon, its fighting backbone; its families at war who were 'proud, when my boys shall first at sea, follow brave Howe to victory'.[4]

The *Naval Chronicle* was positioning its family at war in a time and place that its readership would instantly recognize as being in keenest jeopardy. The 'first of June' could signify only one day in the whole of British history, the Glorious First of June 1794, and the time on that day could only be early morning, minutes before 'Lord Howe made the signal (34) that he meant to pass through the enemy and engage to Leeward',[5] minutes before the cannonade that would herald the start of the first major naval engagement of the Wars.

'Upon deck during action' could indicate only one place: the English Channel, 400 miles from land, on the quarterdeck of the mighty 100-gun *Queen Charlotte*, flagship of the largest British fleet to be assembled for the defence of the homeland since the Spanish Armada. Here was Britain's military power at its most formidable, at its most vulnerable: the 'wooden walls' comprising 25 ships-of-the-line of the Grand Fleet ranged against France's fleet, numbering 26. If Britain's line broke that day, the way would be open for Revolutionary France to overrun the country. For Britain's families at war on that day and in that place, defeat was not an option.

For many of the boys fighting in these Wars, the Glorious First of June was their first battle. Afterwards, exhaustion was total. Joseph Thompson, a midshipman on the 98-gun British ship *Barfleur*, recorded that 'our fatigue was excessive, we lay 5 nights at our quarters.'[6] Yet for all their wounds and aching bones, sailors across the fleet sensed that they had lived history and so still found the energy to dash off letters to their loved ones at home. James Miller, a captain in the Royal Marines aboard 'His Majesty's Ship at Sea'[7] *Leviathan,* was one of the first to put pen to paper. For him, writing the day after the battle, the supreme emotion was one of relief:

> Thank God Almighty My Dear Mother I am in the greatest good health and Spirits after the most glorious Action that ever was fought – we closely engaged with the Enemy three different days and during every one my conduct gave Lord Hugh [Seymour, Captain of the *Leviathan*] so much satisfaction that he has told me I shall ever find in him a very warm and sincere friend. Thank God this is the second Glorious Action I have been in and had the good fortune to escape...[8]

Relief quickly gave way to euphoria. The battle over, now was the time for one and all to bask in the reflected glory of a famous victory. Hyperbole soon followed on hyperbole. For William Parker, now 13 and rated a midshipman on the 74-gun *Orion*, the battle was 'the severest'.[9] For Lieutenant J. Smith of the Queen's Regiment aboard the *Royal George*, it was 'one of the most splendid victories ever fought at sea'.[10] However, the most oft repeated epithet appearing in sailors' accounts was the word 'glorious'. In the words of Joseph Thompson, 'this action is said to be the most glorious & desperate ever fought'.[11] Soon 'glorious' was on everyone's lips. First official mention came in the resolution passed in the House of Lords on 13 June, which referred to 'the glorious victory obtained on the 1st of June'.[12] That same day *The Times* carried an advertisement on behalf of the Theatre Royal, London announcing 'the glorious first of June'.[13] The battle name stuck.

Proud to say that they had been there, sailors across the fleet, from the quarterdeck to the orlop deck, wanted the whole world to know of their part in the events of that glorious day. In a postscript to his letter home, Joseph Thompson urged the relative he was addressing to 'Desire Joy to mention my name when he inserts it'. Henry Joy was no ordinary friend of the Thompson family. As publisher of the *Belfast News-Letter*, he would surely be bound to publish the letter and, in the process no doubt, give Joseph an honourable mention. There was only one problem: in his haste to rattle off his news, Joseph made the mistake of admitting that 'this letter is very incorrect'.[14] It is no surprise that Joy did not publish it.

Just as eager to get his news away by the first available mail was William Parker writing on 3 June:

> My Dearest Mother.
>
> As there is an opportunity of sending you a few lines by a ship that is going with dispatches, I have only five minutes left (as the boat is waiting alongside) to let you know that you will hear by the newspaper of the engagement we have been in, and to tell you not to alarm yourself about me, as I am sound, well, and happy as a king. The engagement was the severest that ever was fought in the whole world. I do not cram you at all by telling you so. Our brave, gallant and steady captain is well. We shall be in port in about a week, when you may expect a letter from me twenty yards long. I forgot to tell you that we have conquered the rascals, and shall bring eight or seven ships of the line-of-battle in with us. Suspend your further curiosity for a short time, and you shall be satisfied in everything by me.[15]

The excitement is palpable: this young boy, who joined the navy at the outbreak of war aged 12, has gone through his do-or-die rite of passage, lived to tell the tale and is 'happy as a king'. Experiencing the immediacy of the moment in a way the young do best, time suddenly distils down to the next 'five minutes left'. Yet, for all his youthfulness and irrepressible exuberance, William displays maturity beyond his years. He is ambitious and what he writes about the battle he knows will be important for him and his career: others on the *Orion* may read what he has to report, hence the gratuitously flattering reference to 'Our brave, gallant and steady captain', which is echoed equally gratuitously in his 20-yard-long letter, when, by then, the captain is 'the brave fighting cool Duckworth'.[16]

Moreover, his parents may show this letter, and the later one he has promised, to his very important uncle, Sir John Jervis, soon to become First Lord of the Admiralty, whose interest had secured William a place on the *Orion* in February

1793 and whose continuing patronage was necessary for William's future career. William's parting remark '…you shall be satisfied in everything by me' is intended to signal that he has done his family credit.

However, William understood that the events of the day were about more than him and how he acquitted himself. His 'I do not cram you' assured his mother that his account was correct. He wouldn't make the same mistake as Joseph Thompson, dashing off a letter full of lots of 'incorrect' information. The promise of a follow-up letter 'twenty yards long' was no idle one. What events of the day he described and how he described them would be crucial. He intended to prepare the fullest and most accurate account of the battle, so that whoever read the letter would see a young gentleman of promise, by rights destined to be a future leader of men.

Yet he was acutely aware that, from his humble vantage-point sent to shelter in the captain's cabin, he had witnessed only a small part of the battle. It would be no excuse that he, like other observers on the day, was hampered by the exceptional circumstances of the battle, which meant that it was 'improper to particularise when clouds of smoke kept the Chief Part of the Fleet totally covered'.[17] The marine artist Nicholas Pocock, writing this in his account of the battle, at least had the advantage that he had hitched a ride in the frigate *Pegasus* for the specific purpose of making a written and pictorial record of the battle. Perched high in the rigging of the *Pegasus* as it circled round the gladiators locking horns, Pocock had a panoramic view and could watch the battle unfold through Lord Howe's orders, as when the Admiral 'made Sig 36', the signal that would have sent shivers of anticipation down the spine of every sailor in the fleet, ordering '…that each Ship was to steer for and engage Independently of each other the Ship opposed on the Enemy's Line'.[18]

If Pocock had a problem capturing an image of the battle in its entirety, William should not have been surprised how limited his vision was. The reality would certainly have struck home as William, like many of the boys and officers who survived the battle, wrote up his daily log:

At 8 bore up to engage the enemy. At 9 the action commenced. At 10 the main-topmast was shot away a few feet above the cap; at half-past, mainyard shot away in two pieces right to the slings. Four of the enemy's ships appeared to be in the greatest confusion;

three of them appeared to direct their fire at us; which, notwithstanding our disabled state was returned with the greatest briskness. The *Gibraltar* and *Culloden* came to our assistance, which gave us an opportunity of getting clear of the wreck. Rove and knotted as fast as possible, and remained in readiness for the enemy's ships as they came up about noon, the enemy's fleet being terribly mauled, began to edge away to leeward gradually, regardless of their disabled hulks; threw cask overboard to clear the decks.[19]

A few desultory references to damage and the repair work and the log concludes with: 'Three men killed, and several wounded, but most of them slightly',[20] a sharp reminder that for all the national importance of the Battle of the Glorious First of June, William, like the hundreds of other young gentlemen at battle stations that day, had been fighting for his life. Casualties on the British side were 287 dead and 811 wounded, and would end up exceeding every other naval engagement during the Wars apart from Trafalgar. French casualties numbered an estimated 3,500 dead and wounded.[21] William had been through the carnage and was alive to tell the tale. Still, it wasn't enough for him to have been there and survived. He had a job to do. He needed intelligence, hard facts about what had happened on that momentous day. News, gossip, rumours were swirling round the fleet, travelling from ship to ship, from wardroom to wardroom. William had been at sea only since February the previous year and this was his first battle. But William was no ordinary boy. During a glittering naval career, he would reach the pinnacle of his profession, being made admiral of the fleet in 1863. Instinctively he knew he must wait, listen, learn, get the full facts, then, and then only, write his letter 'twenty yards long'.

So it was that at 'Three o'clock – Evening, Orion, Plymouth Harbour Tuesday June 17th 1794',[22] fully two weeks after the battle, William finally wrote to give his parents 'an account of most particular things that have happened'.[23] The first inkling his parents had that this would be an account to be proud of comes early on in the letter when William describes Lord Howe's strategy leading up to the battle: on 20 May the British captured a small enemy convoy and 'Lord Howe considered, and thought it the most prudent step he could take to take the prisoners out of them all and burn and destroy the vessels, as it would weaken the Fleet by sending men on board of them, as we expected an action hourly. We then made sail and left the other nine retaken ships in flames.'[24]

It is very doubtful that William came to this conclusion about such a perverse decision all by himself. More likely, as his father, if not his mother, would have understood, was that he heard other officers, maybe even the captain himself, discussing and debating the merits of Lord Howe's decision in the wardroom or at the captain's table. No harm in this; William was doing what was expected of him: learning what it took to become an officer.

A few 'yards' further down William's epistle brings his parents to the time when the main enemy fleet is spotted. It is 28 May. William describes the early skirmishes between the fleets over the next few days: 'A quarter before ten they began firing at our van… The enemy fired chiefly at our rigging trying to dismast us, and we at their hulls, which we thought the best way of weakening them.'[25]

This was another insightful and, this time, tactical observation, and one that his parents could again be forgiven for believing came from listening to the senior officers. After all, such views were common currency in naval circles at the time. Still, it is suspicious that William's account at this point bears a striking resemblance to the log written up two weeks earlier by another young gentleman, Edward Baker, a fellow messmate on the *Orion*: 'The French pointed their guns very high which did a good deal of execution about our rigging but we fired chiefly at their hulls as we thought it best.'[26] Either he and Edward had both been listening to the same senior officers, or William had taken a peek at Edward's log some time between 1 and 17 June.

Alert to the possibility that Captain Duckworth might read Edward's log and see the similarities with his own letter, William may have deliberately gone off at a tangent in the next sentence as he recounts an episode worthy of one of the many burlesque nautical plays that were got up at sea: 'It was surprising to see with what courage our men behaved; there were even some of them so eager that they jumped up in the rigging to huzza, and Captain Duckworth hauled them down by the legs.'[27] For good measure he then adds his dose of flattery in parenthesis: 'I mean the brave fighting cool Duckworth.'[28] If that didn't lay a false scent, nothing would. However, just in case, he further discombobulates his readers in his next sentence when he recounts witnessing his first death: 'We had not fired two broadsides before an unlucky shot cut a poor man's head right in two, and wounded Jno Fane and four other youngsters like him very slightly. The horrid sight of this poor man I must confess did not help to raise my spirits.'[29]

William's letter continues inching ever closer to the day of the great battle, and at last, after more 'yards' of prose, he reaches the moment when the fleets engage. It is here we see William come into his own, setting out the battle positions with effortless clarity. Of all the descriptions of that day, William's is unsurpassed for the clarity of its tactical overview. Further, it captures the mounting tension, the inevitability of confrontation as the fleets take up their places like partners for a waltz:

> At eight the action began and the firing from the enemy was very smart before we could engage the ship that came to our turn to engage, as every ship is to have one because our line is formed ahead, and theirs is formed also. Suppose their first or leading ship is a 100 gun and ours a 74, our ship must engage her. I believe we were the ninth or tenth ship; our lot fell to an 80 gun ship, so we must not waste our powder and shot by firing at other ships, though I am sorry to say they fired very smartly at us and unluckily killed two men before we fired a gun, which so exasperated our men that they kept singing out, 'For God's sake, brave Captain let us fire! Consider, sir two poor souls are slaughtered already'[30]

Next comes the moment of sudden, deadly impact, the instant when battle mutates into the total warfare that the French had promised:

> But Captain Duckworth would not let them fire till we came abreast of the ship we were to engage, when Captain Duckworth cried out: 'Fire my boys, fire!' upon which our enraged boys gave them such an extraordinary warm reception that I really believe it struck the rascals with the panic. The French ever since the 29th (because we so much damaged one of their ships) called us the little devil and the little black ribband, as we have a black streak painted on our side. They made the signal for three or four of their ships to come down and sink us, and if we struck to them to give us no quarter; but all this did not in the least dishearten our ship's company.[31]

Again, the general tactical position William describes could have come from a senior officer, but his understanding is remarkable for a boy so young. As to the exchanges between the captain and the men, he may well have been within earshot of Captain Duckworth, quartered as he was nearby in the captain's cabin.

But what of the two men 'unluckily killed'? Was he a witness to this? He had seen his first death earlier, but with these two men, was he again reliant on other eyes and ears for his information? Edward Baker's log provides a clue:

> The French were very smart at firing with Long Balls which harassed our Ship very much and 1 unfortunate shot came in at the starboard side of the main deck and killed George Graham of the 4th gun and John Leahy belonging to the same gun. Our ship's company were very much enraged at those 2 men falling from the enemy's shot and it disheartened them the more as they were not firing.[32]

It would seem William had taken another peek at his friend's log, and it is the difference between the two accounts that gives the game away: William does not provide the names of the two men 'unluckily killed', whereas Edward does. Edward was down on the main gun deck, where the tragedy occurred, and he, rather than William, was the eyewitness to the two deaths. Edward's knowing the names of the two fallen men and recording them in his log are sure signs that the dead men were in the gun crew he was in charge of when they were hit by the '1 unfortunate shot'. Before any action had started, William had been busy between the decks and was one of the party that 'got up sufficiently of powder and shot to engage the enemy',[33] but once battle was joined, by his own admission later in the letter, he was in the captain's cabin.

Like Edward Baker, William Dillon on the *Defence*, and now aged 14, was also in charge of a gun crew during the battle, and like Edward named fallen men under his command. In his *Narrative* he describes how 'I was quartered on the Lower Deck under Lieut. Beecher. He had the command of the seven foremost guns. And three of them in the bow were under mine.'[34]

In a later passage William Dillon recounts that:

> One of these, John Polly, of very short stature, remarked that he was so small the shot would all pass over him. The words had not been long out of his mouth when a shot cut his head right in two, leaving the tip of each ear remaining on the lower part of his cheek. His sudden death created a sensation among his comrades, but the excitement of the moment soon changed those impressions to others of exertion. There was no withdrawing from the situation and the only alternative was to face the danger with becoming firmness.

The head of this unfortunate seaman was cut so horizontally that anyone looking at it would have supposed it had been done by the blow of an axe. His body was committed to the deep... Several of my men were wounded. Holmes, the Captain of the guns, a powerful fine fellow, had his arm carried away close to the shoulder.[35]

As with William Parker, this is William Dillon's first action and he is alert to the importance of remembering at the time and recording later what went on that day. At one point, before the battle proper gets underway, 'as we could not use the guns below, I availed myself of that circumstance to attend on the Quarter Deck, to witness all that was passing. Never having been present in an action of the kind, my curiosity and anxiety were beyond all bounds... Owing to that desire I saw more than most of the Mids, who kept to their station, and I can now relate what I really did see.'[36]

Also aware that readers of his memoirs might want to know more about the battle than what he has witnessed in person, William Dillon has no hesitation in recounting action he has heard from elsewhere on board the ship, but, unlike William Parker, he makes it clear that he is not an eyewitness:

At ½ past 11 the main mast came down... This information was conveyed to us below by some seamen who had been in the tops. As they could no longer be useful in consequence of two of the masts being shot away, they were ordered down to the guns. They reported the upper end of the Quarter Deck to be dreadfully shattered. The Lower Deck was at times so completely filled with smoke that we could scarcely distinguish each other. And the guns were so heated that, when fired, they nearly kicked the upper deck beams.[37]

Later in the battle, William Dillon is in contact with another source of first-hand information, one of his messmates, Consitt, who 'in a few words ... gave me an interesting account of what had been going on upon the Quarter Deck, as he was one of the Captain's aides-de-camp. He had been sent down to the Lower Deck to ascertain its state and condition.'[38]

When William Dillon is his own witness to events, all the senses are employed to evoke what it was like that day. He starts with having 'never seen a man killed before. It was a most trying scene. A splinter struck him in the crown of the head and when he fell the blood and brains came out, flowing over the deck.'[39] Smell mingles with sight when the 'Lower Deck was at times so completely filled with smoke that we could scarcely distinguish each other.'[40] Sounds and touch come from the same crushing, deafening source when we 'heard most distinctly our shot striking the hull of the enemy. The carved work over his stern was shattered to pieces'[41] and the 'guns were so heated that, when fired, they nearly kicked the upper deck beams. The metal became so hot.'[42] Finally comes taste, left to linger like a pall over the whole battle when, in the aftermath, the 'Fleet was hove to, that the crews might have their breakfasts ... but it was a sorry meal, scarcely deserving the name.'[43]

Writing 25 years after the battle, William Dillon has the advantage over Edward Baker and William Parker of both hindsight and age. He therefore describes more graphically, if with less immediate poignancy, the atmosphere and action down on the gun deck as the battle intensified. Through his eyes we gain a vivid impression of the duties of a young midshipman at battle stations:

> We had instructions to lower the ports whilst loading our guns, that the enemy's musketry might not tell upon our men... After the two or three first broadsides, I became anxious to have a good view of the ship we were engaging. To this effect, I requested the men at the foremost gun to allow me a few seconds, when the port was hauled up, to look out from it. The gun being loaded, I took my station in the centre of the port; which being held up, I beheld our antagonist firing away at us in quick succession. I had not enjoyed the sight long – only a few seconds – when a rolling sea came in and completely covered me. The tars, noticing this, instantly let down the port, but I got a regular soaking for my curiosity. The men cheered me, and laughingly said, 'We hope, Sir, you will not receive further injury. It is rather warm work here below: the salt water will keep you cool.'[44]

Many of the emotions expressed in these passages are those of a grown man looking back through rose-tinted spectacles, but William Dillon *was* in the thick of the action on the *Defence*, as, evidently, was Edward Baker on the *Orion*. But what of William Parker? By contrast with the other two, he appears to have been relatively cocooned from the action. Much as in the anecdote of Lord Howe and the 'blushing boy' in the *Naval Chronicle*, captains often sought to insulate their youngest protégés from the full force of a battle. William Parker seems to have been one of those who was so shielded, as is evident when he describes the moment the battle became personal for him:

> About this time, a musket ball came and struck Captain Duckworth between the bottom part of his thumb and finger, but very slightly, so that he only wrapped a handkerchief around it, and it is now almost quite well... Their firing was not very smart, though she contrived to send a red hot shot into the Captain's cabin where I am quartered, which kept rolling about and burning everybody, when gallant Mears, our first lieutenant, took it up in his speaking trumpet and threw it overboard.[45]

Hardly the intense baptism of fire that his fellow midshipmen had endured, but what came next would more than make up for that. The battle was in its last death throes; victory was assured. Now came the point of reckoning, the moment when William Parker confronted what war means, a moment so horrible that he excised it out of his log, unable to find the words to describe what he had witnessed. It is the moment when the French ship *Le Vengeur* sank. There were many sailors that day who claimed to have seen and heard *Le Vengeur* sinking but accounts vary wildly. Some claimed that 'the air resounded with cries of *Vive la Republique*'[46] as the French sailors went down with the ship. Others said the cries were '*Vive les Anglais*'.[47] So varied are the accounts that it is difficult to distinguish who did or did not witness the horrific event. However, the description William Parker gives in his 'twenty yards long' letter home leaves one in no doubt that he was an eyewitness:

> But I forgot to tell you that the ship that struck to us was so much disabled that she could not live longer upon the water, but gave a dreadful reel and lay down on her broadside. We were afraid to send any boats to help them, because they would have sunk her by too many souls getting into her at once. You could plainly perceive the poor wretches climbing over to windward and crying most dreadfully. She then righted a little, and then her head went down gradually, and she sunk. She after that rose again a little and then sunk, so that no more was seen of her. Oh my dear father! When you consider of five or six hundred souls destroyed in that shocking manner, it will make your very heart relent. Our own men even were a great many of them in tears and groaning, they said God bless them.[48]

For William Parker, Edward Baker and William Dillon, the Wars had just begun. For 15 midshipmen listed as wounded in the *London Gazette Extraordinary* on 11 June, their war was briefly interrupted, even if, as in the case of Hornsby Charles, 'he was a Midshipman of the *Queen Charlotte* in the action of 1st Of June 1794 in which he lost a leg'.[49] Hornsby was soon back at sea and duly promoted to Lieutenant before he died in 1802. Of the numerous lower-deck casualties during the battle, few have been recorded other than on casualty lists. One does stand out: 15-year-old Mary-Anne Talbot, who assumed the disguise of a sailor boy, was 'stationed [a]board the *Brunswick* [where] Captain Harvey, observing her cleanliness and manner to be different from those of many lads on board … promoted her to be his principal cabin boy, in which capacity she continued to serve him until the enemy's fleet came in sight'.[50] Serving in a gun crew, she was wounded several times but still kept 'the concealment of her sex',[51] even when invalided to Haslar Hospital after the battle.

She was lucky. For five midshipmen, Abraham Nelson, William Ivey, John Hughes, David Greig, and James Lucas, all listed as dead, their war was over.

While the Glorious First of June was being fought and won, other young gentlemen and boy sailors were already spread across the globe defending Britain's interests in the Mediterranean, in the West Indies, in the Indian Ocean. Yet others were still awaiting their turn to go into battle, young gentlemen like James Gordon (reputedly the model for Forester's Hornblower), a captain's servant aboard the 74-gun *Arrogant* and aged 12 at the time of the Glorious First of June. Ordered to join the Grand Fleet for the upcoming engagement, the *Arrogant* missed the battle by a day. Years later James recalled the embarrassment of missing the action: 'We went to Plymouth, and from thence to Spithead, where we found the ships' crews which had been in action in high spirits – they would hardly deign to speak to fellows in our squadron.'[52] No matter; his day would come. There would be more battles ahead, some of them not the battles anyone, let alone these youngsters, anticipated. The Wars at sea were about to get ugly.

9

MUTINY, PUNISHMENT
AND PROMOTION

A court martial was held on board the same ship for the trial of John Watson and James Allen, two seamen lately belonging to the *Hermione,* for being concerned in a mutiny on board the said ship, and in carrying her into La Guira. They were sentenced to suffer death, by being hanged by the neck. The prisoner, John Watson, appeared to be nearly 60 years of age, and took a very active part in the mutiny. The prisoner, James Allen, had been servant to the second lieutenant prior to the mutiny, and was then about 14 years of age; but it appeared he had also been very active in the mutiny, and had even assisted in the murder of his own master.[1]

The mutiny being prosecuted took place in September 1797 while the *Hermione* was on station in the West Indies, but mutineers, these two included, were still being brought to trial three years on. Thus on 7 August 1800 'at ten o'clock Watson was launched into eternity; but as the same provost martial was obliged to attend both men, Allen was not executed until eleven o'clock.'[2]

As with many crimes on board ship in the age of sail, there were shades of mutiny and, in turn, degrees of punishment. Some commanding officers, known graphically as 'flogging captains', did not, or chose not to, understand this. Others did, among them Captain Collingwood under whom Jeffrey Raigersfeld served when he first went to sea. Recalling the pre-war days, Jeffrey wrote admiringly: 'During upwards of the three years and a half that I was in this ship, I do not remember more than four or five men being punished at the gangway, and then so slightly that it scarcely deserved the name, for the captain was a very humane man and … made great allowances for the uncontrolled eccentricities of the seamen'.[3]

Captains could afford to be lenient in peacetime. However the outbreak of war in 1793 did little to diminish the seaman's long-standing unhappiness with his lot: bad conduct persisted and indeed increased, despite the sense of ever-present jeopardy. Being on a permanent war footing heightened the need for tight discipline, the inevitable result being that naval justice would be applied with greater intensity.

Corporal punishment was long a fact of life on board ship. William Dillon, in his *Narrative*, recalled himself as a youngster witnessing his first flogging: 'My next trial was to witness the punishment of one of the crew for some act of insubordination, with a cat of nine tails over his bare shoulders. My feelings were touched to the quick in that instance, but in course of time I became used to it, knowing that there was no controlling the bad characters without resorting to such measures.'[4]

Recalling this rite of passage enabled William Dillon to present the officer's point of view. The men also accepted the need for discipline so long as it was fair and even-handed: they understood that there were certain crimes, among them theft and desertion, that went beyond the realms of 'uncontrolled eccentricities' and deserved the severest punishment if a ship was to remain well regulated. Nelson was a caring captain, yet did not spare a Scape Gallowses, 14-year-old Walter Holmes (entry number 7957) from Smithfield, London. Walter, whose Marine Society entry showed that he could read but not write and had marks of smallpox, was also recorded as having spent time at sea prior to joining the *Agamemnon* in 1793. He should know the rules. Caught stealing during a shore raid on Corsica in 1794, he was given a dozen lashes.

The crime of desertion should have been cut and dried. Nevertheless, the punishment could be modulated depending on the circumstances. In an era of hot presses, running from a ship when it was in home port during peacetime was viewed far less seriously than if desertion occurred during wartime into an enemy port. The former occasioned anything from a few dozen lashes to 'being flogged round the fleet'[5] as happened, Jeffrey Raigersfeld recalled, 'whilst the ship lay at Spithead [to] a seaman by the name of Hickery'.[6] Another two Scape Gallowses on the *Agamemnon*, Richard Ferribee (entry number 7951) aged 17, and Charles Waters (entry number 7916) aged 15, both from Houndsditch,

London, were caught by Nelson trying to desert in October 1794 and were flogged.[7] In their case, they were lucky to be caught prior to escaping, especially since they were endeavouring to make their getaway on Corsica. Desertion into enemy territory smacked of cowardice and was tantamount to treason, the assumption being that the deserter would then reveal information to the enemy. The only punishment could be death. Even young midshipmen were not exempt from the extreme sanction. In May 1794, during the bombardment of Bastia, a town on the island of Corsica, Nelson wrote forebodingly to his wife, Fanny: 'It is said a Mid. of mine (a Norfolk lad) is deserted to the enemy, I do not believe it. If he is, to a certainty he will be hanged.'[8]

In a letter dated 13 May 1798, William Parker, by then aged 17, records the crew of the *Hermione* deserting into an enemy port, a crime which was enough alone to guarantee their execution: 'We have been in this place about a fortnight from a second detachment to La Guayra, demanding the crew of the *Hermione* which the Spanish Governor doe [*sic*] not think proper to give up without orders from the Spanish Court. You will be glad to hear that seven more of them have been taken and hanged on our station.'[9]

William, already an acting lieutenant, having spent the past four years in the West Indies, would have been directly responsible for ensuring that 'three were executed on board the *Magicienne* by lot, and four more are taken ready for trial.'[10]

However this was not merely desertion. It was mutiny, surely punishable only by death. Again, not necessarily: in the early years of the Wars, public perceptions of mutiny were dictated substantially by the circumstances of the infamous events on the *Bounty*, which had occurred in 1791 and long divided opinion. The early years of the Wars were studded with a litany of isolated so-called mutinies that never reached public notice: men protesting over poor food rations, heavy-handed punishment or simply to obtain shore leave. Each was punished on its merits, as William Parker sanctimoniously notes in his 'twenty-yards long' letter in June 1794 recounting an incident he witnessed on the *Orion*: '...most of our brave boys have undone all the good they ever did. Last Friday night they contrived to smuggle a great deal of liquor into the ship, and with the joy of having returned safe to port, and of the victory, most of the ship's company got so drunk that they mutinied, they said they would have liberty to go ashore; the Captain almost broke his heart about it.'[11]

Quickly abandoning his holier-than-thou voice, William gleefully indulges in detailed descriptions of the men's humiliation: '…seven of the ringleaders were seized by the officers and twenty other men; they were put in irons, and the next morning when they were told of their night's proceedings they wept like children. The twenty were punished with — lashes each, and the seven were kept in irons, and would have been tried by a court-martial; but Captain Duckworth … said that as he was of a forgiving nature he gave them into the hands of the ship's company.'[12]

The parting shot about the 'ship's company' was a euphemism conveying to a knowing reader the message that the captain had left it to the innocent in the crew to punish the guilty. Whatever punishment this was, it was a far cry from the one handed down to the *Hermione* mutineers by court martial. On a relative scale, therefore, the *Hermione* mutiny must have ranked at the high end seismically, if only to judge by the fact that even 14-year-old James Allen was shown no mercy. In which case, what was it that was so heinous about this one mutiny?

In addition to the mutineers deserting into an enemy port, there were the circumstances of the *Hermione* mutiny itself. These were particularly horrific, the crew, admittedly, driven to desperation by the day-to-day brutality of Captain Pigot, a 'flogging captain'. In another time, another place, acting on the usual mode of complaint – an anonymous letter from the crew – the Admiralty might have quietly reprimanded the *Hermione*'s captain or removed him from his post, thereby defusing a volatile situation with sleight of hand. When in early 1797 the crew of the *Blanche* rose up against their new captain, Henry Hotham, who had a reputation for being a 'damn'd tarter',[13] the mutiny was abandoned after Nelson, commodore of the fleet, came aboard and assured the crew that 'If Capt Hothom [*sic*] ill treats you, give me a letter and I will support you'.[14] Mollified, the crew waited until the *Blanche* returned to Portsmouth in July 1797, and 'the ships company rought a petition to the Admiralty wishing to be draughted, as we did not like the capt.'[15]

However, far away on the West Indies station the crew of the *Hermione* had no such recourse to natural justice close to hand. Frustration boiling over, the crew took matters into their own hands and the ensuing mutiny raged out of control, sucking crew and officers, young and old alike, into its vortex. In the first frenzy of the mutiny 'the Gunroom party put the second Lieutenant and Midshipman to

Death in the most savage manner and as they dragged them up the Hatchway apparently dead they continued cutting and stabbing them with various weapons till they reach'd the Main Deck when they threw them overboard.'[16]

James Allen was servant to the second lieutenant and this was when he 'assisted in the murder of his own master'. As for the 14-year-old midshipman who was killed, maybe he was in the mould of the 'young tyrant' despised by Jack Nastyface, but that did not justify his murder. Nevertheless rogue Mids were everywhere to be found, and seamen were not the only ones to suffer at their hands. David Casey, a lieutenant serving on the *Ambuscade* in the Caribbean in early 1797, but still only 18, fell foul of 'a certain young Midshipman of my watch (a very ill conducted youth, highly connected and a great favourite of the Captain).'[17] As a result, David was court-martialled, demoted to midshipman and transferred out of the *Ambuscade*. He at least had some temporary satisfaction knowing, as he pointed out in the tract he wrote in 1839, that 'the young gentleman who caused my misfortune was soon found so ill conducted and troublesome as to oblige his quitting the Ship; the same evening of my trial he was heard to boast (and was complain'd for it) that he had broke one Lieutenant and would break others.'[18]

Justice was done but, for David, things were about to get worse: his new ship was the *Hermione*, and the 'flogging captain' quickly had David in his sights:

> About a week previous to the unfortunate Mutiny, when reefing topsails at our usual hour in the evening, I was at my station in the Main Top when Captain Pigot who appeared to have drank freely fancied we were not as smart as usual – got into a violent passion at which moment he observed a man going up the lee Main Topmast rigging and instantly in very harsh language desired to know the cause.[19]

David, not one to hold his tongue when injustices were flying around, duly intervened on behalf of the seaman, with the result that the captain 'instantly launched out in the most abusive and unofficer like language calling me a damn'd lubber, a worthless good for nothing fellow… I was then ordered below under arrest'[20] pending a decision on punishment. If David had been a common seaman, he could expect to be 'tried for insolent and contemptuous behaviour to the first lieutenant and taking him by the collar,'[21] as was the case for a Jeremiah Croning serving on the *Ramilies*: 'The charge being proved, the prisoner was sentenced to receive 150 lashes, to forfeit all his pay, and to suffer two years solitary confinement in the Marshalsea.'[22] Even being classed as a boy in the ship's company would not have served to spare David the sharp end of a boatswain's wrath. Boys in a ship's company routinely endured corporal punishment. The ritual, graphically known as kissing the gunner's daughter, involved the culprit being strapped to a gun and flogged, the instrument of punishment graduating from the cane, through the cat of five tails – a boy's cat – to the cat of nine tails, the young miscreant often being obliged to prepare these for himself.

However David was an officer, albeit demoted to midshipman and therefore a mere petty officer. Flogging of officers in public was frowned on. Indeed, any young gentleman could reasonably expect to be spared the humiliation because, as future officer material, he should not lose the respect of the ship's company. Jeffrey Raigersfeld recalled how he and his fellow midshipman ran 'wild and riotous'[23] and 'four of us were tied up one after the other to the breech of one of the guns and flogged upon our bare bottoms with a cat-o'-nine-tails, by the boatswain… No doubt we all deserved it'[24] but, crucially, 'were thankful that we were punished in the cabin instead of upon deck.'[25]

The approved form of summary punishment for a young gentleman, be he a captain's servant – or 'volunteer first class' as he was designated from 1794 onwards or a midshipman, was mastheading: 'to cause to go to or stand at the masthead as a punishment.' The misdemeanours deserving this punishment could be as trivial as Jeffrey Raigersfeld not being 'quick and expert in my answers'[26] on navigation, or being quarter of an hour late on the 4 o'clock watch in William Dillon's case when 'Mr Twysden … ordered me up to the Mast Head. It was a cold morning, with a damp mist. Away I mounted the rigging, and remained aloft till 8 o'clock, when the Lieutenant called me down.'[27] William Parker, the model young gentleman, makes no mention of being punished at any stage in his career.

For the far greater crime of insolence to his captain, David Casey, as a midshipman, could expect a reprimand, further demotion, outright dismissal or, in the case of a midshipman court-martialled for robbing a Portuguese boat in 1798 'sentenced to be turned before the mast, to have his uniform stripped off him on the quarterdeck before all the ship's company, to have his head shaved, and to be rendered for ever incapable of serving as a petty officer.'[28]

David could not complain therefore when he 'was order'd to quit the Midshipman's Mess and to do no more duty but to prepare to quit the Ship the first opportunity. I quitted the Midshipman's Mess and mess'd on my Chest in the Steerage near their Birth.'[29] However, 'on the following morning ... I was brought on the Quarter Deck ... I was seized to the Capstern, the usual place of punishment, and I received one dozen lashes from the Boatswain on my back.'[30]

Meantime, David's plight was about to become submerged into bigger events. The initial spark that lit the mutiny occurred when:

> A few days after my punishment, a melancholy circumstance occurred in reefing topsails which greatly increased the previous dislike of the Captain and no doubt hastened if not entirely decided the Mutiny. Three boys fell from the Mizen Topsail Yard on the Quarter Deck.'[31]

Blaming the crew for these fatalities, Captain Pigot ordered the boatswain 'to start the entire Topmen.' 'Starting' was a common form of punishment at that time. William Dillon called it 'Passing of the Gauntlet'[32] whereby 'the culprit was bare from his trousers upwards, and had to pass through two rows of the Ship's Company, on each side of the Main Deck. Every man, being furnished with a knittle made of rope yarn, struck him on the back as he passed.'[33] Hardened from years in the service, William Dillon still remembered it as a 'very severe punishment'.[34] This was almost certainly the punishment William Parker meant when the captain of the *Orion* 'gave them into the hands of the ship's company'. Starting was an adult punishment, the equivalent meted out by young gentlemen on their peers being cobbing ['to beat on the buttocks'].

The crew of the *Hermione* decided that starting was an inappropriate reaction by Captain Pigot to the affecting loss of three boys. The fire of resentment once lit, the murderous flames soon spread out of control and: 'On 21st September 1797, the Mutiny took place. It commenced about eleven o'clock at night – No resistance being made in any quarter, the Ship was instantly in possession of the Mutineers when the Captain, Second and Third Lieutenants and one Midshipman were at once Murder'd in the most savage and cruel manner.'[35]

After this initial murderous mayhem:

it was then warmly debated how the remaining officers should be disposed of – there was a general cry to put every officer – young and old to Death – the majority of the crew prevailed against them and the remaining unfortunate officers were brought on Deck and disposed of as their fate was decided: some were wounded and thrown overboard and others were thrown overboard unhurt… The Master was principally sav'd by the two principal mutineers placing themselves as Sentinels at his Cabin Door and by his servant Boy (quite a youth and who died in Prison) going through the Ship crying and begging of the Crew most piteously that his Master's life be spared.[36]

Next it was David's turn. 'My life was repeatedly debated.'[37] His life hung in the balance for days while warring factions among the mutineers decided his fate. In the end he was saved because he had been one of the captain's principal victims. Nevertheless, the damage was done, and, at the time of their execution three years later, the *Naval Chronicle* summed up the extent of the crimes that John Watson and young James Allen had committed:

The hand of Providence has evidently shewn itself in the punishment of these atrocious wretches, the shame of England and humanity. They had all made their escape, and were in an enemy's country; yet by various ways, and hidden in unaccountable means, vengeance has pursued and delivered them up to their offended country! – We trust this strong and memorable document will not be lost upon the navy, and that it recur in the very first moment of artful mutiny and political sedition.[38]

According to this, the 'atrocious wretches' were guilty of far more than murder, desertion to the enemy, or indeed mutiny. They committed 'political sedition'. That was why naval bloodhounds, among them William Parker, had been set loose to scour the globe for their scent, and why all the mutineers, James Allen included, had to be brought to justice and executed, even if it took years, as in the case of Mr Wood who was only 'launched into eternity'[39] on 17 October 1806.

If this mutiny had been an isolated incident there might have been clemency for James Allen, young as he was. However, in the eyes of the authorities the *Hermione* mutiny was just the latest in a string of mass mutinies, stretching back six months. 1797 was Britain's *annus horribilis*, the year when Britain came closest at any time during the Wars to following France's descent into anarchy.

To many observers, an insidious canker had bored into Britain's 'wooden walls': a more destructive enemy, if left to flourish unchecked, than all the armies France could muster against Albion. Rip its own entrails apart and Britain would soon suffer the same self-inflicted mutilation as France. In the febrile atmosphere prevailing, the slightest hint of organized unrest on board a ship in His Majesty's Navy smacked of revolution and triggered collective panic through the echelons of power. Thus it was that, when a mass mutiny broke out at Spithead off Portsmouth in April 1797, the Admiralty responded tentatively. At first the softly-softly approach was not only expedient but easy. The principal demand of the mutineers was for an increase in navy pay. Seaman's pay had been static since 1652 yet, with the war, prices of staples such as wheat had skyrocketed. The Quota Acts, passed in 1795 and 1796 to encourage volunteer recruitment, had offered extra bounties to new landsmen recruits, which only served to show how poorly paid the long-serving mariners were. So the demand for better pay was one the Admiralty could readily sympathize with and remedy. Nelson, for instance, commented that 'I am entirely with the Seamen in their first Complaint. We are a neglected set, and, when peace comes, are shamefully treated.'[40] The demand was rapidly conceded, the mutineers returned to active duty and there were no reprisals.

However there was a second wave of mutinies a month later, this time at the Nore, the mooring station off Chatham. The demands of this second group of mutineers were more outrageous and included the right to approve officer appointments. Also, their tactics became more extreme, including firing on two frigates trying to escape the mutineers' blockade. Echoing the sentiments of the officer class that enough was enough, Nelson offered that 'for the Nore scoundrels, I should be happy to command a ship against them.'[41] Ashore, voices began pealing out in alarm, among them Lord Arden, one of the Lords of the Admiralty, whose clarion call was that 'the mutinies were the most awful crisis that these kingdoms ever saw.'[42]

Against this background of incipient panic, when the mutiny finally collapsed, the ringleaders, including a Quota man, Richard Parker, were rounded up and hanged. The voices of propaganda quickly swung into action, and stories were noised abroad that the mutiny was politically motivated: 'The mutineers in another ship were proved to be connected with "Corresponding Societies" at Nottingham.

Their plan was "'to carry the ship into an enemy's port, French, Dutch or Irish", and they meant, in the event of being brought into action with an enemy's ship, to shoot their own officers on the quarter-deck.'[43]

Dark hints were put about that the mutinies were the work of a deeper subversive movement, the United Irishmen, and credence was added to these mutterings when civil rebellion broke out in Ireland in 1798. In this toxic atmosphere of supposed conspiracy, it was not sufficient to hang a few ringleaders. The search was on for other scapegoats, and beware any seaman foolish enough to commit any offence, small or large, during these uncertain times. He could expect more than his fair share of summary and exemplary justice. Thus it was that a macabre scene unfolded in the squadron on blockade duty off Cadiz. Two men happened to be on a charge of committing 'unnatural acts', an aberrant crime by the naval mores of the times, the recognized punishment being death. However, adding fuel to the fires of suspected sedition, the crew of the St George decided to mutiny 'as an execution for such a horrible offence would bring disgrace on the ship'.[44] Having no truck with seamen's finer sensibilities, Sir John Jervis, the admiral commanding the squadron, promptly brought forward the court martial and, dispensing with the usual period of grace after sentencing, had the execution carried out on the first available day, ignoring the fact that it was a Sunday and part of the squadron was skirmishing with Spanish gunboats. The macabre result was that 'the inside division of line a battle ships was engaged by the gunboats, the other division had their penant up at the mizen peak for prayers, and the other division had the yellow flag hoisted, a hanging of two men, all at one time on a Sunday morning'.[45]

Vice-Admiral Thompson complained at this travesty of the Sabbath, but Jervis was having nothing of his sensibilities either and promptly packed him off home. Justice must be done and seen to be done, if necessary with due ostentation. By July, Jervis could write confidently:

We have had five executions for mutiny and a punishment of 300 lashes given alongside two disorderly line-of-battle ships and the frigate to which the mutineer belonged... Two men have been executed for sodomy, and the whole seven have been proved to be the most atrocious villains. At present there is every appearance of content and proper subordination.[46]

Panic over; heavy-handed justice had the desired result for the time being, but news travelled slowly in those days and was easily distorted en route both to and from Britain's far-flung fleets. So it was that strange cross-currents meandered their way across the Atlantic during the summer months of 1797, finally reaching the West Indies in September. There, the disaffected crew of the *Hermione* picked up the scent of something wild in the wind, their legitimate grievances against a 'flogging captain' mushroomed into brutal mutiny and then as quickly mutated into supposed 'political sedition' as news of this latest and bloodiest mutiny sped back home to England. The die was cast.

Yet to join the *Naval Chronicle* in branding the *Hermione* mutineers as enemies of the state is to oversimplify the forces at work during this period and miss the point that the mutineers of Spithead, the Nore and, finally, the *Hermione* were victims of a deeper malaise that had been building in the service for some years and pervaded all levels of the navy, from admirals, including Nelson, down through captains, including Pigot, and ending up with 14-year-old James Allen.

As is all too often the case, the turmoil of 1797 was born not of failure but of success: failure crushes hopes; success raises expectations that must then be satisfied with ever larger doses of success. Limit or reduce the doses and first disaffection creeps in, then impatience, and finally desperation. It is this chain reaction that reached its peak in 1797. The mutinies were the inevitable end-product of the navy's stunning successes so far: it had single-handedly seen off the enemy, not just the French at the Glorious First of June 1794, but more recently the Spanish at the Battle of Cape St Vincent in February 1797. Moreover, these victories were just the tip of an iceberg of innumerable smaller skirmishes and individual ship engagements where, time after time, the British prevailed. In the meantime, any plans France had to invade Britain had been scuppered. All this was down to the navy. By contrast, Britain's efforts at prosecuting the war on land against Revolutionary France were a catalogue of humiliations: the expeditionary force, led by the duke of York and dispatched to the Low Countries to halt Revolutionary France's conquering ambitions, had failed miserably.

All eyes were on Britain's navy and, to add to the rising tide of expectations, the nation discovered in these latest victories at sea a new wave of young heroes everyone could identify with. The name of Earl Howe may have rung out in glorious June of 1794, but a dour, ageing 69-year-old was hardly the stuff of legends.

The Battle of Cape St Vincent brought to the attention of the British public the name of a new and altogether more charismatic young hero, then only a captain.

> We immediately proceeded in the direction of the Spanish Fleet, *of just double our force*, and on the 14th 1797, met them off Cape St Vincent. The weather was rather foggy, and they were not seen at any great distance, and had not time to form a regular line of battle before we broke through cutting off their rear. I had now the opportunity of seeing what could be done by the determination and activity of one man. The main body were about to pass astern of us, to rejoin those cut off, when Nelson left the rear of the line and threw himself single handed directly across their passage… I think I can safely say that had it not been for this act of Nelson's we should probably not have taken a single ship. As it was we captured four – two of three decks and two of two decks.[47]

George Elliot, a young gentleman whose account this was, had gone to sea in 1795 aged 11 and served with Nelson in the Mediterranean for the past two years. Naturally, Nelson was his hero. However, Nelson was not alone in the heroics of that day. Captains Cuthbert Collingwood and Thomas Troubridge, among others, made their names at the battle, and, standing next to their commanding officers on the quarterdeck or below supervising gun crews, there was a phalanx of up-and-coming midshipmen whose individual exploits that day were also recorded in the *London Gazette*, *Gentleman's Magazine* and *Naval Chronicle*. William Hoste and the other Norfolk lads were at the battle and, punishing his parents for their dilatory letter-writing, William said nothing in his letter of 16 February about his own exploits, instead archly reporting that 'I am happy to inform you that on 14th instant we fell in with the Spanish fleet off Cape St Vincent.'[48] It was left to Nelson to sing William's praises: 'You will be anxious to hear a line of your good and brave William after the sharp services of the *Captain* on the 14th. I have hitherto said so much of my dear William that I can only repeat, his gallantry never can be exceeded.'[49]

The feeling grew through the nation that it had found a new generation of heroes, and in their hands there was nothing Britain's navy could not do. Its 'wooden walls' would no longer serve as a mere defensive bastion planted from time to time down the centre of the English Channel to ward off unwelcome invaders. Rather, they could become a battering ram to beat down one enemy after another and project Britain's nascent power wherever the nation chose.

Yet – and here was the rub – among the officers and men aboard Britain's vast navy, which had increased from 498 ships in 1793 to 691 in 1797, success in battle was not being translated universally, and certainly not fairly, into personal success. Patriotism, poverty or the Press may have been the forces that variously impelled Britain's lower-deck men and boys to join the navy in the early years of the Wars, but promotion and pecuniary advantage must sustain them thenceforth.

Opportunities for promotion from the lower-decks were exceedingly limited, but did increase with the Wars, assisted by 'dead men's shoes', literally in some cases, as David Casey came by prior to his debacle on the *Hermione* when 'I reached my Ship in a very exhausted State and with the loss of everything but the Shirt and Trousers I wore; I was consequently put to my Shifts for a new Stock and dependant on my brother Mids for some time; one of them dying about that time I purchased most of his effects at the public sale that followed agreeable to the custom of the Service.'[50]

George Elliot had first-hand experience of seamen promoted into dead men's shoes and gave this cynical assessment:

> I was first entrusted with the charge of the watch (to do lieutenant's duty) in a case of illness, when blockading Malta, before I was quite fifteen years of age … and if I was not as efficient as was desirable, I suspect I was equal to at least two of the lieutenants, who had just been made up from common seamen, and were neither used nor very fit to command. Four out of our five lieutenants were made in that way, the distress for officers was so great – two were efficient, one very good, and the other two very much otherwise.[51]

Among the 'one very good' would have been the likes of Thomas Troubridge, hero of the Battle of Cape St Vincent, who rose to become an admiral but whose father was a baker. Another captain to have risen from humble origins was on the *Alcide*. Arriving on board, William Dillon was told to 'think what you may expect, in selecting the navy for your Profession. Our Captain was a hatter's son. See the position he now holds: therefore you need never despair.'[52] However, both these were sons of tradesmen with at least a modicum of education. From yet more modest roots came 'gallant Admiral Hopson', who from a common sea-boy, rose to an high rank in the navy',[53] and John Pasco, not yet famous as signal-lieutenant on the *Victory* during the Battle of Trafalgar and later promoted to captain, who 'it was said in the papers some time ago … was a midshipman with the King [William IV]. It was not so, he was a boy in the ship, and was the servant in the midshipmen's berth in which I messed; he was by way of promotion handed over to John Baptiste, the Prince's steward.'[54]

Nevertheless, these were exceptions. If 'Jack Tar' had any ambitions to preferment – 'going aft through the hawse-hole', as his prospects were graphically called – more likely he would have been satisfied with some modest elevation that would at least spare him 'from under the lash of the boatswain, a meare tirent, and other officers',[55] as Jacob Nagle, an American impressed into the British Navy, described his relief when told that his meagre knowledge of reading and writing would lead to his promotion to 'act as ships steward under the purser'.

Occasionally there were official attempts to dangle promotion as a carrot in front of a sailor, for instance with a poster in Jamaica announcing: 'Wanted, in consequence of the great promotion of Warrant Officers since her arrival in Port Royal only three months ago, a few Able-bodied seamen who will have every chance to work up and fill vacancies of Petty Officers, and who will be sure of obtaining comfortable livelihood, by entering upon the *Salisbury*.'[56]

However money was what counted: better pay, as the Spithead mutineers first demanded, or, better still, prize money. Yet this was where Jack Tar ran up against forces more powerful than him. At this period of the Wars, there was the occasional prize to be had, but for a sailor to get his hands on his fair share of the prize money was a lottery. There were too many sticky fingers higher up the pole, as Jacob Nagle discovered when:

One morning at 4 am [24 June 1797] we saw a sail coming bearing down upon us with all sail she coud croud… We up English colours and gave hur about 6 or 7 guns nearly at one time. Amediate she hall'd hur colours down… We took hur into Adm'l Jarvis and was made fast a stern of his ship but never received anything for hur. She was a rich loaded ship from the River of Plate, South America, which Jervice put in his own pocket.[57]

This incident was just one example of the pervasive and reckless greed across the officer class at this time. Even Nelson, who only a year earlier was happy to settle for 'honour and salt beef',[58] took leave of his senses following St Vincent, and, albeit briefly until he saw the error of his ways, had only one thought in mind:

prize money. He did not mind who died in the process, as some of his comrades would soon find out to their cost. His next big venture, the assault on the island of Tenerife in late July 1797, had no strategic or naval purpose. He had got wind of a sizeable treasure fleet reaching Tenerife from South America. Capture that and he would be set for life. Greed got the better of his judgement; greed and impatience, for word was going round the squadron that the Spanish were about to sue for peace, in which case better grab what he could double quick.

Nelson and his fellow officers reckoned the Spanish treasure fleet was theirs for the taking. Unfortunately, in their eagerness and arrogance they assumed the 'Dons' would be a pushover and took scant trouble over the planning. So when the assault came it was an unmitigated disaster: the mission failed, many in the landing parties were captured or killed and others, among them Thomas Fremantle, were wounded. For Betsy Fremantle, a passenger on board *Seahorse*, a frigate commanded by her husband, Thomas, and part of Nelson's squadron, 'this is the most melancholy event, I cant help thinking of poor Captain Bowens losing his life just at the end of a war in which he had been so fortunate... Fremantle had a very good night's rest he has no fever at all, his wound was dressed at twelve oclock and Fleming says it looks very well.'[59]

Fremantle was alive; Betsy was lucky. Not so fortunate were the Norfolk lads, they who for the past four years had stood shoulder-to-shoulder with Nelson in the Mediterranean and carried all before them. Suddenly personal tragedy struck at the heart of their merry troop. William Hoste poured out the shared anguish in his letter home of 15 August:

> My Dear Father,
>
> I must now sit down and give you a detail of our unfortunate expedition against the island of Teneriffe. At two, Admiral Nelson returned on board, being dreadfully wounded in the arm with a grape-shot. I leave you to judge my situation when I beheld our boat approach with him who I may say has been a second father to me, his right arm dangling by his side, while with the other he helped himself to jump up the ship's side and with a spirit that astonished everyone told the surgeon to get his instruments ready for he knew he must lose his arm and that the sooner it was off the better... At nine, a flag of truce came off Santa Cruz with a Spanish officer and the captain of the Emerald, who besides other bad news, informed us that Lieutenant Weatherhead was mortally

wounded. This was a stroke I could hardly stand against, however convinced it was not a time to give way I got everything in my power ready for his reception and about eleven he was conveyed on board in a cradle. The surgeon examined his wound and said he thought it was impossible he could live long. I am sorry to say his words proved true. And now am I come to the worst part of my story. He lingered out to Saturday 29 of July, and then expired seemingly without pain. In losing him, I lost a good companion and a true friend – He was the darling of the ship's company and universally beloved by every person who had the pleasure of his acquaintance. His body was committed to the deep on Sunday the 30th three volleys of musketry fired in honour of his memory.[60]

Very much as an afterthought, William mentioned that he was the latest beneficiary of dead men's shoes. There was no rejoicing: 'I had almost forgot to say that on the death of Weatherhead, Adml Nelson give me a commission to act as lieutenant in his vacancy; happy would it have made me, had it been in any other, as I shall ever regret the loss of him.'[61]

The same frenzy of greed that brought about the disaster of Tenerife had inspired an earlier series of pointless attacks on Cadiz harbour. Betsy Fremantle noted in her diary the events of those days of madness: 'July 5th. Dined on board alone with Fremantle and some of the officers. One of the many Fishermen came on board it is said not a woman now remains in Cadiz, but the night before last a bomb went into a house and killed a child in the mothers arms and the woman lost her arm. They again went to bombard the Town tonight.'[62]

This was wanton war on civilians. Nevertheless, out of respect for her husband's profession, Betsy kept her own counsel until, frustration boiling over the next day, she finally let fly in her diary on Thursday 6 July: 'Very much tired and sleepy all day… The Admiral wrote that this bombardment must be given over, Thank god, it was sacrificing men for nothing, he did it out of avarice as he heard 4 millions of piastres should be sent out to him.'[63]

Here was a damning indictment of the nation's new hero. Yet by now Nelson could do no wrong and, when the subsequent Tenerife mission failed and he offered humble pie expecting censure, the response from Jervis was that 'mortals cannot command success: you and your companions have certainly deserved it by the greatest degree of heroism and perseverance that ever was exhibited'.[64] Nelson was forgiven, but Jervis could not turn a blind eye to the increasing incompetence of his fellow officers, incompetence brought on by self-interest and too quick promotion. Charged with restoring discipline after the mutinies, Jervis was in no doubt about the cause of the deep malaise in the service: 'The present indiscipline of the navy originated with the licentious conduct of the officers.'[65] Further symptoms of this indiscipline were apparent in a court martial on Captain Sawyer in which 'the proof being so strong against Capt Sawyer, having a fondness for young men and boys, that he broke from ever serving in His Majesties service.'[66]

Jervis had gone to the heart of the problem: it was the officer corps that was rotten. The fact that in Jacob Nagle's opinion Jervis was, hypocritically, the greediest among the admirals and therefore setting the worst example was academic. No respecter of the 'sprigs of nobility' flooding the navy, Jervis swept away captain after captain whom he did not consider up to the job: Lord Harvey, whose ship *Zealous*, was 'in a most undisciplined state, the people incessantly drunk'[67] was sent home, as was Sir Charles Knowles of the *Goliath*, described by Jervis as 'an imbecile, totally incompetent, the *Goliath* no use whatever under his command.'[68]

Jervis was not the only interested observer to spot bad officers. Betsy Fremantle, who for all her ignorance of matters naval had a sharp eye for flaws in the characters of the officers with whom she rubbed shoulders, quickly set her sights on one rogue captain, recounting in her diary her doubts when 'the *Blanche* took a prize a few days ago off Toulon a French man of war of 12 guns, but parted company in a gale of wind off Cape Corse, and it is feared she is lost. Captain Hotham is vexed, he feels the disappointment more sensibly than other people for he is a stingy young man.'[69] Consumed by greed and described by Jacob Nagle, who served under him, as a 'damn'd tarter', it is little surprise that the crew of the *Blanche* subsequently mutinied in 1797 against Captain Hotham and that he was removed.

The rampant problems in the senior officer corps not only bred resentment among the men and boys of the lower-decks, leading to many of the mutinies at this time of the Wars, but could also cast a pall over the careers of young gentlemen who depended on these senior officers for their promotion. The push to expand the navy following the outbreak of war in 1793 had brought a vast influx of fresh-faced youngsters eager to volunteer for a life of glamour, excitement, fame, wealth and, last but not least, promotion. Promotion was the easiest reward to dispense among young gentlemen: it brought the instantly recognizable personal honour they and their families craved, and with it came enhanced pay. However, to earn promotion beyond midshipman they had to prove they had what it took to be leaders of men. Inevitably, not all were up to the job, but come 1797 the combination of dead men's shoes and the sheer pressure to keep at sea the vast numbers of ships needed to defend Britain's far-interests meant that abuses which had long prevailed in the service were allowed to get out of hand. The result was that some young midshipmen were promoted too rapidly to lieutenant, even captain, where they were called on to make life-and-death decisions for a whole ship's company, decisions which were well beyond their training and competence.

William Parker's path to promotion highlights one obvious abuse in the system of promotion. Made 'acting lieutenant' in October 1796, he was confirmed in the rank in March 1799. His Passing Certificate summarized the basic preconditions to be fulfilled as he 'who appears to be more than 21 years of age, and has been at sea more than six years',[70] of which four had to be as midshipman. All this seemed straightforward enough and the certificate next listed his times in ships and vessels under-mentioned:

Ships	Quantities	Years	Months	Weeks	Days
Orion	Captain's Servant	1	1	1	6
Orion	Midshipman	0	12	0	2
Leviathan	Midshipman	1	7	3	2
Magicienne	Acting Lieutenant	1	6	3	6
Magicienne	Ditto	0	2	0	3
Queen	Acting Lieutenant	0	10	0[71]	

The certificate stated what documentary proof of good service he had provided, namely 'journals kept by himself in the *Orion*, *Leviathan*, *Magicienne* and *Queen* and certificates from Captains Duckworth, Bingham, Ricketts, Ogilvy, and Dobson of his diligence, sobriety and obedience to command'.[72]

Finally came William's list of technical competencies: 'He can splice, knot, reef a sail, work a ship in sailing, shift his tides, keep a reckoning of a ship's way by plain sailing, and Mercator's; observe by the sun or stars; find the variation of the compass; and is qualified to do his duty as an able seaman and a midshipman.'[73]

There was one problem, however: as good an officer as William was, he was not 21. Nor was George Elliot, but he explained how the passing system could be manipulated:

Having completed my six years' of servitude, I was sent with nine other midshipmen to London, to pass the necessary examination for a lieutenant's commission; our examinations before the old commissioners of the navy were not severe, but we were called on to produce certificates that we were twenty-one years of age (I was sixteen and four days). The old porter in the hall furnished them at 5s. a piece, which no doubt the commissioners knew, for on our return with them they remarked that the ink had not dried in twenty-one years. Everybody was promoted ... from sixteen to eighteen ... the distress for officers was such as to insure every midshipman his step the day he became eligible.[74]

The loophole was that William and George only had to appear as if they were 21. If the abuses had been limited to cheating on the age requirement and an examination that was 'not severe', the problem would not have become too serious. However there was a more glaring abuse, false mustering, which, taken to its extremes, could endanger ships and their crews. Again, this abuse had been around since the time the British Navy had been subject to regulation and enabled young gentlemen to cheat on the time they were expected to serve before being granted a lieutenant's commission. The six-year rule was considered sacrosanct. Both William and George met this requirement. It supposedly ensured that patronage and interest only worked so far as enabling a young gentleman to gain entry to a favoured ship and captain. Once aboard and on his way, he still had to prove to his commanding officer that he had what it took to be an officer.

Self-evidently, therefore, in the push for promotion much hung on the captain: a good recommendation from him in the certificate he issued and the examining commissioners could afford to turn a blind eye to any suspected cheating on time. The only problem was that this practice was subject to increasing abuse during the early, harum-scarum years of the Wars: captains issued flawed recommendations either because of pressure from family or patrons, or owing to shortage of officers, or so as to palm a bad midshipman off on to another, unsuspecting, captain.

Nelson was a case in point: he was the key to how his Norfolk protégés –
William Hoste, William Bolton, Josiah Nisbet and the Weatherheads – secured
promotion. Following the Battle of Cape St Vincent he set about his task with gusto,
fortified in the knowledge that his new-found status would enable them to push
hard for their promotion. It all went to Nelson's head. Top of the list for special
attention was Josiah, his stepson. He must show his wife that he was pulling
whatever strings he could for her son. His letter of 3 March 1797 updated Fanny
on his efforts thus far: 'I regret Josiah has not served his time. I have wrote to
Maurice to see if he cannot get a little cheating for him it might be done and would
be invaluable. I am getting from Captain Stirling a certificate and I wish one could
be got from Captain Sotheby for if he will cheat, I shall do the same for the *Boreas*,
for if the war last another year he must be made a Lieutenant and I hope farther…'[75]

This was bare-faced cheating on Nelson's part: Josiah had never served with
either Captain Stirling or Captain Sotheby and would have been a babe-in-arms
when Nelson commanded the *Boreas*. Unabashed, Nelson wrote a month later to
say that his machinations had succeeded: 'When you write to Josiah you may
address yourself to Lieutenant Nisbet and I hope he will be a Captain if the war
lasts till October next.'[76]

Keen to impress Fanny, he compared his success on behalf of Josiah to the
lacklustre progress he made arranging promotion for his other Norfolk protégés:
'William Bolton, and Hoste with Weatherhead will also be promoted by Lord
Jervis but I fear about their time. I have sent to Maurice to take out so much of
Capt. William Bolton's time, that is all fair. Weatherhead, Mr Coke has interested
himself about and I hope will get over his want of time, but I fear he has not
interest for such a thing.'[77]

Ten days on he admitted that he had temporarily failed: 'I want Hoste,
Bolton, Weatherhead to be made when I shall feel easy but as yet I cannot cheat
for their time.'[78]

However, hasty promotion for these three – if necessary by cheating – was
fully warranted and in due course came through, except that by then John
Weatherhead was dead. Notwithstanding, Nelson could rest easy that, in pushing
rapid promotion for these three young gentlemen, he was doing the right thing
by himself, by them and, above all, by the navy: any ship would be in good hands
with them. Not so in the case of Lieutenant Suckling, a relation of Nelson's whom

he had taken under his wing and who was also from Norfolk. The first hints concerning Suckling's unsuitability as an officer came in Fanny's letter of 10 April 1797: 'Maurice Suckling is appointed 5th Lieutenant of the *Neptune*, I have taken into my head that he will not like to remain there. I fancy the Captain of her is anxious to have everything in greater order than before, however I told him Suckling was your relation and had been many years at sea with you, so that if he can be civil I hope he may.'[79]

Nelson considered Maurice 'in some respects … an odd man'[80] and was hoping that an early recall to the family estate would save him and the Sucklings further embarrassment. Too late, for on 14 September 1801 'a Court Martial was held … on Lieutenant Suckling, Commander of the *Furnace* Gun brig, for neglect of duty, and absenting himself without leave. Some part of the charges being proved against him, he was ordered to be superseded from *Furnace*.'[81]

Worse, however, than Suckling was the problem Nelson had stored up for himself pushing the career of his stepson, Josiah. It was not so much the flagrant cheating. There were other far worse examples of the same practice, as when Lieutenant William Walker was court-martialled for, among other offences, 'having answered for his own child, aged one year, rated A.B. and said he was on shore on duty'.[82] Lieutenant Walker's crime, however, was to get caught, so he had to be dismissed the service.

In Josiah's case, Nelson's cardinal sin was that he cheated on his stepson's time knowing full well from first-hand experience that Josiah was not suitable officer material. Worse still, he did it for purely personal reasons. This was one of Nelson's few professional lapses. Fortunately for him, his heroic status would serve to protect him from the worst of censures. Nevertheless he would come to bitterly regret conspiring in what William Hoste termed Josiah's 'pretty quick promotion',[83] the final straw being the personal humiliation heaped on Nelson when, just as he was celebrating his next great, some say his greatest, naval triumph, Jervis wrote threatening a court martial on Josiah.

THE BATTLE OF THE NILE

W hile the British Navy was busy in 1797 successively thrashing the Spanish at St Vincent and the Dutch at Camperdown, at the same time as dowsing the fires of political sedition and rooting out bad conduct in the officer corps, France was quietly plotting its next *coup de main*. Moreover, this time it had a general it could count on to deliver success on the field of battle. In May 1797, Napoleon Bonaparte was dispatched into northern Italy and by October had rolled over the Austrians, forcing them to sign the Peace of Campo Formio ceding Belgium and Lombardy to France. Next came England, and Napoleon was sent to the Channel to assess the viability of an invasion. However he had his sights set on grander prizes. In his words: 'Europe is but a molehill – all the great reputations have come from Asia.'[1] And the gateway to the Orient was Egypt. Conquer Egypt, and the Levant and India were at his mercy.

So it was that in the spring of 1798 a fleet of 13 ships-of-the-line, 14 frigates and 400 transports was assembled at Toulon and in adjacent ports along the French and Italian coasts ready to carry across the Mediterranean the mighty army of Egypt, comprising 31,000 elite troops and nine generals, 9,000 seaman and four admirals. Napoleon would lead this mighty *caravanserai* on his personal quest for imperial glory, travelling in style in the 120-gun *L'Orient*, the largest ship afloat, accompanied by his secretary, Louis Bourriènne, and, acting as aide-de-camp, Napoleon's 16-year-old stepson, Eugène de Beauharnais. Eugène was not the only young Frenchman seeking glory in the sands of Egypt. The French flagship, *L'Orient*, carrying Napoleon and Eugène to Egypt had a complement of

1,010 officers and crew, and there were an estimated 40 boys serving on each of the three gun decks.[2]

The Mediterranean had been vacated by the British the year before, but word had reached London that Napoleon had some grand scheme in mind. Was his destination Malta, the West Indies or Ireland? A small reconnaissance squadron of six ships was dispatched back into the Mediterranean in April 1798 and waited outside Toulon, France's main naval base. Commander of the squadron was Nelson, a surprise choice given that he was the most junior admiral in the navy. Surprise turned to outrage when a further squadron of ten ships was detached from the Channel Fleet and placed under Nelson's command. With these reinforcements came new orders: find Napoleon and destroy him. Sir John Orde, a senior admiral on blockade duty off Cadiz, protested in open letter and was promptly recalled. His mistake was not understanding that the decision to appoint Nelson came from the top. Apart from lacklustre Portugal, Britain was without allies. This made William Pitt, Prime Minister, desperate for a victory, and one momentous enough to cajole erstwhile allies such as Austria and the Kingdom of the Two Sicilies back on to Britain's side. Pitt's judgement was that Nelson was the man for the job. Only he had the flair, the daring, the genius to deliver the hammerblow Pitt craved. The stakes could not be higher as Lord Spencer pointed out in a letter to Admiral Jervis, now Lord St Vincent:

> The appearance of a British squadron in the Mediterranean is a condition on which the fate of Europe may at this moment be stated to depend. I think it almost unnecessary to suggest to you the propriety of putting it under the command of Sir H. Nelson, whose acquaintance with the part of the world, as well as his activity and disposition seem to qualify him in a peculiar manner for that service.[3]

Yet, strangely for Nelson, his whole demeanour at this time was tentative. En route to his station off Toulon, his letters to Fanny betrayed an insidious angst. Absent were the 'activity' and sureness of touch that had suffused Nelson's being at the Battle of Cape St Vincent and ahead of Tenerife. Instead, in a letter to Fanny dated 24 April, he wrote forlornly that 'I pray fervently for peace'.[4] In another letter, of 1 May, he repeated the same prayer 'that it will very soon please God to give us peace'.[5] He seemed bewildered, an impotent bystander watching while

'Bonaparte has gone back to Italy where 80 thousand are embarking for some expedition probably Sicily, Malta, Sardinia and to finish the King of Naples at a blow. There are others who think this mighty army is for Portugal, to be landed at Malaga and march thro' Spain.'[6]

Overwhelmed by the great task set him, Nelson sought refuge in petty resentment of the families of three of his Norfolk lads, William Hoste, William Bolton and another relative, the Cooper boy, all of whose money troubles refused to go away and had him fuming to Fanny that 'I have put myself to great inconvenience in advancing money for his son and desire him to repay you according to my desire.'[7] Nelson decided that enough was enough and, in a letter to the father of one of the new intake of young gentlemen joining him on his flagship, *Vanguard*, wearily laid down the law on money matters:

> I am this moment favor'd with your letter of the 14th: and although you rate my example far too high, yet if you wish to place your son in the *Vanguard* I shall be happy in giving him every protection in my power, it is necessary he should be at Portsmouth next week, and Mr Cambell my Secretary will tell whoever goes with him what is necessary for the Youth and manage his Money concerns for I believe it is almost unnecessary to tell you that lads of that age get no pay and therefore an allowance of money for their Mess & Expenses must be made them and not less than from 30 to 40 pounds a Year.[8]

As if confirming Nelson's grim forebodings, in May the fleet off Toulon was hit by a mighty storm sent by 'Almighty's goodness to check my consummate vanity'[9] leaving his ship 'dismasted, his fleet dispersed and himself in such distress that the meanest frigate out of France would have been a very unwelcome guest'.[10] The same storm swept away one of his new intake of young gentlemen – 'Mr Thomas Meek (who was recommended by Mr Hussey, by brother Suckling etc) is killed'.[11] – and enabled Napoleon's armada to quit Toulon and escape to the open sea, which he did on 19 May. After a brief detour to occupy Malta, the army of Egypt rumbled on to its ultimate destination with Nelson sometimes behind, other times ahead, of the French fleet. At one point, off the coast of Sicily, 'during the night of the 22nd of June, the English squadron was almost close upon us. It passed within six leagues of the French fleet.'[12] The next near-miss came when

'Nelson, who learned of the capture of Malta, on the day we left the island, sailed direct for Alexandria, which he rightly considered as the point of our destination. By making all sail, taking the shortest route, he arrived before Alexandria on the 28th, but on not meeting with the French fleet he immediately put to sea.'[13]

By now angst gave way to panic as Nelson, in this his first fleet-command and unaccustomed to the heavy responsibility that came with that position, began to crumble under the deadweight of imminent failure. He drafted a letter to St Vincent offering that 'if it is decided I am wrong, I ought for the sake of our country to be superseded. I hold I was right in steering for Alexandria and by that opinion I must stand or fall.'[14]

Yet Nelson was wrong to doubt himself. Finding Napoleon's fleet in the vastness of the Mediterranean was a challenge that would have daunted any of Britain's admirals. The difference was that Nelson, as soon as he caught up with the French fleet, would deliver victory. This was not in doubt. Once Nelson cleared his brain of the hubris and greed that followed on his success at St Vincent and the legacy of self-doubt from the disaster at Tenerife, there would be a welcome return of that clarity of strategic and tactical vision William Hoste, now a lieutenant aboard the *Theseus*, had seen Nelson display on that first cruise along the French coast in 1793. Gone would be Nelson's outrageous battle cry 'Westminster Abbey or Victory' at St Vincent as he led the boarders on to the Spanish ship *San Josef*.

Gone too was the mischievousness displayed at St Vincent by the likes of admiral's midshipman George Parsons, now aged 13, whose good fortune it was:

> …to be in great favour with the vice-admiral; so much so, that each day he personally took me to where the grapes clustered his cabin, and the oranges in nettings hung thick above my head, with strong injunctions only to eat what had begun to decay. I was then, not quite 13, and strictly obeyed orders, *while he was in sight to enforce them*, otherwise a tempting peach, with its soft maiden blush, or the coarser red of juicy nectarine, diverted me from the straight and narrow, – I am sorry to reflect how frequently.[15]

The mood among the young gentlemen and boys ahead of the descent on Egypt was quite different. They knew Nelson had his orders and the outcome of the Wars hung on his successful execution of those orders. Let Napoleon run loose now and there would be no end to his ambition. Lord St Vincent had given Nelson the best ships, captains and crews he could spare. Epitomizing the renewed earnestness was James Gordon, who, to his chagrin, had missed the Glorious First of June, but now aged 16 was master's mate on the *Goliath* having decided to turn over a new leaf. As he recalled later: 'At this time of my life I was a complete blackguard. I never wrote home, because I could not write, nor do I remember ever receiving a letter from any of my relations. At last I joined the *Eurydice* and was happy to find mids of my own age on board; they were all fine, smart boys and good sailors. I was soon ashamed of myself and now began to pay attention to my profession.'[16] Fifteen-year-old George Elliot, now a midshipman also on the *Goliath*, recalled that 'as one of the elite of our fleet, we were chosen to proceed and join Nelson up the Mediterranean.'[17]

Failure among this elite was not an option. Nothing must be left to chance. Everything must be subject to meticulous planning. 'Their ships were trained to every exercise of arms',[18] which meant crews being drilled day in, day out in gun practice, and marines regularly exercised musket drill. And as the fleet criss-crossed the Mediterranean, Nelson laid down with his captains a clear plan of battle, including detailed signals, so that every ship would know what its duty was in the hurly-burly of action. Nelson convened regular conferences on board the *Vanguard*, some or all his captains being called to join him in honing a strategic and tactical plan for when the British finally caught up with the French fleet. Nelson skilfully balanced the freedom he knew he must give to individual captains to act tactically as they saw fit in the heat of battle with the overall constraints of a strategic master plan he laid down in advance. Nelson's General Order chillingly spelt out the strategic objective: 'The captains of the ships will see the necessity of strictly attending to **Close Order** and should they compel any of the Enemy's ships to strike their Colours they are at liberty to judge and Act accordingly, whether or not it may be advisable to cut away their Mast and Bowsprit, with this special observance, Namely that **The Destruction of the Enemys Armament is the Sole Object**.'[19]

These words, some of which were written in bold by Nelson, summarized the battle plan: the enemy must surrender or suffer total annihilation. This was not to be a battle for prizes or glory, or half-measures. This was the total warfare France had promised Britain in 1793. Nelson was only responding in kind.

Success in this next battle must be measured in total victory; London demanded nothing less. That was why Nelson had been chosen.

And as if to ram home that success and victory ranked ahead of prizes and personal glory, Nelson continued in his General Order that:

> The Ships of the Enemy are therefore to be taken possession of by an Officer and one Boats crew only in order that the British Ships may be enabled to continue the attack and preserve their stations. The Commanders of the Divisions are to observe that no considerations are to induce them to separate from pursuing the Enemy unless by Signal from me so as to be unable to form a speedy junction with me, and the Ships are to be kept in that Order that the whole Squadron may act as a single ship.[20]

It only remained to find what Nelson called 'the Devil's children'[21] in the deep blue of the Mediterranean. Day in, day out, the search went on. This was midshipman's work, scouring the horizon from the masthead for enemy sail or joining parties sent to board passing vessels and garner crucial intelligence on the French fleet's whereabouts. A ship's lieutenant would generally command these delicate missions, but the general orders were clear: 'You are always to take a midshipman and a man who understands the language with you; and the midshipman is to continue in the boat to prevent the boat's crew from asking questions or giving answers; and not one of the boat's crew to be suffered to come out of the boat.'[22]

After the near miss at Alexandria another month was spent fruitlessly tracking backwards and forwards round the eastern Mediterranean, picking up trails of false or out-of-date intelligence until, finally, on 1 August 'the *Zealous*, after previous signals, announced to the Admiral, at three-quarters past 2 that 16 sail of the line were at an anchor E b S [east-by-south], and in a few minutes after, we all discovered them. At 3, the Admiral made the signal to prepare for battle.'[23]

This was the news the whole fleet had been waiting for. Edward Berry, captain of the flagship, *Vanguard*, described the reaction of the fleet: 'The utmost joy seemed to animate every breast on board the squadron at the sight of the Enemy…'[24] This may have been the mood on the quarterdeck. More likely Jack Tar's mood down below was as described by John Nicol: 'We rejoiced in a general action; not that we loved fighting, but we all wished to be free to return to our homes and follow our own pursuits. We knew there was no other way of obtaining this than by defeating the enemy. "The hotter the war the sooner the peace."[25]

The events of the next 24 hours have been described from many vantage points. There is the chaplain of the *Swiftsure*, who explained seeing preparations for his first battle at sea: '... all means of preservation from fire, leaks, and other casualties, were arranged in order; a bower cable was got out of the after part of the ship, and bent forwards, that she might anchor by the stern; the dreadful engines of destruction ready primed and doubly loaded; the men at their quarters, waiting in silent expectation of the orders of their superiors; the officers respectfully looking towards their captains, and waiting with firmness the awful moment.'[26]

Alternatively, there are the logs of the various ships, including the *Vanguard*, which described those first hours in typically laconic terms: 'Bore up for the French fleet lying Aboukir Roads. Backed main topsail to get Mutine's boat on board. Filled do. Immediately. Soundings 15, 14, 13, 11 and 10 fathoms. 28 minutes past 6, French hoisted their colours and commenced firing on our van ships.'[27] The most detailed technical account with such references to 'at 25 minutes past 4, to prepare for battle, with the sheet cable out of the stern port, and springs on the bower-anchor'[28] comes from Miller, captain of the *Theseus*, writing to his wife. Finding the affection in their relationship requires careful reading between the lines, and the presumption is that his letter was intended for public consumption.

Few letters describing the battle have survived. William Hoste's first letter home with news of the battle was one of many placed on the frigate, *Leander*, charged with bringing official news of the battle back to London. However en route to Britain the *Leander* was captured by the French and three bags of mail, official as well as personal, were dumped overboard before the ship was overrun.

One later account stands out above all the others, George Elliot's *Memoir*, written some years later but the best for a blow-by-blow account of the battle, for the simple reason that 'the *Zealous* and the *Goliath* were the most advanced ships next to the Admiral',[29] as a result of which George, aboard the *Goliath*, was in the thick of the action throughout.

Intentionally or not, his account of the hours leading up to the opening salvoes of the battle cast the *Zealous* and *Goliath* as rival yachtsmen jostling with each other, vying for the best line, one eye on each other, the other eye on the finishing post where lay beckoning the laurels of victory: the French fleet polished, sparkling, gleaming against Africa's setting sun. From the off, George disputes who had the honours of first spotting the enemy fleet:

On 1st August, 1798, being the lead ship of our fleet, in which no order of sailing was kept, but each ship got on as fast as she could, by way of gaining time; I, as signal midshipman, was sweeping round the horizon ahead, with my glass, from the royal yard, when I discovered the French fleet at anchor in Aboukir Bay. The *Zealous* was so close to us that had I hailed the deck they must have heard me; I therefore slid down by the backstay and reported what I had seen. We instantly made a signal, but the under toggle of the upper flag at the main came off in breaking the stop, and the lower flag came down – the compass signal was however clear at the peak; but before we could recover our flag, *Zealous* made the signal for the enemy's fleet – whether from seeing our compass signal or not I never heard – but we thus lost the little credit of first signalizing the enemy, which, as *signal midshipman*, rather affected me.[30]

This was battle action about to become personal. Distilled down to the most insignificant of objects – an 'under toggle' – was the world of a young boy at sea preparing for the battle of his life, yet consumed by thoughts of his moment in history. Underhand tactics or not, the *Zealous* and its signal midshipman had craftily stolen a march on George. Still, George could console himself that he was not the only one to notice the devious trick *Zealous* had pulled. Rivalry between quarterdecks was not uncommon, as George Parsons recalled when, like George Elliot, he was signal midshipman on the *Foudroyant* during a later engagement and Nelson set his flag-captain, Sir Edward Berry, on his mettle, telling him that 'this will not do, Sir Ed'ard: it is certainly *Le Genereux*, and to my flagship she can alone surrender. Sir Ed'ard, we must and shall beat the *Northumberland*',[31] and promptly ordered: 'Youngster, to the masthead.'

As for George Elliot on the *Goliath*, the next twist in his race with the *Zealous* was that:

Captain Foley guessed that the signal would be made to form *the line as most convenient*; that is, to get into line as the ships happened to be at the moment. We were actually first by half the length of a ship; but Captain Hood, of the *Zealous*, was very much senior to Foley, and was a likely man to make a push for the post of honour. Foley gave orders therefore to have our stay-sails and studding-sails ready to run up, to keep our place, and I fortunately saw the flags, under the flagship's foresails, as they left the deck, so that by the time they reached the royal yard, to show over it, our sails were going up, and we got a little more start and took the lead. Hood was annoyed but could not help it. They (Hood and Foley) were fine competitors for such an honour, as I will now show.[32]

George Elliot and the crew of *Goliath* were now firmly in the lead. Nothing, not even a near pile-up back in the trailing pack of British ships was going to stop Foley holding on to pole position:

> Shortly after we were in line, Hardy (afterwards Sir Thomas) in his brig, boarded a coasting vessel, and took out some of the crew to act as pilots for the bay. We were running free, and going about seven miles an hour, and Hardy's small boat being loaded with the Egyptians missed the *Vanguard* (the flag ship) which brought to, but ran a long way in doing so. This caused a delay of upwards of fifty minutes. No signal was made, Foley stood on, and Hood followed him, but the third ship in the *Audacious*, brought to, and of course forced the two ships between her and *Vanguard* to do the same. A gap was thus made between the *Goliath* and the *Zealous* and the rest of the fleet, of about seven miles, for we never shortened sail till we were coming to an anchor.[33]

Foley and Hood did not have to square this 'gap' with Nelson's earlier battle instructions that 'the captains of the ships will see the necessity of strictly attending to Close Order'. Nelson's decision to attack so late in the day meant that the quicker the British arrived and engaged the enemy the better. Accidental though this 'gap' was, George Elliot, needless to say, turned the circumstances to advantage, portraying the eventual sequence of events as a masterly ploy of psychological warfare by the British flaunting their zeal under the noses of the pusillanimous French, who were waiting powerlessly as the British closed in mercilessly for the kill, eager for the honour to strike the first blow on their prostrate victim: 'The battle therefore began by only two ships against the whole of the enemy's van, a fine example of determination, more spoken of by the French than in England, where perhaps it may not have been known – but it turned out, as I shall hereafter show, to be a lucky thing for us, as well as a most important event for the success of the day.'[34]

The point when battle was about to be joined had arrived and by now every member of the crew on the *Goliath* and *Zealous* would have been on tenterhooks, eagerly waiting for the first shots to be fired, after which it would be all din, noise, shot, bullets, blood, smoke, fire and death. George did not describe these moments. Why should he? He had seen and heard it all before and there were greater wordsmiths than him who conjured up the unfolding conflagration, the anonymous poet in the *Naval Chronicle* in 1800 being just one:

> Now issue forth from each tremendous tier,
> Volumes of smoke, and cataracts of fire;
> The roaring cannons, thro' the pitchy gloom,
> Disgorge Death's daemons lurking in their womb;
> Hiss thro' the hurtled air the whirring ball,
> And all is desp'rate rage, and darkness all,
> Save when the vivid lightnings, as they play,
> Flash on the decks a momentary day.[35]

Not for George such vague flights of poetic imagery. There was one final act still to be played out between the *Zealous* and *Goliath* before 'the awful moment', the one act that, he believed, ran counter to the generally accepted version of events.

He started off with an explanation of the challenge facing Captain Foley: 'When we were nearly within gunshot, standing as aide-de-camp close to the Captain, I heard him say to the master that he wished he could get inside of the leading ship of the enemy's line.'[36] Accomplish this manoeuvre and it would do for the French, but it was a manoeuvre fraught with danger, not least because of the formidable defensive position the French fleet had taken up within the bay to counter just such a possibility:

> ...the enemy had 13 large ships anchored in close order of battle, in the form of a bow, with the convex part to us, *l'Orient*, of 120 guns, making the centre of it, the string of the bow being NW & SE, and four frigates a little within them, a gun and mortar

battery on a small island about three quarters of a mile from their van, and three mortar boats placed near the frigates.[37]

To the British ships bearing up to the French line, the landward side of the enemy fleet was blocked off and the British could attack only on the seaward side. This considerably increased the odds in favour of the French, which was why they had anchored as they had. The problem was exacerbated in that 'no one in the fleet had the least knowledge of the bay; nor was any known chart of it existing, except an ill drawn plan found on board the vessel captured on the 29th of June.'[38] Proof of the risks came when Captain Troubridge, 'in his eager desire to gain a forward station in the glorious contest',[39] led his ship, *Culloden*, into the bay and 'just before he struck, had found ten fathoms of water, [but] before the lead could again be hove, the Culloden was fast aground on the rocks.'[40] Add the fact that 'the evening was now closing in'[41] and Nelson's decision to attack at dusk rather than waiting until daybreak must have seemed high risk, the closer the moment came for battle to commence.

Faced with these odds, the master of the *Goliath* must have thought Captain Foley had taken leave of his senses when he started musing how 'he wished he could get inside' the French line. This was the sort of wild scheme masters of His Majesty's ships were there to caution their captains against. And yet the master agreed. Why was this, and why did five other British ships in turn follow suit? After all, Foley was no hothead: he was bred from good landowning stock, with an uncle who had served in the navy and, since himself being promoted to captain in 1790, he had served as flag-captain to three admirals. This was not someone who would surrender to vainglory.

The chaplain of the *Swiftsure* ventured his explanation of events, namely that 'the British admiral, who saw all the advantages the enemy possessed, but saw them with a seaman's eye, knew they must have room to swing the length of their cables: and consequently, that there would be space enough for our ships to anchor between them and the shore.'[42] However this is only half the story. The chaplain should have explained that it was normal for a fleet at anchor to be moored bow and stern, in which case there would be no need for an arc of deep water on the landward side in which to rotate at anchor. Furthermore, for whatever reason, possibly lack of time to complete his reconnaissance of the bay, the French admiral, Brueyes, had placed his ships far apart and ordered them to anchor by the bows only, which meant that there were no shoals within a cable's length round each ship, including on the landward side. The chaplain credited Nelson with this crucial discovery, as did Berry, Nelson's flag-captain on the *Vanguard*. The *Naval Chronicle* gave the credit to Captain Hood of the *Zealous* who 'had been hailed by the admiral, to know if he thought there was sufficient depth of water for our ships between the enemy and the shore; Captain Hood is reported to have replied that he did not know, but that, with the admiral's permission, he would lead in and try.'[43] Nelson in turn is supposed to have told Hood: 'You have my leave. I wish you success.'[44]

Yet the *Zealous* and *Vanguard* were nowhere near each other at the crucial moment when the decision was made to go inside the French line. Furthermore it was the *Goliath*, not the *Zealous*, which went inside first. Stripping away the sycophancy of the chaplain of the *Swiftsure* and Nelson's flag-captain, the general consensus of later historians is that Foley undertook this manoeuvre on his own initiative. This brings the sequence of events back to the quarterdeck of the *Goliath* and that moment when someone on that vessel thought to look for the vital clue that betrayed the French fleet's fatal Achilles heel. Someone saw that the French ships were not anchored both bow and stern. Someone worked out what that meant. Who was it? It is worth asking the question, since the answer goes beyond the personal duel between Foley and Hood and throws light on the most important moment in the Battle of the Nile, that moment when the scales of advantage tipped irretrievably in favour of the British fleet and ensured that victory would go to Britain, whatever deadly cannonades and broadsides would be delivered by either fleet in the hours ahead.

According to George Elliot it was *he*, not Captain Foley, who in the gathering gloom first spotted the flaw in the French mooring system, and it was he who pointed out the significance to his captain. When George heard Foley 'say to the master that he wished he could get inside of the leading ship of the enemy's line,'[45] George's reaction was that:

> I immediately looked for the buoy on her [the leading French ships] anchor, and saw it apparently at the usual distance of a cable's length [i.e. 200 yards], which I reported; they both looked at it, and agreed there was room to pass between the ship and her anchor (the danger was, the ship being close up to the edge of the shoal), and it was decided to do it. The master then had orders to go forward, and drop anchor the

moment it was a ship's breadth inside the French ship, so that we should not actually swing on board her. All this was exactly executed.[46]

A 15-year-old Mid changing the course of history? Not possible. After all, George would surely claim credit. If his *Memoir* were, as he stated, purely 'for my family',[47] rather than for the general public, then there was little chance of anyone coming along years later to contradict him, and he could brag to his children and grandchildren with impunity. Yet why tell his family a blatant untruth, given that his place in history was already sufficiently assured, just by his having been at the battle, and why go against historians of the time who had already accorded the credit to Nelson? As an earlier beneficiary of Nelson's patronage George had no reason to debunk the reputation of the nation's hero, and as the son of a senior diplomat, Lord Minto, who previously had been Governor of Sardinia, George would have understood the foolishness of making false claims. More to the point, he would have enough to be proud of just being a part of the forthcoming battle.

Yet George persists, as he explains the clear advantage that accrued to the British by coming in on the landward side of the French fleet:

> I also heard Foley say, he should not be surprised to find the Frenchman *unprepared* for action *on the inner side* – and as we passed her bow I saw he was right, her lower-deck guns were not run out, and there was lumber, such as bags and boxes, on the upper-deck ports, which I reported with no small pleasure. We first fired a broadside into the bow – not a shot could miss at the distance – the *Zealous* did the same; and in less than a quarter of an hour this ship was a perfect wreck, without a mast or a broadside gun to fire.[48]

Through a myriad of technical details, a close-up, blow-by-blow account of the battle as seen from the *Goliath* places George variously in the bows, on the poop, and on the quarterdeck:

> By this time, having no after bitts to check the cable by (which came in at the stern port) it kept slowly surging [i.e. slipping] through the stoppers, and at last the remaining stoppers broke (our sails had flown loose, by the gear being shot away, we had no time to furl them), and it ran out to the clench [i.e. the end] placing us a little past the second ship in the French line, so as to engage us and the third ship.[49]

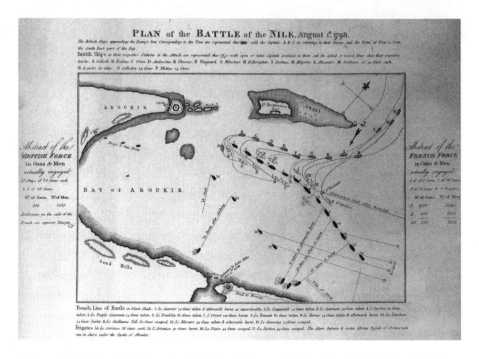

A plan of the battle of the Nile as it unfolded on 1 August 1798 showing the Goliath *marked 'A' and the* Zealous *marked 'B' as the lead ships. (National Maritime Museum, Greenwich, London)*

Briefly stepping back from his close quarters, George pans out to the wider panorama of the battle, in the process reinforcing the truth about *Goliath*'s, if not his, pivotal role in it. 'We were just in this position when the leading ships of the body of the fleet came in.'[50] Persisting in his claim that the *Goliath* and *Zealous* entered the battle well ahead of the other ships, George states later in his account that 'Foley's running on with only one ship to support him, when the fleet brought to for the Egyptians was also most fortunate. The French captains were all on board their admiral's ship, and did not expect us to come in that night.'[51] By giving his captain the credit, he is acknowledging a chain of command. He may have been the one on the spot to have 'looked for the buoy' on the French ships but it is his captain who took the decision to act on his discovery.

As the battle raged there was an incident that, if the stage on which it played out were not so macabre, would have been the stuff of music-hall farce. George starts off in a matter-of-fact way: 'The first ship, the *Audacious*, took up a useless birth between the first and second ships of the enemy's line, both of them being utterly beaten and dismasted; the second ship, the *Theseus*, commanded by as good an officer as we had, Captain Miller ... came inside the French line.' Suddenly the battle closed in and the atmosphere became claustrophobic when:

> ...in passing within ten yards [*Theseus*] gave us three most hearty cheers, which our men returned from their guns pretty well. The French were ordered by their officers to *cheer in return,* but they made such a lamentable mess of it that the laughter in our ships was distinctly heard in theirs – and one of their captains told me that they never could get their men to stand to their guns afterwards.[52]

While the port-side main guns of the *Goliath* were doing battle with the *Conquérant* in the French line, George found himself engaged, along with some of his fellow midshipmen, in a separate skirmish with a French frigate, the *Sérieuse*, attacking the *Goliath* from the landward side:

> Sir James Gordon, myself, and poor Paddy Graves, who was killed soon after, with occasional assistance from a signal-man, worked the foremost gun on the opposite side with round shot at the frigate... The chamber of the howitzer held very little powder, because the gun was very light: the very heavy shot could therefore have but little force; and as she [the *Serieuse*] fell off with her helm hard a port ... one of these large shot[s] wedged itself in above water, between the rudder and sternpost and completely prevented their moving their rudder again, and it consequently brought them round towards the sand bank close to them, on which they run; and on her heeling over water came in at many shot holes, and she filled... Thus those youngsters amusing themselves with a prize gun which could not throw shot with force enough to pass through a ship's side, caused the loss of a fine frigate. Had the shot had more force, it would have passed through and done no injury. It was only want of force that made it stick, and so wedge the rudder and render it immoveable. Such are the chances of war. There was no mistaking the shot – no other ship, English or French, had a larger shot than a thirty-two pounder, and it was the only howitzer used on that side.[53]

This incident over, for George and the crew of *Goliath* their part in the battle was effectively at an end, and they became spectators as the struggle raged on further down the line, reaching its climax in apocalyptic fashion:

Considerably later at night, long after it was quite dark, perhaps about ten o'clock, we saw a ship down the line on fire – it was long before we could judge which party she belonged to – our share of the action was all but over, and we looked on in great suspense – at last, as the fire increased, we saw her *three decks*, which decided the point, as we had but two-deck ships. We wished to send boats down, but, on examination, had not one that could be made to swim, so shattered were they all. It was an awful sight, and when she blew up the firing ceased on all sides, for I believe fully half an hour, or perhaps nearer an hour.[54]

What George was describing was the 'most grand and awful spectacle'[55] of the 120-gun *L'Orient*, flagship of the French fleet, in its death throes, and the tragedy he saw unfolding from a distance others witnessed at close quarters. It came down to the French consul in Palermo to collate these accounts and transmit to Paris the news that 'it was in this situation of affairs that Admiral Brueyes was wounded in the head and the hand, nevertheless he continued to command, till a cannon ball cut him in two: he lived a quarter of an hour afterwards, and would expire upon deck. A moment afterwards, Captain Cassa Bianca, formerly a deputy, was mortally wounded by a splinter; this beautiful vessel then took fire, and every effort to extinguish it proved ineffectual.'[56]

At this point in the great battle there emerged from the enveloping smoke and din the tragic figure of:

…young Cassa Bianca, a boy of ten years old, who during the action had performed prodigies of valour, refused to escape in a boat, being unwilling to leave his wounded father: nevertheless he afterwards put his father upon a mast which was thrown into the sea; himself and the Commissary of the fleet were upon it when *l'Orient*, of 120 guns, blew up with a most horrible noise, and destroyed these unfortunate persons. The explosion was so dreadful, that the town, which was four leagues distance, was shaken with it. The two squadrons thought for ten minutes they would be destroyed with the showers of fire, red-hot cannon etc which fell. For ten minutes, they waited in silence the moment of their destruction: but Englishmen and Frenchmen were in the presence of each other, and again the cannons thundered, and the battle became more bloody than ever.[57]

So affected was the French consul that he recommended that 'if the government act properly … they will honour the memory of Admiral Brueyes, of young Cassa

Bianca, and all those brave men who died fighting'.[58] Sensing that the sinking of *L'Orient* and the apotheosis of this 10-year-old accidental hero were the iconic images of this apocalyptic collision of two mighty empires, Felicia Hemans later immortalized the moment in her poem *Casabianca*:

> The Boy stood on the burning deck …
> Whence all but he had fled;
> The flame that lit the battle's wreck
> Shone round him o'er the dead.
>
> Yet beautiful and bright he stood,
> As born to rule the storm –
> A creature of heroic blood,
> A proud, though childlike form.
>
> The flames rolled on – he would not go
> Without his father's word;
> That father, faint in death below,
> His Voice no longer heard.
>
> There came a burst of thunder-sound
> The boy – oh! where was he?
> Ask of the winds that far around
> With fragments strewed the sea! –
>
> With mast, and helm, and pennon fair,
> That well had borne their part;
> But the noblest thing which perished there
> Was that young faithful heart![59]

The battle over, it was time for the mopping-up operations. For William Hoste on the *Theseus*, this meant prize-taking tasks. Captain Miller 'sent Lieutenant Hawkins to take possession of *Mercure*, and Lieutenant Hoste of *Artemise* [but] when the latter got within about a cable's length of the *Artemise*, perceiving she was set on fire by a train, and that her people had abandoned her on the opposite side, he also returned on board: after burning about half an hour, she blew up.'[60]

For George Elliot, clear-up duties on board *Goliath* came first and 'we were at work all night, trying to save our masts, which were much shattered; and I was so knocked up about three o'clock in the morning, that I actually fell asleep in the act of hauling up a shroud hawser. The old boatswain laid me down in his cabin close by, and two hours after I was all fresh and right again.'[61]

Jobs done, bones rested, it was time for George to tend his wounds as '…the swelling in my neck from a wound had fixed my head very near my left shoulder, in the position I had slept in, and it remained there for several days, though, as far as I remember, without pain.'[62] The official list of wounded on the *Goliath* compiled after the battle mentioned only two midshipmen, Law Graves and James Payne, which meant that George's injury was evidently not considered sufficiently serious to merit being recorded.

Official reports listing battle casualties were generally brief and boys were rarely identified separately. However there was certainly one boy known to have been a casualty on the *Goliath*, a 'lad who was stationed by a salt-box on which he sat to give out cartridges and keep the lid close – it's a trying berth – when asked for a cartridge, he gave none, yet he sat upright; his eyes were open. One of the men gave him a push; he fell all his length on the deck. There was not a blemish on his body, yet he was quite dead and thrown overboard.'[63]

Unsurprisingly there were many casualties on both sides, on the French side roughly 4,000, on the British side 895 dead and wounded at first count, although the number rose during the hours and days after the battle as victims of the surgeon's knife failed to survive. A high proportion of British casualties were midshipmen and master's mates (the same rank as a midshipman). Of the 16 officers and petty officers listed as killed in the returns to the *Naval Chronicle* in its January 1799 issue, seven were midshipmen or master's mates, and of the 37 officers listed as wounded, 14 were midshipmen.

Among these was one who took the 'hit' for James Saumarez, captain of the *Orion*, when 'a large splinter, impelled with the greatest violence, after mortally wounding Mr Miles (one of Sir James' aides-du-camp) wounded Sir James very severely on the side.'[64] Saumarez survived, but the young midshipman's ordeal continued down in the cockpit where a woman, Nancy Perriam, was assisting the surgeon in his gruesome task and recalled how 'the boy bore the operation without a murmur, and when it was over turned to me and said: "Have I not borne it like a man?" Having said this he immediately expired.'[65]

The high proportion of midshipmen among the casualties at this battle has perversely been 'blamed' on Nelson, 'whose example on the breaking out of the war [1793] gave so chivalrous an impulse to the younger men of the service that all rushed into a rivalry of enterprise which disdained every warning of prudence.'[66] So desperate were these 'younger men' to prove themselves and thereby earn promotion that, so the wry joke went, 'a young lieutenant, who was never backward on such occasions, said with some truth, "A fellow has now no chance of promotion unless he jumps into the muzzle of a gun and crawls out of the touch-hole."'[67]

Whether Nelson was to blame or not, he found himself recovering from his own wounds in the days following the battle, just as his step-son arrived with a letter from St Vincent, which began with 'it would be a breach of friendship to conceal from you that he [Josiah] loves drink and low company.'[68] If this were all that Nelson had to worry about concerning his stepson, he could relax. St Vincent was right to root out 'licentiousness' but what sailor didn't love his 'drink' and the occasional indulgence in 'low company', especially after a hard-fought battle. What St Vincent wrote next, however, left Nelson in no doubt how serious the problem, *his* problem, was. Josiah, wrote St Vincent, 'is thoroughly ignorant of all forms of service, inattentive, obstinate, and wrong-headed beyond measure, and had he not been your son-in-law must have been annihilated months ago. With all this, he is honest and truth-telling, and I dare say, will, if you ask him, subscribe to every word I have written.'[69]

War had reached the heart of the Nelson family.

THE NELSON FAMILY AT WAR

Josiah is to have another Ship and to go aboard, if the *Thalia* cannot be got ready. I have
done *all* for him and he may again as he has often done before, wish me to break my
neck, and be abetted in it by his friends who are likewise my enemies; but I have done
my duty as an honest generous man and I neither want or wish for any body to care
what become of me… Living I have done all in my power for you, and if dead, you
will find I have done the same, therefore my only wish is to be left to myself…[1]

The contrast in Nelson's sentiments in this letter of March 1801 with
another written in August 1793 also to his wife, Fanny, speaks volumes:
'The being united to such a good woman, I look back to as the happiest
period of my life; and as I cannot here show my affection to you, I do it doubly
to Josiah, who deserves it, as well on his own account as on yours, for he is a real
good boy, and most affectionately loves me.'[2] What had happened in the
intervening period to bring about the disintegration in the relationship between
Nelson, his stepson, and now his wife?

From the loneliness of the captain's cabin aboard the Agamemnon, Nelson
yearned for companionship that August of 1793 as the British fleet stood off Toulon
harbour on blockade duty, watching night and day for 'whether the French intend
to come out.'[3] In the early days of the conflict with France, hopes rode high of a short
war, and Nelson frequently mused, as he did in his letter of 1 December that year,
that 'before many months are over we shall have peace.'[4] His letters spoke of hope,
love and familial bliss, Fanny relishing them, always responding in kind, as on

6 October 1794 when she wrote, 'how anxious I am to see my dear husband and child, what happiness … my heart is full: may I see you in good health'.[5]

Like many men at sea, Nelson longed for his wife's letters, assuring her in January 1795 that 'I hope we have many happy years to live together'.[6] Hers was a distant and all-important love that dutifully kept the home fires burning for her absent sailor husband, just as thousands of other wives did for their sailor loves. What made that 'love' for hearth and home grow ever stronger as the days at sea passed into months and years was, after all, that it was in the nature of a sailor to marry the sea, yet yearn for the comfort of hearth and home. Nelson was no exception and, mariner through and through, he was steeped in this contradiction of warring 'loves'.

Over the coming years Fanny, like so many other naval wives, would have grown used to the rhythm of Nelson's letters and ever more attuned to his mood swings, – the doom-laden self-pity expressed as the months and years passed with no end to the conflict in sight and the grim foreboding ahead of each anticipated battle, as in March 1795, when he wrote that 'a glorious death is to be envied'.[7] So Nelson's fateful letter of 1801, with its dose of bitter venom, may only have registered initially to Fanny as a warning of yet one more deadly challenge that lay ahead for her husband in the service of their country, this time against the Danes at the Battle of Copenhagen in April of that year.

As for the tone of finality in his letter, she did consult her brother-in-law, who counselled her to ignore the letter 'as his Brother seemed to have forgot himself'.[8] But as days and months merged into years, it became clear that this letter – the one that she would eventually call the 'Letter of Dismissal' – was the last she would receive from her husband. The bonds of the close-knit family, so lovingly portrayed by both husband and wife in the early years of the Wars, had been rent asunder.

All too often one of the 'unseen' casualties of war is the family. The prolonged separations, the loneliness, the dread of bad news, the longing for good news, the interminable waiting, the worlds apart of the home and the battlefield – all prey on the minds and hearts of distant loved ones. Yet many of the family letters from the Wars say nothing of these emotions. In the Parker family there is only eager excitement when William is first off to sea, as on 16 October 1793 when William's brother, George, writes to their father: 'Sir John [Jervis] shewed me a letter from Duckworth this morning dated the 13th instant wherein to the best of my recollection he uses the following expression: "William Parker I have placed under the wing of Mrs D. where I shall continue him till we sail. He is a truly delightful boy and attends to all my admonitions. I sincerely and with reason hope he will continue to merit your patronage and protection to which he is much entitled.'"[9] Writing from his station off Martinique on hearing news of the Battle of the Glorious First of June 1794, Sir John Jervis, William's uncle and patron, writes to George Parker on 2 August 1794: 'Your young tar has had [a] bellyful of fighting under Lord Howe. That battle was the best fought on our side of any since the Dutch war…'[10] This was the news – and tone – families wanted to hear and pass around.

So too for the Austen family. Absent from Jane's letters to her sister Cassandra, which survive from 1796 onwards, are any of the emotions that she later owns up to in her novels. There is no anguish, dread or fear, only playful anticipation when, for instance, good news about her sailor brothers is in the offing. On 24 December 1798 Jane writes about Charles' push for promotion: 'I have sent the same extracts of the sweets of Gambier to Charles, who poor fellow! tho' he sinks into nothing but an humble attendant on the Hero of the peice [sic] will I hope be contented with the prospect held out to him.'[11] Then again, only joy is on display when good news arrives, as on 8 April 1798, and Jane writes jokingly, this time about Francis: 'The Triton is a new 32 Frigate, just launched at Deptford – Frank is much pleased with the prospect of having Capt. Gore under his command.'[12] News from the battlefront is handled in a matter-of-fact manner as on 1 December 1798: '…I have just heard from Frank. He was at Cadiz, alive and well, on October 19…'[13]

All is gentle decorum and understatement in the family letters of the Parkers and the Austens. A few moments of panic apart, even the Hostes' correspondence seems a model of understatement. Contrast these with the rising crescendo of rhetoric between Fanny and her husband as the Wars progress. For all that Fanny's brother-in-law tried to discount the letter sent to Fanny in 1801, Nelson and she had been in mounting crisis for years, and caught squarely in the middle was Nelson's stepson and young gentleman 'boy sailor', Josiah Nisbet, both victim of and, according to Nelson's Letter of Dismissal, the cause of the family's disintegration.

Josiah was not the only boy with a famous stepfather to be so caught. Probably the most apt comparison of how these Wars affected family life can be made with young Eugène de Beauharnais, Napoleon Bonaparte's stepson. When Napoleon, then engaged in the fateful expedition to Egypt, heard the news that his wife, Josephine, had taken Hippolyte Charles as a lover in Italy, he threatened divorce in a series of scathing letters to his wife – letters that were intercepted by the British and published in the British press. Eugène, who was serving with Napoleon in Egypt, not only found himself witness to his stepfather's very public revenge affair with the wife – dubbed 'Our Lady of the Orient'[14] by the British press – of a French Lieutenant, but was also obliged to act as go-between with his warring parents begging discretion and calmer heads.

Still, Eugène was an innocent bystander. Not so Josiah, if Nelson's last letter to Fanny were to be believed. So what could Josiah possibly have done to earn the opprobrium of his stepfather? Hadn't Josiah's career at sea started so well? Having made his decision to follow Nelson into the *Agamemnon*, he had quickly settled into life at sea, and Nelson's early letters were full of Josiah's early excitement, the youngster being 'in high glee to think we are going to sail'[15] and having 'got a Turkish sabre of which he is not a little proud'.[16] Nelson seemed happy to have Josiah with him: 'Josiah … is a good boy'.[17] Josiah's letters home to his mother were soon full of the Wars, as when in October 1793 he wrote: 'I still like being at sea and think I always shall. We have been at Toulon which I think a very strong place. The Spaniards have ran[sic] away every time they have engaged the French and have behaved with the utmost barbarity to all those who laid down their arms and also the Neapolitans have behaved very cruelly in some cases.'[18]

The first major engagement for Josiah and the other young gentlemen aboard the *Agamemnon* came with the capture of the French ship *Ça Ira* in March 1795, and Josiah seems to have risen to the challenge. Afterwards Nelson proudly wrote to Fanny that 'Josiah and Hoste with Bolton were my aide-de-camps and behaved with great courage, and Josiah thinks there is no great danger from a Frenchman's shot… *Agamemnon* was very much cut up today but at this moment we are again ready for action…'[19] It was the same again two years on at the Battle of Cape St Vincent, the next big action in which both Nelson and Josiah participated: after the battle Nelson reported to Fanny that 'I am most perfectly well and rich in honour as is Josiah and Hoste'.[20]

Indeed, it was during the raid on Tenerife in August 1797, 'the night Sir Horatio Nelson lost his arm,'[21] that Josiah truly came into his own. In his letter of 5 August reporting on the outcome of the raid, Nelson laconically acknowledged Josiah's heroics, telling Fanny: 'I know it will add much to your pleasure in finding that Josiah under God's providence was principally instrumental in saving my life.'[22] However grudging Nelson's admission, here, surely, was proof to a mother that the Wars, far from tearing her husband and his stepson apart, had brought them closer together. Here was *her* son saving *her* husband's life. So important was the incident at Tenerife as proof of the good relations between her son and her husband and how the Wars had brought them together that when Fanny was asked to contribute to Nelson's biography in 1806, she wrote a detailed *Memorandum* describing how 'in the act of Sir H. putting his foot over the boat he was shot thro' the elbow. Lieut N. who was close to him saw him turn his head from the flash of the guns, say to him "I am shot thro' the elbow." Upon which he seated him in the boat… Lieut N. took off his coat in order to catch the blood and feeling where the bones were broken he grasped the arm with one hand which stopped the bleeding.'[23]

Taking command of the boat Josiah then ordered the men to strike out for the ship, even though everyone aboard risked being caught in the fire from the Spanish shore batteries, and 'when the boat reached the side of the ship Nisbet called out "Tell the surgeon the Admiral is wounded and he must prepare for amputation", upon which they offered to let down the chair, Sir H said "No I have yet my legs and one arm" and he walked up the side of the ship, Lieut N keeping so close that in case he had slipped he could have caught him.'[24] So how, four years on, could Nelson be telling Fanny that Josiah might 'wish me to break my neck'?

The clues had been in their letters all along, in a mounting crescendo of barbs aimed by Nelson at his stepson. Beginning with constant complaints about Josiah's dilatory letter-writing, the first real inkling that all was not well came a year after they left England when, on 16 January 1794, Nelson wrote announcing that he planned to find Josiah a position outside the navy: 'I think if the Lockharts will get Josiah a good place he has sense enough to give up the sea, although he is already a good seaman.'[25] Nelson's next letter, on 28 February 1794, was more blunt: 'I wish Mr Lockhart could get Josiah a good place on shore I am sure I don't like his going to sea if he can be better provided for, and I am certain Josiah would give up the sea for anything we can wish him to do.'[26] In the event, Josiah remained on the *Agamemnon*, at least for the time being. Meanwhile Fanny tried soothing her husband's mounting frustration, writing on 17 December 1794: 'My child I figure to myself good obedient to you and I hope tells you all the secrets of his heart. If he does you will keep him good. At his time of life much is to be feared, thank you for having a French master. Do make him clean his teeth not cross ways but upwards and downwards.'[27]

However Nelson was becoming increasingly intractable, writing in August 1795 that 'Josiah will be a good officer I have no doubt, but I fear will never be troubled with the graces. He is the same disposition as when an infant. However he has many good points about him.'[28] Unfavourable and invidious comparisons with Nelson's favourite, William Hoste, peppered his letters: 'I am sorry to tell you poor little Hoste has very near broke his leg but it is in a fair way of being very soon well. He was a prize master of a vessel and fell down a scuttle. Josiah is as well as usual.'[29] Finally Nelson turned his venom on both mother *and* stepson, writing in a letter of 23 August 1796: 'You seem to think Josiah is a master of languages. I must say he is the same exactly as when an infant and likes apples and port wine but it will be difficult to make him speak French much more Italian.'[30]

Faced with this mounting onslaught, Fanny may have concluded that her son was falling short in performance of his duties. It would have been natural for her to assume that her husband had her son's best interests at heart, and that it was Josiah – not Nelson, the nation's hero – who was solely at fault. However, this was not the case. Lonely and starved of companionship, Nelson had taken a mistress, Adelaide Correglia, an opera singer who worked out of Leghorn (Livorno), a port on the coast of Italy that was a frequent shore base for the *Agamemnon*. Referred to as Nelson's 'dolly' by one of his fellow captains, Thomas Fremantle, her liaison with Nelson was an open secret and Josiah would surely have known about it. Could perhaps this be why, in his bewilderment about how to handle such a sensitive topic with his mother, he no longer wrote home? Maybe this also explains Josiah's deteriorating conduct.

Wherever fault lay, it was only a matter of time before the tension between Nelson and Josiah boiled over. In December 1796 Nelson was briefly in Gibraltar, taking part in the planned withdrawal of the British from the Mediterranean.

He was leaving the *Agamemnon*, which was to return to England, and transferring to a frigate, *La Minerve*, for 'an arduous and most important mission'. Josiah, Nelson reported, 'stays by choice in the *Captain*'.[31]

News of their parting distressed Fanny, who wrote pleading, 'I long to hear Josiah is with you.'[32] Nelson and Josiah were briefly reunited for the Battle of Cape St Vincent, but soon after it was Nelson who decided to send 'Josiah with Captain Berry who wished to have him and he will learn more with him than he could wish with me and he must be broke of being at my elbow. I assure you I love him and I am confident it's reciprocal, His understanding is manly and his heart is as good as we can wish, but the same shyness is still visible it is his nature and cannot be altered but how much better than if he was forward.'[33]

Doubtless to assuage his conscience, Nelson set about impressing Fanny with his efforts to secure promotion for Josiah and, not satisfied with being able to tell her that 'Josiah is a lieutenant',[34] pressed for further promotion on Josiah's behalf. Four months later he was able to report that St Vincent 'has made Josiah master and commander'.[35] This was patronage above and beyond the call of familial duty: Nelson had done right by his wife and stepson. Yet Fanny was still trying to come to terms with the news of Josiah's enforced move to Captain Berry's ship. With strained fortitude, she wrote to her husband that 'I have never shed a tear on Josiah's account but when I have known he was not with you. You are the best judge. Capt Berry is a gentlemanly man his character is quite established ... I think you have paid him a very handsome compliment.'[36]

By now she clearly realized that matters were not as she would wish them to be. When news came direct from Captain Berry telling her that all was well between Josiah and Nelson and 'that he is good', sensing with a woman's instinct that all was not as it seemed, Fanny nervously wrote: 'I hope it is all truth for therein consists much of my happiness.'[37] Even the news of Josiah's promotions did not quell her anxieties: knowing what Nelson thought of her son, Fanny again wrote anxiously, 'I thank you for my dear Josiah's promotion, my love to him, he shall soon hear from me. I hope you are right in regard to his further promotion. I trust he will do you credit.'[38]

Following the Battle of Tenerife, Nelson was back in England convalescing from the loss of his right arm. What transpired between Fanny and Nelson in the six months that he was home is unknown, but, from the tone of the letters once Nelson returned to sea in March 1798, Fanny must have realized that something irretrievable had broken down between her husband and her son. Loyalty to her hero, to the nation's hero, dictated that her husband was faultless. Letter after letter to Nelson still yearned to 'hear your opinion of Josiah'.[39] Desperate for good news, she latched on to a Mr Pearson who had seen somebody 'from Lord St Vincent's fleet, he says they all speak well of Josiah. I hope its true'.[40] But it wasn't true. Captain Berry had lied to her. Now, it seems, the whole fleet was lying. It had to have been because at that precise moment Josiah was being dispatched by St Vincent, bringing with him the letter that found Nelson recovering from his wounds following the Battle of the Nile. Nelson was merciless as he relayed the news of Josiah's latest ignominy to Fanny, announcing with an air of finality the beginning of the end of Josiah's career at sea: 'Josiah is in the *Bonne Citoyenne*. I see no prospect of his being made post [captain]. I wish he was as great a favourite of Lord St Vincent's as I wish him, but that is not my fault. However, I hope he do well in time. He is young and will not endeavour to make him agreeable for his interest or comfort'.[41]

As bad as this news was for Fanny, yet worse was still to come. She had to stomach in this same letter the announcement that her husband was back in Naples, this time for more than four days, and his announcement that 'I hope one day to have the pleasure of introducing you to Lady Hamilton. She is one of the very best women in this world. She is an honour to her sex… I am in their [the Hamiltons'] house'.[42] As if to rub salt in the wound, the final insult came when Nelson boasted that 'Her ladyship if Josiah was to stay would make something of him and with all his bluntness I am sure he likes Lady Hamilton more than any female. She would fashion him in 6 months in spite of himself. I believe Lady Hamilton intends writing you'.[43]

In later letters Nelson pounded away relentlessly: 'The improvement made in Josiah by Lady Hamilton is wonderful; your obligations and mine are infinite on that score'.[44] Faced with this onslaught, Fanny, a far-off spectator and powerless to do anything, could be forgiven for thinking she was about to lose not just her husband but also her son to the warm embrace of this former strumpet Emma Hamilton.

To make matters worse, desperate to save her marriage Fanny would be moved to choose between husband and son, and chose her husband. Nelson had begun flaunting under his stepson's nose the twists and turns of his never-ending tryst with Emma Hamilton. Josiah's conduct deteriorated. He disgraced himself at a party thrown by the Hamiltons at the Palazzo Sessa in Naples in honour of Nelson's 40th birthday in September 1798. In front of 1,700 guests, drunk and incapable, he had to be ushered from the ballroom by two naval officers, and when later challenged on his conduct, according to Captain Troubridge, blamed Nelson: 'I could obtain no promise of any change. The only answer I could procure [from Josiah] was that he knew it would happen, that you had no business to bring him to Sea, that he had told you so often, and that it was all your fault. I again pointed out to him in the strongest language his black ingratitude to you by making use of such speeches; no arguments I could make use of would induce him to alter his language…'[45]

Josiah went from bad to worse: disobeying orders, alienating Britain's Austrian allies 'by seizing of [their] Privateers and breaking her up for fire wood'[46] and finally embroiling himself in a court martial with fellow officers on the *Thalia*, the ship he captained. Patience rapidly running out, in January 1799 Nelson loosed off a warning shot at Fanny: 'I wish I could say much to your and my satisfaction about Josiah but I am sorry to say and with real grief, that he has nothing good about him, he must sooner or later be broke, but I am sure neither you or I can help it, I have done with the subject it is an ungrateful one.'[47]

In March 1800, in one of the last letters she dared send her husband, Fanny tried desperately pleading that 'I can with safety put my hand on my heart and say it has been my study to please and make you happy, and I still flatter myself we shall meet before very long. I feel sensibly all your kindnesses to my dear son, and I hope he will add much to your comfort.'[48] But that was not to be. Still, when the final Letter of Dismissal came, Fanny took the line of least resistance; she decided her husband was right, and that it was all Josiah's fault. With that decision came a long estrangement between mother and son. As for Josiah's career in the navy, it was finished.

12

LAND AHOY

From its inception in 1799, the *Naval Chronicle* carried a monthly record of routine warship activities through Britain's main naval ports. 'Wind S.E. Sleet and Rain,'[1] one Plymouth report read. This weather report was followed by ship movements: 'Arrived the *Spider* schooner, and *Telegraph*, 16 guns. Lieutenant Corsellis, from Torbay. Also *L'Aventure* privateer of 14 guns and 42 men, of St Maloes, captured by the *Aristocrat* lugger, off the Seven Islands, after a long chase. Sailed the *Fury*, 18 guns, Captain Curry, with a fleet, to the eastwards.'[2] There was nothing extraordinary in this report, other than its date: 'Jan. 1, 1800.'[3] The night before, the rest of Britain may have been celebrating the arrival of the new century, but for the *Spider*, *Telegraph* and many other of the navy's fighting ships still at sea, it was business as usual and any New Year festivities would have been a muted affair, signalled with an extra measure of grog all round and maybe, weather permitting, some theatricals. As for the crew of the *Fury* heading out to sea on New Year's Day, Captain Curry had kept the *Fury* in port overnight so that the men could celebrate in the manner every young tar craved: ashore, in a nearby tavern.

Britain was entering the eighth year of the Wars and there still seemed no end in sight. Peace and a return to the bosom of the family would have to wait. Meanwhile the officers and men of Britain's fighting navy must make do with the next best thing: occasional snatches of shore leave, a privilege fraught with complications. Arriving in port was the moment when a captain's leadership qualities were put to the test: grant his men shore leave and they might never return; deny it to them and they might jump ship or, worse, mutiny, as William Parker had witnessed on the *Orion* in 1794. To combat the problem of men deserting, captains, especially those serving on the West Indies station, devised an arsenal of *ruses de guerre*, including, in Jamaica, enlisting the help of:

> ...a shark of great magnitude, in Port Royal, that swam round the shipping in that port at noon each day, receiving from the men the offal of their dinner, invariably taken at that time. As this shark was a complete check on desertion, the officers would not allow it to be fired at, or in any way molested. In consequence, it regularly at noon might be seen, its fin above water, rapidly making its way to the shipping. He was named Port Royal Lion, and quite domesticated among the mariners that frequented that port.[4]

Needless to say, young gentlemen required no 'Port Royal Lion' to keep them corralled on board ship. As future officers they were to be trusted, therefore subject only to standing orders, and were routinely allowed ashore for brief periods – anything from an evening to a long weekend – when a ship was in port. On foreign stations, shore leave was an opportunity for sightseeing by the youngsters. As a 12-year-old captain's servant, William Hoste's first foreign port was Cadiz and, on 15 June 1793, excited at the prospect of going ashore, he quickly dashed off a letter to 'my dear sister'[5] boasting that 'I expect to go on shore either to-day or to-morrow. There is to be a Bullfight today at Cadiz but the wind blows so fresh that I am afraid I shall not be able to get ashore.'[6] Curiously, given how excited William was at the prospect of this event, there was no follow-up letter saying whether he attended the bullfight, but Nelson's letter of 23 June to Fanny describing the bullfight referred to 'we English':

> A bull feast (for which the Spaniards are famous and for their dexterity in attacking and killing of which the ladies choose their husbands) was exhibited in which we English had certainly to regret the want of humanity in the Dons and Donnas. We had what is called a fine feast for 5 horses were killed and 2 men very much hurt. Had they been killed it would have been quite complete. We felt for the bulls and horses and I own it would not have displeased me to have had some of the Dons tossed by the enraged animal. How women can even sit much more applaud such sights is astonishing. It even turned us sick, and we could hardly sit it out. The dead mangled horses with their entrails...[7]

Taking his cue from Nelson's evident disgust at this 'fine feast', William may have decided that, on reflection, this was not an event worth bragging about to his 'dear sister'. No such qualms on William's next stop, 'four days' in Naples, where 'in so short a time, half the curiosities of the place we could not see.'[8] William regaled his family with the full Baedeker treatment:

> Mount Vesuvius, about six miles from Naples, we have beheld in all its glory, for now its irruptions are most splendid; the lava spreading from the top at a great distance, and rolling down the mountain in long streaks of fire. Captain Nelson was so kind as to present me with two orders of admission to the king's museum, and the ruins of Herculaneum, which were well worth seeing; but it was a mortifying circumstance to us, that our conductors could not speak either English or French; therefore our curiosity was more excited than gratified... The city of Naples is large, but the houses are very irregular; they have some fine buildings, the king's palace and public buildings.[9]

The city and especially its royal court had a notorious reputation so, relieved as William's parents would have been reading about his excursion to Herculaneum, they would have had mixed feelings when their son told them that 'the King of Naples intended to honour us with a visit on board'.[10] Concern would then have turned to relief when 'the day was fixed, and we were all prepared for his reception, but some unexpected business prevented his coming, which was a disappointment to us'.[11] Panic might have set in when William mentioned meeting Lady Hamilton; so the rumour mill ran, this was a woman whose virtue had already been passed around the great houses of England, and now here she was in Naples, and shaking hands with their poor, innocent, sweet William. Still, surely he couldn't have come to any harm. He was in Naples 'only four days' and, hopefully, that would be the last time he would visit the city.

Moreover, at least Naples was a friendly port. Attempting to take shore leave in enemy territory presented a quite different set of risks as two young gentlemen discovered at Bastia on Corsica in April 1796 when:

> ...we came to an anchor in a bay within the town and found the *Blanch* frigate laying there. At this time the Corsekons were verry troublesome to the English... Our first leut't and a midshipman went with there [*sic*] fusees into the next field to shoot birds.

The Cosecans ware laying in ambush in sight of us on board. One Cossican came to them and took both their guns from them, and showing them the men that ware laying ready with their rifels to fire at them if they resisted and then walked off with there guns and left to come on b'd empty handed.[12]

Young gentlemen employed in the Channel Fleet had no such problems when taking shore leave. Back in home port, Prince William Henry had been able to visit 'Farmer Lilington where I drank some milk',[13] and the only 'hazard' William Dillon encountered on special leave in July 1794 shortly after returning home from the Battle of the Glorious First of June was the adulation of the London crowds, occasioned by his father 'insisting upon my appearing everywhere in uniform. I could not move in the streets without being cheered, and many persons came and shook me by the hand.'[14]

Another young midshipman stationed with the Channel Fleet in the early years of the Wars was Charles Austen, fresh from the Portsmouth Naval Academy. Apart from a succession of unremarkable actions along the Irish and Dutch coasts, including the one that earned him promotion to lieutenant in 1797 and involved driving a Dutch straggler from the Battle of Camperdown into the port of Helvoetsluys, Charles' wars started off quietly. This was apparent from the occasional references to Charles in his sisters' letters to one another. The earliest surviving letter from Jane to Cassandra was one written over 9 and 10 January 1796. Charles had been at sea for two years and was already 15. In it, Jane bemoaned the fact that 'we have heard nothing from Charles for some time'.[15] In a letter that September, she made light of the problem: 'What a fine fellow Charles is, to deceive us into writing two letters to him at Cork! I admire his ingenuity extremely, especially as he is so great a gainer by it.'[16]

With so little to crow about, the sisters concentrated instead on Charles' frequent opportunities for home leave, which, to judge by the letters, were taken up almost exclusively with two pastimes: Charles furthering his career and Charles partying. Promotion was a serious business, yet the way Jane describes Charles' manoeuvres it seems more like a party game. In a letter to Cassandra written over Christmas 1798, Jane immediately sets the tone, as she mocks the whole process: 'The lords of the Admiralty will have enough of our applications at present, for I hear from Charles that he has written to Lord Spencer himself to be removed. I am afraid his Serene Highness will be in a passion, & order some of our heads to be cut off.'[17]

Notwithstanding this remark, Charles evidently knew how to manipulate the system, as two days later Jane could write that, 'Lieutenant Charles John Austen is removed to the *Tamar* frigate – this comes from the Admiral. We cannot find where the *Tamar* is, but I hope we shall now see Charles here at all events.'[18] But nothing was ever straightforward in ship movements or naval promotion and, having got his way, a month later Charles changed his mind about joining this frigate. Jane tried to keep up with the twists and turns, in one letter reporting that 'Charles leaves us tonight… The *Tamar* is in the Downs, and Mr Daysh advises him to join her there directly, as there is no chance of her going to the westward. Charles does not approve of this at all, and will not be much grieved if he should be too late for her before she sails, as he may then hope to get into a better station,'[19] only to write soon after that 'he attempted to go to town last night, and got as far on his road thither as Dean Gate, but both coaches were full, and we had the pleasure of seeing him back again. He will call on Daysh to-morrow to know whether the *Tamar* has sailed or not, and if she is still at the Downs, he will proceed in one of the night coaches to Deal.'[20]

Charles was playing a dangerous game of brinksmanship with the Admiralty, which Jane and Cassandra could not hope to fathom, instead only watch with admiration as his gamble paid off. In the same letter, but from two days on, Jane was finally able to report success in that 'I have just heard from Charles, who is by this time at Deal. He is to be Second Lieutenant, which pleases him very well. The *Endymion* is come into the Down, which pleases him likewise. He expects to be ordered to Sheerness shortly, as the *Tamar* has never been refitted.'[21] After all the contortions, Charles' bluff had paid off and he ended up on a frigate more to his liking.

Given how the only one of Charles' skills to improve during his time at the Portsmouth Naval Academy was, according to his school reports, his dancing, it is unsurprising that his other preoccupation was party-going. This fitted in with the sisters' plans. They wished promotion and advancement on Francis and Charles for the honour that brought to the family. However, they wished on their brothers, above all, the whirl of dances and balls for the immediate benefits that would accrue to them in society as sisters of naval heroes. With Charles stationed in the Channel Fleet, whenever he returned from a cruise through the Channel or along the coast of Ireland, the sisters picked up the news along the grapevine and immediately began planning their social calendar accordingly. On 8 and 9 January 1799, Jane warned Cassandra almost breathlessly that 'Charles is not come yet, but he must come this morning, or he shall never know what I will do to him. The Ball at Kempshott is this Evening, & I have got him an invitation, though I have not been so considerate as to get him a *Partner*. But the cases are different between him and Eliza Bailey, for he is not in a dieing way, & may therefore be equal to getting a partner for himself.'[22]

If, however, he struck out on his own, Jane was quick to disapprove, as in a letter written over 8 and 9 November 1800, when she recounted that 'James [Austen] had not time at Gosport to take any other steps towards seeing Charles, than the very few which conducted him to the door of the assembly room in the Inn, where there happened to be a Ball on the night of their arrival. A likely spot enough for the discovery of a Charles; but I am glad to say that he was not of the party, for it was in general a very ungenteel one, and there was hardly a pretty girl in the room.'[23]

Forming an impression of Charles solely from his sisters' correspondence inevitably does not tell the whole story, especially when he was still 'Naughty Charles'[24] and 'our own particular little brother'.[25] However, the fact remains that, serving in the Channel Fleet, Charles had so far been spared the worst of the Wars and had escaped the personal tragedy that, for instance, afflicted William Hoste following the Battle of Tenerife with the near death of his patron, Nelson, and loss of his great friend John Weatherhead. William wrote to his sister, Kate, in April 1798 already many months after Weatherhead's death, and it is evident that these chastening experiences still deeply affected him, casting a shadow over recent shore leave he knew his sister would want to hear about. A letter to his little sister should be all fun, gaiety, frivolity; yet from the outset the tone was languid and resigned. 'My dear sister,' he wrote, 'I shall sit down and inform you of all the news I can gather together, though the dull life we lead at sea will afford very little.'[26] Briefly rallying, William forced himself to enthuse over a sightseeing expedition when he 'arrived safe at Gibraltar with a convoy. I had been there several times before but never had the curiosity to examine the fortifications till now. We made a party on board, and went entirely round it. The caves were wonderful indeed and well worth seeing.'[27] Unlike his time in Naples, however, his heart was clearly not in it. Though 'General O'Hara gave a ball to the officers of the army and navy whilst we were there,'[28] William wrote, 'I was not of the party, though invited; you know I never cut a figure in dancing when in England and I assure you I have not improved much since, for God knows we have something else to do besides dancing.'[29]

After the triumphs of the Battle of the Nile five months on, William perked up considerably and, finding himself back in Naples after five years, he was soon his old self: ebullient, enthusiastic and – as it was shore leave after a famous victory – determined to celebrate and celebrate in style. Furthermore, aged 18, he could begin thinking of more manly pursuits than bullfights and sightseeing. One of his first letters home after the Battle of the Nile shows him caught up in the intrigue-ridden *demi-monde* of Naples court life.

This letter, dated 10 April 1799, was intended to scotch rumours that had reached England about the navy's wild goings-on in Naples. Peddled by scurrilous French gossipmongers, these rumours were in retaliation for the English press pillorying Napoleon over his very public cuckolding by Josephine while he was in Egypt. 'We arrived in Naples,' ran William's letter, 'about three o'clock in the afternoon of the 1st of September and after getting *pratique* Captain Capel and myself proceeded to Sir William Hamilton's.'[30] Next came the news that William's parents must have been dreading: 'Lady Hamilton (whom I suppose you have heard of) received us very kindly indeed. I had a letter of introduction from Lord Nelson to her, so that I soon became acquainted...'[31]

Of course William's parents had heard of Lady Hamilton. Who hadn't heard of Romsey's infamous 'Belle Dame sans Merci'? They will have remembered their son meeting her briefly in 1793. Now, six years on, Lady Hamilton had reappeared and would surely not waste a moment getting her claws into their innocent William. And as the letter continued, sure enough, 'on our leaving the palace we were met by Lady Hamilton who made us get into her carriage and parade through the streets till dark; she had a bandeau round her head with the words "Nelson and Victory". The populace saw and understood what it meant and "Viva Nelson" resounded through the streets… We went to the Opera and were in the Minister's box with him and his lady.'[32] Still, William wasn't alone. He was with his fellow officer Captain Capel. Not for long, as it turned out. In the very next sentence another bombshell dropped: 'The next day Captain Capel proceeded on his passage to England, so I was left alone. We had been so long a cruise before the action that I was in want of almost everything. Lady Hamilton was good enough to assist me until I was completely fitted out. I lived at Sir William Hamilton's house during my stay, and was entertained by him with the most distinguished attention.'[33] William was now all alone, being kitted out by the painted lady, at her mercy, and living under the same roof as her. What more could befall their son?

Unbeknownst to William's parents, at about the same time Lady Hamilton was writing to Nelson telling him that 'dear little Captain Hoste dines with us in the day, for he will not sleep out of his ship.'[34] The question arises why she was lying, if indeed it was her, not William. Maybe she already had her sights set on Nelson and did not want him suspecting for a moment that he might be second in line behind William. Whatever game she was playing, she seems to have been confident enough of her wiles to bait Nelson, still hovering off shore, with the following sweets about William: 'We Love him dearly. He is a fine, good lad. Sir William is delighted with him, and I say he will be a second Nelson. If he is only half a Nelson, he will be superior to all others.'[35]

As for William's parents back in unworldly Norfolk, they could only read on, somehow hoping William's letter would dispel their worst fears about other wild rumours they had heard. Finally William came to the point: 'a few days after I was surprised by an officer arriving from the palace … he gave me a note from the Queen (but whom I was to consider incog) and a small box with a very handsome diamond ring inclosed in it.'[36]

Whatever his mother's fears regarding Lady Hamilton, they were nothing to compare with this affair of the ring. William's explanation had better be good: 'Such my dear mother is the history of the ring which my father said you were afraid was for private service, but I hope you are convinced now it was out of regard for the English nation.' Knowing his mother, William sensed that this was not explanation enough. So, to deflect attention away from him and the diamond ring, he added the news that the queen also gave 'two hundred guineas for the brig's company and six pipes of wine and two calves for the same purpose'[37] and that, by way of thanks, 'I returned an answer which was not adequate to the occasion, and on her birthday, which happened a few days after, I dressed the Mutine completely in colours, which is reckoned as token of respect.'[38]

There was no point William carping bitterly that: 'such is the immense reward mentioned by the French to the officer who brought the account of the victory.'[39] To back William up, Nelson had written to Fanny on 16 September referring to 'the elegant diamond ring value at least £500',[40] which he said was reward for William bringing the good news from Egypt. Fanny's task was to pass this titbit back to the Hostes. Nonetheless, as far as William's parents were concerned, the French rumourmongers were right: William had caught the eye of none other than Maria Carolina, Queen of the Kingdom of the Two Sicilies, daughter of Empress Maria Theresa of Austria and sister of the executed Queen Marie Antoinette of France. The queen from the most notorious court in Europe had given their son a diamond ring, and that surely could mean only one thing.

As bad as Naples was, Palermo, the twin capital of the Kingdom of the Two Sicilies, was worse. While William was savouring the sweets of Naples, George Parsons was taking advantage of his shore leave to sample 'Palermo – there to receive the incense of refined Italian flattery, incessant balls and feedings, the smiles of beauty, and the witchery of music'.[41] For George and his fellow 14 midshipmen, shore leave was an opportunity to go on the rampage, which they did when they decided to gatecrash a royal ball.

Remembering his time in Palermo, George conjures in his *Reminiscences* an imaginary dialogue of himself and the other midshipmen primping themselves up beforehand:

'Two dirty shirts nearly new, for one clean one,' shouts a midshipman.

'Who will lend a pair of uniform breeches? For mine are worn out by pipe-clay and cleaning,' cries a second reefer. 'John, yours will fit, and you are not on turn for going. Do – there's a good fellow!'

'Excuse me, Jack, for you ruined my number one coat at your last turn-out, by rolling in the gutter, when you received that ugly cut of the stiletto from the cut-throat Italian who calls himself a marquis.'[42]

Bargains struck, foppery suitably indulged, the next problem for the young dandies was the question of transport to the ball, since between them they only had 'a paulo, value fivepence'.[43] They couldn't travel far on the odd paulo, so:

…the leader proposed seizing the first carriage, which he called, putting it into requisition for his majesty's service – viz., *to convey his midshipmen*. A nobleman's splendid vehicle that was standing at his palace door for the purpose of conveying the family to the royal ball, was the first that we encountered, and after a little scuffle in displacing the coachman and footman, we succeeded in lining it, inside and out, with young English midshipmen in training for future Nelsons. This notable exploit created much amazement, and, from their exclamations, displeasure in the minds of our Italian allies, and the upset of another coach, from the careless driving of our leader.'[44]

Arriving at the ball, the 15 midshipmen revelled in the festivities and fireworks. As for George, when 'dancing recommenced … I made some awkward attempts, as partner to the youngest Princess of Castlecicallo, who good-naturedly endeavoured to get me through the Saltarella, but I fancied was glad when she exchanged me for the Prince of Palermo.'[45] The festivities over, in a final flourish the midshipmen ran riot when:

…this splendid entertainment was concluded by some of the wildest of our youngsters attempting to break through his Majesty's foot guards, who refused to give way to their orders. They were instantly charged by the midshipmen with their dress dirks, and broken. One of the savages fired, and shot a fine boy through the thigh, who did well. For this notable and ill-timed feat, Lord Nelson stopped our leave for six months; and many an anathema was showered on us by equally unfortunate contemporaries of the squadron.[46]

Nelson quickly commuted this punishment and the midshipmen's shore leave was only 'stopped till the *capture* of the *Guillaume Tell* again restored it'.[47] The hand of 'Fair Emma'[48] is clearly visible in this reduced punishment: she frequently interceded with Nelson to request leniency, and not just on behalf of midshipmen. According to George, lower-deck sailors also benefited from her influence over Nelson: 'The men when threatened with punishment for misconduct, applied to Lady Hamilton, and her kindness of disposition, and Lord Nelson's known aversion to flogging, generally rendered the appeal successful.' Lady Hamilton 'was much liked by everyone in the fleet, except Captain Nesbit [Nisbet], Lady Nelson's son, and her recommendation was the sure road to promotion.'[49]

George also experienced Lady Hamilton's influence in the matter of his promotion. To judge by his *Reminiscences*, George had had to make his own way in the world and had no natural interest to guide his promotion through the navy. Advancement was slow and his career was stalled at the crucial moment when, in common with vast numbers of sailors, 'on the peace of Amiens taking place I was paid off from the frigate *Batavia*'.[50] The Peace of Amiens, signed in October 1801 and ratified in March 1802, was born of 'financial, political and strategic exhaustion',[51] at least as far as Britain was concerned. People desperately wanted to believe that the peace would be lasting. As a result, much of the fleet was brought back to home ports, ships were laid up and crews paid off. For the French, peace provided Napoleon with a respite in which to consolidate his power base at home and prepare for further foreign conquests.

Yet peace could be a mixed blessing for those in the navy: for crew it meant instant unemployment but a welcome chance to return home to family. For midshipmen with their sights set on the relative, half-pay security of a commission, the key was to have received the necessary 'step-up' *prior* to peace being declared. George Elliot, already a lieutenant, could retire on half pay and happily 'remained on shore till the war broke out again in April or May 1803'.[52] Other young gentlemen, William Parker, William Dillon, William Hoste, even Josiah Nisbet, had gone one stage further by 1802 and made captain or commander. William Hoste went home to Norfolk for a well-deserved rest after ten years without home leave.

Returning from six years in the West Indies, William Parker had other ideas: he went to London. After so long an absence from the seat of power and patronage, the first thoughts of this ambitious young man were not home but his future prospects, which, as he explained to his parents, meant sticking close to his powerful patron, Lord St Vincent, whose 'express wish that I should not quit London prevents me setting off immediately for Staffordshire. I fancy he has something particular in view for me'.[53] While waiting for this 'something particular' from his uncle, William whiled away his spare time going 'three times to the theatre, where Mrs Siddons nearly beguiled me of my tears, in the character of Belvidera, in "Venice Preserved"'.[54] He also 'commenced taking lessons in the violin yesterday, from the 2nd violin player in Drury Lane'.[55] This was not what he had joined the navy for. But his patience was rewarded and, a rarity in peacetime, he was given command of a ship, first the *Alarm*, then, later in the peace, the *Amazon*. William Parker's career was on its way again, and peace would prove little more than a temporary lull in his steady rise to the pinnacle of the service. However there was many a naval officer laid off in peacetime who was 'daily put to his shifts how to get up a dinner'.[56] A career that 'requires years of experience, service, and application to fit him for his duty'[57] could suddenly hit the buffers.

Officers were not the only ones left to shift for themselves come the peace of 1802. The Marine Society was besieged by requests from former Society boys desperate to dredge up interest wherever they could, and the Society was not found wanting. Writing in September 1802, the Society made its case to the Admiralty on behalf of one boy:

> I am requested by the General Court of the Marine Society to acquaint you for the information of the Rt. Hon. The Lords of the Ad. that John Smith sent by this Society 18 September 1797 to HMS *Dromedary* has served as Midshipman and Master's Mate as appears by a number of certificates from the Commanders he served under for the last four years and it appears to the Court that his conduct has been uniformly diligent sober and obedient. They beg their Lordships will please order him to be employed in his Majesty's Navy that he may have an opportunity of Promotion to which he seems by his merit to be entitled.[58]

Despite Britain no longer being on a war footing, the Society was successful in securing promotion for John, which encouraged him to enlist the Society's interest further on his behalf in February 1805, by which time hostilities had resumed and John was back serving at sea. As a result, the following letter was sent to the Admiralty:

> I am ordered by the General Council to state to you that the bearer of this letter, Mr John Smith who was fitted out by the Society about seven years ago and who is master's mate of HMS *Valorous* has passed at the Navy Board for a Lieutenant but unfortunately he is situated much the same as the last young Man you was so good as to interest yourself in his promotion, that of having no Friends. He has requested the Society to use their interest for obtaining a Commission. I therefore convey this request that you will please to use your interest with the Board in such manner as you shall think needful.[59]

John Smith was lucky. He may not have had the patronage that young gentlemen such as George Elliot, William Hoste and William Parker could command, but at least he had the Marine Society he could call on. Not so George Parsons. With no obvious interest available to him, the peace of 1802 caught him in the worst of possible worlds: 'I had been appointed lieutenant by Lord Keith, and served as such during the Egyptian expedition ... and retired, from full pay to nothing.'[60] His problem was that his promotion had been made at sea, but still needed to be confirmed by the Admiralty for it to be effective. Once his commission was confirmed, at least he could retire on half pay. However until then he was only an acting lieutenant, which meant he was still rated as a midshipman, and midshipmen drew no pay once their ships were taken out of service.

On returning to England, George found his worst fears realized: 'the peace promotion had taken place, and there was no hope for me.'[61] If he were not careful he could end up like the midshipman who lamented: 'I have no trade; I have got my trade for to chuse: I will go to St James' Park gate, and there I'll set blacking of shoes.'[62] Without any natural patronage to fall back on within his family, George decided to cast around for someone in the service to put in a good word for him. So it was that, 'as a last resource and "forlorn hope", I went to Lord Nelson's seat, at Merton, and fortunately gained admission to his lordship, through his well-known and favourite servant, Tom Allen, who approached his study door under some apprehension of the nature of our reception.'[63] Tom Allen was right to be apprehensive: George was about to get a rude lesson in the vagaries of patronage: 'The voice of Lord Nelson, denoting vexation, reprimanded my friend, and declared, most truly, that he was pestered to death by young gentlemen, his former shipmates.'[64] Mercifully George's anguish was brief. Interest appeared in the nick of time in the person of 'Fair Emma' who appeared and declared that 'His Lordship must serve me' and must 'set aside his scruples of asking a favour of the first Admiralty Lord, by dictating a strong certificate, which, under her direction, he wrote.'[65]

George ended up lucky. However, among the next generation of young gentlemen eagerly trying to thrust their way up through the service, there were those who had made midshipmen but, with or without patronage, had no prospect of making that next vital step to lieutenant when peace came in 1802. They were simply too young to have served their time or, cruelly in the case of one young gentleman, William Guido Anderson, were only just too young. For him, every day he could serve at sea counted. Son of a marine painter, and a budding artist in his own right, he had joined the navy in 1798 and was ordered to the West Indies in January 1802, despite the fact that the preliminaries of peace had already been signed.

William should not have been going to the West Indies. He had been badly wounded at the Battle of Copenhagen in April 1801. The injuries he described in the letter he wrote to his parents after that battle must have put them in fear for his life: '...I can now seize my pen and in spite of all the misfortunes and dimness which blindness, sickness, lameness or disability of any kind can throw in my way I resolve to write you as long a letter as at last I am able....'[66] William was not exaggerating about his injuries. He had also 'received a violent Blow upon the left knee by a piece of the gun that blew me up which [caused] a bad contusion, but by the help of crutches am able to walk about a little'.[67] The earlier exhortations from his father to 'sketch the whole Fleet every day as Van de Velde used to do'[68] would have to wait.

William should have been invalided home when 'the Captain wished me to go because I was so long ill'.[69] However, William had other ideas. He was adamant that he 'did not wish to go home in the Hospital Ship as we all expected to be ordered home shortly and that I should only be losing my time'.[70] William had a willing accomplice in this travesty, the 'Physician of the Fleet [who] told the Surgeon that he was glad to see that there were young Men that wished to persevere and get on in the Service'.[71] These were famous last words indeed. William's determination to accrue as much time at sea was commendable but foolhardy. Remaining on board the *Bellona* meant he followed where it went, which, as it turned out, was the disease-ridden West Indies. Somehow he survived his six months there. For others out there at the same time, however, it was, as William noted, their graveyard: 'We just left that unhealthy country in good time. The people on shore were dying like rotten sheep. It would really shock you to walk over the Burial Ground; the place for miles is covered with dead bodies.'[72] The *Bellona* finally reached home port, and later in the same letter William could announce with relief, 'we expect to be paid off in the course of a few days.'[73] Sadly, peace and home brought little succour. The injuries he suffered at the Battle of Copenhagen had never properly healed in the unhealthy climate of the West Indies and he died at home in early 1803.

Another young midshipman who had also fought at the Battle of Copenhagen was John Franklin. Unlike William Anderson he was unscathed, but remembered how he 'saw a prodigious number of the slain at the bottom of the remarkably clear water in that harbour – men who had perished on both sides in that most sanguinary action'.[74] John was from the same generation as William Anderson but had very different ideas how best to advance his career as peace loomed in 1802.

He had first gone to sea in 1800 at the age of 14. The decision was very much John's own and 'it was not either youthful whim of moment, or the attractive uniforms, or the hopes of getting rid of school that drew me to it. No! I pictured to mind both the hardships and pleasures of the Sailor's life (even to the extreme) before it was ever told to me… My mind was then so steadfastly bent on going to sea, that to settle to business would merely be impossible'.[75] However, his idea of a career at sea was to go exploring. His childhood hero was his uncle, Matthew Flinders, and listening to his earlier adventures in the South Seas had given John wanderlust. With his uncle having no immediate plans for a voyage of exploration, John, undaunted, joined the navy instead. Through interest, he gained a place on the 64-gun *Polyphemus*, only to hear, just as the *Polyphemus* was about to set off from Yarmouth Roads for the Baltic in January 1801, that 'Lieut Flinders [is] to be a commander, and is appointed to the *Investigator* (late *Xenophon*), now fitting for a Voyage of Discovery'.[76] Before the *Polyphemus* departed, John dashed off a letter begging his parents that 'if we do return before the *Investigator* sails, I shall thank you to use your interest for me to go'.[77] He could only hope and pray he returned from the Baltic in time.

John was following in a long tradition of young gentlemen who had gone to sea on voyages of discovery, youngsters like Alexander Hood whose 'first voyage [aged 14] was with that distinguished officer Captain James Cook, whom he accompanied in the *Endeavour* during the voyage of discovery, which commenced in the year 1772, and returned to England with that celebrated navigator in 1775'.[78] Captain Cook was the beacon light for a whole generation of young gentlemen. On his third and fatal voyage, which started in 1776, Captain Cook had, in echoes of Drake's voyage of circumnavigation, 'several young men amongst my officers who, under my direction, could be usefully employed in constructing charts, in taking views of the coasts and headlands near which we should pass, and in drawing plans of bays and harbours in which we should anchor'.[79]

Among the young gentlemen on board the *Resolution* were three Academites, James Trevenen, James Ward and William Charlton. For James Trevenen, the emotion uppermost in his mind as he anticipated that voyage with Captain Cook was 'what pleasure is seeing foreign countries and exploring new worlds'.[80] On the sister ship, *Discovery*, were a number of midshipmen including 13-year-old Edward Riou and Alexander Home, the latter recounting how:

> When we were in New Zealand, Neddy Rhio, one of my messmates had got hold of a New Zealand dog, as savage a devil as the savages from whom he had got it, and this same dog he intended to bring home to present to the Marchioness of Townend. But one day, when Neddy was on shore on duty, a court martial was held on the dog, and it was agreed [unanimously] that, as the dog was of cannibal origin and was completely cannibal itself, having bit every one of us, and shewn every inclination to eat us alive if he could, that he should be doomed to death, and eat in his turn, we being short of provisions at the time. The sentence was immediately executed, the dog cooked, dressed, and eat, for we were so confoundedly hungry.[81]

These were the 'hardships and pleasures of the Sailor's life' that lay ahead for John Franklin joining his uncle the moment he returned from the Baltic. On 19 July 1801 the *Naval Chronicle* announced in its Portsmouth port report, 'Sailed… *Investigator*, of 14 guns, Captain Flinders, on a voyage of discoveries round the world'.[82] The preliminaries of peace were announced on 1 October 1801, but by then the *Investigator* was long gone and with it 'two young gentlemen more than allowed'.[83] John had caught up with the *Investigator* and would soon be writing from the other end of the world that 'Captain Flinders has instructed me in different points of navigation, which tends to prepare me for promotion; he also when at sea prevents me from keeping time-watch purposely to attend him in working his Time-pieces, Lunars etc.'[84] Flinders came to count heavily on John: the problem was Flinders' brother, Samuel, 'who was much older than Franklin; he too was a midshipman. He was not without talent, but totally without industry or capability of applying it, so he made John Franklin do all the work which he was expected to in making observations etc. All these matters were regularly and most methodically carried on by Franklin, for which Samuel Flinders had the credit, and J. Franklin all the advantages.'[85]

The *Investigator* began leaking from the moment it hit the open sea. After running repairs in Madeira, False Bay at the southern end of Africa, and again on reaching Australia in May 1802, first at Port Jackson, then in the Gulf of Carpentaria, Matthew finally decided that the leaks in the *Investigator*'s hull were 'quite alarming'.[86] In addition, despite adhering to Captain Cook's model dietary regimen, sailors starting dying of scurvy. In June 1803, Matthew admitted defeat and, returning to Port Jackson, condemned the *Investigator*. Transferring as passengers to the *Porpoise*, he, John and the other officers of the *Investigator* prepared to wend their way home. In its periodic articles, entitled *Correct Relation of Shipwrecks*, the *Naval Chronicle* took up the story: 'The *Porpoise* sailed from Port Jackson about the 10th of August 1803, having under her convoy the Merchantmen *Cato* and *Bridgewater*, bound to Batavia. The intended track was through Forrest's Straights [*sic*], between the coast of New Holland and New Guinea, and so getting into the Indian seas, to follow the usual track of the Indiamen, instead of the circuitous route by Cape Horn.'[87]

Passing through the Forrest's [Torres] Strait, disaster struck. The journal of the *Cato* took up the story from there:

> On August 18, 1803, at a quarter past one, saw a sandbank, bearing S.W. about three leagues … struck the reef aft at a quarter before ten pm about a cable's length from the *Porpoise*, who had been ashore for some time … at 9 ½ am she [*Bridgewater*] tacked and stood to the Southward again, and we never saw her more… At two o'clock, on the 19th, we all got away from the Ship, but unfortunately three Seamen, Robert Kay, William Tindall, and George Philliskirk, were lost in the surf. The rest landed in safety, but naked, and joined the Crew of the *Porpoise* upon a sand bank, about 250 yards long and 100 yards broad…[88]

Matthew Flinders in his *A Voyage to Terra Australis*, published in 1814, went into more dramatic detail describing the scramble to get the crew of both the *Cato* and the *Porpoise* safe to where:

> …a number of seabirds eggs scattered over the bank showed that it was above high-water mark, and I sent the gig back with this intelligence to Lieutenant Fowler. Seeing that the *Bridgewater* did not approach, he ordered the boat to lie opposite to the *Cato*;

and Captain Park and his men, throwing themselves into the water with any pieces of spar or plank they could find, swam to her through the breakers; and were then taken to the *Porpoise* where they received food and some clothing. Several were bruised against the coral rocks, and three young lads were drowned. One of these poor boys, who, in the three or four voyages he had made to sea, had been each time shipwrecked, had bewailed himself through the night as the persecuted Jonas who carried misfortune wherever he went. He launched himself upon a broken spar with his captain; but having lost his hold in the breakers, was not seen afterwards.[89]

Matthew Flinders immediately began planning how the survivors might return to civilization. While he and a scratch-crew headed back to Port Jackson, some 94 men and boys, John Franklin included, spent the next two months enduring their own special 'shore leave' on this sandbank whose 'general elevation [was] three or four feet above the common level of high water. It consists of sand and pieces of coral, thrown up by the waves and eddy tides on a patch of reef five or six miles in circuit.'[90]

Meanwhile, on 18 August, the day of the shipwreck, far away across the other side of the world, in his cabin on board *Victory* at the head of the Mediterranean fleet blockading the port of Toulon, Admiral Nelson was writing to Sir Evan Nepean, secretary of the Admiralty, to advise him that 'You will be pleased to acquaint the Lords Commissioners of the Admiralty, that Rear-Admiral Campbell joined me yesterday off this place in his Majesty's Ship *Canopus*, and that I have received by him their Lordships' printed orders.'[91] Britain had already been at war three months when John Franklin fetched up on the sandbank opposite what Matthew Flinders called 'Wreck Reef'.[92] War had been declared on France on 16 May 1803. Nelson had hoisted his flag on the *Victory* on 18 May. The slow countdown to Trafalgar and Westminster Abbey had begun.

TRAFALGAR

According to the *Naval Chronicle* for 1811:

> …the following letter was sent from Mr Bulkely [*sic*], midshipman of the *Victory*, who was wounded in the action off Trafalgar, on 21st of October 1805, in whose arms Lord Nelson died, in answer to one from Admiral (then Captain) Bertie, asking him for a part of the lock of hair, which he accordingly sent, and which Admiral Bertie has now in his possession:
> 'Dear Sir,
> …I regret extremely not to be able to send as much hair as I could wish, owing to my having given away a greater part of it; but I hope you will find sufficient for a ring… His Lordship's body was this day shifted into spirits of wine, and a coffin, and the surgeon extracted the ball which had lodged in the spine … his body is complete but his countenance is entirely altered, nor could I perceive any remaining feature that could call him to my recollection, but his upper lip.'[1]

After the Battle of the Glorious First of June, it was an unknown 'blushing boy' attending Earl Howe ahead of the battle. Following the Battle of the Nile, it was the turn of the French boy hero, Cassa Bianca, drowned when the *L'Orient* sank. Now, with the Battle of Trafalgar, it would be Midshipman Bulkeley recorded lifting his 'trophy' from the nation's hero. After each major battle it seems that, fulfilling its mission to record the whole history of the Wars, the *Naval Chronicle* sought out some young sailor whose exploits it could immortalize.

Boy sailors seemingly were everywhere, ready to fight and die for King and Country, and never more so than in the two years leading up to 21 October 1805 and Trafalgar. This would be the Great Battle, a confrontation that was in the planning the moment William Pitt decided peace with France was impossible so long as Napoleon was in power.

When hostilities broke out in 1793, it was France that declared war on Britain. Ten years on, after the brief lull orchestrated by the Peace of Amiens, significantly it was Britain, turned furious aggressor, that declared war on France, on 18 May. In 1793 it was the king, George III, fired up with moral outrage at the travesty that was the execution of a fellow royal, King Louis XVI, who led the call to arms. Parliament trailed behind, ritually intoning its loyal addresses. In May 1803, by contrast, the voice of the king was barely audible over the deafening sound of Parliament, and the ship of state preparing to weigh anchor in the final thrust for victory. Strike hard and strike now was the rallying call. Yet as loudly as Parliament thundered, the voices of millenarianism roared even louder, reaching a crescendo across the country as the people of Britain demanded nothing less than a war of annihilation.

But how to administer the scything death blow? Britain's war machine did not yet reach into the heartland of Europe. Any land campaign was still dependent on fickle, pusillanimous, weak-kneed allies such as Austria, Prussia, even distant Russia, any of whose appearance on the field of battle was surely guarantee of yet another French victory. So the mantle of massacre must devolve to Britain's navy, and the country's fighting mariners were more than ready to ride to the rescue. Although the navy had been stood down during the brief peace, it still had over 67,000 sailors borne on warships around the globe.

From seaport to seaport, the recruiting machinery swung into action, helped, of course, by the obligatory Press Gangs as 'gentle' reminders to those who might have mislaid their patriotic duty. By December 1803 the fleet of first- to sixth-rate warships back in service numbered 410, and come 1804 the number of men borne on ships was back nudging 100,000 and rapidly closing on its pre-peace peak strength of 130,000.

The Marine Society was, much as in 1793, called on once again to do its bit, though this time the call to arms came well in advance of the declaration of war. By 10 January 1803 the Society was responding to a discreet request from the

Admiralty for boys, noting: 'I am favoured with yours requesting to know if the Society have any boys they wish to dispose of; there is between fifty and sixty boys on Board the Ship.'[2]

Nevertheless, the Society's recruitment drive did not really kick into gear until after the formal declaration of hostilities. In the quarter ended 21 April 1803, the Society's *Book of Boys Received and Boys Discharged* logged 95 boys clothed for the sea service, of which 53 were in the 'King's Service'[3] and 42 in the merchant service. By contrast, the corresponding figures for the quarter ending 21 July were 552 in aggregate, of which 479 went 'in the King's Service' and 11 only into the merchant service. A further 61 remained on board the Society's ship ready for future delivery. One boy was listed as 'run'. After this brief flurry of activity, discharges in the next quarter tailed off and only 127 were sent to the 'King's Service'. However, the number of those marked as 'run' surged to 14, evidence maybe that patriotism was not universally distributed.

The first boy to be discharged into the King's Service from the Marine Society ship on the day war was declared was Stephen Kase, Number 4194, aged 14, described as '4ft 4in.' with 'brown hair, amber eyes, fresh, fair, jolly' but 'cannot read'.[4] He had been on the Society's ship since 24 April and was sent as a servant to Sir James Saumarez of the *Zealand*.

In the *Register of Boys sent as Servants to Officers*,[5] which logged boys passing through the Society merely to be clothed and dispatched immediately to the King's Service, the first boy to be sent after the declaration of war was John Ivey, Number 13108, aged 13, marked down as 4ft 1in. and described with the familiar acronyms 'p r w'.

Many Society boys ended up on ships bound for the Channel Fleet and eventually the Great Battle. These included nine boys sent to the *Bellerophon* on 29 October 1804 and entered in the Society's books as follows:

Name	Age	Stature	Reads: r, Writes: w, S.pox: p
Thomas Larnder	13	4ft 2in	p r
Richard Petty	14	4ft 5in	p r
James Petty	13	4ft 4in	p
Henry Smith	13	4ft 4in	p r w
James Storey	18	5ft	p

William Russell	15	4ft 9in	p r
Philip Jacobs	15	4ft 7in	p r w
George Neale	16	4ft 9in	p
George Nash	16	4ft 7in	p

Under the column headed 'Parish connections and where living', George Neale was listed as 'destitute' but the remaining boys were from London. Under the column 'How he was employed', two had already been to sea, two came directly from school and the remainder had variously worked as 'errand boy', in the 'fields', to the 'plough' or as 'turn wheel'.

The Society seemed determined to keep better track of its boys than in the past, and discharging boys to the King's Service was no longer considered the end of the Society's responsibilities, as evidenced by a letter sent in April 1804 to the 'Captain of the Ardent, Captain Winthrop, Cork or elsewhere'.[6] The background to this letter was that four Society boys had gone missing and Captain Winthrop was the last person known to have received the boys. In their letter of 7 April, the Society explained why it was making their disappearance Captain Winthrop's problem:

> This Society sent 12 boys to Portsmouth on 7th June last… I am also informed that 8 of them were discharged from the *Endymion* 16th June last to HMS *Ardent* and only four of them appear on the *Ardent*'s books, namely William Chapel or Chapman, R.Town, J. Lascoleet alias Gleak, R. Endersby alias Andersby, the remaining four whose Names are undermentioned do not appear on the *Ardent*'s Books. I am ordered by the Committee to make enquiry whether the under Boys did join the *Ardent* as stated in the *Endymion*'s Books and if so whether they are now on Board or to what ship they have been sent and to request your reply as soon as convenient. The Friends of the Boys being anxious to know where they are.[7]

All these were new boys to the war effort. As for the 'veteran' young gentlemen, some, like William Parker, were already at sea, in his case commanding the frigate *Amazon*. Others drifted back to sea slowly as suitable commands became available. George Elliot was given a new command almost as soon as war broke out in May 1803, in his case on the *Termagant*. Francis Austen did not have long to wait either and was appointed captain of the *Canopus*, but William Hoste had to wait

Master Blockhead seeking the Bubble Reputation. (National Maritime Museum, Greenwich, London)

Johnny Newcome cobbed: 'And once again, like eagle spread, across the table he was laid.' (The Adventures of Johnny Newcome in the Navy)

Johnny Newcome turning in and out again: 'And out he rolled, midst peals of laughter, with bed and bed-cloaths rolling after.' (The Adventures of Johnny Newcome in the Navy)

Johnny Newcome sent to hear the dog-fish bark: 'They sent him that very night as soon as ever it was dark to hear the little dog-fish bark.' (The Adventures of Johnny Newcome in the Navy)

Johnny Newcome succumbing to sea-sickness: 'Each lurch the staggering frigate gave he thought must bring him to his grave.' (The Adventures of Johnny Newcome in the Navy)

Midshipman Blockhead mastheaded – or enjoying the fresh air for the 304th time. (National Maritime Museum, Greenwich, London)

The Point of Honour by George Cruickshank, 1825. The whole ship's company, youngsters included, were on deck to witness a flogging at sea. (National Maritime Museum, London)

Battle of the Nile: Destruction of L'Orient, 1 August 1798. According to one eye-witness 'when she blew up the firing ceased on all sides, for I believe fully half and hour.' (National Maritime Museum, Greenwich, London)

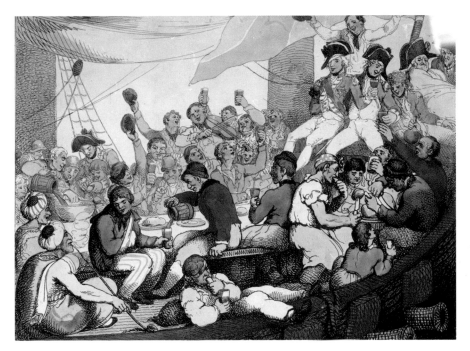

Admiral Nelson recreating with his brave tars after the Battle of the Nile, 1798. (National Maritime Museum, Greenwich, London)

Nelson, his officers, men and boys attending a service of thanksgiving aboard the Vanguard *after the Battle of the Nile, 1798. (The Nelson Museum, Monmouth)*

An illustrated letter from William Guido Anderson serving as a midshipman on the Bellona *in 1800 to his father, the marine artist William Anderson. (National Maritime Museum, Greenwich, London)*

The death of Admiral Nelson: Nelson was struck by a musket shot fired from the Redoubtable *around 1.30pm. In this idealised image he is shown dying on deck surrounded by, amongst others, midshipmen Collinwood, Roberts, Buckley, Rivers, Lancaster, and two signal midshipmen, Robins and Randal. (Bridgeman Art Library)*

Boarding and taking the American ship Chesapeake by the officers and crew of the Shannon, commanded by Captain Broke, June 1813. (National Maritime Museum, Greenwich, London)

Napoleon on board the Bellerophon *watching the receding French coast. (Copyright © Tate, London, 2009)*

The Bellerophon *at anchor in Torbay, 24 July 1815. (National Maritime Museum, Greenwich, London)*

until November 1804 before he secured an appointment to command the frigate *Eurydice*. As for John Franklin, finally in August 1804 he returned home from his enforced 'shore leave' on a sandbank; he would hardly have time to draw breath before returning to active duty as signal-midshipman, joining Marine Society boys Thomas Larnder et al. on the *Bellerophon*. Of these 'veterans', John Franklin was alone in making it to the Great Battle; both William Hoste and Francis Austen expected to, only for their ships to be sent away on important missions just before the battle. Both rued in later correspondence that they were not *there*, 'not to have been in it, is enough to make one mad',[8] to repeat the words of William Hoste.

Among the new generation of young gentlemen eager to go to sea after war broke out again in 1803, 13-year-old Norwich Duff would join his father, George Duff, ahead of the Great Battle. Recently appointed captain of the 74-gun ship-of-the-line *Mars* and known affectionately in the navy as 'Worthy Duff', George came from a naval family and, 'as a boy he was sprightly, active and enterprising; and so bent towards the navy, that seeing his father was averse from his going to sea, he endeavoured, when about nine years of age, to escape by concealing himself on board a small merchant ship, in which he actually sailed to a neighbouring port'.[9] His father finally relented and in 1777 Worthy Duff, aged 13, joined his great-uncle's ship. Worthy Duff's association with the *Mars* only dated back to April 1804, when, in its 'Promotions and Appointments' section, the *Naval Chronicle* laconically announced 'Duff to the *Mars*'.[10] Just as Nelson had done with his Norfolk lads in the *Agamemnon* in 1793, Worthy Duff immediately set about making the *Mars* his own, surrounding himself with as many officers and crew from his native Scotland as possible.

He was not the only Scot to forge a home from home on board ship. In 1798 Thomas, then Lieutenant, later Admiral Lord Cochrane, served on the *Barfleur*, nicknamed the 'Stinking Scotch ship'[11] in part because 'we purchased and killed bullocks on board the *Barfleur*, for the use of the whole squadron [and] raw hides, being valuable, could be stowed away in her hold in empty beef-casks, as especial perquisites to certain persons connected with the flag-ship; a natural result being, that, as the fleshy parts of the hides decomposed, putrid liquor oozed out of the casks and rendered the hold of the vessel so intolerable'.[12]

Wherever captains hailed from around Britain, they understood the virtues of natural loyalty, the ties that bind, but in Worthy Duff's case, he took this to the extreme, gathering round him a veritable Clan Duff. Including himself, there were no fewer than five of his namesakes on board the *Mars* at the Great Battle: a cousin, 20-year-old Alexander Duff, joined in August 1804, and a year on Worthy Duff's son, Norwich, aged 12, and Alexander Duff's brother, Thomas, aged 14. There was also the son of Sergeant William Duff, a very distant relative, who was already in the navy, but, as he was in the wrong ship according to his father, Worthy Duff took up the boy's case and arranged his transfer to the *Mars*. Given this evident partiality and Worthy's dismal experience of the Marine Society sending him seven boys, six of whom were destitute, when he was crewing up the *Nemesis* in 1793, it is unsurprising that there is no record of the *Mars* calling on the Society to supply boys ahead of the Great Battle. No longer a junior captain, Worthy knew where to find the best officers and men.

For all the millenarian forces swirling around Britain as it went back to war in 1803, there are no traces of the apocalyptic emotions in the correspondence between Worthy and his wife Sophia during the 17 months starting from the moment he went on board the *Mars* in May 1804 through to the day of the Great Battle. The letters are instead a picture of calm and normality. The first one written from the *Mars*, on 25 May 1804, as Worthy waits to set sail from Plymouth Docks, tells his wife how 'I am glad to find our little George is better, and that you have got into your own house. Many happy days I hope we shall enjoy in it together, and I trust the prospect is not very distant.'[13]

Seventeen months on and 30 letters later, his final words, written just before the first shots of the Great Battle were unleashed at midday on 21 October, are again only of his family. He hurries to tell his wife that 'I have just time to tell you we are going into action with the combined fleet. I hope and trust in God that we shall all behave as becomes us, and that I may yet have the happiness of taking my beloved wife and children in my arms. Norwich is quite well, and happy. I have however ordered him off the quarter-deck.'[14] In the intervening months, it is all business as usual, the correspondence recounting the routine of life on blockade duty and watching for any and every movement by enemy ships, the monotony broken by the occasional special moment to be remembered, as on 9 November 1804 when he writes to his wife:

You cannot imagine how gay we are to-night. About a week ago I received a petition from the gentlemen of the cockpit, requesting to be allowed to perform the tragedy of Douglas, with the pantomime of Harlequin and the Miller; and last night a ticket was sent to me, with a bill of the play. The performance to commence at 5 o'clock. What think you of these fine things? It is an innocent amusement, much better than being idle and drinking.[15]

The next day he can report that:

This is a proper gloomy November day, but not much wind. I went to the theatre last night, and I can assure you it was no bad performance. Between the play and the farce we had a most excellent Irish song, from one of the sailors. The music indeed was very good, and the entertainment for the night concluded with God save the King. The whole was over a quarter before eight o'clock. They had several scenes not badly painted. The ladies' dresses were not very fine, but did credit to their invention. Lady Randolph was all in black, made out of silk handkerchiefs; and I believe Anne's dress was made of sheets: but upon the whole they looked remarkably well.[16]

Worthy Duff also records numerous meetings with 'the Admiral'. Historians choose to record these as evidence of Nelson's close attention to strategic and tactical planning ahead of each of his major battles. Worthy, on the other hand, portrays them to his wife more by way of passing events in his social calendar, as on 23 November 1804 when 'we Captains have all been on board the Admiral to make our bow. He wanted us so much to dine with him; but I was glad to get off, as it is too late in the season to dine out of the ship at sea.'[17] Then again, on 26 May 1805, 'I went on board our Admiral to-day, as it was calm, and like a good boy staid there to church, as I have no Parson here.'[18]

What could be more normal than theatricals and her husband dining 'on Tuesday with our Admiral on a turtle I had shot with my gun a day or two before, and sent to him; and very it good it was'?[19] So when it comes to the decision what to do for their young son, Norwich, still not yet 13, Sophia, sitting at home back in Edinburgh, can have had few qualms about sending him to join his father. Husband and wife may have discussed this eventuality before Worthy left to join the *Mars*, but his silence on the subject in these letters points to Sophia alone making the final decision together with Norwich. Indeed, from a letter Worthy writes to his father-in-law, Brigadier-General Dirom, in August 1804, it appears that there had originally been other plans for Norwich. What those alternative plans were is unclear as Worthy only writes giving 'many thanks for your attention to Norwich. I hope, poor fellow, he will do well: he has not much to look forward to but what he must make for himself.'[20]

So it comes as a surprise when news reaches Worthy that Norwich is to join the *Mars*. Writing on 23 September 1805, just a few short weeks before the battle, Worthy enthuses to his wife:

> My dearest Sophia will readily believe how much I rejoiced on Saturday last to see our boy. He is very well, and has not been in the least sick. All the rest are also well, though they have been sick during the passage. It was very fortunate my meeting with the *Aurora*, as I was ordered by the Admiral to speak to a frigate off the Gut, before I went to Tangier; and in doing so, I fell in with our boy, and got him out, otherwise it might have been some weeks before he had joined me.[21]

It is clear from this that Norwich had not arrived alone and that a draft, certainly of young gentlemen if not of other crew, had arrived with him, brought from England by the *Aurora*. This is unsurprising: from the frequent official requests by Worthy, it is evident that, for all his efforts to pack the *Mars* with his own before setting sail, he still left Plymouth 16 months earlier with the *Mars* well down on its optimum complement of 640. This latest delivery shows the Admiralty's determination to ensure that the ships in the Channel Fleet were up to full strength ahead of what must, one day soon, be the final showdown with the enemy.

Worthy's primary concern, however, is to reassure Sophia that 'our son' is among friends, safe in his new home away from home:

> I have for the present taken him into the cabin to mess, and sleep. He seems very pleased with his choice of profession, and I hope will continue so. I had the pleasure of receiving by the *Aurora*, yours of 27 July, 2d, and 12 August, but I was informed a week before of Norwich's coming. It is very odd, that on Sunday before he joined, our Captain of marines, who is a very pleasant fellow, told me when I went down to dine in the ward-room, that

he seldom dreamt, but he could not resist telling me his dream of last night, that my son had arrived, and that he was taking him all over the ship to show it to him. So when Master Norwich made his appearance, the dream came into my head immediately.[22]

Over the next month, Worthy makes occasional references to Norwich, as on 7 October when 'I have just time to tell you that Norwich and all of us are well',[23] but, as a naval wife, Sophia might have sensed that the pace of events was quickening when her husband wrote that 'the Admiral has for some days past detached me with three sail of the line under my command, as the advance squadron.'[24] The first of October brought welcome news from her son, his first letter home:

I take the opportunity of the Nimble cutter brig going to England to write to you, as I should not wish to lose a single opportunity. I received your kind letter of the 25th August yesterday, and the next day one from John Dirom [his ten-year-old cousin]. Although I liked the *Aurora* very much, yet I like the *Mars* twenty times better. We had a pleasant voyage in the *Aurora*, though a very long one, on account of a very large convoy, and contrary winds. I was not the least sick during the whole voyage.[25]

An eerie calm then descended. The next two letters from Worthy to Sophia, dated 8 and 17 October, were about 'dining with Brown, of the Ajax,'[26] the politics of the navy and Duff's prospects for promotion to Admiral. Norwich was silent; instead Thomas Dalrymple, ship's purser and instructor to the young gentlemen on the *Mars*, wrote chattily with news that: 'Norwich and all the young gentlemen are making proficiency. We have got an excellent globe which we shall study occasionally; every morning … a certain number of words. Learn English grammar once a week, and in the evening read geography, history, etc, and after pored over their navigation, French, arithmetic etc the greater part of the day.'[27]

All seemed normal. Yet whatever thoughts were going through Sophia and Worthy's minds in those early October days, the warning signs of what lay ahead were there: William Pitt's choice of Nelson as standard-bearer for this mission of annihilation was no accident. This was the man whose do-or-die reputation preceded him, who led from the front, who cared nought for his own safety. Where he led, others not only must, but also wanted to, follow. Moreover, this time, Pitt had placed at Nelson's disposal the mightiest weapon of war he could assemble in Britain's arsenal. No longer the makeshift squadrons Nelson had somehow cobbled together into the semblance of a fighting fleet to hunt down Napoleon in 1798 and win the Battle of the Nile. Instead, Nelson had at his disposal the full might of the Channel Fleet, comprising in all 84 ships-of-the-line and frigates.

Yet, as if unable to comprehend the enormity of the task that Pitt had set his standard-bearer, Worthy could only remark flippantly to Sophia 'that we shall have more than we want',[28] as he watched the remorseless build-up of Britain's Home Fleet in the Channel. From behind these awesome 'wooden walls', nominally Nelson's orders were to blockade the French and Spanish Atlantic ports and prevent the enemy fleets from combining and assisting in Napoleon's reborn plan for the invasion of Britain. Napoleon should have learnt the lessons of Egypt, yet still had no grasp on realities when, back in July 1804, he had mused: 'Let us be masters of the Straits but for six hours, and we shall be masters of the world',[29] only to increase the time he needed from six to 24 hours a month later. What changed in his planning to make him plump first for six hours then for 24? Why not make it 25, even 26 hours?

Few in the navy seriously believed that Napoleon could achieve this hare-brained scheme. As the First Lord of the Admiralty declared: 'I don't say the French won't come, I just say they can't come by sea.'[30] Still, overblowing the threat added the frisson of jeopardy needed to make the job of recruitment at home that much easier. For Pitt had a mightier task in mind for his weapon of choice. No longer would the Home Fleet's task be merely defensive, to plant Britain's long-standing 'wooden walls' down the middle of the Channel. Rather, it must strike at the enemy's jugular, if not its heart, and destroy for ever its ability to wage war at sea. Hidden deep in the Admiralty's instructions to Nelson was the apocalyptic message: the implicit challenge to bring the enemy to battle come what may. Trick, tease, taunt, tempt Napoleon, do whatever was necessary so he would lose patience and recklessly order the Combined Fleets of France and Spain out of what Worthy called the 'snug'[31] safety of those French and Spanish havens and deliver them into the murderous crossfire that would await them on Britain's seas.

Ahead of this showdown, nothing must be left to chance and, if only as a precautionary measure, there was deemed a preemptive need to stiffen Britain's fighting spirit. In echoes of 1757, when 'in consequence of a dubious sentence,

Admiral John Byng, was shot at Portsmouth, for cowardice,[32] the Admiralty once again went looking for sacrificial lambs to impale on the altar of its new-found zeal. And, as luck would have it, one soon came begging. On 23 July 1805, Vice-Admiral Sir Robert Calder at the head of a fleet of 15 sail-of-the-line met the Combined Fleet comprising 23 French and Spanish sail-of-the-line. He captured two enemy ships. Expecting accolades back home, he instead found himself facing a court martial.

At a loss to comprehend the true forces at work, Worthy could only comment in bewilderment: 'I am sorry to find there have been two opinions of Sir Robert Calder's conduct, when in sight of the enemy. I regret it very much, as he is a very worthy gallant officer. As the situation of the enemy's fleet, and the orders he was under, were known only to himself, I am glad to find a court martial is to take place; I hope it will completely clear him.'[33]

Instead of being cleared, Calder found himself judged to have failed to do 'his utmost to renew the said engagement [on 24 July 1805] and to take and destroy every ship of the enemy'[34] and would be 'severely reprimanded'. Once again, in Voltaire's words, government policy was being dictated *pour encourager les autres*. And Calder's crime? Two enemy ships captured were not deemed enough. Forget the minor detail that Calder's fleet was outnumbered 23 to 15. The Admiralty was sending a message: total annihilation meant just that: 'destroy every ship of the enemy'.

Of course, Nelson needed no such message. Briefly back in England in August 1805 after a fruitless chase across the Atlantic in search of the French fleet, which the ill-fated Calder subsequently found but then failed to destroy, Nelson quickly picked up on the political mood. Writing two weeks before Trafalgar, he summed up what was at stake: 'It is, as Pitt knows, annihilation that the Country wants, and not merely a splendid Victory of twenty-three to thirty-six – honourable to the parties concerned, but absolutely useless in the extended scale to bring Buonaparte to his marrow.'[35] He at least understood why he had been chosen and what his duty was.

Arriving off Cadiz on 27 September and confident that he would be victorious if only the Combined Fleet of 33 ships – 18 of them French, 15 Spanish – holed up in port could be tempted out, Nelson ostentatiously sent six ships, including the *Canopus*, captained by Francis Austen, into Gibraltar for watering and restocking. Nelson knew that Spanish spies there would carry the news back to Cadiz and hoped thereby to trick Admiral Villeneuve, commander of the enemy fleet, into making a dash for the open seas. The ploy worked, but little did Nelson know that his trickery was just one small component in the game of blind-man's bluff, and that the real reason why Villeneuve decided to come to battle was exactly the one Pitt had surmised would trigger the Great Battle. Napoleon finally lost patience and, in his frustration, dispatched orders to Villeneuve, relieving him of his command. Getting wind of these orders and faced with imminent humiliation, Villeneuve had no alternative but to take his chances at sea.

William Pitt's plans to trick, tease, taunt, tempt Napoleon had finally paid off. The game of cat and mouse that had begun the day Nelson sailed from Portsmouth aboard his flagship *Victory* in 1803 finally reached its climax on 21 October 1805 off the coast of Spain, so close to Cadiz that people would have been able to watch and listen as the Great Battle raged on the horizon.

In the early morning on that day, the Combined Fleet sailed remorselessly towards Nelson's killing seas: now the massacre could begin. Aboard each one of the 27 ships-of-the-line in the British fleet, officers and men, young gentlemen and boys waited. Among *Victory*'s complement of 850 men, there was one ten-year-old boy, four aged 12 and six aged 13.[36] Rallying his midshipmen ahead of the battle, Nelson gave the following speech: 'Tomorrow, I will do that which will give you young gentlemen something to talk and think about for the rest of your lives. But I shall not live to know about it myself.'[37]

Ignorant these youngsters may have been of the mighty battle that Pitt, the Admiralty and Nelson envisioned for them, but one thing they were sure of was that Nelson would deliver success. Thomas Aikenhead, a Midshipman on the *Royal Sovereign*, wrote his last ever letter four hours before the battle. He sums up the mood bent on sacrifice:

> We have just piped to breakfast; thirty-five sail, besides smaller vessels, are now on our beam, about three miles off. Should I, my dear parents, fall in defence of my King, let that thought console you. I feel not the least dread on my spirits. Oh my parents, sisters, brothers, dear grandfather, grandmother, and aunt, believe me ever your!
>
> Accept, perhaps for the last time, your brother's love; be assured I feel for my friends, should I die in this glorious action – glorious no doubt it will be. Every British heart pants for glory. Our old Admiral [Admiral Collingwood] is quite young with the thoughts of it. If I survive, nothing will give me greater pleasure than embracing my

dearest relations. Do not, in case I fall, grieve – it will be to no purpose. Many brave fellows will no doubt fall with me on both sides.[38]

With the superior training of the men, their more rapid rate of fire, and the fighting readiness of every officer, seaman and boy in the British fleet, the outcome of the battle would never be in doubt, especially when heading towards the British were two allies reluctantly fighting side by side, each commanded by an officer corps with an equally sclerotic tactical mindset. After a long history of defeats at the hands of the British Navy, the French had asked time and again why they kept losing and had concluded that it was the British strategy of 'killing as many as possible of the enemy, rather than of injuring their ships'.[39] This was Nelson's objective at Trafalgar; he would not be bringing any new strategy to the battle. It would be the ruthless way he executed the strategy and the specific tactics that he employed in setting up his killing seas that was novel. Villeneuve even correctly foretold the tactics Nelson would adopt, yet seemed powerless, paralysed, to do anything to prevent them.

Formed up in one long line of battle as was their convention, the French and Spanish offered themselves up as easy prey for the British fleet approaching at right angles and dividing into two parallel columns ready to break the enemy line at its weakest points. Nelson in *Victory* commanded one division, Admiral Collingwood in *Royal Sovereign* was at the head of the other. Sketches showing the opposing battle formation minutes before impact conjure an air of order and calm, so precise, so simple, so perfect was the linear geometry of the competing battle plans. As if mesmerized by the moment, Captain Codrington on the *Orion* could only wonder later in awe that 'I suppose no man ever before saw a sight of such beauty'.[40]

Within minutes all that would change. The first shots of the Great Battle were unleashed on the *Royal Sovereign* by the *Fougueux* at midday. 'Move' the hour-glass forward to 1.15pm to the time when the master of the *Mars*, Thomas Cook, recorded that 'Captain Duff was killed',[41] and all 'beauty' had disappeared. Instead, all was exactly as Nelson had ordered it: 'pell-mell' chaos with, for instance, 'the poop and quarter-deck [of the *Mars*] almost left destitute, the carnage was so great'.[42] No more 'wooden walls' here. Only the sickening, bludgeoning thud of three great empires – Spain, France and Britain – colliding cataclysmically.

The Battle of Trafalgar would be like no other battle of the Wars. When all hyperbole was stripped away, the Battle of the Glorious First of June had been a timid, honourable draw, the Battle of Cape St Vincent an opportunistic flash in the pan signifying little beyond a much-needed shot in the arm for British morale, and the Battle of the Nile, in many ways the most overwhelming of Nelson's victories, as good as over before it started. By contrast, in those fateful morning hours of 21 October 1805, as the British fleet slowly descended on its prey desperately skirting the Spanish coast past Cape Trafalgar, the stench of impending massacre stalked the air and with it, for each man and boy in the fleet, the simple lottery of 'Death or Glory',[43] as was etched on the cannons of the *Bellerophon*. But for Nelson there was no such choice. Ahead of the Battle of Cape St Vincent, his cry had been 'Westminster Abbey! or glorious victory'.[44] Ahead of the Battle of the Nile, his last letter to Fanny had said, 'Glory is my object and that alone'.[45] Come the Great Battle, his war cry would be Westminster Abbey *and* glorious victory: death and glory were to become one.

Urged in the heat of the battle 'not to appear so conspicuously, in full uniform, to the mark of the topmen of the enemy',[46] Nelson shot back: 'No... Whatever may be the consequence, the insignia of the honours I now wear I gained by the exertion of British seamen, under my command in various parts of the world; and in the hour of danger, I am proud to show them and the enemies of England, I will never part with them; if it please God I am to fall, I will expire with these trophies entwined round my heart'.[47]

Would that it were he alone meeting his apotheosis! But on his remorseless funeral march to the great doors of Westminster Abbey, this mighty sea-horseman of the apocalypse would draw many into his vortex of death and destruction, among them the midshipmen and fresh-faced young volunteers serving as his aides-de-camp on the quarterdeck of *Victory*, from where they sent signals, ran messages and brought news, as when, minutes before being felled by a French sharpshooter, Nelson 'observed the act of throwing his Secretary over board, and said, as if doubtful, to a Midshipman who was near him, "Was that Scott?" The Midshipman replied, he believed it was. He exclaimed, "Poor fellow!"'[48] After Nelson was fatally wounded and lying on the middle-deck, still he issued orders to his aides-de-camp, as when 'his Lordship observed that the tiller-ropes were not yet replaced, and desired one of the Midshipmen stationed there to go upon the quarter-deck and remind Captain Hardy of that circumstance'.[49] Many midshipmen would not only have been trained in swordsmanship, but would have learnt how to fire a pistol or musket, so that when Nelson was down in the cockpit, slowly dying of his wounds, 'the Frenchman by whose hand this matchless hero fell, was soon afterwards shot by Mr Pollard, Midshipman of the *Victory*, and was seen to fall out of the mizzen-top'.[50]

Down in the *Victory*'s cockpit, with the wounded and dying waiting in line for treatment, 'the Surgeon, finding it impossible to render his Lordship any further assistance, left him to attend Lieutenant Bligh, Messrs Smith and Westphall, Midshipmen, and some seamen recently wounded'.[51] Robert Smith would die from his wounds, as would another midshipman on the *Victory*, Alexander Palmer. George Westphall survived along with two other midshipmen, William Rivers and Richard Bulkeley, both wounded, the latter evidently not seriously enough to prevent him cutting off the 'lock of hair' from Nelson's head. Among boys from *Victory*'s lower-decks, three volunteers, third class, died: Stephen Sabine, George Welch and Collin Turner; and John Saunders was wounded. Elsewhere in the British fleet, casualties among midshipmen ran high. In all, 13 midshipmen died in the British fleet and a further 45 were wounded, among whom were some volunteers, first class.

Despite being only the fifth ship in the lee division, the *Bellerophon* soon sought out the heat of action, locking on to the French 74-gun *L'Aigle* and trading murderous musket and cannon shot at close quarters until, as John Franklin later described, 'our people took the quoins out and elevated their guns, so as to tear her decks and sides to pieces: when she got clear of us, she did not return a single shot whilst we raked her, her starboard quarter was entirely beaten in, and, as we afterwards learnt, four hundred men hors de combat, so that she was an easy conquest for the *Defiance*, a fresh ship...'.[52] John survived the battle unscathed, dodging the bullets of the French sharpshooter high in the rigging of the *L'Aigle*, whose 'features he vowed he would never forget so long as he lived'[53] as he sprinted along the upper deck with a message. However, other midshipmen on board the *Bellerophon* were not so lucky, William Jewell, James Stone, Thomas Bant and George Pearson all being wounded.

Aboard the *Mars*, the carnage was exceptional. On the morning of the battle, Worthy Duff had received 'the signal ... to lead the lee division of our fleet and to break the enemy's line'.[54] However, because it 'sailed ill ... the Mars, notwithstanding every exertion, was passed by the *Royal Sovereign* ... then the *Belleisle* also shot a-head, and they were in action a few minutes before the *Mars*: each ship breaking through a different part of the enemy's line'.[55]

Minutes before entering the battle, Worthy Duff wrote telling his wife that 'I have just time to tell you we are going into action with the combined fleet. I hope and trust in God that we shall all behave as becomes us, and that I may yet have

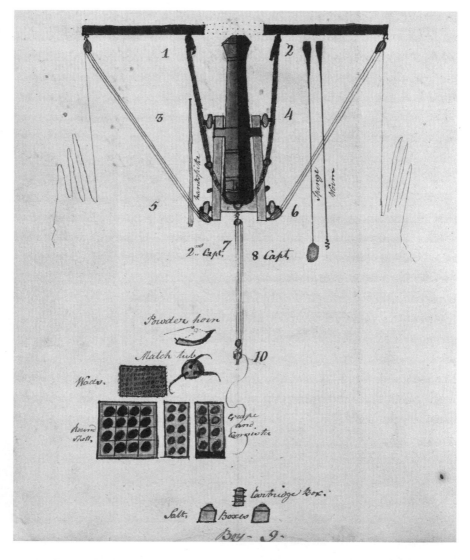

Layout showing the order and preference of men, including a boy (No 9) at battle stations around an 18-pounder gun of the frigate Amazon, *1802. (National Maritime Museum, Greenwich, London)*

the happiness of taking my beloved wife and children in my arms. Norwich is quite well, and happy. I have however ordered him off the quarter-deck.'[56] Very solicitous, but where to send their 13-year-old son to safety on a warship about to go into battle? Surely not down to the cockpit where the 'medical tribe' would soon start the work of Aesculapius?

Where to then? Why not the relative safety of the captain's cabin, which is where Captain Duckworth had quartered William Parker and the other young gentlemen too young to fight during the Battle of the Glorious First of June? Doubtless that is where Worthy Duff intended to send his son, but that is not where Norwich ended up. Instead: 'Captain Duff's son, and three other boys who went out with him, were stationed on the lower-deck during the action, where,' their schoolmaster writes, they behaved like *Young Nelsons*.'[57]

On his way down to the lower gun deck, Norwich would have passed other 'young Nelsons', Royal Marine boys William Gill, John Hall and Francis Parish, whose task at battle stations would have been to keep the gangways clear of dead bodies and report any shirkers. Once down on the lower-deck, Norwich would have fought alongside the gun crews, teaming up with more young Nelsons: boys such as Peter Black and Charles Niles, volunteers second class, and William Crump and John Jarvis, volunteers third class, busy as powder monkeys fetching and carrying supplies for the gun crews.

Worthy Duff had made the right decision when he ordered Norwich off the quarterdeck, otherwise, as William Hennah, lieutenant on *Mars*, later explained in a letter home, the youngster would have been caught up in the ensuing carnage when 'the Quarter-Deck suffered more than any other part of the Ship and I must consider myself as a lucky man in having escaped without the smallest injury'.[58] Not so lucky was:

Captain Duff [who] walked about with steady fortitude and said, 'My God, what shall we do, here is a Spanish three-decker raking us ahead, a French one under the stern.' In few minutes our poop was totaly cleared, the quater deck and forcastle [*sic*] nearly the same, only the Boatswain and myself and three men left alive. It was then the gallant Captain fell. I saw him fall. His head and neck were entirely off his body, when the men heard it, they held his body up and gave three cheers to show they were not discouraged, and then returned to their guns.[59]

In all, according to young Banffshire midshipman T. Robinson, the *Mars* 'had an hundred and ten men killed and wounded, four midshipmen and Captain of Marines'.[60]

Down on the lower-deck, Norwich was spared death or injury, but not the pain he must later bear writing to 'My Dear Mamma' after the Great Battle, to inform her that:

> ...you cannot possibly imagine how unwilling I am to begin this melancholy letter. However, as you must unavoidably hear the fate of dear Papa, I write you these few lines to request you to bear it as patiently as you can. He died like a Hero, having gallantly led his ship into action, and his memory will ever be dear to his King, his Country, and his Friends. It was about fifteen minutes past twelve in the afternoon of the 21st of October, when the engagement began, and it was not finished till five. Many a brave Hero sacrificed his life upon that occasion to his King and his Country.[61]

The Great Battle over, the dead needed to be 'buried'. The log of the *Mars* for 22 October read: 'At 5.30, committed the body of Captain Duff to the deep'.[62] Elsewhere round the victorious fleet, similar ceremonies were underway. Surely now the victors could at last enjoy the spoils of war, the prize money that it was every sailor's right to receive in victory. However the survivors of Trafalgar, be they the defeated French and Spanish or the victorious British, had one more battle to fight. The log of the *Mars* for 22 October had already sounded the grim warning when it recorded the order to 'set storm staysails'.[63] Later that same day Thomas Cook, the ship's master, recorded a further entry in the log of the *Mars*: 'At 12, strong winds and heavy rain'.[64]

In one final apocalyptic twist of fate, a mighty storm had descended on the wreckage of the fleets of three great empires, wreaking more damage than even the Great Battle had done. During that storm, the gods of war surrendered to the gods of the firmament, completing the work of 'annihilation that the Country wants', which Nelson had started but, now dead, could not finish. The victorious British fleet, each ship fighting its own battle for survival, could only watch helplessly as, one by one, 15 French and Spanish prize-ships sank, ran aground or were scuttled in the storm. Britain's sailors, some of whom had waited for years for their share of the spoils of war, would have to wait a little longer.

SPOILS OF WAR

From the Glorious First of June 1794 to Trafalgar 1805, take any battle, action or skirmish in these Wars so far, and whatever homage officers and crew paid to God, King and Country ahead of each engagement, never far from every sailor's thoughts was the yearning for prize money. Time and again, their letters and memoirs betray the desperation.

Prize money was the immediate reward for all the hardships and dangers a sailor had endured over days, months, years at sea. More, however, than its value in worldly riches, there to be spent, enjoyed or squandered in the immediate rapture of victory, prize money was a passport out of society's 'great law of subordination'. From the king downwards, there was always someone lower on the social pyramid who must be kept there, otherwise the fabric of society would unravel. The Wars did not change this. What they did do was afford a select few – those who dared, those who survived – the opportunity to put their past behind them and reach out to a bright new future. Money – uniquely the vast injections of it that came by the spoils of war – yielded that vital 'step up' so desperately sought after by all those somewhere lower down the social orders, bringing at a stroke respect, status and marriage.

There were marriages without love and marriages with love, but there must be money. Without money, there could only be romance, as 17-year-old Betsy Wynne was to discover in the early years of the Wars, when prize money was extremely hard to come by. Betsy was one of three sisters, born to an English émigré family with strong *Ancien Régime* connections. The Wynnes had been wandering the courts and spas of Europe since 1789, always, it seemed, only one small step ahead of the French republican armies. In June 1796, their luck finally running out, Betsy and her father, mother and 15-year-old sister Eugenia were forced to flee Florence, their latest refuge, in the dead of night. Affecting an air of insouciance, Betsy described in her diary the 'pleasant journey the night being light and beautiful'[1] as the family made a moonlight dash for the coast.

Reaching Leghorn on 22 June 1796, 'we went to Mr Udney's and found there a most terrible bustle and noise – All packing up and getting on board the ships. We hardly had time to get a little breakfast, they hurried us so terribly to quit the place.'[2] Betsy was torn by the prospect of what lay ahead, noting in her diary that 'I have not the least wish of going a sea voyage'.[3] However, she had no choice. She might lament the fact that only weeks before she had been playing the harpsichord for Louis XVIII in the gardens of a Veronese palace, but all round her there were 'Republicans who entered Leghorn and fired for some time'.[4] With their only means of escape being by sea, 'Captain Fremantle took us on board his Frigate the *Inconstant*, a most beautiful ship'.[5]

It wasn't long before Betsy was noticing 'how kind and amiable Captain Fremantle is. He pleases me more than any man I have yet seen. Not handsome, but there is something pleasing in his countenance and his fiery black eyes are quite captivating.'[6] As for 'the sea voyage' she had been dreading just days before, now she could only gush how 'the sight of the sea gave me great joy I had not seen it so long'.[7] Marooned on board the *Inconstant*, the diary that she had written up faithfully day in, day out for seven years suddenly had a new purpose: to record what Captain Fremantle did next, as on 5 July when he 'arrived early in the morning – he immediately sent to ask us to dine with him – he came himself to take us and we spent the day and evening with them on board the *Inconstant*. The Ball we were to have yesterday he gave us to-day, the deck was most elegantly drest up and looked like a charming large Ball room all the guns being removed.'[8]

The war could not have been further away. Everyone caught the mood of gay abandon, as 12-year-old George Elliot remembered when recording those days in his *Memoir*:

One thing struck me as a beginner. We had a family on board, who had lately and narrowly escaped from Leghorn, in an English frigate, as the French were entering the town (Dowager Lade Freemantle was the eldest daughter) and we were dancing on the quarter deck at night. It was lit up for the occasion, and being nearer the shore than we supposed, the French opened their fire on us; about the third shot passed through the canvas screens, on each side of the deck, a few feet over the heads of the dancers, but this was not allowed in any way to interfere with the dance – perhaps the ladies may not have been aware, at the moment, what took place.[9]

Betsy had fallen head over heels in love, and she would soon discover that her love was returned, her diary entry for 12 July coyly noting that 'the many proffs [sic] of kind friendship I had received from Captain Fremantle the attention he paid to me filled me with gratitude'.[10] With happiness came pain also, for the captain's attentiveness 'caused me to be excessively sorry in the idea of quitting him soon and perhaps never see him again…' However it wasn't her quitting him, as her diary suggested. Quite the reverse: Freemantle 'acknowledged to M [Mamma] that he was partial to me, and as his fortune at present was not sufficient enough for him to maintain a family he said he could not keep us any longer with him, for he feared that the later we would part the more unfortunate he would feel at the separation.'[11] The bald facts were there: before asking Betsy's parents for their daughter's hand in marriage, the gallant Captain Fremantle must first go out and seek his fortune.

So off the captain went in search of enemy ships, leaving Betsy to fend off the innumerable other more eligible naval bachelors dancing attendance on the family as the squadron cruised along the north coast of Italy during the late summer of 1796, among them, the 'old Gentleman',[12] Betsy's acerbic description for the luckless 40-year-old Captain Foley, whose gauche attempts at wooing only increased Betsy's determination to wait for Captain Fremantle's return, surely bringing with him the news she most craved, that 'he may make some good prize money'.[13]

Listening to the other officers on board ship, however, she would have heard only dire grumblings that these were not 'pleasant days'[14] for prize-taking. A few exceptional actions apart: 'this is not a war of profit: much gain is not to be expected in it',[15] was how Captain, later Admiral, Collingwood summed up prospects in those early years of the Wars. So for Betsy, much as she might wish for prize money, the chances of her captain striking rich were slim, and with no good news to buoy her up she was soon despairing: 'Alas, how will this matter end. If he does not make prize money, it will never do, I should not mind it but my parents would never consent to it, without he gets a pretty good fortune.'[16]

Nevertheless, the Wynnes were wealthy, Betsy was young, and her beau could reappear any day with the news she craved. In these circumstances, she and her parents could afford to be patient. For another family back home in England that same year, waiting was a luxury that could be ill afforded. The Austen family had 'interest' but little money and after three long years of war, still no prize money had come the way of either Francis or Charles. Until that happened, the prospects for sisters Jane and Cassandra attracting suitors were slim indeed. Much longer without good news and they would end up spinsters. Jane understood how dependent she and Cassandra were on their brothers' success, as when she wrote reminding her sister that 'Edward [another brother but not in the navy] & Frank are both gone out to seek their fortunes; the latter is to return soon & help us seek ours.' [17] Come 1800, seven years into the Wars and with Jane already 27, a note of impatience creeps into her letters when, writing on 1 November, she first complains that 'of his Promotion he knows nothing', then sarcastically adds that 'of Prizes he is guiltless.' [18]

Her impatience is understandable, and her disappointment on this occasion may well have been accentuated by the report carried in the January issue of the *Naval Chronicle* for that same year, which tantalizingly regaled its readers with that rarest of events at the time: a truly bumper prize. Naval families across the country would have been left to salivate enviously at the '£40,730 18s 0d' [19] (somewhat in excess of £1.3 million/US$1.95 million in today's money) that each of the four captains received as their share of the prize money for the capture of the Spanish frigates *Thetis* and *Santa Brigida* the previous year. Lieutenants each received £5,091 10s 3d, and even humble 'midshipmen and their Class' [20] earned the princely sum of £791 17s ¾d. With Francis on a lieutenant's pay of £7 per month and Charles on a midshipman's pay of £2 10s 6d per month, the sisters must have been asking themselves where was their *Thetis*, where was their *Santa Brigida*? And to rub salt in the wound, 'able and ordinary seamen and marines' [21] each received £182 4s 9 ¾d, more than double what Francis stood to earn in a year.

On 11 February 1801 it was Charles' turn to catch the impatient end of Jane's tongue as she remarked caustically that his ship 'the *Endymion* has not been plagued with any more prizes.' [22] When at long last there was a prize worth mentioning, still it was not enough, only buying the sisters some baubles. Announcing the happy news, Jane's cheeriness echoes with hollowness: 'He [Charles] has received 30£ for his share of the privateer and expects 10£ more – but of what avail is it to take prizes if he lays out the produce in presents to his Sisters. He has been buying Gold chains and Topaze Crosses for us.'[23]

Money: with the happiness of so many womenfolk – brides-to-be, mothers and sisters – hanging for so long on the endeavours of Britain's officers and young gentlemen, it is no wonder that, come Trafalgar, patience was wearing thin. Worthy Duff certainly felt the frustration. Being the loyal trooper that he was, he dutifully suspended the yearning for pecuniary advantage in the name of King and Country, but it was never far below the surface. He briefly let his guard slip a few months ahead of the Great Battle when recounting to Sophia an incident that promised much: 'I have taken a prize today!'[24] he gaily announced. The exclamation mark, intimately bespeaking irony, should have warned Sophia what was coming next:

> About two o'clock a cask went close to us, and as I could easily get into my station again, I sent after it, when at last we got it on board with a good deal of trouble. It proved I think to be a hogshead of claret; which from the state of, and a number of barnicles upon, the cask, must have been at least several years in the water. The wine is quite sound, and I hope when settled it will turn out well. I wish it was in Castle Street such as it is; of course it is very thick at present, but a little time will let us know what our prize is.[25]

A prize, but hardly worth speaking of, and Worthy knew it. He was just trying to keep their spirits up. Sophia would have understood: married since 1790, she had been a sailor's wife long enough to have seen the ups and downs of the naval profession. Her husband's latest appointment as captain of the 74-gun *Mars* might be very prestigious, but command of a ship-of-the-line was notoriously unprofitable. Forced to operate for long periods in cumbersome fleets on blockade duty and only occasionally blessed with the winner-takes-all of a pitched battle, opportunities for prize money were few and far between.

Likewise, young gentlemen entering the navy and blinded by the zeal of patriotism thought that joining a ship-of-the-line was the be all and end all, but soon saw how misguided they were. An early stint in *Defence* and, as he explained in his *Narrative*, William Dillon, then aged 13, and his fellow midshipmen could not wait to move ships: 'Several of the Mids became dissatisfied with the duty of a line of battle ship. They were not only anxious for more active service, but also to touch some Prize money. Their applications to the Captain to remove them into frigates annoyed him, as he used frequently to declare, "You are all frigate mad."[26]

So 'frigate mad' was the service from top to bottom in the early days of the Wars that the Admiralty had to introduce measures in 1799 limiting the time officers could have command of frigates. For Worthy Duff stuck on the *Mars* ahead of the Great Battle, it was a case of making do with being 'long told that a promotion is to take place; but I will never believe it till I see it in the Gazette, as I cannot see how they can make one, when we have so many on the Admirals' list already.[27] His misfortune was to die before he could enjoy the promotion, the hogshead of claret and the outrageous fortune that must surely come the way of the victors in the Great Battle once the enemy's resistance had been broken.

When it came to the spoils of war everyone knew how the system operated. Prize money was big business and therefore subject to rafts of regulations covering all stages of prize-taking from capture to distribution of the prize money. For the officers and men, capturing a prize was only the beginning of their travails. The next step was to remove it safely to a friendly port, which could be equally, if not more, hazardous. This is where midshipmen came into their own. Often nominated as prize-masters for small captures, young midshipmen had their first real opportunity to shine in an independent, if temporary, command. The problem for the prize-master was that his prize-crew was drawn from the very ship that had just engaged the enemy ship and taken casualties in the process. The end result invariably was that prizes were manned by scratch-crews, which had to operate the captured ship *and* keep watch on its prisoners.

At Trafalgar, the problems for prize-masters were especially acute because of the sheer number of prizes taken, their size and crew numbers and the heavy casualties on both sides. The atrocious weather that engulfed the stricken fleets as the battle drew to a close further compounded the nightmare. Midshipman Henry Walker from the *Bellerophon* found himself in the eye of this gathering maelstrom. As part of the prize-crew assigned to the stricken Spanish ship, *Monarca*, partway through the Great Battle, his first problem was that the initial prize-crew comprised just 'our second lieutenant, myself, and eight men'[28] to man a 74-gun-ship-of-the-line whose original complement was 750, before 250 were killed during the battle. Henry explained his plight in a letter to his mother written on 22 November: 'In the ensuing night a storm came up, such as I had never witnessed, and for the four following days, we had a much severer struggle against the elements than the enemy. You will imagine what will have been our sufferings in a crippled ship, with 500 prisoners on board and only 55 Englishmen, most of whom were in a constant state of intoxication.'[29]

There was little Henry and the second lieutenant could do. The *Monarca* sank. Henry and some of the Spanish prisoners were rescued by the *Leviathan*, from where he recounted that: 'We were more fortunate than several of our countrymen, who were lost in the prizes; others were taken prisoners by the French and Spaniards who rose upon and carried them into Cadiz.'[30]

It only remained for Henry to count the cost and tally up his dwindling winnings. The Great Battle had yielded 19 captures, promising a bonanza of prize money, but only four of these survived the storm, the rest being shipwrecked, deliberately sunk or burned. The arithmetic made sorry reading: 'I suppose I have made about 20£ prize money in the late action, which would have brought me upwards of 100£ had we not met with the dreadful storm which destroyed our prizes.'[31] Twenty pounds (*circa* £640/US $960 in today's money)[32] was scant reward for his work at Trafalgar, bearing in mind that, as midshipman on a first rate, his monthly pay would have been £2 10s 6d.

Henry Walker's predicament as member of a prize-crew is echoed time and again in the annals of the Wars. In an anecdote entitled 'Remarkable Intrepidity of a boy, evinced in the recapture of the *Fame*', the *Naval Chronicle* gives a vivid illustration of the plight of prize-crews, only this time it was the British who were captured but managed to turn the tables on their captors:

At one am on the 25th of October [1811], the *Fame* of Carron, was captured off Shields on her voyage from London to Arbroath, laden with flax and hemp by the French privateer... The privateer left two of the *Fame*'s crew on board, viz an old man and a boy, and put six Frenchmen in her to carry her to a port in France; but a south-east gale ... drove her into the mouth of the Forth, with the navigation of which, the Frenchmen, as well as the old man, were unacquainted ... they allowed the vessel to go before the wind ... till the boy luckily recognized the light of Inchkeith, when he assumed command of the *Fame* and on passing close to the *Rebecca*, lying at anchor in St Margaret's Hope ... he hailed aloud that he had six French prisoners and demanded assistance to get them secured. The moment that the *Rebecca*'s boat reached the *Fame*, the boy seized the Frenchmen's pistols, as his right by conquest, and would not give them up to the *Rebecca*'s crew. The prisoners acknowledged the boy to be an excellent steersman, and consider themselves indebted to him as the means of saving their lives.[33]

Rounding off its anecdote, the *Chronicle* cannot resist attaching an ironic moral intended to highlight the vast gulf between the prospects for a boy from the lower-deck and a midshipman from the quarterdeck: 'Conduct like this, in a boy only of about thirteen years of age, is truly British, and certainly ought not to be allowed to pass without its due reward… Perhaps the most gratifying reward to the boy, would be to enter him as a midshipman on board one of his Majesty's ships. He would then have a chance of becoming an Admiral!'[34]

Once a capture was safe in a friendly port – Gibraltar, in the case of many of the Trafalgar prizes – the next step was to value the ship, which was done based on her tonnage. All the goods and chattels on board were also valued: everything from the guns and other hardware of war down to the slops and provisions. In addition, there was 'head money': £5 for every sailor listed in a captured ship's muster books. The valuation completed, next came the process of distribution. As with all enemy actions, everyone fighting at Trafalgar, from Admirals Nelson and Collingwood down to the youngest of young gentlemen such as Norwich Duff on the *Mars*, and the meanest of Marine Society boys such as the Petty brothers, Richard and James, on the *Bellerophon* – all could expect to 'touch some Prize money'.

The Admiralty had a fixed scale, established in 1708, for dividing up prize money in the event of a successful capture. Although it changed in 1808, veterans of Trafalgar received their prize money based on the old scale, which ranked them according to five classes of mariner. A captain received three-eighths of the total. As a captain's widow Sophia Duff received £2,389, which was her dead husband's share of the special award granted by the government for the action. She would further have collected £973: her dead husband's share of the money pooled from the prizes. Sophia would also have benefited from the Patriotic Fund set up by Lloyd's, which 'Resolved: be afforded to the Widows, Orphans, Parents, and Relatives, depending for support on the Captains, Officers, Petty Officers, Seamen and Marines who fell in these glorious engagements, as soon as their respective situations shall be made known to the Committee.'[35]

One-eighth each of the total went to lieutenants, warrant officers, and petty officers, which included midshipmen, like John Franklin on the *Bellerophon*. This was not John's first prize money. In addition to what he received from his service at the Battle of Copenhagen, returning from his enforced shore leave on the Terra Australis sandbank, he had hitched a ride home with an East India convoy en route from China, which met and bested a French squadron of five warships on 15 February 1804 near the straits of Malacca. So valuable was the cargo saved from the enemy fleet and so grateful was the East India Company that it voted a reward – 'the whole will amount to 50,000l'[36] – to the British crews in the convoy and, as signal-midshipman on the *Earl Camden*, the fleet commodore's flagship, John would have received £30. The £6 reward granted by the East India Company to 'Seamen and servants'[37] makes the £6 9s 6d that Norwich Duff received from Trafalgar seem paltry. As a volunteer-by-warrant, his entitlement to prize money would have been the same as an ordinary seaman's, sharing equally the two-eighths not already granted to the other four senior classes of mariner.

In addition to receiving prize money, the now fatherless Norwich may also have been a beneficiary of the Lloyd's Patriotic Fund, established in 1803, which had taken care of his mother. As a widow, Sophia Duff would have also received a pension from the Charity for the Relief of Poor Widows of Commission and Warrant Officers of the Royal Navy. One youngster who definitely did benefit from the Patriotic Fund, receiving £40, was George Pearson, a 13-year-old volunteer first class who entered the navy in May 1805 and was wounded on the *Bellerophon*. Lieutenant Pryce Cumby, who took over command of the ship when the captain was killed, described George's ordeal:

I met on the quarter-deck ladder little Pearson in the arms of the Quarter-Master who was carrying him to The Surgeon in the Cockpit... When the signal was made to prepare for battle and our drums had beat to quarters for the purpose, the first person that caught my eye on the Quarter-Deck was little Pearson dragging with difficulty one leg after another. I said to him. 'Pearson, you had better go below.' 'I should be very sorry to be below at a time like this.' I instantly said, 'Indeed I will not order you down and if you live you'll be a second Nelson.' Poor fellow he did live to be a lieutenant and then died of fever.[38]

George Pearson had been at sea six months, Norwich only two. Both earned prize money. Yet, Francis Austen, a veteran of 17 years at sea, missed out on the Great Battle by days and so touched no prize money. This was his worst fear realized. In a letter to his fiancée, Mary Gibson, dated 15 October 1805, Francis gives a running commentary of his movements ahead of the anticipated battle, including how he: 'rejoined the Commander in Chief on the morning of the 5th, only to be again dispatched in the course of the day [and was unable] to reach Gibraltar until the 9th when every exertion was made to get on board such supplies of stores and provisions…[in order to] to get back to the fleet…'[39]

Confident that Mary and he were of like minds, he makes no bones about why he was so anxious to be part of the action: 'Having borne our share in a tedious chace and anxious blockade, it would be mortifying indeed to find ourselves at last thrown out of any share of credit and emolument which would result from an action.'[40] Further on in the same letter, by which time, without knowing it, he is writing on the very day of the Great Battle, his resentment finally gets the better of him and he bemoans how his:

> …situation is peculiarly unpleasant and distressing… As I have no doubt but the event would be highly honourable to our arms, and be at the same time productive of some good prizes, I shall have to lament our absence on such an occasion on a double account, the loss of pecuniary advantage as well as of professional credit. And after having been so many months in a state of constant and unremitting fag, to be at last cut out by a parcel of folk just come from their homes, where some of them were sitting at their ease the greater part of the last war, and the whole of this, till just now, is particularly hard and annoying.[41]

In the space of a few lines, 'share of credit and emolument' has become 'loss of pecuniary advantage as well as of professional credit' as money replaces honour in Francis' list of priorities. It cannot have made pretty reading for Mary. Still, at least Francis was being honest. All too often, senior officers claimed, as did Admiral Pellew serving on the East Indies station in 1805, that 'I never cared much about riches and we have enough to make me comfortable'.[42] Usually, such protestations meant exactly the opposite, or that the officer had already made his fortune, as was the case with Pellew, and therefore could afford to adopt a lofty moral tone.

The strength of feeling behind Francis' letter is evident in the side-swipe at the 'parcel of folk just come from their homes', a mean reference to the likes of new arrivals like Norwich Duff and George Pearson, who collected prize money for just a few months' work. This was a common barb. William Dillon referred to this when he touched his first prize money in 1793, still aged only 13: 'The fact of our being bound for St Helena gave us great range over the ocean, and we in consequence made the most favourable calculations upon capturing of the enemy's ships, their homeward bound Indiamen etc. The Elderly Mids did not fail, now and then, to let out a sharp rub at me on account of being rated, which gave me 5 shares in prize money.'[43]

Poor Francis Austen. No matter; his turn would come. He may have missed out on what spoils there were from the Great Battle, but, with the French and Spanish navies virtually destroyed, the world was Britain's oyster. Its navy could range with impunity across the globe plundering land from the French, the Dutch, the Spanish, step by step setting a seal on its soon-to-be-vast empire. After Trafalgar, the European mainland may still have been off limits to Britain, but the enemy coastline, inland as far as Britain's naval cannons could reach, and stretching from the Baltic in the north through the Straits of Gibraltar all the way down to the Greek islands, was open season for Britain's marauding sailors.

Further afield, however, there were still pockets of resistance from the enemies' depleted navies dotted around the globe, as George Parsons, stationed in the West Indies at the tail end of 1805, discovered to his cost. He was serving on 'his Majesty's sloop *Elk*.'[44] Sloops being some of the smallest ships in the navy's fighting rates, they were often proving grounds for young gentlemen, the navy's way of testing fitness to command bigger ships. As ill-luck would have it, George was landed with a 'very youthful commander (for I do not think he had numbered sixteen years)'[45] whose ideas on how to lay his hands on prize money proved bigger than his brains. They entailed giving the squadron commander, 'Old Snuffy', the slip and 'as soon as the sun goes down, up stick and make all sail for the Gulf of Mexico, where we are sure to make our fortunes'.

With the lure of prize money, and no longer fettered by duty to King and Country, it was no surprise that 'this was a clincher, and no person disputed the propriety of such conduct, which was pursued to the very letter, as his Majesty's sloop *Elk* made the town of Carthagena on the succeeding night'. With orders from his youthful commander to 'pick up all you can',[46] George soon spotted a likely target, 'yonder lateen-rigged boat'[47] except that the cargo was 'Melons and pumpkins'. This wasn't quite what the youthful commander had had in mind embarking on his marauding expedition. Still, if George Elliot had been happy with 'his captures [of] market vessels going to Cadiz with very fine fruit, vegetables, poultry, honey, eggs and things we were ready to eat our share of and be thankful'[48] and Worthy Duff had made do with his 'hogshead of claret', the crew of the *Elk* had better be satisfied with their melons and pumpkins. So the order went out: '"Select a supply of the best melons for the boats, and let them go anywhere but to Carthagena." And we lay on the oars, and indulged in a mortal gorge on melons, letting the boat drift at the caprice of the currents. This was employment very passable in a West India night.'[49]

Come daylight, however, and caught unawares, the *Elk* found itself surrounded by 11 enemy gunboats, whereupon 'the heavy report of a gun, the whistle, the crash, the death groan of Richard Bennet, our senior mate, and the agonised shriek of our steward, Saunders Lackey, whose legs were shot off, were all heard the next instant. The cabin boy had likewise his arm broken by this most disastrous shot…'[50] Somehow the survivors got away and, 'having got sail on the brig – for a light breeze had sprung up – I went below to contemplate a most melancholy sight, the mutilated remains of our steward and Richard Bennet. Here was my young commander, weeping bitterly over the bodies, and accusing himself as the cause of their destruction.'[51]

George's withering verdict on this episode makes clear where he thought the blame lay: 'This is not a solitary instance, in the good old times, of boys being appointed to command men.'[52] To compound George's outrage, 'my youthful commander was thanked in public orders for his skill and bravery in the gunboat attack, made a post-captain, and I was sent home second lieutenant of the convoy ship, to be paid off on my arrival…'[53] However disgruntled George may have been at his lack of progress through the ranks, he was only echoing a complaint made frequently in the service as when the *Naval Chronicle* published a letter in 1808 from an anonymous correspondent who described himself as 'a professional man' and referred to 'that sort of patronage by which boys have made a sudden jump to the command of frigates at 17 years of age, or similar exertions of family or borough influence'.[54]

Whatever the failings of the youthful commander on the *Elk*, his big mistake was to assume that Trafalgar had driven the enemy from the seas. Trafalgar had destroyed the Spanish Navy's fighting capacity, but it would take two further sea battles to eliminate France as a sea power: the first by Sir Richard Strachan in his action of 4 November 1805, which began off Cape Finisterre and, with the capture of four French ships, yielded more prize money even than Trafalgar; the second at the Battle of Santo Domingo on 5–6 February 1806 when, as Francis Austen described, 'three of the enemy's ships were in our possession and the other two dismasted and on the rocks'.[55] As captain of the *Canopus*, this action finally brought Francis the 'pecuniary advantage' he had so long craved and enabled him to marry Mary Gibson on his return to Britain in July of the same year.

Santo Domingo was the last major sea battle of the Napoleonic Wars, as first the Spanish, then the French realized the suicidal futility of confrontation with Britain's unbeatable navy on the high seas. Reduced to a rear-guard action skulking in coves, inlets and harbours, the enemies of Britain could only wait for their ships – fighting and merchant – to be picked off as if at will. Away from the politics of mighty imperial ambitions, every officer, seaman, young gentleman and cabin boy, wherever he was serving at sea, could finally stop dreaming of his *Thetis*, his *Santa Brigida*, his Trafalgar, and instead embark on his own private treasure hunt. As everyone knew, the best place for this was a frigate, and that included James Gordon, veteran of St Vincent and Nile who, after leapfrogging various minor frigate commands, finally, in 1808, was appointed captain of the 38-gun frigate *Active* serving in a squadron commanded by William Hoste with orders to cruise in the Adriatic.

With James on the *Active* was Norwich Duff, finally released from his servitude on a succession of ships-of-the line. In one of these, Norwich had narrowly escaped death when on 14 February 1807, as the *Naval Chronicle* recorded acknowledging Norwich's new-found fame, the *Ajax* 'took fire in the bread-room; in ten minutes she was in a general blaze'[56] when 'of forty-five Midshipmen of every description, about twenty are saved; a son and a nephew of the late Captain Duff, and who were with him in the *Mars* when he gloriously fell in the action off Trafalgar, are among the survivors'.[57]

Of all the stations to be sent to along Europe's endless coastline, the Adriatic was a prime spot for plunder. Supposedly a French lake, if control of the shoreline were the measure, the Adriatic was in reality first come, first served for anything caught beyond the range of shore batteries, and it became a prize turkey shoot for the crews of the British frigates hunting its length and breadth. Robert Wilson, a lower-deck sailor with some education who was a seaman on the *Unité* frigate and rose to midshipman before deserting in 1811, served in the Adriatic from 1807, and as far as he was concerned the Adriatic was as much a free-for-all for Jack Tar as it was for the officers. In an entry in his journal for 21 April 1807 he noted: 'It is necessary here to remark that we so closely annoyed the trade in the Adriatic that scarcely a single vessel could pass without our examining them, especially those bound for Trieste, which made our favour courted and our sway dreaded.'[58]

His journal is a seemingly endless tally of captures, as his entry for 27 January 1807 records: 'Detained a ship under Imperial colours. She turned out to be a valuable prize, called the *Istria*, and mounting fourteen guns, laden with a cargo of brandy and wines, and a Venetian built ship… Gave the crew of the detained brig her longboat; they went to Trieste.'[59] In between captures came the tally of prize money being distributed, as on 12 July 1807 when 'each single-share man received three dollars prize money'.[60] At the end of each cruise came the big pay day when, arriving back in Malta, 'each man received as single share six lechins of prize money from agent and twelve dollars from captain from prize money on board'.[61]

With sudden influxes of money on this scale, the thoughts of the men and boys of the lower-decks may have reverted to what lay in store for them if they brought their prize money back home. If not, there were ballads to remind them:

> Don't you see the ships a-coming?
> Don't you see them in full sail?
> Don't you see the ships a-coming?
> With prizes at their tail.
> Oh! My little rolling sailor,
> Oh my little rolling he;
> I do love a jolly sailor,
> Blithe and merry might he be
> Sailors they get all the money,
> Soldiers they get none but brass[62]

Make it past the port-trollops eying 'the ships a-coming' and, if the Royal Academy exhibition of 1803 is any indication of contemporary perceptions, they would next have had to run the gauntlet of footpads skulking down dark alleyways and highwaymen lurking by the roadside. The description in the catalogue of two paintings exhibited by W. R. Bigg that year tells its own story: Exhibit number 173 was listed as 'The gallant sailor, returning home with his mother and sister, attacked by robbers, bravely defends his prize-money',[63] and Exhibit 186 was listed as 'The sailor boy rescued, and his prize-money restored'.[64]

With so many vultures waiting to pounce on the returning sailor, it is no surprise that Robert Wilson, arriving in Malta in July 1808 with pockets full of prize money, decided it was better he 'had glorious fun there… They hired every horse, jackass and coach, that they could find. They formed themselves into fleets (opponents) and performed several nautical manoeuvres on horseback, which of course must be very diverting'.[65]

Easy come, easy go. The cliché could just as well have applied to William Hoste, only it was his parasitical father who fed off William's winnings. From the moment William first went to sea in 1793 it seems that his career was about the prize money he could bring home for his father. In the early years there were no prizes, but still William was expected to report back to his father. As his sea-daddy on the *Agamemnon,* Nelson could have – should have – warned William how unreliable Dixon, William's father, was. Letter after letter to Fanny had Nelson complaining about Dixon Hoste's delinquency, as in early 1796 when he explodes in outrage: 'Extraordinary, I have not had a line from Mr Hoste since I drew the last bill, although it must be known I advanced the money every day for 14 months before I asked for it, and another is rising very fast, I am very angry.'[66]

Yet, instead of warning William, Nelson kept his own counsel. So come the dog-days of 1800, when there were prizes to be had but they were still few and far between, William began dutifully handing over to his father whatever prize money he received: 'I remitted to my agent, some few months back, £1000, and I intend to do the same with this when I get it. I hope my dear father will excuse me when I say the money is of no use to me, as my pay, with very little addition, serves me; and will take the trouble to put it to any purpose he thinks proper.'[67]

Now returning to the Mediterranean in 1808 it was more of the same, only this time there was to be a *lot* more of the same, because, as William proudly announced to his mother, 'Lord Collingwood has been good enough to give me the best cruise in his command':[68] the Adriatic. Ever mindful of his obligation to his father, William spelt out in his next letter home exactly what the Adriatic would mean for his father: 'I have at last got on good ground for pewterising; and I trust, if the war lasts, and I remain on this station a couple of years, to be able to give my good father a lift over the stones.'[69]

William continued to send his prize monies home, and his father continued to spend them. Some of his letters home were only about prizes – taken, to be taken or missed. As the years went by, Dixon's habits only got worse and, as quickly as William amassed his fortune, so, just as quickly, his father frittered it away. For years, William apparently turned a blind eye to his father's profligacy, but, writing in 1813 concerning interest on a loan of £3,400 he had made to his father the previous year, there is no doubting that the scales had finally fallen from the devoted son's eyes: 'I have received a letter from my Agent, which gives me much concern. It grieves me to find that my Father should deceive me, that even the Interest of the money I came forward with two years ago should not be paid, how then can the Principal? I assure you I feel quite hurt that there should be occasion for me to say a word on the subject.'[70] Of the £60,000 William is estimated to have earned from 'pewterising' in the Adriatic, by the time he married in 1817 there was a mere £12,000 he could offer up as capital to the marriage.

William was not the only son of Dixon's 'pewterising' in the Adriatic. In the tradition of naval families, William brought along the next generation, his younger brother Edward, 'Ned', aged 12 when the *Amphion* left England in January 1808. The letters home from William and Ned read much like a reprise of William's own early, innocent days going to sea in the *Agamemnon* with Nelson back in 1793, but this time it is William, 'the sea-daddy', crowing proudly that 'Our dear little sailor is very well and in high feather… It is the most beautiful day I ever saw; and the Isle of Wight on one side, and the coast about Lymington and Southampton on the other, form altogether the most beautiful prospect I ever beheld. Dear little Edward was in Raptures.'[71]

Next come the usual complications of adjusting to the new accommodation: 'Ned slept in his proper hammock for the first time last night. I was obliged to lift him in after several unsuccessful attempts on his part to accomplish it.'[72] Following that comes the Bay of Biscay, the Rubicon that must be crossed: 'Our little sailor … was not at all sea sick during the whole gale which was very sharp and a most tremendous sea running. He laid on my sofa singing … quite unconcerned as if he had been in the drawing room at Godwick. All our passengers were terribly sick.'[73] Finally it is Ned's turn to chip in, a 'wish you were here' postscript aimed at their younger brother Charles, with the sole intention of making him green with envy: 'We had famous fun the other day when it blew so hard. I am sure you would have laughed to see us toppling about the ship. William has got the prettiest little goat you ever saw.'[74]

Watchful of any apparent nepotism, William assures his parents that:

> Our dear little Edward is all you yourself could desire. He will make an excellent officer, and sailor, and is partial to the profession he has chosen. I keep him pretty tight at it, I assure you, and some say, his being my brother is the hardest duty of any youngster in the ship. I try to make him an example to all the other boys, and he has pride enough to see and to act up to my warmest wishes. He is first at everything: I need say no more. When you write to him, give him a hint how necessary it is he should be acquainted with history in general. He is so fond of the practical business, that I am obliged to exert fraternal authority to get the theory.'[75]

Ned's early experiences at sea were very much like William's own first innocent days on the *Agamemnon* with Nelson back in 1793. It was only on entering the Mediterranean that it becomes apparent how much the world had changed for Britain's young sailors. Close on the border between Spain and France came Ned's first taste of action when the *Amphion* encountered a French 30-gun frigate, the *Baleine:* 'Not a moment was lost. We had every man ready for boarding her… In all the actions I have been in, I never saw more cheerfulness and confidence than was expressed by my gallant crew. The poltroon, seeing our intentions, gave way to his fears, and rather than await an attack where he had every advantage, cut his cables and ran her on shore under the batteries of Fort Bouton… "Oh! had I been able to bring him out, what a chance it would have been for your boys."'[76]

The frenzy of anticipation is palpable in this letter of William's from May 1808. No wonder. The days of the patriotic call to arms were long gone. This was payback time and, whether the hunt for prizes was for the 'boys' or their father, it was on in earnest, but the enemy was not playing fair: it ran for cover. Even young Ned had caught the bug: 'I think it will make you happy to hear your boys have done their duty. My little Ned behaved like a hero, and will be everything you could wish him. He tells me he could beat a dozen French frigates now.'[77]

William was soon carrying Ned with him on prize raids, as in August 1809 when he recorded that 'Dear Little Edward was in one of the boats, and shared in the glory and danger of the day. I am in hope [he] will make the first lieutenant; he richly deserves promotion, and if I had any interest, or any of my friends, I would make no scruple of asking their assistance.'[78]

However, as exciting and rewarding as prize-taking was in the Adriatic at this time, the enemy still had some fight in it, as Ned soon found out. In April 1811 William Hoste's squadron was in a particularly hard-fought action against 11 French and Italian warships off the island of Lissa. Under the command of James Gordon and with Norwich Duff among the Midshipmen, the *Active* took numerous casualties: nine killed, including 'Thomas Tracey, boy',[79] and 26 wounded. The casualty list for the *Amphion* was '15 killed, 47 wounded'.[80] Two midshipmen, J. R. Spearman and Charles Hayes, died, and among the wounded were William and younger brother 'T. E. Hoste, midshipman'.[81]

Four months later, on 27 July 1811, there was a further action off the town of Ragosniza. Following this action, Norwich was mentioned in dispatches as one of ten midshipmen that James Gordon decided to 'recommend ... to the notice of the commander-in-chief'.[82] In fleet actions, disputes could often arise between captains, each one claiming a ship captured as his prize. In such cases, the captain of the ship captured was called on to offer his opinion as happened in November 1811, when 'Mr. Norwich Duff, midshipman of the Active, having arrived on board [*La Pomone*], intimated (by orders) a desire to know to which of the ships the frigate had struck; on which, the question was put to the French captain'.[83]

The duty of prize-master was especially hazardous in the Adriatic. Without explaining why, Robert Wilson gave the bald facts in an entry for 31 January 1807: 'We received intelligence from Captain Parker of *Melpomene*, that only four of the prizes that sailed with her on the 25th ult. had reached Corfu ... the other eight they feared were lost; two of them they actually saw go down, [and] saved the people. Of our people missing were Ishmael Goodall, William Jervey, Laurence Flannagan and Richard Jones; the rest sent away arrived in *Melpomene*. Two midshipmen of hers and some of the *Weazle*'s men were missing.'[84]

Three of Ned's fellow midshipmen, Charles Anson, Edward Pocock and Cornwallis Paley also died, each on separate prize-master missions. Ned survived the lottery that was a prize-master duty, possibly because his brother kept him close at hand: 'Dear little Edward was again in one of the boats, and came out prize-master of one of the gun-boats. I think if ever a midshipman deserved his commission as lieutenant, for putting himself in the way of shot, my young friend richly deserves it.'[85]

The problem of casualties among prize-crews was especially acute in the Adriatic and the root cause seems to have been that the British had become victims of their own success. The more prizes they took, the fewer officers and men they had to place on prize-ships. Midshipman Cornwallis Paley fell foul of this when he was given a scratch-crew of three men and a boy for the prize he was to take to Corfu, but in addition was assigned three Italian prisoners, who, unsurprisingly, at their first opportunity turned on the prize-crew, stabbing the boy and slitting Paley's throat.

The problem of scratch-crews wasn't new, only more acute in the Adriatic. The obvious solution was the one William Dillon says was advocated to Captain Hartwell when he was crewing up the 38-gun frigate *Thetis* back in January 1793: 'His officers wanted him to apply for 50 additional men, in case of taking prizes...'[86] According to William, Captain Hartwell refused the suggestion. One captain who had no such qualms, however, was Thomas Cochrane. Given the opportunity, and with one eye fixed on the business of prize-taking, Thomas overmanned his ships. The port-admiral at Plymouth was obviously wise to the antics, so, on one occasion, ordered Thomas to quit port even though his new ship, the frigate *Impérieuse*, was 'in a very unfit condition for sea.'[87] In his memoirs, Thomas tries to claim that it was common practice for port-admirals to use strong-arm tactics: 'The alacrity of the port authorities to obtain praise for despatching vessels to sea before they were in fit condition was reprehensible.'[88]

In a further attempt to deflect attention from what, given the scale of his future prize-taking activities, was in essence the recruitment of a private navy, Thomas enumerates a long list of equipment deficiencies that meant that 'the safety of the frigate might have been compromised'[89] but, tellingly, leaves out any reference to shortage of crew – not because he had or had not reached his official complement of 284, but because he must have known his ploy to overman had been rumbled.

As it was, Thomas promptly captured 15 ships in a three-week period: not a bad haul for a ship that was, according to Thomas, in a very unfit condition for sea.

During his time as a frigate commander from 1800 to 1809, it would be this 'private' navy that would sustain his desperate drive for outrageous fortune, enabling him to attack and take prizes at will, but then also bring them back to port in one piece to be condemned. His desperation for prize money is understandable if not excusable. Much like William Hoste, Thomas was a victim of his father's bad habits, the only difference being that Thomas' father had squandered the Cochrane family fortune on risky business ventures before Thomas even set foot on board ship. Imminent penury drove Thomas into the navy at the outbreak of war in 1793. He was then aged 17, but, on paper, had been at sea since the age of five, in another instance of false-mustering, appearing on the books of a succession of ships that never once heard the patter of Thomas' tiny feet on their decks. With money troubles casting a long shadow over the family, inevitably Thomas' whole naval career and that of his younger brothers, Archibald and Basil, who served under him at various times, must be seen through the prism of fortune-hunting.

Thomas had an uncanny ability to sniff out and capture prizes, some of them snared in melodramatic 'Goliath and David' actions. In a single-ship action on 6 May 1801, which brought his name to the lips of every thrill-seeking father, mother and child in Britain, the *Speedy* sloop of war, mounting 14 guns with a crew of 'fifty-four officers, men and boys'[90] stormed and captured the Spanish 32-gun frigate *Gamo*, with a crew of '274 officers, seamen, boys, and supernumeraries, forty-five marines. Total 319.'[91] Given the obvious disparity in numbers, Thomas needed every man for the boarding party, so left the *Speedy* in the hands of the ship's surgeon and two boys. Having captured the *Gamo*, he next had to solve the problem that had confronted Henry Walker on the *Monarca* after Trafalgar: what to do when the prize-crew was heavily outnumbered by the prisoners captured. His solution was nothing if not cavalier: 'It became a puzzle what to do with the 263 unhurt prisoners now we had taken them, the *Speedy* having only forty-two men left. Promptness was however necessary; so driving the prisoners into the hold, with guns pointing down the hatchway, and leaving thirty of our men on board the prize – which was placed under the command of my brother, the Hon. Archibald Cochrane, then a midshipman – we shaped our course to Port Mahon.'[92]

In his report, which eventually found its way into the *London Gazette* and *Naval Chronicle*, Thomas made certain the world knew what a brilliant action he had masterminded and rammed home the message by mentioning, not just once but twice, his younger brother, Archibald 'the Honourable Mr Cochrane', as deserving 'all the approbation that can be bestowed'.[93] Henceforth the 'Cochrane' name would be inextricably linked with all that was swashbuckling about these Wars. Thomas was a great showman, and he made sure that every heartbeat of every exploit was recorded in the papers of the day. Even before the *Gamo* action, he was forcing his attentions on the public. The *Queen Charlotte* caught fire and sank on 17 March 1800, and Britain was still mourning this tragedy when Thomas had his father plant in the April issue of the *Naval Chronicle* the following piece of unabashed flummery: 'Captain Cochrane has received a Letter from his nephew Lord Cochrane, who was a Lieutenant on board His Majesty's ship *Queen Charlotte*. Some time previous to her blowing up, he had been appointed to the *Speedy* brig; but she not being ready, he was put into the *Généreux*, Lord Nelson's prize, to carry her into port, so that he has escaped.'[94]

In the circumstances, this announcement seems extraordinary. There were other survivors, only they did not 'shout it from the roof-tops'. More to the point, there were 636 obituaries to record. Surely one lieutenant more or less to have cheated death made little difference … except to Thomas. Again, in 1804 when he was putting together a crew for his latest appointment, the *Pallas*, Thomas, ever the showman, issued a poster, almost burlesque in its tone, calling for volunteers. Forget duty, forget patriotism, forget Napoleon trampling all over Europe. The 'Flying' *Pallas* was a frigate and this meant only one thing to Thomas: prizes. So: 'None need apply, but SEAMEN, or Stout Hands, able to rouse about the Field Pieces, and carry an hundred weight of PEWTER, without stopping, at least three miles.'[95]

The requirement for 'Stout Hands' did not mean he was excluding boys from the ship's complement. The Admiralty had allowed him to take only a dozen men from his previous ship. With the *Pallas* requiring a crew of 215 to bring it up to its official complement, and rumours swirling round that Spanish treasure ships were on the move from the West Indies, there was no time to lose. Needs must, and if he had to resort to the Press and boys, 'Stout Hands' or not, so be it; anyone so long as he was off and away on the trail of his next fortune.

The first cruise of the 'Flying' *Pallas* more than lived up to the promises on the poster. It is estimated that Thomas' share of the prize money from this cruise was in excess of £40,000. The Port Report for Plymouth for the period 24 February to 23 March 1805 records four prize-ships captured by Thomas and brought into port. Once more the ultimate showman, Thomas ensured that the Port Report for 24 February recording the arrival home of one of his prizes, the *Caroline*, carried the following personal message from him: 'His lordship declaring if ever it was in his power he would fulfil his public advertisement (stuck up here) for entering Seamen, of filling their pockets with Spanish *pewter* and *cobs*, nick names given by Sailors to silver ingots and Spanish dollars.'[96]

In *The Autobiography of a Seaman* published in 1859–60, Thomas repeated this and other extracts culled from the *Naval Chronicle*, quoting almost verbatim to add an official gloss to what was an unashamed exercise in self-congratulation. The colourful version of his past life that he presented in his *Autobiography* added the final layer of myth essential to the process of immortalization.

And when he wasn't singing his own praises at the time or 50 years on, he could count on those who had served under him to do the job for him. Frederick Marryat's novel *Frank Mildmay or The Naval Officer*, published in 1829, reprises many of Thomas' great exploits. Frederick's father was Chairman of the Lloyd's Patriotic Fund, so had the pick of captains when deciding where to place his son. Frederick entered the navy in September 1806 aged 14 and, initially as a boy volunteer first class, served under Thomas on the *Impérieuse* over the next three years, the heyday of his prize-taking exploits. A fellow volunteer first class was Henry Cobbett, son of William Cobbett the radical parliamentary reformer.

These were the years when Britain's war policy was to progressively take the fight to the French, which meant ever more land operations culminating, from 1808 onwards, in the Peninsular War in Portugal and Spain. At this time, the navy was being increasingly relegated to the role of 'packhorse' fetching and carrying for the land forces under the command of the Duke of Wellington. In a precursor of this trend, many of the *Impérieuse*'s actions combined land with sea operations but, with his usual panache, Thomas turned them to personal advantage. In a typical prize-taking action on 7 January 1807, Thomas reported that 'Lieutenant Mapleton volunteered his services to bring out with the boats whatever vessels might be found there, and, as a preliminary step, attacked Fort

Roquette... A large quantity of military stores was destroyed, four thirty-six pounders, two field pieces, and a thirteen inch mortar spiked, the platoons and carriages burnt, and the fort laid in ruins.'[97]

Midshipmen were in the thick of these actions, among them 'the Honourable Mr Napier and Mr H Stewart, Midshipmen, [who] accompanied Lieutenant Mapleton...'[98] as well as some of the youngest among the crew, who were on one occasion ordered by Thomas to execute a diversionary manoeuvre:

> We now passed close to a small fishing town, where other guns were observed in position ... these being manned by regular troops and backed by hundreds of armed peasantry... By way of feint, to draw off the attention of the cavalry, both *Spartan* and *Impérieuse* manned their small boats and the rocket boats with the ships' boys, dressed in marines' scarlet jackets, despatching these at some distance towards the right, as though an attack there were intended. The device was successful, and a body of cavalry ... promptly set off to receive them.[99]

It is doubtful if one of these 'ships' boys' was Frederick, otherwise he would surely have used the incident in his fictional account of Frank Mildmay, so ingenious is this ruse devised by Thomas. One prize action at which Frederick was present, however, occurred on 21 February 1808 off the town of Almeria when, the boarding parties descending into the boats in preparation for the mission, in Frederick's words 'they found many of the younger midshipmen, who although not selected for the service, had smuggled themselves into the boats... The Captain pretended not to see them when he looked over the side and desired the boats to shove off.'[100] Thomas is silent on this point, but takes up the running in his *Autobiography*, describing how 'the boats, having been previously got in readiness, were forthwith hoisted out, and the large pinnace, under the command of Lieutenant Caulfield, dashed at the French ship, which, as the pinnace approached, commenced a heavy fire, in the midst of which the ship was gallantly boarded, but with the loss of poor Caulfield, who was shot on entering the vessel.'[101]

Thomas hated taking casualties among his crew, so his account glosses over the details of Caulfield's death, instead describing the activities of 'the other pinnace'. It was down to Frederick, the novelist, to supply the gory details in his memoirs: 'Half of our boat's crew were laid beneath the thwarts; the remainder boarded. Caulfield was the first on the vessel's deck – a volley of musketoons received him and he fell dead with thirteen bullets in his body.'[102]

The occasional casualty apart, these were halcyon days: for prize-taking, for the swashbuckling Thomas, and for Frederick, the impressionable young boy in search of his own fortune. He later remembered how:

> …the cruises of the *Imperieuse* were periods of continued excitement, from the hour she hove up her anchor till she dropped it again in port: the day that passed without a shot being fired in anger, was with us a blank day: the boats were hardly secured on the booms than they were cast loose and out again; the yard and stay tackles were for ever hoisting up and lowering down. The expedition with which parties were formed for service; the rapidity of the frigate's movements night and day; the hasty sleep snatched at all hours; the waking up at the report of guns, which seemed the keynote to the hearts of those on board, the beautiful precision of our fire, obtained by constant practice; the coolness and courage of our captain, inoculating the whole of the ship's company; the suddenness of our attacks; the gathering after the combat, the killed lamented, the wounded almost envied; the powder so burnt into our faces that years could not remove it; the proved character of every man and officer aboard, the implicit trust and adoration we felt for our commander; the ludicrous situations which would occur in the extremest danger and create mirth when death was staring you in the face, the hair-breadth escapes, and the indifference to life shown by all – when memory sweeps along these years of excitement even now, my pulse beats more quickly with the reminiscence.'[103]

With prose like this, Frederick found his own unique seam of outrageous fortune.

15

THE WAR OF 1812

The *Little Belt* has arrived off New York, where she has had a sad beating by the American frigate *President*. Some time early in the month, the *Guerrier* [sic] impressed a man on board an American on her passage from one port in the United States to another, whom they took to be an Englishman, as he had no protection, which made a great noise in New York. In consequence of it, the *President* was ordered immediately to sea to demand from the *Guerrier* the man so impressed; this was on the 14th [May 1811]; on the 15th she fell in with the *Little Belt*... Commodore Rodgers [gave] directions that one of the bow guns should be fired into the *Little Belt*, which struck her under the cut water... The *President* mounted 52 guns and 420 men; the *Little Belt* only 18, and 120 men.[1]

One sailor of questionable nationality wrongly impressed and suddenly two nations were at each other's throats: a flimsier pretext for a bloody encounter it is not possible to imagine and yet there was more to come, as America and Britain turned up the volume of rhetoric surrounding the incident. First it was the turn of Captain Bingham of the *Little Belt* to cry foul in the newspapers: 'A boat, accordingly, came with an officer, and a message came from Commodore Rodgers, of the *President*, United States frigate, to say that he lamented much the unfortunate affair (as he termed it) that had happened, and that had he known our force to be inferior, he should not have fired at me. I asked his motive for having fired at all; his reply was, that we had fired the first gun at him, which was positively not the case.'[2]

231

In the opening salvo of this war of words, he who 'had fired the first gun' was to blame. Next it was the turn of the American press to weigh in, the *New York Evening Post* reflecting how:

> …it is said the sloop of war fired a gun, and that was a threat of the most unequivocal kind. Doubtless it was, and deserved a gun in answer. But if we go a little farther back, we will find that the sloop of war hailed before she fired, and received no answer; the commodore, who had before hailed also, conceiving he had a right to the first answer. If he had, there can then be no question but he was perfectly correct in refusing to take any notice of the sloop's hail. It would seem, therefore, that strictly speaking, the whole resolves itself into this very question – Which of the two ought, in the first instance, to have answered the inquiries of the other? Those who maintain that the sloop of war ought first to have answered, instead of returning the hail back, say, that as the *President* got the advantage of hailing first, she … was on an equal footing with the English, and equally entitled to respect.'[3]

In the desperate search for the moral high ground, it had now come down to who had 'the advantage of hailing first'. Yet, morally justified or not, there were still casualties: on the *President*, Commodore Rodgers could boast that 'the injury sustained by the ship under my command is very trifling … no person killed, and but one (a boy) wounded'.[4] Captain Bingham had less palatable news to report: 'The *Little Belt* had 11 killed and 21 wounded; a midshipman had his head shot off, the first lieutenant and master wounded; the latter has, or will be obliged to undergo amputation, his arm being dreadfully shattered.'[5] Among the list of 21 'wounded, most of them mortally'[6] were three boys: William Fern, William Weston and George Roberts. In all, a quarter of the ship's complement had been killed or wounded.

Little Belt was just the latest in a string of fractious incidents between the two countries, originally triggered by Britain exercising its prerogative to board and search American ships for so-called deserters. In some instances, Britain had a genuine grievance, as when it discovered 'John McDonald, alias Samuel Higgins who had been for some time on board an American schooner',[7] put him on trial and hanged him in 1801 'for aiding and assisting in carrying his majesty's late ship *Danae* into a French Port, and delivering her up to the Enemy'.[8] McDonald had 'an American Protection, and was disguised as an American with ear-rings in his ears'.[9] The moral of the story? Beware Americans bearing earrings.

More often than not, however, the search for deserters was a ploy by the British Navy to supplement the work of the Press Gang and flesh out its service with any able-bodied seaman it could lay its hands on, irrespective of their age or nationality. These were murky waters indeed, where nationality and age hung on a scrap of paper that could be forged, torn up, lost or simply ignored. Jacob Nagle recalled the captain aboard the *St Lucia* brig back in 1783 who 'kept the jolly boat for his own use, with 4 little American boys to pul [*sic*] him about, as he new they could not run a way'.[10]

Jacob's career at sea is its own case in point. Born in Reading, Pennsylvania, he served in Washington's army in 1777 aged 15 and three years later enlisted in the fledgling American Navy to fight the British, albeit with his heart very much elsewhere, or so he recalled later: 'while the schooner was laying at Sandy Point, I made a practice of walking the deck till 2 or 3 in the morning, crying and fretting for the loss of my parents, never being so long from home before, when 14 or 16 shells would be flying in the air at one time'.[11] Taken prisoner when the American privateer he was on board was captured in 1781, Jacob 'transferred' his allegiances to the British, serving in its navy for the next 20 years, many of those voluntarily. Jacob was not alone in his voluntary-cum-enforced servitude. American sources claimed in 1800 that 'the number of seamen [in the US Navy] is between 40 and 50,000, including about 5,000 impressed on British ships of war'.[12] It is estimated that 373 Americans alone fought in British ships at Trafalgar.

The tension over so-called 'deserters' briefly reached incendiary levels in 1807 over an incident on 23 June 'off the Capes of Virginia'.[13] News of it even reached Robert Wilson two months later in the Adriatic where he was busy on prize-taking duties but, nevertheless, was in no doubt as to the possible ramifications: 'Received intelligence that the *Constellation* (American frigate) was taken by HMS *Leopard*, and likelihood of American war ensuing'.[14] Robert's information was wrong on one point: the name of the American frigate was *Chesapeake* not *Constellation*. His intelligence was also quickly out of date, as he found out two weeks later when he was one of those who 'boarded an American ship from Boston to Trieste. Heard from her that there was no likelihood of an American war ensuing; and concerning the affair ... it seemed that four men deserted from HMS *Melampus* into the American service'.[15]

Robert was not the only one keeping a weather-eye open at this time for signs of tension between the two countries. In its January 1808 edition, the *Naval Chronicle* reported that: 'Our relations with America are still in a state of great uncertainty; but the proceedings of the senate, and of the house of representatives, as far as they are known, are rather pacific than hostile.'[16] The Americans had evidently backed down, at least for the time being.

Meanwhile, the 'deserters' from the *Melampus* had to be punished, and, with both countries having respect for due process, the ensuing court martial was an ideal forum where Britain could make its case. Midshipmen were often the conduit transmitting orders from a captain to his men on a ship and, accordingly, their evidence could be crucial in courts martial. Two midshipmen gave evidence in this case: Robert Townsend, because he was in command of the jolly-boat (a medium-sized boat used for general tasks) when the four men deserted, and George Tincombe, because he could identify the deserters and was therefore one of 'several midshipmen [who] went on board the *Chesapeake* to search for deserters'.[17] The following questions and answers during George's evidence illustrate how murky the waters surrounding the issue of nationality had become:

Q: Were there many Englishmen mustered on board her? –

A. About twelve men and boys.

Q: Were any of those Englishmen demanded, or any other men demanded, or taken out, except known deserters? –

A: No.[18]

The British were making a fine legal point: an English man or boy was only a deserter if he absconded from a British naval ship and not just because he was English. The powers-that-be in America may have decided to back off, but such legal hair-splitting was lost on the American public. Resentment rumbled on and when the *Little Belt* affair broke three years later, a poem published in the December 1811 issue of the *Naval Chronicle* and subtitled 'Tit for Tat; Or the *Chesapeake* paid for in British blood'[19] left Britain in no doubt that *Little Belt* was payback for *Chesapeake*. The following excerpts give some indication of how high emotions were running in America:

You all remember well, I guess
The *Chesapeake* disaster
When Britons dared to kill and press,
To please their royal master.

But still for this we manned no ship
But used expostulation;
They murder'd Peirce – they fired On *Trip* –
We bore the degradation

But finding injuries prolong'd
Become a growing evil,
Our Commodore got leave, if wrong'd
To blow 'em to the devil

Then having chastis'd the foe,
And wounded thirty British
We gave the rascals leave to go,
They felt so deuced skittish.[20]

'When Britons dared to kill and press' was a clear reference to *Chesapeake*, but this was not the only running sore between the two countries. They 'fired On *Trip*' is an allusion to another bloody encounter and yet another long-standing bone of contention: taking as prizes American ships caught trading with Britain's latest enemy. As resident translator-at-large while aboard the *Seahorse* in 1797, Betsy Fremantle, née Wynne, witnessed the process at close quarters, when her services were enlisted in a prize-taking action against an American merchant ship: 'Sunday February 5th: Took a prize in the morning under American colours laden with grain from the coast of Barbary to Marseilles, tho' the Master, Captain Richard Smith swears he was going to Genoa, his papers and letters prove the contrary. A great bore to examine these papers…'[21] Two days later 'Michael Smith begins to acknowledge that he was going to Marseilles and the cargo was condemned as French',[22] with the result that on Thursday 9 February 'the *Blanche* is going to Porto Ferrajo with the prize'.[23]

Jacob Nagle was serving on the *Blanche* at this time but, judiciously, his journal makes no mention of the prize-action. By the time he came to write up his journal in the late 1830s, he was back on home soil and would have judged it unwise to mention any actions he might have been involved in, even remotely, against his fellow Americans. Not that the captain of the *Blanche* would have obliged Jacob to take part. Captains, like James Dacres of HMS *Guerrière*, understood the prevailing convention and, in his case, relieved ten impressed American sailors of battle duties during a later action against an American warship.

The poet who wrote 'Tit for Tat' was not the only American to remember that 'they fired On Trip'. For one youngster, the *Trip* incident was his first experience of the English. David Farragut, future first Admiral of the US Navy, was only eight when the *Trip* action occurred in 1809, but he vividly recalled the 'bad feeling' in his later journal. Referring to the circumstances of his adoption after his mother's death by Commander David Porter, David described how:

This was after my mother's death. I returned with Commander Porter to New Orleans, where I met Mrs Porter for the first time… I continued to reside with Commander Porter, occasionally accompanying him on excursions and boat expeditions, and sometimes going with my father across the Lake to his plantation; so that I soon became fond of this adventurous sort of life.

Porter was at length relieved, and returned to Washington in the bomb-ketch *Vesuvius*, I accompanying him. It was then that I took leave of my kind parent for ever. We touched at Havana, where we learned that the brig *Vixen*, Captain Tripp, had been fired into by a British vessel of war. I mention this merely because I believe it was the first thing that caused bad feeling in me toward the English nation. I was too young to know anything about the Revolution; but I looked upon this as an insult to be paid in kind, and was anxious to discharge the debt with interest.[24]

If it is possible to find a moment when the US Navy came of age, this is it. Previous generations of young American sailors had cut their teeth in the American Revolution or, as in the case of Stephen Decatur and Oliver Perry, in the wars of the late 1790s against North African pirates. But these were haphazard affairs in naval terms. For David Farragut to have the mighty British Navy already in his sights at the age of eight was a seminal moment: a window into the future.

And if eight-year-old David was thinking like this in 1809, it is no wonder that, two years on, dark forces ambitious to capitalize on Britain's preoccupation with France and make a lunge for Canada would work their magic and ensure that 'the unfortunate affair' of the *Little Belt* must rumble on, gathering momentum towards an inevitable and bloody conclusion.

The *New York Evening Post* had had its say, as had the 'Tit for Tat' bard. Next, an American Court of Inquiry 'calling every deck officer, as well as captains of guns, now on board the *President* who were present during the action'[25] was convened in late 1811 to investigate the *Little Belt* affair. And 'every deck officer' meant just that, young and old alike, and as with the *Melampus* affair, once again crucial evidence would be submitted by midshipmen, including Joseph Smith, who testified that he:

> Heard Commodore R [Rodgers] hail, and no reply for five seconds. Heard second hail, and was looking at the *Little Belt* when the first gun was fired by her, before a shot or any provocation was given from the *President*. The Commodore fired one gun, then the *Little Belt* three, and action continued. Thought the *Little Belt* a frigate. The duration of the action, and orders to cease as before stated. The last order to stop firing was received by three different officers – Commodore R's statement confirmed.[26]

Another midshipman, Richard Carson, gave his version, as seen from where he 'was on the forecastle and gang-ways. Commodore R. hailed, and was answered by repeating his words; second hail was answered by a shot. Was looking at the *Belt*, and saw and heard the gun, before any provocation from Commodore Rodgers, Gun from the *President* was followed by the *Belt*'s broadside, as stated by other. Commodore's account confirmed.'[27] Finally 'Matthew C. Perry, Silas Duncan and John McClack, midshipmen, gave their evidence to the same effect'.[28]

Five young midshipmen being called to give evidence in a Court of Inquiry whose verdict, everyone by then knew, would have huge political ramifications: no surprise then that the evidence of each of the five midshipmen was almost identical. Rodgers had a reputation for having a 'tyrannical and blustering disposition'.[29] Known as 'Bully Rodgers', he had form with junior officers and, in his early days as a captain, a 'court of enquiry was held upon him for unofficer-like conduct in striking one of his midshipmen [and] he was dismissed the service by the President'.[30] Of course, these reports in the September 1811 edition of the *Naval Chronicle* ahead of the Court of Inquiry could be dismissed as the normal propaganda attendant on a highly charged incident, except that the *Chronicle* claimed it was only relaying what had been reported in the 'American papers'.

Forget the original grievance that had brought the might of the *President* down on *Little Belt* in the first place. Forget the heavy British casualties. Forget even that it was all 'an accident' according to John Russell, who served in the *President* and made an affidavit on 25 July 1811 that stated 'that the first gun was fired from the *President*, but he believes from an accident, as no orders were given from the quarter-deck to fire; the guns had locks, and were all cocked. After the action he was informed by the men in the waste, that a man was entangled with the lan-yard of the lock, that occasioned the gun to go off.'[31] What had or had not happened before or during the action no longer mattered. The Court of Inquiry had done its work: everyone on the *President* agreed that it was the *Little Belt*'s fault, and President James Madison now had the legal vindication he needed to beat the war drums, which he did when he had the government newspaper, the *National Intelligencer*, declare on 3 June 1811 that:

> We understand that the conduct of Commodore Rodgers, in repelling and chastising the attack so causelessly and rashly made on the United States frigate *President*, by the British ship of war *Little Belt* has the approbation of the President of the United States … and we assert, that it may be confidently expected by our naval commanders, that in supporting the dignity of our flag, they will be rewarded with the applause of the American government.[32]

It seems there is a point of no return ahead of any war. With *Little Belt*, that point had been reached. Yet to call what was declared on 18 June 1812 a 'war' is, arguably, to elevate it beyond its true magnitude. Officially, the conflict lasted not far short of three years, yet for two of those years President Madison was frantically trying to extricate himself from what soon became apparent was a near disaster of his own making. Nine months after declaring war he was already nominating commissioners to go to Europe in search of peace. Skirmishing, on land and at sea, continued during the peace negotiations. So bizarre are the proportions of this 'war' that the Battle of New Orleans, the biggest of the conflict, took place after peace negotiations had been concluded. As for the Battle of Bladenburg, which was fought on 24 August 1814 and opened the way for 4,000 British troops to enter Washington, the Americans could muster only 6,500 militia to defend the capital. American casualties were 26 killed, 51 wounded; British casualties amounted to 64 killed and 185 wounded.[33]

At sea it was the same story. There were only two major battles, both on lakes and both won convincingly by the Americans: the Battle of Lake Erie in September 1813 and the Battle of Lake Champlain in September 1814. The combined total of ships, American and British, engaged in these two battles was 19 and total casualties were a mere 496. This compares with Trafalgar where there were 27 British ships-of-the-line alone engaged, carrying not far short of 21,500 officers and men, and combined French, Spanish and British casualties exceeded 12,000, of which 449 dead and 1,214 wounded were British.[34]

Most of the sea engagements of this conflict were single-ship actions and it was only the repeated success of the Americans in these encounters that gave them any wider significance. These American successes have been attributed to many factors, one of which was the growing preponderance of boys and young gentlemen in the crews of British ships by this time. To what extent this is the case or an excuse for other failings is debatable. At the court martial to explain the loss of HMS *Guerrière* in September 1812, Captain Dacres gave evidence that 'the absence of the third lieutenant, second lieutenant of marines, three midshipmen, and twenty-four men considerably weakened our crew, and we only mustered at quarters two hundred and forty-four men and nineteen boys'.[35]

These ship-to-ship actions typify the tit-for-tat nature of this conflict. *Chesapeake* versus *Leopard* in 1807 was avenged by *Little Belt* versus *President* in 1811, which was punished in turn by *Shannon* versus *Chesapeake* in 1813. And there were others. The list seems endless. These single-ship actions were often preceded by the preliminaries of a formal challenge, a gesture very much in keeping with the spirit of the times, given that America's Vice-President Aaron Burr had killed his political rival, Alexander Hamilton, in a duel back in 1804 and that the English and Americans were, certainly man-to-man, reluctant adversaries. Prior to the action leading to the capture of the USS *Chesapeake* by the British frigate *Shannon* on 1 June 1813, Philip Broke, a contemporary of Francis Austen's from the Portsmouth Naval Academy and captain of the *Shannon*, wrote to James

Lawrence, the captain of the *Chesapeake*, blockaded in Boston harbour, challenging him to what amounted to a duel. Broke first described the weapons that he had at his disposal and planned to use:

> I am, therefore, induced to address you more particularly, and to assure you that what I write, I pledge my honour to perform to the utmost of my power. The *Shannon* mounts twenty-four guns upon her broadside, and one light boat-gun – eighteen-pounders upon her maindeck, and thirty-two-pound carronades on her quarterdeck and forecastle, and is manned with a complement of 300 men and boys (a large proportion of the latter), besides thirty seamen, boys and passengers, who were taken out of recaptured vessels lately.[36]

There were to be strict rules of engagement to ensure that it was a fair fight, and, in this spirit, Broke offered his American antagonist the privilege of choosing where the duel should take place:

> …I will send all other ships beyond the power of interfering with us, and meet you wherever it is most agreeable to you, within the limits of the under-mentioned rendezvous, viz., from six to ten leagues east of Cape Cod lighthouse; from eight to ten leagues east of Cape Ann's light… If you will favour me with any plan of signals or telegraph, I will warn you (if sailing under this promise) should any of my friends be too nigh, or anywhere in sight, until I can detach them out of my way; or I will sail with you under flag of truce, to any place you think safest from our cruisers, hauling it down when fair to begin hostilities.[37]

Finally Broke elevated the duel almost to the status of a jousting match, grandiosely portraying their imminent combat as two warriors representing their respective countries, the outcome of which would decide the wider conflict:

> You must, sir, be aware that my proposals are highly advantageous to you, as you cannot proceed to sea singly in the *Chesapeake* without imminent risk of being crushed by the superior forces of the numerous British squadrons which are now abroad. You will feel it as a compliment if I say that the result of our meeting may be the most grateful service I can render to my country; and, I doubt not, that you, equally

confident of success, will feel convinced that it is only by repeated triumphs, in even combats, that your little navy can now hope to console your country for the loss of trade it can no longer protect.[38]

The American captain did not receive the letter, but in any event came out to meet his opponent, accompanied by a number of pleasure-boats eager to watch the match. Broke duly abided by the terms of his challenge. This was one of the few 'duels' that the British won, and with the large proportion of boys in the *Shannon*'s complement, it is inevitable that British youngsters figured heavily in the heat of the action. An account by Provo Wallis, a British officer on the *Shannon*, described how:

A severe encounter has been raging in the tops. The midshipmen – Smith in the fore and Cosnahan in the main – had vastly distinguished themselves. Smith boarded the enemy off the foreyard of the *Shannon*, and after hard fighting, chased his last remaining adversary down the foretopmast backstay on the deck. Cosnahan, in the maintop, finding the foot of the topsail intervene between the enemy and himself, laid out on the mainyardarm, and receiving loaded muskets handed down to him through the 'lubber's hole', shot three men from thence. These were midshipmen indeed![39]

Being in the heat of the action meant that youngsters took their fair share of casualties: 'The British returns state the loss of the *Shannon* to be: twenty-seven killed, fifty-eight wounded.'[40] Among the list of killed were:

Thos Barry – 1st Class boy: Cut in two by star shot
J McLoughlin – Boy: Grape shot in the neck
Wm Perrey – Boy: Grape shot in the body[41]

Among the wounded were:

Mr Samwell – Midshipman – Musket ball through the upper part of the left thigh, [Died in hospital]
John Gormand – Boy 3rd Class – Cut on the head; part of the ear carried away by a musket shot.[42]

For these British youngsters there would have been a note of desperation as they thrust themselves forward into battle: the British Navy was increasingly crowded out with young midshipmen bumping up against the upper echelons of a service that, after 20 years of almost continuous warfare, was top-heavy with admirals, captains and lieutenants. The navy had created intermediate ranks such as sub-lieutenant to give youngsters the impression that they were advancing through the service. However there was no escaping the fact that the naval war against the old enemy, France, had been won and that time was fast running out for these young gentlemen to secure for themselves the vital commission that their predecessors had come by so much more easily. The American theatre of operations was maybe their last opportunity.

Recovering in his hospital bed in Halifax, Nova Scotia after the action, Broke wrote giving his wife news of the young gentlemen on board whom she would have known personally through family connections back home. Their prospects for promotion featured as much as their convalescence. In his first letter Broke wrote that 'Samwell had a musket shot through the flesh of his thigh, but is doing extremely well... I have no doubt Etough, Smith and Leake will be made lieutenants directly, and some more soon. Samwell should have his time sent out, though, I fear, he is not of age yet. Tommy Fenn is well, and shot at the enemy bravely with a little gun... Driscoll getting on fast. I have recommended him strongly...'[43]

In his next letter, however, he was obliged to report that:

> I open this again for a cruel task. I know how my beloved L—— will feel for a person who has been so kind and attentive to her and to the dear children; but poor Mrs Samwell's son is gone. Only the night before, the doctors considered him safe, and I thought of nothing but his promotion; but his wound took a sudden turn from breaking a blood-vessel, and he went off whilst supposed to be asleep. The same surgeon attended him as has care of me, and every attention was shown him. I grieve for her and for my L——. I will write a letter to her for you to send; it may be relieving you, though she will come to you the same for comfort, and to vent her grief.[44]

This was the softer side of Broke. The harsher side came earlier in this same letter where, duellist to the end, he could not help crowing that 'the foolish Americans have been publishing a thousand absurd lies. Not liking to believe that their ship was bigger than *Shannon*, and got such a terrible beating by fair play, as she did, the simpletons say we used infernal machines. They are sadly disappointed. They had fetters for us all upon deck ready, which came to their use.'[45]

With two evenly matched ships, it was inevitable that casualties would be heavy on both sides. For the *Chesapeake*, the returns were: 'Killed, forty-seven; wounded ninety-nine; wounded since dead – fourteen.'[46] Among these were seven midshipmen listed as:

Killed: Midshipman Pollard Hopewell
             Midshipman John Evans
             Midshipman Courtland Livingston
Wounded: Midshipman Francis Nichols
             Midshipman Walter Abbott
             Midshipman Wm. A Weaver
             Midshipman Edmund M. Russell[47]

From these lists and the following description, American midshipmen were as much in the thick of the action as their British counterparts, as is further evident from the following account obtained by the *Naval Chronicle* from 'authentic sources of information'[48]: 'Captain Broke did not fall, but staggered back, and sat down on a coil of rope, when one of the *Chesapeake's* midshipmen, who had been in the foretop, slid down a rope and alighted close to him; the poor fellow was saved from the fury of the boarders, by the Captain, who brought him with him back to the quarter-deck.'[49]

For many of these American youngsters, conflict with Britain was a first opportunity to shine in an expanding service and they were not going to miss out. David Farragut was one who, early on, saw his chance of glory, following his adoptive father into the *Essex*, a 32-gun frigate being made ready for war in August 1811. David was ten years old at the time and in his later journal described those first days at sea as the battle lines were drawn:

The war with Great Britain was declared just after we began overhauling. The declaration was read to the crew on three successive days, and the Captain put the question to them, whether any one wished his discharge on the plea of being British subjects. No one answered until the third day, when, in the act of taking the oath of allegiance to the United States, one man refused, saying he was an Englishman.[50]

Years of resentment spilt over for all to see: 'Unfortunately for him, there was a sailor on board who offered to make oath that the fellow was an American… The crew were enraged to such a degree that violence would have been done if the Captain had not interfered. He determined to gratify them to a certain extent, and allowed the man to be tarred and feathered and put on shore at New York as a coward.'[51]

Three years of skirmishing around the coasts of South America finally brought David his big moment during this war. In February 1814 the *Essex* found itself trapped by the British in the Chilean port of Valparaiso and Captain Porter challenged the British frigate *Phoebe* to a ship-on-ship duel. The British captain declined the challenge and, together with the sloop of war *Cherub*, maintained the blockade. David described the initial manoeuvres:

> It was understood in our ship, one day, that Captain Porter had sent word to Captain Hillyar that, if he would send the *Cherub* to the leeward point of the harbour, he would go out and fight him. We all believed the terms would be accepted, and everything was kept in readiness to get under way. Soon after the *Phoebe* was seen standing in with her motto flag flying, on which was God and our Country! British Sailors' Best Rights! This was in answer to Porter's flag, Free Trade and Sailors' Rights. She fired a gun to windward, and the *Cherub* was seen running to leeward.[52]

The duel was on but, according to David, the British were not playing by the rules:

> …when within two miles of our position, the *Phoebe* bore up and set her studding-sails. This I considered to be a second breach of faith on the part of Hillyar; for by his manoeuvres in both instances, it was evident that he was either wanting in courage or lacked the good faith of a high-toned, chivalrous spirit to carry his original intention… He was dealing with a far inferior force, and it was ignoble in the extreme, on his part, not to meet his foe, when he had the ghost of an excuse for doing so, ship to ship.[53]

Outnumbered and outgunned, it was only a question of time before the *Essex* struck. David described the battle from his vantage point, starting out with the usual 'baptism' – literally, in his case – by fire:

> I shall never forget the horrid impression made upon me at the sight of the first man I had ever seen killed. He was a boatswain's mate, and was fearfully mutilated. It staggered and sickened at first; but they soon began to fall around me so fast that it all appeared like a dream, and produced no effect on my nerves. I can remember well, while I was standing near the Captain, just abaft the mainmast, a shot came through the waterways and glanced upwards, killing four men who were standing by the gun, taking the last in the head and scattering his brains over us. But this awful sight did not affect me half as much as the death of the first poor fellow. I neither thought of nor noticed anything but the working of the guns.[54]

David took his readers through his duties, some he was expecting, others not. His account stands comparison with those from the Battle of the Glorious First of June: where William Dillon is ponderous, David's is clear and succinct; where William Parker's lacks immediacy, it is the sheer proximity to the heat of battle that David conveys. Keeping up with David as he rushes here, there and everywhere leaves the reader quite breathless:

> During the action I was like 'Paddy in the cat-harpins', a man on occasions. I performed the duties of Captain's aid, quarter-gunner, powder-boy, and in fact did everything that was required of me… On one occasion Midshipman Isaacs came up to the Captain and reported that a quarter-gunner named Roach had deserted his post. The only reply of the Captain, addressed to me, was 'Do your duty, sir.' I seized a pistol and went in pursuit of the fellow, but did not find him… Soon after this, some gun-primers were wanted, and I was sent after them… When my services were not required for other purposes, I generally assisted in working a gun; would run and bring powder from the boys, and send them back for more, until the Captain wanted me to carry a message; and this continued to employ me during the action… When it was determined to surrender, the Captain sent me to ascertain if Mr — had the signal-book, and if so, to throw it overboard. I could not find him or the book for some time; but at last saw the latter lying on the sill of a port, and dashed it into the sea… Isaacs and I amused

ourselves throwing overboard pistols and other small arms, to prevent their falling into the hands of the enemy.[55]

However, amid the mayhem, David still found time to note the heroism, the patriotism, the emotions that stir men at such moments of intense danger:

It was wonderful to find dying men, who had hardly ever attracted notice among the ship's company, uttering sentiments, with their last breath, worthy of a Washington. You might have heard in all directions. 'Don't give her up Logan!' – a sobriquet for Porter – 'Hurrah for liberty!' and similar expressions. One of the crew of the bow gun told me of a singular act of heroism on the part of a young Scotchman, named Bissley, who had one leg shot off close to the groin. He used his handkerchief as a tourniquet and said to his comrades:

'I left my own country and adopted the United States to fight for her. I hope I have this day proved myself worthy of the country of my adoption. I am no longer of any use to you or to her, so good-by!' With these words, he leaned on the sill of the port and threw himself overboard.[56]

The battle over and lost, next came the moment for calm reflection. Recalling his thoughts as a youngster aged 13 in the heat of the action, David's first impulse was how unchivalrous Captain Hillyar had been. Yet, as a retired admiral of the US Navy writing his memoirs years later, he soberly concludes with the benefit of hindsight that:

…it has been quite common to blame Captain Hillyar for his conduct in this affair; but when we come to consider the characteristics of the two commanders, we may be inclined to judge more leniently… Porter was about thirty-two years of age at the time, and the 'pink of chivalry' of an ardent and impetuous temperament; while Hillyar was a cool and calculating man, about fifty years old, and … as he had the superior force, he had determined not to leave anything to chance, believing any other course would call down on him the disapprobation of his government.[57]

Herein, we see the shift in British thinking that characterized the later stages of this conflict and ultimately determined its outcome. Eight months earlier America had been an irritating sideshow and Philip Broke could indulge himself challenging the *Chesapeake* to a duel off Boston harbour. Come 1814, those days were over. The Duke of Wellington expressed the need for change in blunt, military terms: 'I do not know where you could carry on such an operation which would be so injurious to the Americans as to force them to sue for peace.'[58] There was little enthusiasm for this fight with the Americans, yet fight the British must. Hillyar had the answer: forget challenges, duels and jousts; he had the superior force, he would use it.

Nevertheless, capturing one American frigate in the backwaters of the South Pacific might be great for naval morale, but it was not going to end this nuisance conflict. So it was with a heavy heart that Britain packed off ships and troops aplenty in search of Wellington's 'injurious' operation. They found it in the waterways of Chesapeake Bay. Lieutenant-Colonel James Napier summed up what a joyless experience this next phase of the conflict was: 'It is quite shocking to see men who speak our language brought in wounded; one feels as if they were English peasants and that we are killing our own people. Strong is my dislike to what is perhaps a necessary part of our job, namely plundering and ruining the peasantry. We drive off all their cattle – it is hateful to see the poor Yankees robbed.'[59]

Those who converged on America for this mission included 'old Nelsons' like Francis, long since 'Captain' Austen, James, now 'Captain' Gordon, Frederick, now 'Lieutenant' Marryat and John, now 'Lieutenant' Franklin. With them came a whole new generation of 'young Nelsons', among them Frederick Chamier and Charles Abbott, the latter a graduate of what was by 1812 called the 'Royal Naval College at Portsmouth'.[60] Charles served briefly with William Hoste in the Adriatic and during the summer of 1814 joined, aged 16, 'a large expedition preparing to sail for the Chesapeake [but] was instead ordered on to Halifax' from where he joined an 'expedition ... which was to reduce that portion of the province of Maine which is situated between the river Penobscot and the British frontier'.[61]

Charles had little else to say in his memoirs about his 'war' in America. Quite the contrary in the case of Frederick Chamier. He had joined the navy aged 13 in 1809 and in *The Life of A Sailor*, a thinly disguised autobiographical novel written in 1832, Frederick describes in detail his time as a midshipman serving on the *Menelaus*, including participating in the expedition up the Chesapeake to Baltimore. For him the futility of a tit-for-tat conflict the British did not believe in is evident from the outset: 'Our voyage across the Atlantic was short and pleasant and we arrived in the Chesapeake amid that general war of conflagration and devastation, which half ruined the fertile shores of Virginia and Maryland. That this war, or rather the means by which it was carried on, was disgraceful to a civilised nation, no man doubts now.'[62]

As Frederick and his fellow sailors, marines and soldiers landed, they fanned out, some towards Washington, as in the case of James Gordon, and others, like Frederick, towards Baltimore. John Franklin, in a later influx, did not join this expedition, instead making his way to New Orleans where he was injured in the subsequent battle there.

With heavy irony Frederick describes how Wellington's 'injurious' operation was interpreted on the ground:

> The hue and cry always was 'Respect private property'; 'pay for what you take, but take care to take all you can'; and under this wholesome legislation we burnt and destroyed right and left. If by any stretch of argument we could establish the owner of the house, cottage, hut etc., to be a militia-man, that house we burnt, because we found arms therein; that is to say, we found a duck-gun, or a rifle. It so happens that in America, every man must belong to the militia; and, consequently, every man's house was food for a bonfire. And so well did we act up to the very spirit of our orders, that if the Americans who bounded the shores of Virginia and Maryland do not entail upon their posterities the deepest hatred and the loudest curses upon England and her marauders, why, they must possess more Christian charity than I give them credit for... The ruin, the desolation, the heartless misery, that we left them to brood over, will for ever make the citizens of the United States, in spite of the relationship of the two countries, hate us with that hatred no words can allay, or time eradicate.[63]

Burn, burn, and burn again, that was Britain's grand strategy. And when they reached the White House, they were to burn it too. Frederick Chamier explained the moral justification for this strategy:

> Because, forsooth, some savages, or perhaps men dressed one degree better than savages, commence a system of barbarity and desolation in the north; we, pretending to be the most civilised nation on the face of the earth, must imitate their ravages in the south: because in Canada, some huts and hovels were burnt, we in the Chesapeake

were to burn and destroy some noble mansion, desolate some magnificent estate, and turn a land of plenty and prosperity into a bleak desert of starvation and misery.[64]

In 1812 the Americans had plundered Canada and burnt the Canadian seat of government in York. So the British had the right to burn Virginia, Maryland and the White House. Tit for tat, pure and simple, yet for all that this was a conflict characterized by seemingly endless retaliation, both sides preferred to measure their responses: the British made sure to burn only government buildings in Washington, except for the one private home in the city that was burnt because a sniper fired on the British.

Still, the longer the tit for tat went on, the more likely it was that the combatants would forget who 'fired the first gun', and would therefore be unable to decide who should 'fire the last gun'. Frederick Chamier had no such problems. The final hurrah started out as follows:

> As I have bored the reader with real attacks on men and ships, I think it right to give a very short sketch of a land fight – against neither landmen nor soldiers, but against something equally formidable – because
> Where no honour's to be gain'd
> Tis thrown away in being maintain'd.
>
> It was at the plunder of the town of Tappahanock, where, as usual, the cry of 'Respect private property' had particularly been impressed by a certain tall captain whose gig went off to the tender actually laden with boots and shoes… We were particularly desired not to land; but seeing boots and shoes walking into a captain's gig – half a butcher's shop in another, the cockswain of a third with two geese dangling to his hands – we became hungry from fancy… The boat was soon laden deeply, and we all re-embarked like good boys, with the exception of young Martin, who had strayed a little away.[65]

Intentional or not on the part of Frederick, this anecdote with which he ends the account of his war reads like a tall story, though it is perhaps an allegory of the wider conflict in which these youngsters had found themselves embroiled:

> We had scarcely shoved off our station, before Mr Martin appeared, cutlass in hand, running at an uncommon pace, closely pursued by a large pig, which kept capering at

his heels, with its back rounded, bristling and grunting like a hog in a high wind. Our gallant messmate having seen the delinquent grubbing up some cabbages, thought he would be revenged upon the pig for its violation of all 'respect of private property' and prepared to kill and capture the animal. It appears the enemy allowed Martin to get within reach, for it was made sensible of this by receiving a pretty sharp thrust from a cutlass; whereupon, like Hudibras' horse, –

Which, straight, in wrath did then resent

The wrongs done to his fundament

It turned round, and ventured to taste a part of the midshipman's legs. This untoward event disheartened the assaulter, who seemed now to be in the situation he had destined for his enemy, saving the roasting.'[66]

So far this is all giant whopper, unless the midshipman is recast as Britain bent only on violating America's sovereignty, and the pig as America running out of patience and turning the tables on Britain, with the result that: 'A speedy flight was begun; but finding the pig gain upon him in his retreat, the gallant young hero occasionally turned and struck his pursuer over the head with the aforesaid cutlass.'[67] In this allegorical no-man's land, suddenly every sentence resonates with hidden meanings: for the pig snapping at Martin's heels, read America's frigates harrying the mighty British Navy. For the aimless cutlass thrusts, read Britain's odd victory as with the *Shannon* versus the *Chesapeake*. But the allegory does not end there: 'Mr Hog, by no means intimidated, continued his attack – and had he been one inch further in advance, the calf of the midshipman's leg would have been missing. It became anything else but a joke; and some of the sailors, who saw their favourite likely beaten and discomfited by the pig, stepped on shore, and four hours afterwards were busily employed in devouring the enemy.'[68]

This is Britain finally realizing that America is no ordinary foe, and that the only way to defeat it is with overwhelming numbers. So ends the 'allegory', and with it the War of 1812, at least so far as midshipmen Chamier and Martin were concerned, as, soon after, 'we sailed, and arrived at Bermuda as the *Menelaus* was standing out on her way home. I was instantly taken on board, and in eighteen days was at anchor in Portsmouth.'[69]

And yet, allegory or no allegory, it does seem unfair on America that Britain should have ended up, in this war of tit for tat, one pig to the good – unless, of course, Britain was still owed one pig because of what David Farragut had done after the *Essex* struck to the *Phoebe* six months earlier when:

> I went on board the *Phoebe* about 8 am on the morning of the 29th and was ushered into the steerage. I was so mortified at our capture that I could not refrain from tears. While in this uncomfortable state, I was aroused by hearing a young reefer call out:
>
> 'A prize! A prize! Ho, boys, a fine grunter, by Jove!'
>
> I saw at once that he had under his arm a pet pig belonging to our ship called 'Murphy'. I claimed the pig as my own.
>
> 'Ah', said he, 'but you are a prisoner, and your pig also.'
>
> 'We always respect private property', I replied, and, as I had seized hold of Murphy, I determined not to let go, unless compelled by superior force. This was fun for the oldsters, who immediately sung out:
>
> 'Go it, my little Yankee! If you can thrash Shorty, you shall have your pig.'
>
> 'Agreed!' said I.
>
> A ring was formed in the open space, and at it we went. I soon found that my antagonist's pugilistic education did not come up to mine. In fact, he was no match for me, and was compelled to give up the pig. So I took master Murphy under my arm, feeling I had, in some degree, wiped out the disgrace of our defeat.[70]

With 'master Murphy' rescued and 'Shorty' unfairly deprived of his 'fine grunter', in this tit-for-tat war about so little it is no wonder that 'young Martin', the mighty British Army and Navy in tow, went up Chesapeake Bay to Baltimore, then back down again, then up the Rappahannock estuary to the little town of Tappahanock in August 1814. Martin was looking for a grunter, and until he found a grunter the War of 1812 could not be over.

With due apologies, therefore, to the memory of David Farragut, he may have a lot answer for. Had he done the 'honourable' thing and let Shorty keep his prized 'fine grunter', this little war, surely, could have been over six months earlier.

NAPOLEON ON THE
BELLEROPHON

'The barge approached, and ranged alongside. The first lieutenant came up the side, and to Maitland's eager and blunt question, "have you got him?" he answered in the affirmative. After the lieutenant, came Savary, followed by Marshal Bertrand, who bowed and fell back a pace on the gangway to await the ascent of their master.'[1]

George Home, writing in his *Memoirs of an Aristocrat* published in 1838, was recording events he witnessed as a midshipman on 'the morning of 15th of July'[2] 1815. Why the excitement and anticipation? Another of Britain's enemies capitulating? Surely there was nothing unusual about this one. After all, hundreds of French, Spanish, Dutch and Danish officers, even the occasional American, had surrendered to the all-conquering British Navy over the past 22 years. Another midshipman there to witness the moment of capitulation. What was so special about that? Wasn't George just the latest in a long line of youngsters who had seen these Wars in all their manifestations – William Hoste, William Dillon, William Parker, Josiah Nisbet, George Elliot, George Parsons, John Franklin, Norwich Duff, Frederick Marryat, Frederick Chamier, to name just a few so far. What could George Home possibly have to say about these Wars that had not been said 100 times before?

Little enough, if the early years of his career in the navy were anything to go by. Born on 8 December 1794, six months after the Battle of the Glorious First of

June, George was a child of the Wars and the 'youngest of five comely sons',[3] one of whom joined the army, another the Marines and 'my third … was sent off to the navy, where he was rapidly rising, when he burst a blood-vessel and expired instantly'.[4] Their father, Alexander, was 'an old naval officer who had faced death and danger from Hawke's action off Brest'[5] and 'circumnavigated the globe under the great Cook, and was with him when he was killed at Owyhee.'[6] Indeed, it was their father who masterminded the infamous court martial on Neddy Rhio's 'dog…of cannibal origin'[7] aboard *Discovery* during that voyage.

With this fighting pedigree to live up to, there was no question that 'the moment I expressed a wish to go to sea, the Commodore lost no time to take me at my word'[8] and that the commodore would eschew the type of cerebral homily Francis Austen received from his father back in 1788 on how to act in the 'little world of which you are going to become an Inhabitant',[9] preferring some plain-speaking instead: 'You're scarcely old enough to be of any use at a gun-tackle, but d—n me, George, you'll make a capital powder monkey… Mark you, George, never jink about when you hear the report of a cannon, shying does no good; if you are to be knocked on the head, it will be done before you hear the report; and it's d—d cowardly like to see a fellow put the ship's side between him and the bullets.'[10]

Working the Scottish patronage network, an introduction to the port-admiral of Leith was arranged, which encounter George ensured came suitably remembered with all the appropriate vernacular customary for such occasions:

> 'I say you d—d young spalpeen, what are you grinning at there with your white-washed baby face? Make a sailor of you, eh! Never mind, you're the son of a brave old officer, and that is a better recommendation to me than twenty earls' letters.' So saying, he… swore I was a young Nelson, and immediately ordered me to be appointed to the T—t sloop of war, then on a cruize off the coast of Norway, but soon expected into port.[11]

Going to sea in 1809 aged 15 with 'a sea-chest, stuffed full of shirts, stockings, jackets, trousers, shoes, a Bible, pewter wash-stand, bason, soap, combs and brushes, before I was a month at sea, the spoons disappeared. The boy of the berth was suspected, and finding he was about to be detected, he committed them, crest and all, to the safe custody of the sea, which tells no tales.'[12] Yet, tales of larceny aside, George's description of his early days at sea suggests that the navy had come on by leaps and bounds since the early years of the Wars. Not only was 'the midshipman's berth neat and clean handsomely painted, with all "appliances and means to boot" in the shape of buffet, glasses, decanters clean towels etc [but] the young gentlemen, as the midshipmen are designed, clean as new pins.'[13]

However, on closer examination it seems that George was one of the lucky ones to have 'such a gentlemanly set of officers. There were no tricks played off upon new comers, none of those beastly practices which I have seen exercised upon poor youngsters which at once disgusted them with the Service, and made them take the first opportunity of escaping on shore, bag and baggage never to return.'[14] By contrast, Frederick Marryat, going to sea just three years earlier, could only recall how: 'there was no species of tyranny, injustice, and persecution, to which youngsters were not compelled to submit from those who were their superiors in bodily strength.'[15]

George's early luck continued even into his first action and prize-taking: 'We had not been out a week before we had taken several paltry prizes, and sent in two Yankee brigs suspected of malpractices. I was sent off prize-master of a wretched privateer... An old quarter-master and four hands were sent on board with me to take the prize into Leith under direct superintendence of old Stewart the quarter-master. Arrived at Leith, Stewart took care to have me equipped in my best uniform to carry the account of the prize, and the logbook of our proceedings since we left his Majesty's ship...'[16]

Assuming George's memory did not let him down, this account was still from 1809, which would have made him barely 15, young for prize-master duty, as the port-admiral noted when George reported in: '"So", says he, "youngster, I am glad to see you, but what the devil tempted J—s to send you in with a prize? By G—d you can no more keep a ship's way that you can fly; but I see an old fellow outside there, that, I suppose, had charge of both you and the prize."'[17]

It seemed that George's career was set fair from the outset. However, with fewer enemies to engage as the Wars began winding down and the opportunities for glory, promotion and 'pewter' dwindling, George's career tailed off. During the conflict with America there were a couple of brushes with 'Brother Jonathan',[18] including 'a six hours' chase after the famous *Wasp* of the Yankees, which made more captures during the short war than any of the American cruisers',[19] but even then George's star was crossed. Orders came through 'to proceed to Cove of Cork to join a fleet bound for America and in four days [we] came to anchor in Cove harbour, where a great many transports full of troops with the Boyne ninety-eight and several frigates were lying wind-bound under orders for America. The wind, however, continued direct in our teeth for several weeks and at last blew home the news of peace with the Yankees.'[20]

On that downbeat note it seemed as if George's Wars would be over before they had begun. However, there remained one more defining chapter in George's naval career, which began on that 'morning of 15th of July [when] it was finally agreed that the Emperor should come on board the *Bellerophon*'.[21] So defining was what followed for George that he prefaced his account with an assurance that:

> …how vivid is my recollection of these events, now that nearly the fourth part of a century has passed away since the scene took place; but who that possessed the feelings of rational being could witness it, and lose one trace of the wonderful circumstance. My log-book, kept at the moment, is now lying on the table before me; yet I find I do not need to refer to it, even for dates, or the very hours of the day when the very events took place, so completely stamped is the whole on my memory.[22]

Yet, as with so many memoirs of these Wars, two voices obtrude as the memories are recalled: there is George, the 'aristocrat' and 44-year-old retired naval officer, delivering a political polemic on how rudely 'the fallen Emperor'[23] was treated, not by Britain and its people, but by 'Castlereagh and his Holy Allies'[24] from the Continent. There is the other voice of the 'Midshipman of the *Bellerophon*'[25] and it is this one that compels and informs readers as he recounts how:

> …the evening of the 14th was calm and delightful … as we lay at single anchor in Basque Roads, awaiting the event of the morrow. All was expectation and excitement. The first lieutenant was engaged seeing all the belaying pins get an extra polish, and that every rope was coiled down with more than usual care, while every hush from the shore, or speck on the water, was listened to and watched with intense anxiety, lest our prey should escape us. I confess, while all this was going on, young and thoughtless as I was, I still believed the event beyond the compass of possibility. I had the middle watch, and just as I was relieved about half-past four in the morning of the 15th, and a lovely morning it was, we saw a man-of-war brig get under weigh from Aix Roads, and stand out towards us, bearing a flag of truce. The wind, however, was blowing direct in her teeth, so that

she made little of it, and it became evident that it would be several hours before she reached us. While the other midshipmen of the watch slipped off to their hammocks to have a snooze before breakfast, I could not think of sleep, but stood anxiously watching the short tacks of *Le Epervier*, which now 'carried Caesar and his fortunes.'[26]

The anticipation is palpable. After 22 years of almost non-stop warfare, time had come down to hours and parts thereof. What had started out back in 1793 as a mighty clash of ideologies – revolution versus the old order – had distilled down to one man, and what he did next. After battles on sea and land ranging across the globe, where mighty storms, human waves and artillery blasts drove mankind's destiny, now all was suspended in a 'lovely morning', waiting on a wind 'blowing direct in her teeth'. And in case his readers are misguided enough to think that all the quivering excitement aboard the *Bellerophon* was confined to the mind of one impressionable young midshipman with an overactive imagination and yearning quest after his own self-importance, George lays bare the petty ambitions of those more senior to him. He first creates a sense of imminent jeopardy when 'about six in the morning, the look-out man at the mast-head announced a large ship of war standing direct in for the roadstead...'[27]

Could this be some remnant of the French Navy arriving at the eleventh hour to rescue Napoleon and whisk him off to some redoubt from where he could contemplate another triumphal return to power? How long before this ship-of-the-line showed its colours? Would the *Bellerophon*, hero of the Glorious First of June, the Nile and Trafalgar have to fight one last battle? Yes, but this would a 'battle' of a different kind, as quick-thinking 'Captain Maitland, suspecting [the ship of war] to be the *Superb*, bearing the flag of Admiral Sir Henry Hotham, he gave immediate orders to hoist out the barge, and dispatched her, under the command of the first lieutenant...'[28]

Yet it was not to the *Superb* that the barge was dispatched. A 38-year-old Scottish aristocrat, Maitland had seen enough admirals manoeuvring for glory in lines of battle. Napoleon Bonaparte was the *Bellerophon*'s, not the admiral's, prize. Accordingly, the barge was dispatched 'to the French brig, being apprehensive that if the Admiral arrived before the brig got out, that Napoleon would deliver himself up to the Admiral instead of us, and thus have lost us so much honour. As our barge approached, the brig hove to, and from the moment she came alongside, we watched every motion with deep anxiety. Like all Napoleon's movements, he was not slow even in this, his last free act...'[29]

George and the whole crew of the *Bellerophon* watched spellbound, eager to witness the exact point in time when Napoleon stepped from a French brig on to an English barge and in the process surrendered his destiny irretrievably into the hands of his enemy. 'The barge had not remained ten minutes alongside, before we saw the rigging of the brig crowded with men, persons stepping down the side into the boat, and the next moment she shoved off, and gave way from the ship; while the waving of the men's hats in the rigging, and the cheering which we heard faintly in the distance, left no doubt that the expected guest was approaching.'[30]

All now became bustle as the *Bellerophon* made final preparations for the arrival:

> ...a general's guard of marines was ordered aft on the quarter-deck, and the boatswain stood, whistle in hand, ready to do the honours of the side. The lieutenants stood grouped first on the quarter-deck, and we more humble middy's behind them, while the captain, evidently in much anxiety, kept trudging backwards and forwards between the gangway and his own cabin, sometimes peeping out at one of the quarter-deck ports, to see if the barge was drawing near.[31]

Yet at the very instant when this almost theatrical drama was reaching its climax, on to the monumental stage strode, like the gravediggers in Shakespeare's *Hamlet*, the ship's prankster hell-bent on acting the giddy-goat:

> A young midshipman, one of the Bruce's of Kennet, I think, walked demurely up to Manning, the boatswain, who was standing all importance at the gangway, and after comically eyeing his squat figure and bronzed countenance, Bruce gently laid hold of one of his whiskers, to which the boatswain good-humouredly submitted, as the youngster was a great favourite with him. 'Manning', says he, most sentimentally, 'this is the proudest day of your life; you are this day to do the honours of the side to the greatest man the world ever produced, or ever will produce.' Here the boatswain eyed him with proud delight. 'And along with the great Napoleon, the name of Manning, the boatswain of the *Bellerophon*, will go down to the latest posterity; and, as a relict of that great man, permit me, my dear Manning to preserve a lock of your hair.' Here he made an infernal tug at the boatswain's immense whisker and fairly carried away a part of it, making his way through

the crowd, and down below with the speed of an arrow. The infuriated boatswain, finding he had passed so rapidly from the sublime to the ridiculous, through the instrumentality of this imp of a youngster, could vent his rage in no way but by making his glazed hat spin full force after his tantalizer, with a 'G—d d—n your young eyes and limbs.' The hat, however, fell far short of Bruce, and the noise and half burst of laughter the trick occasioned, drew the attention of the Captain, who, coming up, with a 'What, what's all this?' the poor boatswain was glad to draw his hat and resume his position.[32]

Comic interlude over, the moment everyone had been waiting for arrived, 'and now came the little great man himself, wrapped up in his gray greatcoat buttoned to the chin, three cocked hat and Hussar boots, without any sword, I suppose emblematic of his changed position.'[33] George watched Napoleon's every movement while 'the captain again moved his hat, and turned to conduct the Emperor to the cabin. As he passed through the officers assembled on the quarter-deck, he repeatedly bowed slightly to us, and smiled.'[34] Star-struck, George could only wonder at 'what an ineffable beauty there was in that smile, his teeth were finely set… I marked his fine robust figure as he followed Captain Maitland into the cabin, and, boy as I was, I said to myself, "Now have I a tale for futurity."'[35]

Later that same day, when he wasn't 'engaged … bringing on board the suite and luggage of the Emperor from *La Epervier* brig',[36] George made sure he was within earshot watching and listening as Napoleon 'made the round of both decks, complimented Maitland, on the excellent order of the ship … asked questions at any of the men who came in his way, and a young middy who, boy-like, had got before the Emperor, and was gazing up in his face, he honoured with a tap on the head, and a pinch of the ear, and, smiling, put him to a side, which the youngster declared was the highest honour he had ever received in his life, viz. to have his ears pinched by the great Napoleon!!!'[37]

Soon the *Bellerophon* was overwhelmed by its passengers as 'the fine figure of Lady Bertrand, with her charming children, adorned our quarter-deck. A great many officers in rich uniforms came off with Napoleon… These were all grouped about this fine morning, making the deck of the old ship … look as gay as a drawing-room on a levee day.'[38] Baggage safely stowed and 'the Emperor and his faithful few' suitably accommodated, the *Bellerophon* now made its seven-day journey across the English Channel. During its passage, opportunities abounded for George to witness Napoleon at close quarters. One occasion stood out above all others: 'I shall never forget that morning we made Ushant [on the coast of Brittany]. I had come on deck at four in the morning to take the morning watch, and the washing of decks had just begun, when, to my astonishment, I saw the Emperor come out of the cabin at that early hour, and make for the poop-ladder.'[39] Finally, came George's own moment to remember when:

> from the wetness of the decks, he [Napoleon] was in danger of falling at every step, and I immediately stepped up to him, and tendered my arm, which he laid hold of at once, smiling, and pointing to the poop, saying in broken English, "the poop, the poop;" he ascended the poop-ladder leaning on my arm; and having gained the deck, he quitted his hold and mounted upon a gun-slide, nodding and smiling thanks, for my attention, and pointing to the land he said "Ushant, Cape Ushant." I replied, "Yes sire," and withdrew.[40]

From a respectful distance, George watched as Napoleon 'took out a pocket-glass and applied it to his eye, looking eagerly at the land. In this position, he remained from five in the morning to nearly mid-day, without paying any attention to what was passing around him, or speaking to one of his suite, who had been standing behind him for several hours.'[41] It was then that Napoleon realised his Wars were over, or at least that was how George saw it when recalling how 'he thus gazed, it was the last look of the land of his glory, and I am convinced he felt it such. What must have been his feelings in those few hours, how painful the retrospect, and how awful the look forward! There still lay before him that land which he made so famous...'[42] Others thought so to: William Quiller Orchardson, in his oil painting *Napoleon on board the Bellerophon*, painted in 1880, also sought to capture that same moment.

The stage was now set for the final act in this tragedy, but, faithful to the exact chronology of those days, George shows Napoleon rallying one last time in the belief that he would be granted exile in Britain, his attempts to make light of the few days remaining on the *Bellerophon* assisted in some small part by George and his fellow midshipmen who:

> Amongst other plans for killing time, and lightening the tedium of a sea passage to the refugees, we bethought us of getting up a play. This was managed by one of the lieutenants of marines, a fellow of great taste, and some one or two of the midshipmen, who pretended

to skill in the Shakespearian art. What the piece was I do not recollect, but when it was announced to the Emperor, by Captain Maitland, and the immortal honour of his imperial presence begged, for a few minutes, he laughed very heartily, consented instantly; and turning to Lady Bertrand, told her that she must stand his interpreter. The stage was fitted up between decks, more, I am afraid, in ship-shape than theatrical style; and sure enough, Napoleon and his whole suite attended. He was much amused with those who took the female parts, which, by the way, was the most smooth-chinned of our young gentlemen, remarking that they were rather a little Dutch built for fine ladies; and after good-naturedly sitting for nearly twenty minutes, he rose, smiled to the actors, and retired.[43]

Making landfall at Torbay, the priority was to send news of Napoleon's capture to the government, the first lieutenant being charged as messenger. Once again the burlesque intruded on the solemnity of the moment, George recounting being 'the midshipman on the boat, which conveyed the lieutenant on shore, and no sooner had we got clear of him, than I was taken prisoner by some twenty young ladies, marched off to a fine house in the little town, regaled with tea and clouted cream and bored with five thousand questions about Napoleon, the ridiculousness of which I have often laughed at since. "What like was he – was he really a man? Were his hands and clothes all over blood when he came on board?"'[44]

Burlesque descended to farce once the *Bellerophon* moved to Plymouth Sound, there to await the government's decision on Napoleon's fate. 'The Sound was literally covered with boats'[45] full of curious sightseers, and it was the crew's task to keep the overeager at bay; cue 'a plan of some of our wise-headed young gentlemen. Being in want of amusement, they bethought them of priming the fire engine, which happened to be standing on the poop, and after clapping a relay of hands ready to ply it to advantage, we uncovered, and waited the approach of the boats. No sooner were they within reach, than off went the water-spout, which fell "alike on the just and the unjust" for both the dockyard men and the spectators who came within its compass got a good ducking.'[46]

All the while, the government was deciding what Napoleon's fate should be. At length the fatal news arrived and all was gloom and misery. 'From that hour to the day of his leaving the ship, Napoleon never again appeared on deck, and the broken expressions, and despairing looks of the members of his suite, but too well bespoke the feelings of their doomed master.'[47]

As well as Napoleon being sent into exile on St Helena, it had been decided by the government that the ship to convey him on the last leg of his journey would not be the *Bellerophon*. Ostensibly the reason was that the *Bellerophon* was deemed unfit to make the long journey. However, preying on the minds of the government might have been the fear that the crew of the *Bellerophon* had formed too close an affinity with Napoleon and his entourage during the crossing from France. Certainly George's memoirs betray these sympathies when he laments: 'Had I known what human misery is as well as I do now, the restlessness of Napoleon, or his being unable to close an eye, would have in no way surprised me. If a petty care can break our sleep, what must have been his feelings who had lost the fairest empire on the face of the globe; nay, who had lost a world?'[48]

Whatever the government's concerns, the day came when Napoleon was to leave the *Bellerophon*:

> The 7th came; it was a dull cloudy sunless day, and every countenance was overcast with gloom... At length Napoleon appeared, but oh, how sadly changed from the time we had last seen him on deck. Though quite plain, he was scrupulously cleanly in his person and dress, but that had been forgot, his clothes were ill put on, his beard unshaved, and his countenance pale and haggard... Before leaving the ship he turned to us on the quarter-deck, once more waved his hand in token of adieu, took hold of the man-ropes, and walked down the side, taking his seat in the Northumberland's barge...[49]

George's last sight of Napoleon was him 'looking back to the ship [where] he saw every head, that could get stuck out of a port, gazing after him: even the rough countenances of the men bespoke a sympathy for his cruel fate, and apparently conscious of their feelings, the exiled chief again lifted his hat, and inclined his head to the gazing ship's company.'[50]

Napoleon was about to embark on the last leg of his journey into oblivion, where, in one final macabre irony, it would be the task of another 'young Nelson' to draw a veil down over the man who had been Britain's nemesis ever since that day back in October 1793 when, as a young lieutenant in the Revolutionary Army, he helped liberate Toulon and the sorry remnants of France's navy from the clutches of Lord Hood, Captain Nelson and Britain's Mediterranean fleet, and thereafter set France on its mightiest of all wars with the old enemy.

The following extracts from Frederick, by then 'Captain', Marryat's logbook tell a small part of this final act:

1821. March 7th. Came to an anchor at St Helena.

May 1st Weighed and made sail to cruise to windward; but was recalled in consequence of being attacked with dysentery and cholera morbus on 3rd.

—5th Napoleon Bonaparte died.

—9th Exchanged into HM sloop *Rosario*. Attended the funeral of Bonaparte.

—16th Sailed for England with despatches.[51]

Frederick's reputation as a sketch-artist had preceded him and when the *Beaver*, the brig he commanded, was ordered to guard St Helena and watch for any attempts to liberate Napoleon, he was invited by the governor of the island, Sir Hudson Lowe, first to attend the lying-in-state of Napoleon, and then, there being no death-mask skills on hand on the island, to draw him in death and record the funeral procession of French and British officers. For good measure, Frederick Marryat also sketched Sheikh, the dead Emperor's charger.

Florence Marryat, widow of Frederick, filled in some of the gaps in his log in her *Life and Letters of Captain Marryat* published in 1872, and described how:

on the afternoon of the day on which Napoleon died, Captain Marryat took the well-known sketch of him in full profile, which was afterwards engraved both in France and England. It represented the dead emperor lying on his camp bed with his hands crossed above the crucifix upon his breast, and has been considered one of the most striking likenesses preserved of him. After the emperor's death, being attacked by dysentery, Captain Marryat exchanged from the *Beaver* into the *Rosario* sloop, and returned home in her on the 9th of May 1821.[52]

A young Nelson had touched Napoleon Bonaparte in life. Now another had touched him in death.

17

'AH! THE PEACE HAS
COME TOO SOON'

'I get impatient to have done with this part of my story.'[1] With this ominous preamble, George Home launched into the final depressing chapter of his Wars, describing how the *Bellerophon*, mighty warhorse of so many battles, was to be 'laid up in ordinary' and have its 'rigging stripped, the guns taken out, the ballast, mast, spars etc etc, in short, the fine old ship made a mere hull, with an empty bottle hung at her figure-head, to show that the grog was out.'[2] Simultaneously came 'the kindly purpose of being paid off … the pay-captain [coming] on board, the men going off by fifties at a time, some blessing, and some cursing their officers, every one taking off his own glad way.'[3]

Next it was the turn of the officers to go their separate ways and 'without any outward show of sorrow, I bade adieu to my messmates, who, all joyous and unthinking (perhaps they had less to think of than me) shook hands with me, and wished me a happy passage home.'[4]

Such bittersweet partings were being repeated in ports all round the country during the latter months of 1815, as ship after ship was decommissioned and, within three years of the end of the Wars, manpower was reduced from 145,000 to 19,000. All ranks and ratings faced an uncertain future, cast adrift, possibly even shipwrecked, on the shores of a now alien land some had not known for many years. For commissioned officers there was a desperate scramble for appointment to any of the few ships remaining in service. Among those were some of the young

Nelsons whose careers have been followed most closely. Certain among them remained constantly, or with only short intervals, in service after the Wars, and once made post-captain, only had to stay alive long enough, and outlive their fellow captains on the seniority list, to ensure that they would reach the illustrious rank of admiral, as did Charles Austen, Jeffrey Raigersfeld and James Gordon, if not admiral of the fleet, as did both Francis Austen and William Parker, the latter also being made a baronet in 1844. Others surely would have attained these heights if ill-health, brought on by the rigours of harsh service, had not cut short first their careers, next their lives. Among these, William Hoste at least had the consolation of being knighted in 1815 and, despite the dead weight that bore down on him from his father's profligacy, prospered with a high-society marriage to Lady Harriet Walpole, from one of the leading patrician families in the country.

Whether George Parsons, another casualty of the Wars, would have reached the rank of captain if ill-health had not forced him out in 1810 is questionable, given that he seemed caught between the quarterdeck and the lower-deck. He at least was granted a Greenwich Hospital pension, albeit late on in life, in recognition of his services. Josiah Nisbet, a casualty of a different kind from the Wars, was, once shorn of the millstone that had been his fate as stepson of the greatest living hero of the times, finally able to make peace with his mother and, embarking on a business career outside the navy, settled in Exmouth where his mother eventually joined him.

For those commissioned officers who remained in good health but did not immediately find postwar re-employment in the navy, there was the unenviable prospect of joining the growing heaps of flotsam washed up on the shore-lines of society. There they must await a fresh wave of appointments or, preferably, another war to carry them back out to sea, neither of which might ever come, leaving them with only their half pay to sustain them in the meantime, and at the mercy of salon predators, such as sharp-tongued Fanny Burney, itching, since before the Wars had even started, to pick over the withering carcasses of Britain's spent heroes. Criticized for the burlesquing of her Captain Mirvan, as 'surly, vulgar, and disagreeable'[5] in *Evelina; or, A Young Lady's Entrance into the World*, published in 1778, Fanny had lashed back: 'the more I see of sea captains, the less reason I have to be ashamed of Captain Mirvan; for they have all so irresistible a propensity to wanton mischief, – to roasting beaux, and detesting old women, that I quite rejoice I showed the book to no one ere printed, lest I should have been prevailed upon to soften his character.'[6] Likewise 'having been tormented and vexed in a most cruel way by C. Foley'[7] there was little chance that Betsy Fremantle would spare swipes at Captain Charles Foley in her diaries, should he ever dare cross her path back in England.

No such prospect for John Franklin. Still only a lieutenant at the end of the Wars, he was a man of destiny who had navigated his way through enough shoals and reefs around the globe to know that England was not for him. The moment the tide was in his favour, he weighed anchor and was off back to his first love, exploration, carving out new frontiers for Britain's ever-expanding empire.

As for those young Nelsons who, come 1815, were still trapped by their age if not their lack of patronage in the humble rank of midshipman, they risked, as George Parsons had feared was his fate following the earlier Peace of Amiens in 1802, being left with no past and no future. For those lucky midshipmen with connections, such as Charles Abbott, the advent of peace in 1815 hardly registered. He joined the navy's work helping consolidate the vast colonial gains wrung out of the Wars. For him, the onset of peace came when 'this was Bacchante's last service; we were ordered into Portsmouth Harbour and there paid off.'[8] This was followed by a brief sightseeing 'tour of Paris and Brussels, visiting the recent battle-field of Waterloo,'[9] which interlude ended when 'Captain Stanfell having been appointed to command the *Madagascar* 38, very kindly offered to take me with him.'[10] In a few short sentences Charles dispensed with the end of *his* Wars.

Noticeably, in a navy so heavily shorn of numbers, the key was not just interest, but the right interest, in Charles' case the binding association he had with his commanding officer both before and after the Wars ended. By contrast, George Home found his wagon hitched to the wrong horse, Captain Maitland, his commanding officer on the *Bellerophon*, who warned him on their parting: 'I cannot offer you a ship just now, but should I get a command again, which I am afraid will not be soon, you have only to show your face, and you shall have what vacancy I can give you.'[11]

Captain Maitland did not come by an appointment for another three years, by which time George's life had taken a different turn, and writing years later he could only echo the sentiments of despair felt by those of his fellow midshipmen shipwrecked on the shores of Britain that 'it is a glorious scene of confusion to him who blesses himself free of the bondage; but if I entered the navy with a heavy heart, I left it with a sorer. All hope of promotion was blasted with the peace. With Waterloo fell my hopes, and well did I know, that in my own country, great as my connexions were, I had no friend to look to but my poor old father, who still survived, though in a very helpless condition.'[12]

As for those other youngsters, the boys who never escaped the lower-decks during the Wars, there were among them 'the forsaken dogs' who had come to the doors of the Marine Society at some point during the Wars. Twenty-two years of virtually non-stop warfare changed nothing for them. They still remained officially as 'friendless' as the day they were first entered as such in the column headed 'Parents or Fatherless' in the Society's *Register*. They had been society's castaways for however long they were at sea, and returning 'home', they would still be 'Strangers to Beds', unless proper measures were taken to forestall the looming human tragedy. Fortuitously for many of these youngsters, unlike after previous wars, 'swallowing the anchor', as it was called, was less painful. The navy decided in its own interests that in future it needed a steady and reliable supply of boys to serve 'before the mast'. Despite the reduction of the navy to a peace-time level, Britain had ever-growing commitments to its far-flung empire and had continuing ambitions to reach out into unexplored, unexploited corners of the globe. With these forces at work, the fabric of a new volunteer navy was conceived in the aftermath of the Wars and some at least of the boys from the lower-deck found security as the permanent heartbeat of a professional standing navy.

EPILOGUE

MADE FOR EVER

The Wars had ended, and with it the careers of many young Nelsons whose whole professional life so far had been dedicated to the service of King and Country. The story they have told, which, little did they know it, began in the dawn of the British Navy with a boy with no name on the shores of the island of Mocha, deep in the South Pacific, would soon be drawing to a close. For some, like the grandson of Sir Archibald Drew spotted by Anne Elliott and Admiral Croft on Bath's Milsom Street in *Persuasion*, 'the peace has come too soon for that younker'.[1] The Wars had been the making of so many young Nelsons. Peace might now cast many of them into oblivion. Yet in time new memorials would be erected in the memory of these young Nelsons: naval literature, mixing fact and fiction, would recall their lives, their exploits and their scars, letting the Wars live on long after they were over.

For those from the lower-decks it was invariably the scars that would be remembered, as the likes of William Robinson, alias Jack Nastyface, came forward determined to make their case against the evils of the navy. William had not waited for peace before parting company with the navy; instead, as early as 1811, 'having safely landed our freight, and bearing no orders to go on any particular service, we prepared for our return to old England, and arrived at Portsmouth in the latter end of the year, when I quitted, and took my leave of the naval service'.[2]

For 'quitted', read 'deserted', taking William into a twilight world from which he only dared re-emerge in 1836 when, under his eccentric pen name, he sought, along with many former sailors with an axe to grind, to lay bare the iniquities of Britain's navy during the Wars. Whether it was William Robinson, Pel Verjuice, Jacob Nagle or Robert Wilson, all had 'deserted' and each had their story to tell, be it about the Press Gang in its various manifestations, which had consigned them to a lower-deck 'servitude', or the regime of harsh and arbitrary punishment, close confinement and poor pay, which made life in the navy more or less 'a hell afloat'.

From the other end of the spectrum there simultaneously emerged a steady trickle of glossy, swashbuckling novels, more or less fictional, all eager to capitalize on the public's newly revived appetite for all things naval and set to glorify if not sanctify the world of the quarterdeck and immortalize the lives of the navy's officers and, with it, their time as young volunteers and midshipmen. Captain after captain turned his hand to these accounts, beginning with William Glasscock and *The Naval Sketch Book* in 1826, Frederick Marryat and *Frank Mildmay or The Naval Officer* in 1829 and Frederick Chamier, whose *The Life of A Sailor* published in 1832 so enlivened the final chapter of the War of 1812. Upwards of 50 naval novels were written over a 30-year period beginning in the mid-1820s.

Following hard on the heels of these early forays into semi-fictional naval literature came nothing short of a tidal wave of sometimes venerable, often self-serving, occasionally witty memoirs and journals from retired naval officers, each of which, with its own personal stories and anecdotes to recount, gave little more than a snapshot of the Wars, but when aggregated into a collage of images and memories reveal the epic proportions of these Wars.

However, with so many story-tellers at large, each full of their own self-importance and their own perspective on life in the navy, discerning the truth in the fiction, or indeed the fiction in the truth, would be like navigating through a maritime maelstrom, 'terra firma' for the uninitiated coming just occasionally from some supposedly unimpeachable corroborative source as when William Mark, a purser who served under Admiral Lord Nelson, declared in his memoirs entitled *At Sea with Nelson* published in 1846 that 'Marryat has shown what a middy's berth may generally considered to be'.[3]

Believe William Mark or not on this one fine point, what is beyond dispute is that by 1829 Frederick Marryat already had the credentials to make his fiction believable to an audience both in and well beyond naval circles. That was what would count if Frederick were to steer *his* ship safely to port after the Wars, rather than end up shipwrecked on the nearest reef lurking in the murky waters awaiting each sailor, whatever his rank, as he made landfall in the autumn of 1815. In addition to having been 'there' and served with Captain Lord Cochrane, recognizable to contemporaries as every man's epitome of the swashbuckling hero, Frederick had already, long before putting pen to paper, carved out a name for himself as a pictorial commentator with the requisite keen eye for what the public – its landlubbers as well as its seafarers – could instantly relate to in the lives and adventures of the nation's naval heroes, especially its young heroes.

Soon after the Wars ended, Frederick had begun collaborating with George Cruickshank the caricaturist, the result of which was two series of cartoons depicting life at sea, more especially those seminal moments that surely the landlocked sections of the public wanted to believe every young midshipman had experienced: *The Sailor's Progress* and *The Life of a Midshipman, or The Life of Mr Blockhead*. The images of the career of Mr Blockhead instantly captured the key rites of passage in the lives of the nation's wartime generation of young Nelsons: their call to arms, first impressions, baptism by fire, punishment and promotion. Only their 'pewterising' was missing.

No problem. Frederick was about to find, first with these caricatures, later with his novels, his own source of 'pewter'. The caricatures instantly made Frederick famous, so much so that he began moving in royal circles, being elected, somewhat eccentrically, a member of the Royal Society and in 1820, shortly after being promoted to the rank of commander, being invited on board the royal yacht to meet King George IV and converse with the Duke of Clarence, the latter only too eager to reminisce about his own days at sea as Midshipman Prince William Henry, as he was some 40 or so years earlier.

Frederick was the archetypal naval novelist but he was not the first to fictionalize the wartime efforts of Britain's sailors. Plays were being written and performed throughout the Wars, often in celebration of the latest victory. Naval poems, songs, ballads and shanties were regularly published in wartime editions of the *Naval Chronicle* and duly filtered out into other publications such as the

Gentleman's Magazine, which, in 1794 for instance, printed a poem about a young naval surgeon entitled 'Lines on the Death of a Young Gentleman who caught the fever at Gosport in the discharge of his medical Duty'.[4]

One of the most elaborate of these early fictional forays was a poem in four cantos entitled *The Adventures of Johnny Newcome in the Navy*, written in 1818 by John Mitford, whose distant uncle, Lord Redesdale, had had John placed in the navy aged 11, at the outbreak of the Wars. John was present at the Battles of Toulon in 1795, Tenerife in 1797 and the Nile in 1798, rising steadily through the officer ranks from midshipman to commander, until he became one of the casualties of the Wars, being discharged deemed insane.

This poem, written under a pseudonym 'Alfred Burton', had Johnny going through his own rites of passage, each key event accompanied by a cartoon conceived by the other great naval caricaturist of the times, Thomas Rowlandson. As with the first sketch in Frederick Marryat's *The Life of a Midshipman, or The Life of Mr Blockhead*, entitled *Leaving Home*, so too Rowlandson had his own version of the same theme, similarly entitled *Leaving Home*, to accompany Mitford's moment in Johnny's story when:

> The Coach stopp'd at the garden gate
> And first the Father took his seat;
> John paus'd to share a last embrace,
> Then blew his nose, and took his place.–
> The steps tucked up, the door bang'd tight
> The Guard roar'd out, 'All right, all right';
> 'Yaw! Babies, hip!' The Driver cried,
> With whistle, stamp, and lash thrown wide;
> And on the reeling carriage passed:
> John thought it went confounded fast:
> His Mother, as it left her view,
> And his young sisters waved adieu[5]

Both Rowlandson and Marryat conjured up 'young sisters' as integral components in their pictorial image of the moment. Yet by leaving them behind as, respectively, Johnny Newcome and Frank Mildmay departed for the coast and a naval career,

---

John Mitford and Frederick Marryat ensured that their fiction would remain stories of the sea. Their works would therefore never have the universal appeal of another author, Jane Austen, who was as intimately associated with the navy as John Mitford's 'young sisters' and confidently deployed naval characters in her fiction, but positioned them in Bath and the country houses of southern England. This was the world she knew: 'There, you will be quite at home'[6] was the advice she gave her niece, who had her own writing ambitions. Against these settings, Jane Austen's novels start where the poem by John Mitford and the novels of Frederick Marryat leave off – as 'his young sisters waved adieu' – and end only when Jane's last naval heroine, Anne Elliot, can with self-satisfaction declare in *Persuasion* that 'she gloried in being a sailor's wife'.[7]

For Jane Austen, the novels were an escape, an attempt at filling a void that no reality could possibly hope to fill, especially as day to day life came down too often to the lament that 'we have heard nothing from Charles for some time'.[8] These few spare words written in 1796 in Jane's first letter to have survived from the Wars sum up the anguish of a family marooned at home, left waiting each day for news of not just one but, in the case of the Austen family, two sailor brothers fighting far away. Out of this emptiness emerged a vein of creative energy that attempted to bring to life the drama of a family at home in wartime.

Unlike Frederick Marryat, Frederick Chamier and the other naval novelists, Jane Austen placed the sailor characters that she created in amongst a wider pantheon of characters – the military, ecclesiastical, noble, gentry – of all ages and within a milieu never far from the normality of the drawing room of a country house. This was her contemporary appeal, making her naval heroes and anti-heroes, and their setting, instantly recognizable to a wider reading public than just the naval fraternity. Among her contemporaries she tapped into a fascination with the plight of those left at home as the Wars raged somewhere far over the horizon, with how those families interreacted with their sailor sons or brothers when they briefly returned home on shore leave, and with how, on retirement at the end of the Wars, these sailors, whatever their ages, reintegrated into the society they had left behind when they went to sea.

However, her novels, at least those with a naval content, did more than fill a void. They were in part a cathartic release of her own inner pain as she sought to bring her brothers, Francis and Charles, back home safe and sound; in part a sister communicating, in the way she knew best, her love for her brothers. Three of Jane Austen's works stand out for their naval content, each in their turn reflecting the Wars at the time they were written, each in their own way immortalizing the ideal of the sailor brother, who must never quite grow up.

First came *The Adventures of Mr Harley*, described by Jane as 'a short, but interesting Tale',[9] written some time in the period 1788–91 and therefore just before the Wars proper had started, but after Francis had embarked on his naval career. This 'interesting Tale' is so short it can be quoted in full:

> Mr Harley was one of many Children. Destined by his father for the Church & by his Mother for the Sea, desirous of pleasing both, he prevailed on Sir John to obtain for a Chaplaincy on board a Man of War. He accordingly cut his Hair and sailed. In half a year he returned & set off in the Stage Coach for Hogsworth Green, the seat of Emma. His fellow travellers were, A man without a Hat, Another with two, An old maid & a young Wife. This last appeared about 17 with fine dark Eyes & an elegant Shape; in short Mr Harley soon found out, that she was his Emma & recollected he had married her a few weeks before he left England. FINIS[10]

This 'Tale' is one of 16 minor works comprising Jane's youthful output of short stories, poems and plays, 14 of which were dedicated to one or other of her family or friends, the whole extending to 92 leaves in the original manuscript. In the case of this tale it was: 'with all imaginable Respect inscribed to Mr Francis William Austen Midshipman on board his Majestys Ship the *Perseverance* by his Obedient Servant. THE AUTHOR.'[11]

Ignoring its limited literary merits, *The Adventures of Mr Harley* is important for what it reveals about how a young girl, aged somewhere between 13 and 17, imagined the navy, a world that the Austen family had no experience of until Francis went to sea in 1788. Coming from a clergy family, Jane will have seen her first task in this tale as being to reconcile the moral dilemma of a brother serving on a man-of-war, which she does by making her fictional hero a chaplain, the message to Francis being that, since he is not a chaplain on board his real-life frigate, he should at least do as one would.

When alluding to the contrary pulls of father and mother, Jane may have been evoking the, doubtless, frequent family conferences deciding what career should be chosen for each of her six brothers, all of whom, unusually in an age still plagued with high mortality rates, survived to adulthood, including one who was mentally retarded. The 'half a year' cruise is telling: a young girl would have had no concept how long a cruise, let alone a war might last, and, for her, half a year was quite long enough for Francis to begin and end his naval career.

If there is a deeper message in this tale, it is the plight of the 'young Wife' forgotten by Mr Harley in the half a year that he has been away at sea. Emma is '17 with fine dark Eyes & an elegant Shape'. Jane could have already been 17 herself when she wrote this 'Tale'. Whether this is how she imagined a sailor's bride might feel, or how she herself might be as a sailor's bride, is unimportant. She ends up conveying in a few sharp words what it was like for her left behind, while the carefree naval hero, in this case her brother Francis, was away at sea, thinking only of himself and his career. She was not alone in trying to comprehend the alien world into which the Austen family had been thrust by Francis' new career. Sister Cassandra was simultaneously penning a portrait ostensibly of Henry V for another of Jane's early creative experiments entitled *The History of England*. The uniform and pigtail speak more of a young midshipman than of a king of England.

The next of Jane's works of fiction with a naval content was *Mansfield Park*, begun in 1811 when she had already completed three novels. By then Britain had been at war off and on for 18 years, during which time she had enjoyed the intermittent returns home of her two brothers, only to endure their subsequent departures.

Unlike in the confabulated narrative of *The Adventures of Mr Harley*, where the hero sounds suspiciously young to be a married chaplain, come *Mansfield Park* there is no doubt that the naval hero, William Price, is firmly anchored in the 'real' world of a volunteer, going to sea aged 11 and thenceforth graduating through the rank of midshipman to become a lieutenant in his early twenties. If William has a career thereafter, it is lost from view. Choosing this career span, Jane would have had ample opportunities to tap into her brothers' immediate first-hand knowledge of the navy, yet does so only sparingly, preferring instead to stay 'quite at home'. It is strictly from that vantage point that she presents her brothers' naval careers.

In a reprise of the dilemma that she resolved by legerdemain in *The Adventures of Mr Harley*, Jane initiates a long debate on the merits of a naval career versus one in the clergy. First comes the allusion to the pivotal importance of natural interest whereby 'it is the same sort of thing ... as for the son of an admiral to go into the navy, or the son of a general to be in the army, and nobody sees any thing wrong in that. Nobody wonders that they should prefer the line where their friends can serve them best...'[12] Later on in the story, the matter of 'interest' is revisited at frequent intervals, especially by Sir Thomas Bertram who has interest, but only enough to secure his nephew, William, his first berth at sea, As to the next steps in William's career, Sir Thomas, 'the uncle who had done most for his support and advancement',[13] understands that more powerful interest is required and, therefore, that 'his nephew's introduction to Admiral Crawford might be of service. The Admiral he believed had interest.'[14] When the admiral duly procures William's promotion to lieutenant, Sir Thomas in turn acknowledges that 'it is very uncertain when my interest might have got William on. He has done it already.'[15]

Having put on display the mechanics by which a young gentleman might enter and then rise in the profession, Jane proceeds to set out the reasons why a career in the navy might be chosen, beginning with the blunt affirmation that 'the profession, either of navy or army, is its own justification. It has everything in its favour; heroism, danger, bustle, fashion. Soldiers are always acceptable in society.'[16] Viewed from the outside, which is where Jane is 'quite at home', it is a service, at least for midshipmen and their sibling sisters, which is chosen for its glamour and excitement. She expands further on this when William is called on to talk about his time at sea: 'Young as he was, William had already seen a great deal. He had been in the Mediterranean – in the West Indies – in the Mediterranean again – had been often taken on shore by the favour of his Captain, and in the course of seven years had known every variety of danger, which sea and war together could offer. With such means in his power he had a right to be listened to.'[17]

Here is a perfect moment for Jane to bring into her narrative the details of some exciting action that she may have heard Francis or Charles recount. Instead she stops short with an airy reference to some 'account of a shipwreck or an engagement'.[18] Bring on Marryat. Bring on Chamier. And it is not as if there aren't any details. William has them in abundance: *vide* one of his audience swooning, 'Dear me! how disagreeable – I wonder any body can ever go to sea',[19] and another briefly feeling 'the highest regard for a lad, who, before he was twenty, had gone through such bodily hardships, and given such proofs of mind. The glory of heroism, of usefulness, of exertion, of endurance, made his own habits of self-indulgence appear in shameful contrast; and he wished he had been a William

Price, distinguishing himself and working his way to fortune and consequence with so much self-respect and happy ardour, instead of what he was!'[20]

Far away as Mansfield Park is from the quarterdeck of a frigate or ship-of-the-line, the interconnected naval themes of rank, patronage and promotion are translated into what they mean for the families left behind. In William's case, the initial announcement to the family comes simply enough: 'He is made. Your brother is a Lieutenant. I have the infinite satisfaction of congratulating you on your brother's promotion',[21] the directness of the announcement echoing how Jane recorded Francis' real-life promotion: 'Frank is made. – He was yesterday raised to the Rank of Commander...'[22]

However, as unalloyed as the delight was over the real-life promotion of Francis, it is not as easy to enjoy William's fictional promotion for its own sake, the naval content being firmly suborned to the author's onshore plotline. William's promotion becomes a poison chalice for his sister Fanny, who discovers that the interest exerted to secure his promotion has brought with it an obligation: an unwanted suitor expects her hand in marriage in return.

Occasionally Jane allows her pantheon of naval characters in *Mansfield Park* to expand outwards to embrace senior ranks, but only so as to emphasize how the rigid hierarchy at sea would be enacted on shore. Asked by Edmund Bertram, 'Do you know any thing of my cousin's captain?'[23] Miss Crawford responds, much in echo of Betsy Fremantle, that her circle of acquaintances is 'among Admirals ... we know very little of the inferior ranks. Post captains may be very good sort of men, but they do not belong to us. Of various admirals, I could tell you a great deal; of them and their flags, and the gradation of their pay, and their bickerings and jealousies. But in general, I can assure you that they are all passed over, and all very ill used.'[24] Firmly rooting this knowledge where she is 'quite at home', Jane has Miss Crawford conclude her discourse: 'Certainly, my home at my uncle's brought me acquainted with a circle of admirals. Of Rears and Vices, I saw enough.'[25]

Contrast Miss Crawford and her lofty admirals with humble Fanny and lowly midshipman William Price, who, home on leave, bemoans the fact that 'I could not expect to be welcome in such a smart place as that – poor scrubby midshipman as I am'.[26] He reverts to this when telling Fanny about possible plans to go to a dance: 'I do not know that there would be any good in going to the Assembly, for I might not get a partner. The Portsmouth girls turn up their noses at any body who has not a commission. One might as well be nothing as a midshipman. One is nothing indeed. You remember the Gregorys; they are grown up amazingly fine girls, but they will hardly speak to me, because Lucy is courted by a Lieutenant.'[27]

However, these forays into naval generalities, important though they are for an understanding of how those close to the service, but not in it, viewed it, are digressions from the main naval relationship in the novel: Fanny and William's sibling bond. As brother and sister, they are the lynchpin round which Jane expresses her idealized vision of the relationship between the younger generations of a family at war. From the outset, the intermittent separations that are the natural rhythms of any naval career become the essential dramatic device needed to heighten the emotional tension. This manifests itself in a rivalry between the two of them as to who can feel the strongest regard for the other. Initially they vie for who will take the lead in that most important of lifelines in any naval family: the letter-writing. Fanny starts off by claiming that William 'had promised he would, but he had told her to write first'.[28] Jane revisits the subject some years into the story when the brothers are being condemned for being the bad letter-writers that they are and has Fanny intervene in defence of her absent brother, protesting that 'when they are at a distance from all their family...they can write long letters'.[29]

Another way in which the siblings compete is at the moment of separation, when they vie for who can feel the pain of it most keenly as when 'William determining soon after her removal, to be a sailor, was invited to spend a week with his sister in Northamptonshire, before he went to sea. Their eager affection in meeting, their exquisite delight in being together, their hours of happy mirth, and moments of serious conference, may be imagined; as well as the sanguine views and spirits of the boy even to the last, and the misery of the girl when he left.'[30]

After the separation comes the long wait until William's return, a wait interspersed with such reminders of the longings every sister left at home should feel: 'Upon the whole, it was a comfortable winter to her; for though it brought no William to England, the never failing hope of his arrival was worth much.'[31] Even in this brief allusion Jane displays, with the lightest of touches, the instinctive understanding of the rhythm of the navy, which only personal experience could engender: ships generally chose to winter in home port if possible.

William remains ever-present as, when describing her bedroom, Fanny mentions that there was '...pinned against the wall, a small sketch of a ship sent four years ago from the Mediterranean by William, with HMS *Antwerp* at the bottom, in letters, as tall as the main-mast'.[32] With these small allusions, Jane brings to bear her own experience of life as the sister of two sailors off at war, the whole building to a crescendo with William's brief homecoming, when a veritable cascade of emotions tumbles out:

> William, her brother, the so long absent and dearly beloved brother, was in England again, She had a letter from him herself, a few hurried happy lines, written as the ship came up the Channel and sent into Portsmouth, with the first boat that left the *Antwerp*, at anchor, in Spithead. There could be no doubt of his obtaining leave of absence immediately, for he was still only a midshipman; and his parents, from living on the spot [in Portsmouth], must already have seen him and be seeing him perhaps daily, his direct holidays might with justice be instantly given to the sister, who had been his best correspondent through a period of seven years...[33]

With these few statements Jane airily discards all the technicalities of a ship at sea returning to port. Just as her brother, Charles, seemed capable of bending the Admiralty to his will, so too does Fanny's brother, William. More important for her is what William's homecoming means to the siblings. This is to be the reunion of two – in all but reality – lovers, as Fanny describes how 'she found herself in an agitation of a higher nature – watching the hall, in the lobby, on the stairs, for the first sound of the carriage which was to bring her brother ... the first minutes of exquisite feeling had no interruption...'[34]

Thus reunited, the competition is renewed for which of the two can feel the strongest emotion. For William 'she was the first object of his love, but it was a love which his stronger spirits, and bolder temper, made it as natural for him to express as to feel.'[35] Fanny is also his deepest confidante, '...opening all his heart to her, telling her all his hopes and fears, plans and solicitudes respecting that long thought of, dearly earned and justly valued blessing of promotion – who was interested in all the comforts and all the little hardships of her home.'[36]

Fanny takes up the running, betraying that, beneath these tangible, innocent manifestations of a perfect sibling bond, lies something much deeper, inspired by William who is the only one:

…with whom (perhaps the dearest indulgence of the whole) all the evil and good of their earliest years could be gone over again, and every former united pain and pleasure retraced with the fondest recollection. An advantage this, a strengthener of love, in which conjugal tie is beneath the fraternal. Children of the same family, the same blood, with the same associations and habits, have some means of enjoyment in their power, which no subsequent connections can supply; and it must be a long and unnatural estrangement, by a divorce which no subsequent connection can justify, if such precious remains of the earliest attachments are entirely outlived. Too often alas! It is so – Fraternal love, sometimes almost every thing, is at others worse than nothing. But with William and Fanny Price, it was still a sentiment in all its prime and freshness, wounded by no opposition of interest, cooled by no separate attachment, and feeling the influence of time and absence only in its increase.[37]

This was to be no passing love for, on a subsequent reunion, Jane comes back to the subject of fraternal love and where it would end in practical terms:

Everything supplied an amusement to the high glee of William's mind, and he was full of frolic and joke in the intervals of their high-toned subjects, all of which ended, if they did not begin, in praise of the *Thrush* [William's ship] – conjectures how she would be employed, schemes for an action with some superior force, which (supposing the first lieutenant out of the war – and William was not very merciful to the first lieutenant) was to give himself the next step as soon as possible, or speculations about prize-money, which was to be generously distributed at home with only the reservation of enough to make the little cottage comfortable in which he and Fanny were to pass all their middle and later life together.[38]

Here is an emotional dimension that is far away from the real world of a naval family as conceived by Francis and Charles, and it is no surprise that neither brother could bring himself to praise *Mansfield Park*. Asked for his opinion, Charles was blunt and dismissive, saying that he 'did not like it near as well as P & P. [*Pride and Prejudice*] – thought it wanted Incident.'[39] Charles may have found the novel especially embarrassing in view of the fact that Jane chose to have William give Fanny a very pretty amber cross that he had brought her from Sicily, reprising a present that Charles had given Jane, which she referred to in her letter to Cassandra of 27 May 1801 remarking that 'he has been buying Gold chains and Topazes Crosses for us'.[40]

As for Francis – possibly the more likely of the two brothers to be the object of her 'love' – he could not but deflect the cloying sentiments as diplomatically as possible, using the 'we' as a deliberate device to distance himself from Jane when he wrote that 'we certainly do not think it as a whole, equal to P & P – but it has many & great beauties. Fanny is a delightful Character! And Aunt Norris is a great favourite of mine. The Characters are natural & well supported, & many of the Dialogues excellent.'[41] There is praise, but faint indeed, since there is no mention of William or the naval content of the novel.

Jane the spinster had bared her soul, declared a love that was reciprocated in fiction but an embarrassment in real life. Still, she could comfort herself that a first venture into naval fiction had caught the attention of one very special admirer, who had his personal chaplain, James Stanier Clarke, write to Jane in November 1815:

> It is certainly not incumbent on you to dedicate your work now in the Press to his Royal Highness; but if you wish to do the Regent that honour either now or at any future period, I am happy to send you that permission which need not require any more trouble or solicitation on your Part. Your late Works, Madam, and in particular *Mansfield Park* reflect the highest honour on your Genius & Principles; in every new work your mind seems to increase its energy and powers of discrimination. The Regent has read and admired all your publications.[42]

This was high 'naval' praise indeed given that the prince regent was possibly a patron of the *Naval Chronicle* and James Clarke had served as a naval chaplain in the Channel Fleet aboard *Impétueux* for four years from 1796 to 1799 and was intimately associated with the *Naval Chronicle*. By the time she received this letter Jane had already begun work on *Persuasion*, the third in this 'trilogy' of naval fictions and, with the Wars at an end, its story neatly completed the life cycle of a sailor: his retirement. She confidently filled *Persuasion* with a rich cast of naval characters, albeit still setting them firmly in her 'quite at home' environment of Bath and its surrounding stately homes. Here is an older generation of naval characters, Frederick Wentworth, the novel's hero, taking over where William

Price's career left off. Frederick begins his fictional career as a lieutenant recently promoted to commander and thence to post-captain, in the process graduating, by dint of prize money, from one who 'had no fortune'[43] to someone who 'with five-and-twenty thousand pounds, and as high in his profession as merit and activity could place, was no longer nobody'.[44]

Whereas prize money appeared only fleetingly in *Mansfield Park* and was barely discernible as a reason for William entering the navy, Frederick, by contrast, is senior enough to touch his share of outrageous fortune. Prize money is a constant theme in *Persuasion*, competing only with honour and service in earning naval officers the right to respect from their fellow citizens since 'the navy, I think, who have done so much for us, have at least an equal claim with any other set of men, for all the comforts and all the privilege which any home can give. Sailors work hard enough for their comforts, we must all allow.'[45]

In this new world inhabited by senior naval officers, Jane has long lost sight of those earlier days of youthful innocence epitomized by Mr Harley and William Price, indeed so much so that the one young midshipman whom she does incarnate in *Persuasion* is a caricature, more grotesque even than Fanny Burney's Captain Mirvan. Jane venomously describes how:

…the Musgroves had the ill fortune of a very troublesome, hopeless son; and the good fortune to lose him before he reached his twentieth year; that he had been sent to sea, because he was stupid and unmanageable on shore; that he had been very little cared for at any time by his family, though quite as much as he deserved; seldom heard of, and scarcely at all regretted when the intelligence of his death abroad had worked its way to Uppercross, two years before… He had, in fact, though his sisters were now doing all they could for him, by calling him 'poor Richard', been nothing better than a thick-headed, unfeeling, unprofitable Dick Musgrove, who had never done anything to entitle himself to more than the abbreviation of his name, living or dead. He had been several years at sea, and had, in the course of those removals to which all midshipmen are liable, and especially such midshipmen as every captain wishes to get rid of, been on board Captain Frederick Wentworth's frigate, the *Laconia*, and from the *Laconia*, he had, under the influence of his captain, written the only two letters which his father and mother had ever received from him during the whole of his absence, that is to say, the only two disinterested letters; all the rest had been mere applications for money.[46]

'Poor Richard'. No young Nelson he. To think that he had eluded the attentions of the *Naval Chronicle* and all the memorialists, biographers and autobiographers who had been busy sanctifying the nation's young naval heroes throughout the 22 long years of the Wars, only to be picked off, mocked and pilloried just as the Wars ended. This was a cruel epitaph indeed for all those young Nelsons who had fought so bravely for King and Country, crueller still for another 'Richard', the one whose Mother Marsinghall was so blissfully ignorant of what a 'sea of trouble' her 'little Richard' was about to endure sending him to sea, otherwise she 'wouldst not have supposed by his being a midshipman he was made for ever. Though literally it was the case, for poor fellow, he never was made anything else, but died before he had served his time.'[47]

NOTES

ABBREVIATIONS

MM: Mariner's Mirror
MSY: The Marine Society
NC: Naval Chronicle
NMM: National Maritime Museum
NRS: Navy Records Society
RA: Royal Archives
RNM: Royal Naval Museum

PROLOGUE

1   *Naval Chronicle*, Vol. XV p.293
2   Ibid.
3   Kennedy, Ludovic, *Nelson's Band of Brothers*, London (1951), p.314
4   Pocock, Tom, *Remember Nelson: The Life of Captain Sir William Hoste*, Newton Abbott (1978), p.117
5   Laughton, J. K., ed., *Journal of Rear-Admiral Bartholomew James 1752–1828*, NRS Vol. VI, 1896, p.7
6   Ibid.
7   Ibid., p.6
8   Shakespeare, William, *2 Henry IV* 3.1.18
9   Rodger, N. A. M. *The Safeguard of the Sea: A Naval History of Britain Vol. 1 660–1649*, London (2004), p.141
10 Laughton, p.4

CHAPTER 1

1   Hampden, John, ed. *Francis Drake Privateer. Contemporary Narratives and Documents*, London (1972), p.62
2   Ibid.
3   Ibid., p.128
4   Rodger, Appendix IV pp.498–501
5   Hampden, p.26
6   Ibid., pp.215–6
7   Ibid., p.214
8   Ibid.
9   Robinson, C. N., *The British Tar in Fact and Fiction*, London (1909), p.65
10 Ibid.
11 Ibid.

12 Irving, Laurence, ed., *A Selection of the Principal Voyages, Traffiques and Discoveries of the English Nation by Richard Hakluyt*, London (1927) pp.82–3
13 Ibid., p.86
14 Ibid., p.87
15 Ibid., p.101
16 Hazlewood, Nick, *The Queen's Slave Trader: John Hawkyns, Elizabeth I and the Trafficking in Human Souls*, New York (2004), p.180
17 Ibid.
18 Hampden, p.227
19 Ibid.

CHAPTER 2

1   MSY/K No.1, 13 September 1786
2   Ibid.
3   MSY/A/1, 25 June 1756
4   MSY/A/1, 12 August 1756
5   MSY/H/1, No.3, 5 August 1756
6   MSY/K, No.3, 13 September 1786
7   MSY/K, No.2, 13 September 1786
8   MSY/A/1, 25 June 1756
9   MSY/A/1, 29 July 1756
10 Ibid.
11 MSY/A/1, 12 August 1756
12 *Naval Chronicle*, Vol. XXXVIII p.148
13 Ibid.
14 Woodman, Richard, *…of daring temper. A History of the Marine Society*, London (2006), p.24
15 Fielding, John, *An Account of the Origin and Effects of a Police Set on Foot by His Grace the Duke of Newcastle in the year 1753, upon a Plan Presented to His Grace by the Late Henry Fielding, Esqr. to which is added a Plan for Preserving those Deserted Girls in this Town, who Become Prostitutes from Necessity*, London (1758), p.21, in Pietsch, Roland W. W., *Ships' Boys and Charity in the Mid-Eighteenth Century: The London Marine Society (1756–1772)*, London, Ph.D. thesis (2003), p.38
16 Woodman, p.18
17 *Regulations of the Marine Society: Historical Accounts*, London (1772), p.41 also in Pietsch, p. 43
18 Woodman, p.13
19 Ibid., p.25
20 Ibid., p.26
21 Pietsch, p.118

22 MSY/K, No. 2, 13 September 1786

23 Pietsch, p.187

24 Ibid.

25 *Regulations of the Marine Society: Historical Accounts*, London (1772) pp.12–14, in Pietsch, p.162

26 Fielding, John (1758), p.21 in Pietsch, p.38

27 Ibid., pp.17–19, in Pietsch, p.43

28 Fielding, Henry, *The History of Tom Jones, a Foundling*, London (1749, 1997) in Pietsch, p.43

29 Fielding, John, *An Account of the Receipts and Disbursements Relating to Sir John Fielding's Plan, for the Preserving of Distressed Boys, by Sending them to Sea*, London (1769) pp.2–5, in Pietsch, p.44

30 Hanway, Jonas, *Three Letters: Letter I* (1758), p.6, in Pietsch, p.187

CHAPTER 3

1 Pocock, Tom, *Sailor King The Life of King William IV*, London (1991), p.38

2 Ibid.

3 Ibid.

4 RA/GEO/MAIN/2944, Papers of King George III

5 RA/GEO/MAIN/16346, King George III to Admiral Hood, 16 April 1783

6 Laughton, J. K., ed., *The Naval Miscellany Vol. 1*, NRS Vol. 20 (1902), p.225 King George III to Admiral Hood, 27 May 1779, in Pocock, p.9

7 RA/GEO/MAIN/16147, Admiral Hood to King George III, 15 July 1778

8 Ibid.

9 *Prince George's Logg Book*, LOG/N/B/7, B/8, B/9

10 Ibid.

11 *Oxford English Dictionary*: a definition first identified in the *Experienced Eng. Housekeeper*, Raffald, E., 1769

12 *Prince George's Logg Book*, LOG/N/B/7, B/8, B/9

13 Ibid.

14 Ibid.

15 Ibid.

16 Laughton, p.225, King George III to Admiral Hood, 27 May 1778, in Pocock, p.10

17 RA/GEO/MAIN/16154, King George III to Admiral Digby, n.d.

18 RA/GEO/MAIN/16156–7, King George III to General Budé, 11 June 1779

19 RA/GEO/MAIN/16158–9 King George III to Prince William, 13 June 1779

20 *Prince George's Logg Book*, LOG/N/B/7, B/8, B/9

21 Ibid.

22 Ziegler, Philip, *King William IV*, Bungay, Suffolk (1971), p.29

23 *Prince George's Logg Book*, LOG/N/B/7, B/8, B/9

24 Ziegler, p.29

25 Ibid., p.30

26 RA/GEO/MAIN/16154, King George III to Admiral Digby, n.d.

27 Digby, Admiral Robert Archives: Admiral Digby to Admiral Hood, in Pocock p.46

28 *Prince George's Logg Book*, LOG/N/B/7, B/8, B/9

29 Ibid.

30 Ibid.

31 Ibid.

32 Ibid.

33 RA/GEO/MAIN/44600–1, Prince William to King George III, 11 July 1779

34 RA/GEO/MAIN/44604–5, Prince William to King George III, 18 October 1779

35 RA/GEO/MAIN/44602–3, Prince William to King George III, 3 September 1779

36 *Prince George's Logg Book*, LOG/N/B/7, B/8, B/9

37 RA/GEO/MAIN/44609–10, Prince William to King George III, 9 January 1780

38 Ibid.

39 RA/GEO/ADD15/749 Admiral Hood to General Budé, 20 March 1783

40 *Prince George's Logg Book*, LOG/N/B/7, B/8, B/9

41 Ibid.

42 RA/GEO/MAIN/44611–2, Prince William to King George III, 26 January 1780

43 *Prince George's Logg Book*, LOG/N/B/7, B/8, B/9

44 Ibid.

45 Wright G. N., *The Life and Reign of William the Fourth*, two vols (pp.106–9) reproduce the text of J. Watkins biog op. cit., London (1837), in Ziegler, p.33

46 Ibid.

47 RA/GEO/ADD4/122, King George III to Prince William, 2 March 1780

48 *Prince George's Logg Book*, LOG/N/B/7, B/8, B/9

49 Pocock, p.27

50 Ziegler, p.34

51 Ibid., pp.33–4

52 RA 44600, Prince William to King George III, 11 July 1779

53 RA 44606–7, Prince William to King George III, 24 November 1779

54 Aspinall, A., ed., *The Later Correspondence of King George III* (Vols 1–3), Cambridge (1938), Vol.1, p.77 King George III to Prince William August 1784, in Pocock, p.68

55 Aspinall, p.107, King George III to Prince William, 28 October 1784, in Pocock, p.68

56 *Prince George's Logg Book*, LOG/N/B/7, B/8, B/9

57 Ibid.

58 Ibid.

59 Pocock, p.36

60 *Prince George's Logg Book*, LOG/N/B/7, B/8, B/9

61 Ibid.

62 RA/GEO/MAIN/44638–9, Prince William to King George III, 27 September 1781

63 *Prince George's Logg Book*, LOG/N/B/7, B/8, B/9
64 Ibid.
65 RA/GEO/MAIN/44632, Prince William to King George III, 28 September 1781
66 Ibid.
67 Ibid.
68 RA/GEO/MAIN/44633-4, Prince William to King George III, 10 November 1781
69 *Prince George's Logg Book*, LOG/N/B/7, B/8, B/9
70 Ibid.
71 Pocock, p.39
72 Clarke, James Stanier & M'Arthur, John, *The Life of Admiral Lord Nelson K.B. from his Lordship's Manuscripts*, London (1809), 2 vols, Vol. I p.53, in Hibbert, C., *Nelson A Personal History*, London (1994), p.35
73 RA ADDL 4/15, Prince Frederick to Prince William, 4 January 1782

CHAPTER 4

1   Laughton, J. K., ed., *Journal of Rear-Admiral Bartholomew James 1752-1828*, NRS, Vol. 6 (1896), p.4
2   Sullivan, F. B., *The Royal Academy at Portsmouth 1729-1806* (MM LXIII 1977), p.312
3   MSS195
4   Lloyd C. & Anderson R. C., eds., Penrose, C. V., *A Memoir of James Trevenen*, NRS, Vol. 101 (1959), p.5
5   Robinson, C. N., *The British Tar in Fact and Fiction*, London (1909), p.77
6   MSS195
7   Ibid.
8   Lloyd, p.9
9   MS.AUS/14
10 Ibid.
11 Ibid.
12 Ibid.
13 Ibid.
14 Hubback, John H. & Edith C., *Jane Austen's Sailor Brothers*, London (1906), p.20
15 Lloyd, p.10
16 Digby, Admiral Robert Archives in Pocock, Tom, *Sailor King The Life of King William IV*, London (1991), p.45
17 Lloyd, p.5
18 MS.AUS/14
19 Sullivan, p.314
20 Ibid.
21 MSS195
22 MS.AUS/14
23 Ibid.
24 Southam, Brian, *Jane Austen and The Navy*, London (2005), p.39
25 Sullivan pp.316-9
26 Ibid.
27 Ibid.
28 Ibid.
29 Ibid.
30 Ibid.
31 Ibid.
32 Lloyd, pp.8-10
33 Ibid.
34 Ibid.
35 Ibid.
36 Ibid.
37 *Webster's Third New International Dictionary*, Chicago (1976)
38 Lloyd, pp.8-10
39 MS.AUS/14
40 *Naval Chronicle*, Vol. XXX p.449
41 Hamilton, Sir Richard Vesey, ed., *Letters and Papers of Admiral of Fleet Sir Thos Byam Martin GCB*, NRS, Vol. 24, (1903), p.23
42 Lloyd, p.7
43 NMM 355.231.1 (422.7) p.19, c.f. P.C.R.O. S3/103 sessions file for April 1736 deposition dated 29 October 1735 in Thomas, J. H., *Portsmouth Naval Academy: An Educational Experiment Examined*, Portsmouth Archive Rev, Vol. 3 (1978)
44 Sullivan, p.319
45 Hamilton, Sir Richard Vesey & Laughton J. K., eds., *Recollections of James Anthony Gardner*, NRS, Vol. 31 (1906), p.15
46 *Naval Miscellany*, NRS, Vol. IV, p.472
47 Laughton, J. K., ed., *Letters and Papers of Charles, Lord Barham. Admiral of the Red Squadron, 1758-1813*, NRS, Vol. 39 (1910)

CHAPTER 5

1   *Naval Chronicle*, Vol. I, p.212
2   Fremantle, Anne, ed., *The Wynne Diaries*, Oxford (1935-40), 3 vols, Vol. I, p.231
3   Hathaway, W.S., ed., *The Speeches of the Right Honourable William Pitt in the House of Commons*, Vol. II, p.103, in Hague, William, *William Pitt the Younger*, London (2004), p.331
4   Ibid.
5   Bodleian Library: House of Commons Papers 1793
6   Ibid.
7   Ibid.
8   NC, Vol. II, p.488
9   Sainsbury, Capt A. B. & Phillips, Lt Cdr F. L., *The Royal Navy Day by Day*, Stroud (2005), p.43
10 MSY/O/7
11 Robinson, William, *Jack Nastyface. Memoirs of an English Seaman*, London (1973), p.11
12 Ibid., p.135
13 Robinson, C. N., *The British Tar in Fact and Fiction*, London (1909), p.122

14 White, Colin, ed., *Nelson: The New Letters*, London (2005), p.157

15 Ibid.

16 Ibid., p.151

17 Nicolas, Sir Nicholas Harris, ed., *Dispatches and Letters of Vice-Admiral Lord Viscount Nelson*, 7 vols, London (1844–6), Vol. I, p.294

18 White, p.153

19 Nicolas, Vol. I, p.294

20 Matcham, M. Eyre, *The Nelsons of Burnham Thorpe*, London, (1911), p. 99

21 Nicolas, p.301

22 AGC/17/1

23 MSY/O/7

24 MSY/O/7, No. 7910

25 MSY/O/7, No. 7911

26 MSY/O/7, No. 7913

27 Ibid.

28 MSY/O/7

29 MSY/O/7, Nos. 7914, 7952, 7958

30 MSY/O/7

31 Ibid.

32 MSY/K No. 7, 13 September 1786

33 Ibid.

34 Ibid.

35 MSY/K No. 9, 13 September 1786

36 Ibid.

37 Ibid.

38 Woodman, Richard, *...of daring temper. A History of the Marine Society*, London (2006), p.25

39 MSY/K No. 1946, 2 February 1793

40 MSY/K No. 1945, 1 February 1793

41 MSY/K No. 1950, 7 March 1793

42 MSY/K No. 1982, 17 January 1794

43 MSY/K No. 1948, 22 February 1793, No. 1949, 28 February 1793

44 MSY/K No. 1813, 31 August 1792, No. 1946, 2 February 1793

45 Nicolas, Vol. I, p.298

46 Robinson, William, p.25

47 Ibid.

48 Ibid.

49 Nicolas, Vol. I, p.298

50 Ibid.

51 Ibid., p.299

52 ADM/L/A/51

53 Ibid.

54 BGY/W/3

55 Robinson, C. N., pp.358–9

56 Ibid., p.85

57 Nicolas, Vol. I, pp.80–1, Hibbert, Christopher, *Nelson, A Personal History*, London (1994) pp.38,

58 Matcham, p.100

59 Naish, George P. B., ed., *Nelson's Letters to his Wife and other Documents 1785–1831*, NRS, Vol. 100 (1958), p.75

60 Nicolas, p.302

61 Naish, pp.73–4

62 Ibid., p.75

63 Ibid.

64 Lloyd C. & Anderson R. C, eds., Penrose, C. V., *A Memoir of James Trevenen*, NRS, Vol. 101 (1959), p.10

65 Hoste, Lady Harriet, *Memoirs and Letters of Captain Sir William Hoste*, London (1833)

66 Keate, E. M., *Nelson's Wife*, London (1939), p.66

67 NC, Vol. XXX, p.3

68 Parsons, G. S., *Nelsonian Reminiscences*, London (1843), p.199

69 Ibid.

70 Ibid.

71 Hoste, p.8

72 Ibid., p.49

73 Parsons, p.205

74 Southam, Brian, *Jane Austen and The Navy*, London (2005), p.35

75 Ibid., p.34

76 Ibid.

77 Ibid.

78 Ibid.

79 Ibid.

80 Ibid.

81 Ibid.

82 Ibid.

83 Hubback, John H. & Edith C., *Jane Austen's Sailor Brothers*, London (1906), p.20

84 Ibid.

CHAPTER 6

1 Hamilton, Sir Richard Vesey, ed., *Letters and Papers of Admiral of Fleet Sir Thos Byam Martin GCB*, NRS, Vol. 24 (1903), p.14

2 Ibid., p.15

3 Ibid., p.28

4 Lewis, Michael, ed., Sir William Henry Dillon, *A Narrative of My Professional Adventures 1790–1839*, NRS, Vol. 93 (1953), p.12

5 Ibid., p.8

6 Ibid.

7 Ibid., p.12

8 Ibid.

9 PAR 188/1

10 Raigersfeld, Jeffrey Baron de, *The Life of a Sea Officer 1783–1828*, ed. Laughton, L. G Carr, London (1929), p.8

11 Lewis, p.13

12 Ibid., p.14

13 Ibid.

14 Ibid.
15 Ibid.
16 Ibid., p.15
17 Ibid., p.16
18 Ibid., p.17
19 Raigersfeld, p.10
20 Lewis, p.17
21 Hoste, Lady Harriet, *Memoirs and Letters of Capt Sir William Hoste*, London (1833), 2 vols, Vol. I, p.9
22 Nicolas, Sir Nicholas Harris, ed., *Dispatches and Letters of Vice-Admiral Lord Viscount Nelson*, London (1844–6), 7 vols, Vol. I, p.305
23 Hamilton, p.24
24 Naish, George P. B, ed., *Nelson's Letters to his Wife and other Documents 1785–1831*, NRS, Vol. 100 (1958), p.81
25 Ibid., p.75
26 Ibid., p.80
27 Ibid., p.77
28 Hoste letters on microfiche: letter dated 19 May 1793
29 Raigersfeld, p.8
30 Ibid., p.6
31 Ibid., p.7
32 Ibid.
33 Ibid., p.8
34 Phillimore, Augustus, *The Life of Admiral of the Fleet Sir William Parker*, London (1876–80), 3 vols, Vol. I, p.10
35 PAR 188/1
36 Ibid.
37 Phillimore, Vol. I, p.11
38 Pemberton, Charles Reece, *The Autobiography of Pel Verjuice*, London (1929), p.136
39 Ibid.
40 Ibid., p.154
41 Ibid.
42 Robinson, William, *Jack Nastyface. Memoirs of an English Seaman*, London (1973), pp.32–3
43 Ibid., p.28
44 Ibid., p.26
45 Raigersfeld, p.10
46 Ibid., p.7
47 Ibid.
48 Ibid., p.9
49 PAR188/1
50 Phillimore, Vol. I, p.56
51 Hoste letters on microfiche: letter dated 5 August 1793
52 Hoste, p.10
53 Phillimore, Vol. I, p.10
54 Ibid.
55 Raigersfeld, p.7
56 Ibid.
57 Hoste letters on microfiche: letter dated 5 August 1793
58 Hoste, p.29
59 Phillimore, Vol. I, p.11
60 Ibid.
61 Ibid.
62 Lewis, p.13
63 Phillimore, Vol. I, p.11
64 PAR188/1, 23 April 1793, letter

CHAPTER 7

1 Hamilton, Sir Richard Vesey, ed., *Letters and Papers of Admiral of Fleet Sir Thos Byam Martin GCB*, NRS, Vol. 24, (1903), p.25
2 MSS195
3 Pemberton, Charles Reece, *The Autobiography of Pel Verjuice*, London (1929), p.138
4 Hamilton, p.24
5 *Naval Chronicle*, Vol. XXX, pp.4–5
6 Ibid.
7 Ibid.
8 Hoste, Lady Harriet, *Memoirs and Letters of Capt Sir William Hoste*, London (1833), 2 vols, Vol. I, p.14
9 Naish, George P. B., ed., *Nelson's Letters to his Wife and other Documents 1785–1831*, NRS, Vol. 100 (1958), p.94
10 Lewis, Michael, ed., Sir William Henry Dillon, *A Narrative of My Professional Adventures 1790–1839*, NRS, Vol. 93 (1953), p.28
11 Ibid., p.19
12 Ibid., p.21
13 Ibid., p19
14 Ibid., p.21
15 Ibid., p.27
16 Ibid., p.25
17 Ibid., pp.22–3
18 Ibid., p.23
19 Hoste letters on microfiche: letter dated 5 August 1793
20 Sullivan, F. B., *The Naval Schoolmaster During the Eighteenth Century and the Early Nineteenth Century* (MM LXII 1976), p.318
21 Ibid.
22 Ibid., p.321
23 Hamilton, p.57
24 Ibid., p.58
25 Ibid., p.59
26 Ibid.
27 Phillimore, Augustus, *The Life of Admiral of the Fleet Sir William Parker*, London (1876–80), 3 vols, Vol. I, p.5
28 Ibid., p.6
29 Lewis, p.45
30 Ibid., p.33
31 Ibid., p.35
32 Ibid.

33 Ibid., p.41
34 Ibid., p.20
35 Naish, p.291
36 Lewis, p.41
37 Ibid., p.25
38 Raigersfeld, Jeffrey Baron de, *The Life of a Sea Officer 1783–1828*, ed. Laughton, L. G Carr, London (1929), p.10
39 Lewis, p.30
40 PAR182, letter of George Parker, 16 October 1793
41 Lewis, p.89
42 Robinson, William, *Jack Nastyface. Memoirs of an English Seaman*, London (1973), p.35
43 Lewis, p.76
44 Raigersfeld, p.18
45 Lewis, p.21
46 Ibid.
47 Ibid.
48 Ibid.
49 Raigersfeld, p.15
50 Ibid., p.12
51 Ibid.
52 Ibid., p.13
53 Ibid.
54 Pocock, Tom, *Remember Nelson: The Life of Captain Sir William Hoste*, Newton Abbott (1978), p.49
55 Lewis, p.46
56 NC, Vol. VI, p.256
57 Lewis, p.21
58 Ibid., p.14
59 Robinson, p.35
60 Lewis, p.21
61 Ibid., p.38
62 Ibid.
63 MSS195
64 Phillimore, Vol. I, p.41
65 Lewis, p.45
66 Ibid.
67 Parsons, G. S., *Nelsonian Reminiscences*, London (1843), pp.47–8
68 Ibid., p.32
69 NC, Vol. II, p.525
70 Parsons, pp.44–5
71 NC, Vol. II, p.525
72 Lewis, p.60
73 Laughton, J. K., ed., *Journal of Rear-Admiral Bartholomew James 1752–1828*, NRS, Vol. 6 (1896), p.7
74 Hamilton, p.59
75 Robinson, p.55
76 Ibid.
77 NC, Vol. I, p.261
78 Robinson, p.55
79 Lewis, p.69

80 Ibid., p.83
81 NC, Vol. II, p.527
82 Parkinson, C. Northcote, *Portsmouth Point The Navy in Fiction 1793–1815* Liverpool (1949), p.58
83 Ibid.
84 Parsons, p.48
85 NC, Vol. IX, p.419
86 NC, Vol. X, p.73
87 Ibid.
88 NC, Vol. II, p.527
89 Ibid.

CHAPTER 8

1 *Naval Chronicle*, Vol. I, p.25
2 Ibid., frontispiece
3 Ibid., p.21
4 Ibid., p.416
5 JOD/12, *Nicholas Pocock: Notes and Sketches on Board HMS Pegasus*, 1/6/1794
6 MM, Vol. 8 (1974), pp.335–8
7 AGC/8/33
8 Ibid.
9 Phillimore, Augustus, *The Life of Admiral of the Fleet Sir William Parker*, London (1876–80), 3 vols, Vol. I, p.45
10 Jackson, T. Sturges, ed., *Logs of the Great Sea Fights 1794–1805*, NRS, Vols 16 & 18 (1899-1900), Vol. 16 (1899), p.54
11 MM, Vol. 8 (1974), pp.335 8
12 Ibid.
13 Ibid.
14 Ibid.
15 Phillimore, Vol. I, p.44
16 Ibid., p.52
17 JOD/12
18 Ibid.
19 Phillimore, Vol. I, p.43
20 Ibid.
21 Cordingly, David, *Billy Ruffian The Bellerophon and the Downfall of Napoleon*, London (2003), p.85
22 Phillimore, Vol. I, p.49
23 Ibid.
24 Ibid., p.51
25 Ibid., p.52
26 BRK/14, *Logbook of the Orion. Capt Duckworth Apr–Jun 1794*
27 Phillimore, Vol. I, p.53
28 Ibid.
29 Ibid.
30 Ibid., p.54
31 Ibid.
32 BRK/14
33 Phillimore, Vol. I, p.53

34 Lewis, Michael, ed., Sir William Henry Dillon, *A Narrative of My Professional Adventures 1790–1839*, NRS, Vol. 93 (1953), p.125
35 Ibid., p.130
36 Ibid., p.125
37 Ibid., p.131
38 Ibid., p.133
39 Ibid., p.125
40 Ibid., p.131
41 Ibid., p.129
42 Ibid., p.131
43 Ibid., p.128
44 Ibid., p.130
45 Phillimore, Vol. I, pp.54–55
46 NC, Vol. I, p.22
47 Ibid.
48 Phillimore, Vol. I, p.55
49 NC, Vol. VIII, p.88
50 NC, Vol. XI, p.443
51 Ibid.
52 Perrett, Bryan, *The Real Hornblower. The Life and Times of Admiral Sir James Gordon GCB*, London (1998), p.25

CHAPTER 9

1 *Naval Chronicle*, Vol. IV, p.156
2 Ibid., p.166
3 Raigersfeld, Jeffrey Baron de, *The Life of a Sea Officer 1783–1828*, ed. Laughton, L. G Carr, London (1929), p.20
4 Lewis, Michael, ed., Sir William Henry Dillon, *A Narrative of My Professional Adventures 1790–1839*, NRS, Vol. 93 (1953), p.23
5 Raigersfeld, p.7
6 Ibid.
7 Woodman, Richard, *...of daring temper. A History of the Marine Society*, London (2006), p.42
8 Naish, George P. B., ed., *Nelson's Letters to his Wife and other Documents 1785–1831* NRS, Vol. 100 (1958), p.111
9 Phillimore, Augustus, *The Life of Admiral of the Fleet Sir William Parker*, London (1876–80), 3 vols, Vol. I, p.123
10 Ibid.
11 Ibid., p.57
12 Ibid.
13 Nagle, Jacob, *The Nagle Journal: A Diary of the Life of Jacob Nagle, Sailor, from the Year 1775 to 1841*, ed. John C. Dann, New York (1988), p.209
14 Ibid.
15 Ibid., p.211
16 BGR/12: *Rough Statement from other imperfect recollections of Lieutenant David O'Brien Casey's service and sufferings in Her Majesty's Navy*, 22 November 1839

17 Ibid.
18 Ibid.
19 Ibid.
20 Ibid.
21 NC, Vol. IV, p.515
22 Ibid.
23 Raigersfeld, p.22
24 Ibid.
25 Ibid.
26 Ibid., p.21
27 Lewis, p.105
28 Hubback, John H. & Edith C., *Jane Austen's Sailor Brothers*, London (1906), p.29
29 BGR/12
30 Ibid.
31 Ibid.
32 Lewis, p.23
33 Ibid.
34 Ibid.
35 BGR/12
36 Ibid.
37 Ibid.
38 NC, Vol. IV, p.166
39 NC, Vol. XVI, p.343
40 MM, Vol. 21 (1935), pp.428–49
41 Rodger, N. A. M., *The Command of the Ocean. A Naval History of Britain 1649–1815*, London (2004), p.448
42 Ibid.
43 *Annual Register* 1799, Appendix to *The Chronicle*, p.176
44 Rodger, p.451
45 Nagle, p.211
46 Kennedy, Ludovic, *Nelson's Band of Brothers*, London (1951), p.90
47 Elliot, Sir George, *Memoir of Admiral the Hon. Sir George Elliot, written for his children*, p.p. London (1863), p.7
48 Hoste, Lady Harriet, *Memoirs and Letters of Capt Sir William Hoste*, London (1833), 2 vols, Vol. I, p.66
49 Ibid.
50 BGR/12
51 Elliot, p.5
52 Lewis, p.19
53 NC, Vol. III, p.111
54 Hamilton, Sir Richard Vesey, ed., *Letters and Papers of Admiral of Fleet Sir Thos Byam Martin GCB*, NRS, Vol. 24 (1903), p.28
55 Nagle, p.60
56 Laffin, John, *Jack Tar The Story of the British Sailor*, London (1969), p.29
57 Nagle, p.211
58 Naish, p.90
59 Fremantle, Anne, ed., *The Wynne Diaries*, Oxford (1935–40), 3 vols, Vol. II, p.186

60   Hoste letters on microfiche: letter of 15 August 1797
61   Ibid.
62   Fremantle, p.183
63   Ibid.
64   Kennedy, p.98
65   Ibid.
66   Nagle, p.204
67   Kennedy, p.98
68   Ibid.
69   Fremantle, p.171
70   Phillimore, Vol. I, p.122
71   Ibid.
72   Ibid.
73   Ibid.
74   Elliot, p.25
75   Naish, p.319
76   Ibid., p.322
77   Ibid.
78   Ibid., p.323
79   Ibid., p.361
80   Ibid., p.297
81   NC, Vol. VI, p.247
82   NC, Vol. IV, p.75
83   Hoste, p.77

CHAPTER 10

1   Bourrienne, F. de, *Memoirs of Napoleon Bonaparte*, ed. Sanderson, E., London, p.68
2   Lavery, Brian, *Nelson and the Nile*, London (1998), p.80 & Rawson, Geoffrey, *Letters of Lord Nelson*, St Albans (1949), p.188
3   Pocock, Tom, *Horatio Nelson*, London (1988), p.153 in Cordingly, David, *Billy Ruffian The Bellerophon and the Downfall of Napoleon*, London (2003), p.125
4   Naish, George, P. B., ed., *Nelson's Letters to his Wife and other Documents 1785–1831*, NRS, Vol. 100 (1958), p.394
5   Ibid., p.395
6   Ibid.
7   Ibid., p.393
8   White, Colin, ed., *Nelson: The New Letters*, London (2005), p.209
9   Naish, p.396
10   Ibid.
11   Ibid., p.397
12   Bourrienne, p.70
13   Ibid.
14   Lavery, p.127
15   Parsons, G. S., *Nelsonian Reminiscences*, London (1843), p.254
16   Perrett, Bryan, *The Real Hornblower. The Life and Times of Admiral Sir James Gordon GCB*, London (1998), p.26

17   Elliot, Sir George, *Memoir of Admiral the Hon. Sir George Elliot, written for his children*, p.p. London (1863), p.9
18   *Naval Chronicle*, Vol. VIII, p.229
19   White, p.213
20   Ibid.
21   Rawson, Geoffrey, *Letters from Lord Nelson*, St Albans (1949), p.185
22   Patton, Philip, *Strictures on Naval Discipline*, Edinburgh (1807), p.140 in Lavery, p.118
23   Jackson, T. Sturges, ed., *Logs of the Great Sea Fights 1794–1805*, NRS, Vols 16 & 18 (1899–1900), Vol. 16 (1899), p.39
24   NC, Vol. I, p.44
25   Baynham, Henry, *From the Lower Deck: The Old Navy 1780–1840*, London (1969), p.41
26   NC, Vol. VIII, p.229
27   Jackson, p.53
28   Ibid., p.40
29   Ibid.
30   Elliot, p.9
31   Parsons, p.12
32   Elliot, p.9
33   Ibid., pp.10–11
34   Ibid., p.11
35   NC, Vol. IV, p.61
36   Elliot, p.9
37   Jackson, p.41
38   NC, Vol. VIII, p.229
39   Ibid.
40   Ibid.
41   Ibid.
42   Ibid., p.230
43   Ibid.
44   Ibid.
45   Elliot, p.11
46   Ibid.
47   Ibid., p.1
48   Ibid., p.11
49   Ibid., p.12
50   Ibid.
51   Ibid., p.17
52   Ibid., p.12
53   Ibid., p.16
54   Ibid., p.13
55   Jackson, p.44
56   NC, Vol. III, p. 194
57   Ibid.
58   Ibid.
59   Hemans, Mrs, *The Poetical Works of Mrs Hemans*, London, p.455
60   Jackson, p.46
61   Elliot, p.13
62   Ibid.

63 Baynham, p.46
64 NC, Vol. VI, p.103
65 Kennedy, Ludovic, *Nelson's Band of Brothers*, London (1951), p.132
66 Hamilton, Sir Richard Vesey, ed., *Letters and Papers of Admiral of Fleet Sir Thos Byam Martin GCB*, NRS, Vol. 24 (1903), p.65
67 Ibid.
68 Pocock, Tom, *Remember Nelson: The Life of Captain Sir William Hoste*, Newton Abbott (1978), p.80
69 Ibid.

CHAPTER 11

1 Rawson, Geoffrey, ed., *Letters from Lord Nelson*, St Albans (1949), p.309
2 Nicolas, Sir Nicholas Harris, ed., *Dispatches and Letters of Vice-Admiral Lord Viscount Nelson*, London (1844–6), 7 vols, Vol. I, p.316
3 Naish, George P. B., ed., *Nelson's Letters to his Wife and other Documents 1785–1831*, NRS, Vol. 100 (1958), p.86
4 Ibid., p.95
5 Ibid., p.254
6 Ibid., p.192
7 Ibid., p.199
8 Russell, Jack, *Nelson and the Hamiltons*, London (1969), p.181
9 PAR182
10 Phillimore, Augustus, *The Life of Admiral of the Fleet Sir William Parker*, London (1876–80), 3 vols, Vol. I, p.96
11 Le Faye, Deirdre, ed., *Jane Austen's Letters*, London (2003), p.29
12 Ibid., p.13
13 Ibid., p.23
14 Stuart, Andrea, *The Rose of Martinique*, London (2003), p.239
15 Naish, p.77
16 Ibid., p.90
17 Ibid., p.84
18 Ibid., p.94
19 Ibid., p.201
20 Ibid., p.314
21 Ibid., p.374
22 Ibid., p.332
23 Ibid., p.374
24 Ibid., p.375
25 Ibid., p.100
26 Ibid., p.104
27 Ibid., p.265
28 Ibid., p.220
29 Ibid., p.221
30 Ibid., p.302
31 Ibid., p.310
32 Ibid., p.349
33 Ibid., p.318
34 Ibid., p.323
35 Ibid., p.333
36 Ibid., p.360
37 Ibid., p.367
38 Ibid., p.358
39 Ibid., p.428
40 Ibid., p.445
41 Ibid., p.401
42 Rawson, p.199
43 Naish, p.401
44 Rawson, p.204
45 Russell, p.64
46 Ibid., p.95
47 Ibid., p.64
48 Ibid., p.138

CHAPTER 12

1 *Naval Chronicle*, Vol. III, p.77
2 Ibid.
3 Ibid.
4 Parsons, G. S., *Nelsonian Reminiscences*, London (1843), p.171
5 Hoste letters on microfiche: letter dated 15 June 1793
6 Ibid.
7 Naish, George P. B., ed., *Nelson's Letters to his Wife and other Documents 1785–1831*, NRS, Vol. 100 (1958), p.84
8 Hoste, Lady Harriet, *Memoirs and Letters of Capt Sir William Hoste*, London (1833), 2 vols, Vol. I, p.16
9 Ibid.
10 Ibid.
11 Ibid.
12 Nagle, Jacob, *The Nagle Journal: A Diary of the Life of Jacob Nagle, Sailor, from the Year 1775 to 1841*, ed., John C. Dann, New York (1988), p.198
13 *Prince George's Logg Book*, LOG/N/B/7, B/8, B/9
14 Lewis, Michael, ed., *Sir William Henry Dillion, A Narrative of My Professional Adventures 1790–1839*, NRS, Vol. 93 (1953), p.155
15 Le Faye, Deirdre, ed., *Jane Austen's Letters*, London (2003), p.1
16 Ibid., p.6
17 Hubback, John H. & Edith C., *Jane Austen's Sailor Brothers*, London (1906), p.51
18 Ibid., pp.51–2
19 Ibid., pp.52–3
20 Ibid., p.53
21 Le Faye, p.39
22 Ibid., p.33
23 Ibid., p.56
24 Ibid., p.35
25 Ibid., p.38

26   Hoste, p.84
27   Ibid.
28   Ibid.
29   Ibid.
30   Ibid., p.104
31   Ibid.
32   Ibid.
33   Ibid.
34   Pocock, Tom, *Remember Nelson: The Life of Captain Sir William Hoste*, Newton Abbott (1978), p.83
35   Ibid.
36   Hoste, p.104
37   Ibid.
38   Ibid.
39   Ibid.
40   Naish, p.400
41   Parsons, p.14
42   Ibid, p.16
43   Ibid.
44   Ibid.
45   Ibid., p.19
46   Ibid., p.20
47   Ibid., p.226
48   Ibid., p.35
49   Ibid., p.36
50   Ibid., p.8
51   Rodger, N. A. M., *The Command of the Ocean. A Naval History of Britain 1649–1815*, London (2004), p.472
52   Elliot, Sir George, *Memoir of Admiral the Hon. Sir George Elliot, written for his children*, p.p. London (1863), p.35
53   Phillimore, Augustus, *The Life of Admiral of the Fleet Sir William Parker*, London (1876–80), 3 vols, Vol. I, p.188
54   Ibid.
55   Ibid.
56   Robinson, C. N., *The British Tar in Fact and Fiction*, London (1909), p.127
57   Ibid.
58   MSY/G/1, letter of 30 September 1802
59   MSY/G/1, letter of 7 February 1805
60   Parsons, p.8
61   Ibid.
62   Robinson, p.412
63   Parsons, p.8
64   Ibid.
65   Ibid., p.9
66   MM, Vol. 15 (1929), p.241
67   Ibid., p.242
68   Ibid., p.240
69   Ibid., p.246
70   Ibid.
71   Ibid.

72   Ibid., p.249
73   Ibid.
74   PST/44
75   Beardsley, Martyn, *Deadly Winter. The Life of Sir John Franklin*, Rochester (2002), p.10
76   NC, Vol. V, p.183
77   Beardsley, p.6
78   NC, Vol. VI, p.175
79   Lloyd C. & Anderson R. C., eds., Penrose, C. V., *A Memoir of James Trevenen*, NRS, Vol. 101 (1959), p.15
80   Ibid., p.12
81   *Daily Telegraph*, 27 September 2006
82   NC, Vol. VI, p.83.
83   Beardsley, p.9
84   Ibid.
85   PST/44
86   Beardsley, p.12
87   NC, Vol. XII, p.303
88   Ibid., p.304
89   Flannery, Tim, ed., *A Voyage to Terra Australis*, Melbourne (2000), p.241
90   Ibid., p.249
91   Nicolas, Sir Nicholas Harris, ed., *Dispatches and Letters of Vice-Admiral Lord Viscount Nelson*, London (1998), Vol. V, p.168
92   Flannery, p.248

CHAPTER 13

1   *Naval Chronicle*, Vol. XXVI, p.202
2   MSY/G/1, 10 January 1803
3   MSY/K/3
4   MSY/K/3, No. 4194, 24 April 1803
5   MSY/0/10
6   MSY/G/1, letter of 7 April 1804
7   Ibid.
8   Pocock, Tom, *Remember Nelson: The Life of Captain Sir William Hoste*, Newton Abbott (1978), p.117
9   NC, Vol. XV, p.265
10   NC, Vol. XI, p.420
11   Cochrane, Admiral Lord, *Memoirs of a Fighting Captain*, London (2005), p.20
12   Ibid.
13   NC, Vol. XV, p.277
14   Ibid., p.293
15   Ibid., p.281
16   Ibid.
17   Ibid., p.282
18   Ibid., p.285
19   Ibid., p.286.
20   Ibid., p.279
21   Ibid., p.288
22   Ibid.

23 Ibid., p.290
24 Ibid.
25 Ibid.
26 Ibid., p.291
27 Lavery, Brian, *Nelson's Fleet at Trafalgar*, NMM (2004), p.76
28 NC, Vol. XV, p.287
29 Rodger, N. A. M., *The Command of the Ocean. A Naval History of Britain 1649–1815*, London (2004), p.529
30 Howarth, D., *Trafalgar, The Nelson Touch*, London, (1969) in Beardsley, Martyn, *Deadly Winter. The Life of Sir John Franklin*, Rochester (2002), p.20
31 NC, Vol. XV, p.287
32 NC, Vol. XVII, p.109
33 NC, Vol. XV, p.291
34 Ibid., p.175
35 Lewis, Jon E., *The Mammoth Book of How it Happened. Trafalgar*, London (2005), p.143
36 Hibbert, Christopher, *Nelson, A Personal History*, London (1994), p.325
37 Kennedy, Ludovic, *Nelson's Band of Brothers*, London (1951), p.314
38 NC, Vol. XV, p.119
39 NC, Vol. IV, p.145
40 Warwick, Peter, *Voices from the Battle of Trafalgar*, Newton Abbot (2005), p.141
41 Jackson, T. Sturges, ed., *Logs of the Great Sea Fights 1794–1805*, NRS, Vol. 16 (1899), p.246
42 Ibid.
43 NC, Vol. XVII, p.361
44 Naish, George P. B., ed., *Nelson's Letters to his Wife and other Documents 1785–1831*, NRS, Vol. 100 (1958), p.276
45 Ibid., p.398
46 NC, Vol. XV, p.14
47 Ibid.
48 Ibid, p.38
49 NC, Vol. XVII, p.193
50 NC, Vol. XIV, p.485
51 NC, Vol. XVII, p.196
52 Warwick, p.185
53 Ibid., p.184
54 NC, Vol. XV, p.271
55 Ibid.
56 Ibid., p.293
57 Ibid.
58 AGC/H/18
59 Tayler, Alistair & Henrietta, eds., *Book of the Duffs Vol. II*, Edinburgh (1914), p.263
60 Ibid.
61 NC, Vol. XV, p.293
62 Jackson, p.247
63 Ibid.
64 Ibid.

CHAPTER 14

1 Fremantle, Anne, ed., *The Wynne Diaries*, Oxford (1935–40), 3 vols, Vol. II, p.97
2 Ibid., p.97
3 Ibid., p.96
4 Ibid., p.99
5 Ibid., p.97
6 Ibid., p.98
7 Ibid., p.97
8 Ibid., p.102
9 Elliot, Sir George, *Memoir of Admiral the Hon. Sir George Elliot, written for his children*, p.p. London (1863), p.6
10 Fremantle, p.106
11 Ibid.
12 Ibid., p.111
13 Ibid., p.116
14 Austen, Jane, *The Complete Novels of Jane Austen: Persuasion*, London (1983), p.1181
15 Hill, Richard, *The Prizes of War: The Naval System in the Napoleonic Wars 1793–1815*, Stroud (1998), p.14
16 Fremantle, p.119
17 Le Faye, Deirdre, ed., *Jane Austen's Letters*, London (2003), p.5
18 Ibid., p.52
19 *Naval Chronicle*, Vol. III, p.79
20 Ibid.
21 Ibid.
22 Le Faye, p.80
23 Ibid., p.91
24 NC, Vol. XV, p.284
25 Ibid.
26 Lewis, Michael, ed., Sir William Henry Dillon, *A Narrative of My Professional Adventures 1790–1839*, NRS, Vol. 93 (1953), p.110
27 NC, Vol. XV, p.292
28 Jackson, T. Sturges, ed., *Logs of the Great Sea Fights 1794–1805*, NRS, Vol. 18 (1900), p.325
29 Ibid., p.326
30 Ibid., p.327
31 Ibid.
32 Historical conversions courtesy of the Bank of England. Contemporary exchange conversions at £1=US$1.50
33 NC, Vol. XXVI, p.453
34 Ibid., p.454
35 NC, Vol. XIV, p.466
36 NC, Vol. XII, p.139
37 Ibid.
38 Warwick, Peter, *Voices from the Battle of Trafalgar*, Newton Abbot (2005), p.274
39 Hubback, John H. & Edith C., *Jane Austen's Sailor Brothers*, London (1906), pp.149–50
40 Ibid., p.150

41 Ibid., pp.154–5

42 Parkinson, C. Northcote, *Edward Pellew, Viscount Exmouth, Admiral of the Red*, London (1934), p.327 in Hill, p.69

43 Lewis, p.71

44 Parsons, G. S., *Nelsonian Reminiscences*, London (1843), p.91

45 Ibid.

46 Ibid.

47 Ibid.

48 Elliot, p.32

49 Parsons, p.92

50 Ibid., p.96

51 Ibid., p.97

52 Ibid., p.101

53 Ibid., p.104

54 NC, Vol. XX, p.116

55 Hubback, p.174

56 NC, Vol. XVII, p.320

57 Ibid., p.321

58 Thursfield, H. G., ed., *Five Naval Journals 1789-1817*, NRS, Vol. 91 (1951), p.168

59 Ibid., p.165

60 Ibid., p.186

61 Ibid., p.240

62 Laffin, John, *Jack Tar The Story of the British Sailor*, London (1969), p.189

63 NC, Vol. IX, p.463

64 Ibid.

65 Thursfield, p.240

66 Naish, George P. B., ed., *Nelson's Letters to his Wife and other Documents 1785–1831*, NRS, Vol. 100 (1958), p.291

67 Pocock, Tom, *Remember Nelson: The Life of Captain Sir William Hoste*, Newton Abbott (1978), p.97

68 Hoste, Lady Harriet, *Memoirs and Letters of Capt Sir William Hoste*, London (1833), Vol. I, p.316

69 Ibid., p.317

70 Pocock, p.192

71 Hoste, pp.303–4

72 Pocock, p.134

73 Ibid.

74 Ibid.

75 Hoste, p.314

76 Pocock, p.135

77 Hoste, p.311

78 Ibid., p.347

79 NC, Vol. XXV, p.434

80 Ibid., p.433

81 Ibid.

82 NC, Vol. XXVI, p.493

83 NC, Vol. XXXVII, p.35

84 Thursfield, p.161

85 Hoste, Vol. II, p.110

86 Lewis, p.66

87 Cochrane, Admiral Lord, *Memoirs of a Fighting Captain*, London (2005), p.85

88 Ibid.

89 Ibid., p.86

90 NC, Vol. VI, p.151

91 Ibid.

92 Cochrane, p.43

93 NC, Vol. VI, p.151

94 NC, Vol. III, p.323

95 Cochrane, p.67

96 NC, Vol. XIII, p.329

97 NC, Vol. XVII, p.167

98 Ibid.

99 Cochrane, p.117

100 Pocock, Tom, *Captain Marryat. Seaman Writer and Adventurer*, London (2000), p.32

101 Cochrane, p.96

102 Pocock, *Captain Marryat* p.32

103 Hannay, David, *Life of Frederick Marryat*, London (1889), p.23

CHAPTER 15

1 *Naval Chronicle*, Vol. XXVI, pp.34–5

2 Ibid., p.82

3 Ibid., p.33

4 Ibid., p.40

5 Ibid., p.34

6 Ibid., p.83

7 NC, Vol. V, p.533

8 Ibid.

9 Ibid.

10 Nagle, Jacob, *The Nagle Journal: A Diary of the Life of Jacob Nagle, Sailor, from the Year 1775 to 1841*, ed. John C. Dann, New York (1988), p.63

11 Ibid., p.53

12 NC, Vol. III, p.76

13 NC, Vol. XVIII, p.64

14 Thursfield, H. G., ed., *Five Naval Journals 1789-1817*, NRS, Vol. 91 (1951), p.195

15 Ibid., p.197

16 NC, Vol. XIX, p.66

17 NC, Vol. XVIII, p.117

18 Ibid., p.339

19 NC, Vol. XXVI, p.488

20 Ibid.

21 Fremantle, Anne, ed. *The Wynne Diaries*, Oxford (1935–40), 3 vols, Vol. II, pp.166–7

22 Ibid.

23 Ibid.

24 Farragut, Loyall, *The Life of David Glasgow Farragut*, New York (1879), p.11

25 NC, Vol. XXVI, p.426

26 Ibid., p.425

27 Ibid.
28 Ibid.
29 Ibid., p.282
30 Ibid.
31 NC, Vol. XXVII, p.63
32 NC, Vol. XXVI, p.41
33 NC, Vol. XXXI, p.340 & Borneman, W. R, *1812: The War that forged a Nation*, New York (2004), p.229
34 Ibid.
35 NC, Vol. XXVIII, p.348
36 Brighton, Rev. J.G., ed., *Admiral Sir P.B.V. Broke Bart: A Memoir*, London (1866), p.160
37 Ibid., pp.160–1
38 Ibid., p.161
39 Ibid., p.171
40 Ibid., p.219
41 Ibid., p.204
42 Ibid., pp.205–7
43 Ibid., p.264
44 Ibid., p.265
45 Ibid.
46 Ibid., p.219
47 Ibid., p.218
48 NC, Vol. XXX, p.160
49 Ibid., p.161
50 Farragut, p.14
51 Ibid.
52 Ibid., p.34
53 Ibid., pp.34–5
54 Ibid., p.40
55 Ibid., pp.40–1
56 Ibid., p.42
57 Ibid., p.39
58 Forester, C. S., *The Age of Fighting Sail*, New York (1956), p.154
59 Perrett, Bryan, *The Real Hornblower. The Life and Times of Admiral Sir James Gordon GCB*, London (1998), p.105
60 Colchester, Admiral Charles Lord, *Memoranda of my Life*, London (1869), p.3
61 Ibid., pp.6–7
62 Chamier, Frederick, *The Life of a Sailor*, London (1832), p.175
63 Ibid., p.177
64 Ibid., p.175
65 Ibid., p.195
66 Ibid., pp.195–6
67 Ibid., p.196
68 Ibid.
69 Ibid., p.205
70 Farragut, p.44

CHAPTER 16

1 Home, George, *Memoirs of an Aristocrat and Reminiscences of the Emperor Napoleon by a Midshipman of the Bellerophon*, London (1838), p.219
2 Ibid., p.213
3 Ibid., p.14
4 Ibid., p.62
5 Ibid., p.2
6 Ibid., p.4
7 *Daily Telegraph*, 27 September 2006
8 Home, p.62
9 Hubback, John H. & Edith C., *Jane Austen's Sailor Brothers*, London (1906), p.20
10 Home, p.130
11 Ibid., p.65
12 Ibid., pp.69–70
13 Ibid., pp.132–3
14 Ibid.
15 Marryat, Florence, *The Life and Letters of Captain Marryat*, 2 vols, London (1872), Vol. I, p.16
16 Home, pp.137–41
17 Ibid., p.141
18 Ibid., p.148
19 Ibid., p.183
20 Ibid., p.200
21 Ibid., p.213
22 Ibid., pp. 213–4
23 Ibid., p.214
24 Ibid.
25 Ibid., p.1
26 Ibid., pp.215–6
27 Ibid., p.217
28 Ibid.
29 Ibid.
30 Ibid.
31 Ibid., p.218
32 Ibid., pp.218–9
33 Ibid., p.219
34 Ibid., p.220
35 Ibid., p.225
36 Ibid., p.224
37 Ibid., p.225
38 Ibid., p.224
39 Ibid., p.233
40 Ibid.
41 Ibid., pp.233–4
42 Ibid.
43 Ibid., pp.238–9
44 Ibid., p.239
45 Ibid., p.243

46 Ibid., p.245
47 Ibid., pp.245–6
48 Ibid., p.233
49 Ibid., pp.250–3
50 Ibid., pp.253–4
51 Marryat, p.83
52 Ibid., p.85

CHAPTER 17

1 Home, George, *Memoirs of an Aristocrat and Reminiscences of the Emperor Napoleon by a Midshipman of the Bellerophon*, London (1838), p.259
2 Ibid.
3 Ibid.
4 Ibid., p.260
5 Burney, Fanny, *Evelina; or, A Young Lady's Entrance into the World*, Oxford (1982), p.38
6 Ibid., Introduction p.xxx
7 Fremantle, Anne, ed., *The Wynne Diaries*, Oxford (1935–40), 3 vols, Vol. II, p.119
8 Colchester, Admiral Charles Lord, *Memoranda of my Life*, London (1869), pp.8–9
9 Ibid.
10 Ibid.
11 Home, p.260
12 Ibid.

EPILOGUE

1 Austen, Jane, *The Complete Novels of Jane Austen: Persuasion*, London (1983), p.1241
2 Robinson, William, *Jack Nastyface. Memoirs of an English Seaman*, London (1973), p.134
3 Mark, William, *At Sea with Nelson, being the Life of William Mark, A Purser who served under Admiral Lord Nelson*, London (1929), p.82
4 *Gentleman's Magazine*, Vol. LXIV, p.1036
5 Burton, Alfred, *The Adventures of Johnny Newcome in the Navy*, London (1904), p.19
6 Le Faye, Deirdre, ed., *Jane Austen's Letters*, London (2003), p.269
7 Austen, *Persuasion*, p.1290
8 Le Faye, p.2

9 Chapman, R. W., ed., *Minor Works*, Vol. VI of the Oxford Jane Austen (1954) revised edition by B.C. Southam (1969), p.40
10 Ibid.
11 Ibid.
12 Austen, *Mansfield Park*, pp.510–511.
13 Ibid., p.580
14 Ibid., p.600
15 Ibid., p.627
16 Ibid., p.511
17 Ibid., p.582
18 Ibid.
19 Ibid.
20 Ibid.
21 Ibid., p.618
22 Le Faye, p.32
23 Austen, *Mansfield Park*, p.482
24 Ibid.
25 Ibid.
26 Ibid., p.587
27 Ibid., p.590
28 Ibid., p.456
29 Ibid., p.482
30 Ibid., p.459
31 Ibid., p.467
32 Ibid., p.535
33 Ibid., p.580
34 Ibid.
35 Ibid., p.581
36 Ibid.
37 Ibid.
38 Ibid., p.662
39 Southam, Brian, *Jane Austen and The Navy*, London (2005), p.223
40 Le Faye, p.91
41 Southam, p.223
42 Le Faye, p.296
43 Austen, *Persuasion*, p.1158
44 Ibid., p.1288
45 Ibid., p.1154
46 Ibid., p.1172
47 Laughton, J.K., ed., *Journal of Rear-Admiral Bartholomew James 1752–1828*, NRS, Vol. VI (1896), p.7

BIBLIOGRAPHY

MANUSCRIPTS

ADM/L/A/51, NMM

AGC/8/33, NMM

AGC/H/18 NMM

BGR/12 *Rough Statement from other imperfect recollections of Lieutenant David O'Brien Casey's service and sufferings in Her Majesty's Navy* (1839), NMM

BGY/W/3, NMM

BRK/14 *Logbook of the Orion. Capt Duckworth Apr–Jun 1794*, NMM

HOSTE Letters on microfiche: letter dated 19 May 1793, NMM

JOD/12, *Nicholas Pocock: Notes and Sketches on Board HMS Pegasus 1/6/1794*, NMM

LOG/N/B/7, B/8, B/9 *Prince George's Logg Book*, NMM

The Marine Society – NMM:

MSY/A: Fair Minutes of the Committee of The Marine Society 1756–74

MSY/B: Fair Minutes of the Committee with account of the Annual General Meetings 1774–1975

MSY/G: Letter books 1802–92

MSY/D: Fair Minutes of the General and Extraordinary Court of The Marine Society, minutes of the Sub-committee and Routine Grants and rough minutes

MSY/H: Entry of boys admitted 1756–63

MSY/K: Registers of boys received and discharged from the Marine Society's ship 1786–1874

MSY/O: Registers of boys entered as servants of the King's Ship 1770–1873

MS.AUS/14 *A Plan of Mathematical Learning Taught in the Royal Academy Portsmouth performed by Francis Austen. A student there 1788.* NMM

MSS195 Royal Naval Academy, Portsmouth 1729–1816: RNM

PAR182 Letter of George Parker 16 October 1793, NMM

PAR188/1 23 April 1793 Letter, NMM

PST/44 NMM

RA/GEO/MAIN, RA

RA/GEO/ADD, RA

RA/ADDL, RA

BOOKS

Andrews, Kenneth R., *Trade, Plunder and Settlement*, Cambridge (1984)

Annual Register 1799

Austen, Jane, *The Complete Novels of Jane Austen*, London (1983)

Bawlf, Samuel, *The Secret Voyage of Sir Francis Drake*, London (2004)

Baynham, Henry, *From the Lower Deck: The Old Navy 1780–1840*, London (1969)

Beardsley, Martyn, *Deadly Winter. The Life of Sir John Franklin*, Rochester (2002)

Bonner Smith, D., *The Naval Mutinies of 1797*, MM 1935 pp.428–49, MM 1936 pp.65–86

Borneman, W. R., *1812: The War that Forged a Nation*, New York (2004)

Bourrienne, F. de., *Memoirs of Napoleon Bonaparte*, ed. E. Sanderson, London

Brighton, Rev. J. G., ed., *Admiral Sir P.B.V. Broke Bart: A Memoir*, London (1866)

BIBLIOGRAPHY

Burney, Fanny, *Evelina; or, A Young Lady's Entrance into the World*, Oxford (1982)

Burton, Alfred, *The Adventures of Jonny Newcome in the Navy*, London (1904)

Chamier, Frederick, *The Life of a Sailor*, London (1832)

Chapman, R. W., ed., *Minor Works* Vol. VI of the Oxford Jane Austen (1954) revised edition by B. C Southam (1969)

Cochrane, Admiral Lord, *Memoirs of a Fighting Captain*, London (2005)

Colchester, Admiral Charles Lord, *Memoranda of my Life*, London (1869)

Corbett, Julian S., *Drake and the Tudor Navy*, Aldershot (1988)

Cordingly, David, *Billy Ruffian The Bellerophon and the Downfall of Napoleon*, London (2003)

Elliot, Sir George, *Memoir of Admiral the Hon. Sir George Elliot, written for his children*, p.p. London (1863)

Farragut, Loyall, *The Life of David Glasgow Farragut*, New York (1879)

Flannery, Tim, ed., *A Voyage to Terra Australis*, Melbourne (2000)

Forester, C. S., *The Age of Fighting Sail*, New York (1956)

Fremantle, Anne, ed., *The Wynne Diaries*, 3 vols, Oxford (1935–40)

Gentleman's Magazine

Gore Allen, W., *King William The Fourth*, London (1960)

Hague, William, *William Pitt the Younger*, London (2004)

Hamilton Sir R. Vesey & Laughton, J. K., eds., *Recollections of James Anthony Gardner*, NRS, Vol. 31 (1906)

Hamilton, Sir Richard Vesey, ed., *Letters and Papers of Admiral of Fleet Sir Thos Byam Martin GCB*, NRS, Vol. 24 (1903)

Hampden, John, ed., *Francis Drake Privateer. Contemporary Narratives and Documents*, London (1972)

Hannay, David, *Life of Frederick Marryat*, London (1889)

Hazlewood, Nick, *The Queen's Slave Trader: John Hawkyns, Elizabeth I and the Trafficking in Human Souls*, New York (2004)

Hemans, Mrs, *The Poetical Works of Mrs Hemans*, London

Hibbert, Christopher, *Nelson, A Personal History*, London (1994)

Hill, Richard, *The Prizes of War: The Naval System in the Napoleonic Wars 1793–1815*, Stroud (1998)

Home, George, *Memoirs of an Aristocrat and Reminiscences of the Emperor Napoleon by a Midshipman of the Bellerophon*, London (1838)

Hoste, Lady Harriet, *Memoirs and Letters of Capt Sir William Hoste*, London (1833)

Hubback, John H. & Edith C., *Jane Austen's Sailor Brothers*, London (1906)

Irving, Laurence, ed., *A Selection of the Principal Voyages, Traffiques and Discoveries of the English Nation by Richard Hakluyt*, London (1927)

Jackson, T. Sturges, ed., *Logs of the Great Sea Fights 1794–1805*, NRS, Vol. 16 (1899)

Keate, E. M., *Nelson's Wife*, London (1939)

Kelsey, Harry, *Sir John Hawkins: Queen Elizabeth's Slave Trader*, Yale (2003)

Kennedy, Ludovic, *Nelson's Band of Brothers*, London (1951)

Laffin, John, *Jack Tar The Story of the British Sailor*, London (1969)

Laughton, J. K., ed., *Journal of Rear-Admiral Bartholomew James 1752–1828*, NRS, Vol. 6 (1896)

Laughton, J. K., ed., *Letters and Papers of Charles, Lord Barham. Admiral of the Red Squadron, 1758–1813*, NRS, Vol. 39 (1910)

Laughton, J. K., ed., *The Naval Miscellany Vol. 1*, NRS Vol. 20 (1902),

Lavery, Brian, *Nelson and the Nile*, London (1998)

Lavery, Brian, *Nelson's Fleet at Trafalgar*, NMM (2004)

Le Faye, Deirdre, ed., *Jane Austen's Letters*, London (2003)

Lewis, Jon E., *The Mammoth Book of How it happened. Trafalgar*, London (2005)

Lewis, Michael, ed., Sir William Henry Dillon: *A Narrative of My Professional Adventures 1790–1839*, NRS, Vol. 93 (1953)

Lloyd, Christopher, *The Royal Naval Colleges at Portsmouth and Greenwich*, MM LII (1966)

Lloyd C. & Anderson R. C., eds., Penrose, C.V. *A Memoir of James Trevenen*, NRS, Vol. 101 (1959)

Mark, William, *At Sea with Nelson, being the Life of William Mark, A Purser who served under Admiral Lord Nelson*, London (1929)

Marryat, Florence, *The Life and Letters of Captain Marryat*, 2 vols, London (1872)

Matcham, M. Eyre, *The Nelsons of Burnham Thorpe*, London (1911)

Nagle, Jacob, *The Nagle Journal: A Diary of the Life of Jacob Nagle, Sailor, from the Year 1775 to 1841*, ed. John C. Dann, New York (1988)

Naish, George P. B., ed., *Nelson's Letters to his Wife and other Documents 1785–1831*, NRS, Vol. 100 (1958)

Nautical Magazine, Vol. 2 (1833) pp.721–34

Naval Chronicle, 40 vols, London (1799–1818)

Navy Records Society: *Naval Miscellany*

Nicolas, Sir Nicholas Harris, ed., *The Dispatches and Letters of Vice-Admiral Lord Viscount Nelson*, 7 vols, London (1844–6)

Parkinson, C. Northcote, *Edward Pellew, Viscount Exmouth, Admiral of the Red*, London (1934)

Parkinson, C. Northcote, *Portsmouth Point The Navy in Fiction 1793–1815*, Liverpool (1949)

Parsons, G. S., *Nelsonian Reminiscences*, London (1843)

Patton, Philip, *Strictures on Naval Discipline*, Edinburgh (1807)

Pemberton, Charles Reece, *The Autobiography of Pel Verjuice*, ed., Eric Partridge, London (1929)

Perrett, Bryan, *The Real Hornblower. The Life and Times of Admiral Sir James Gordon GCB*, London (1998)

Phillimore, Augustus, *The Life of Admiral of the Fleet Sir William Parker*, London (1876–80), 3 vols

Pietsch, Roland W.W., Ships' Boys and Charity in the Mid-Eighteenth Century: The London Marine Society (1756–1772), London Ph.D. thesis (2003)

Pocock, Tom, *Captain Marryat. Seaman Writer and Adventurer*, London (2000)

Pocock, Tom, *Horatio Nelson*, London (1988)

Pocock, Tom, *Remember Nelson: The Life of Captain Sir William Hoste*, Newton Abbott (1978)

Pocock, Tom, *Sailor King The Life of King William IV*, London (1991)

Raigersfeld, Jeffrey Baron de, *The Life of a Sea Officer 1783–1828*, ed., L. G Carr Laughton, London (1929)

Rawson, Geoffrey, ed., *Letters of Lord Nelson*, St Albans (1949)

Robinson, C. N., *The British Tar in Fact and Fiction*, London (1909)

Robinson, William, *Jack Nastyface. Memoirs of an English Seaman*, ed. Oliver Warner London (1973), first published as *Nautical Economy, or Forecastle Reflections of Events during the Last War* (1836)

Rodger, N. A. M., *The Safeguard of the Sea. A Naval History of Britain Vol. 1 660–1649*, London (2004)

Rodger, N. A. M., *The Command of the Ocean. A Naval History of Britain 1649–1815*, London (2004)

Russell, Jack, *Nelson and the Hamiltons*, London (1969)

Sainsbury, Capt A. B. and Phillips, Lt Cdr F. L., *The Royal Navy Day by Day*, Stroud (2005)

Southam, Brian, *Jane Austen and The Navy*, London (2005)

Stuart, Andrea, *The Rose of Martinique*, London (2003)

Sugden, John, *Sir Francis Drake*, London (1996)

Sullivan, F. B., *The Royal Academy at Portsmouth 1729–1806*, MM LXIII (1977), pp.311–26

Sullivan, F. B., *The Naval Schoolmaster During the Eighteenth Century and the Early Nineteenth Century*, MM LXII (1976) pp.311–26

Tayler, Alistair & Henrietta, eds., *Book of the Duffs Vol. II*, Edinburgh (1914)

Thomas, J. H., *Portsmouth Naval Academy: An Educational Experiment Examined*, Portsmouth Archive Rev Vol. 3 (1978), see NMM 355.231.1 (422.7)

Thursfield H. G., ed., *Five Naval Journals 1789-1817*, NRS, Vol. 91 (1951)

Warwick, Peter, *Voices from the Battle of Trafalgar*, Newton Abbot (2005)

White, Colin, ed., *Nelson: The New Letters*, London (2005)

Woodman, Richard, *...of daring temper. A History of the Marine Society*, London (2006)

Wright, G. N., *The Life and Reign of William the Fourth*, London (1837)

Ziegler, Philip, *King William IV*, Bungay (1971)

INDEX